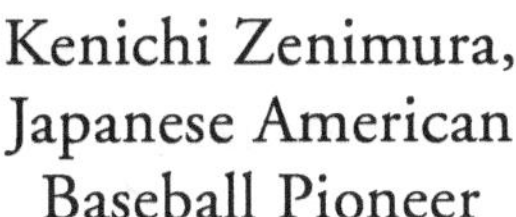

Kenichi Zenimura, Japanese American Baseball Pioneer

K. Zenimura
Capt. of the F. A. C.

Kenichi Zenimura, Japanese American Baseball Pioneer

BILL STAPLES, JR.

Foreword by Don Wakamatsu

McFarland & Company, Inc., Publishers
Jefferson, North Carolina, and London

Frontispiece: Signature of Kenichi Zenimura, Captain of the Fresno Athletic Club (Zenimura Family Archive)

LIBRARY OF CONGRESS CATALOGUING-IN-PUBLICATION DATA

Staples, Bill, Jr., 1969–
Kenichi Zenimura, Japanese American baseball pioneer / Bill Staples, Jr. ; foreword by Don Wakamatsu.
p. cm.
Includes bibliographical references and index.

ISBN 978-0-7864-6134-9
softcover : 50# alkaline paper ♾

1. Zenimura, Kenichi, 1900–1968.
2. Baseball players — United States — Biography.
3. Japanese American baseball players — Biography.
I. Title.
GV865.Z46S73 2011 796.357'092—dc23 [B] 2011025744

BRITISH LIBRARY CATALOGUING DATA ARE AVAILABLE

On the cover: Kenichi Zenimura, center, flanked by Lou Gehrig (left) and Babe Ruth after an exhibition game at Fresno's Firemen's Ballpark on October 29, 1927. Photograph by Frank Kamiyama (Nisei Baseball Research Project)

Manufactured in the United States of America

McFarland & Company, Inc., Publishers
Box 611, Jefferson, North Carolina 28640
www.mcfarlandpub.com

To my beautiful family, Kyra, Joshua and Alison,
who inspire me every day to learn, live, laugh, love
and do my part to make the world a better place.

Table of Contents

Acknowledgments ix
Foreword by Don Wakamatsu 1
Preface 3
Introduction 11

1 — Athlete in the Making (1900–1920) 13
2 — Breaking Down Barriers (1920–1924) 30
3 — Only the Ball Was Small (1925–1929) 51
4 — The Twilight Era (1930–1941) 78
5 — Relocating and Rebuilding Hope (1942–1943) 114
6 — A Taste of Freedom (1944) 146
7 — Rounding Third and Heading Home (1945) 164
8 — Passing the Torch (1946–1968) 183

Appendix A: Select Box Scores 209
Appendix B: Who's Who in Zenimura's Career 215
Appendix C: F.A.C. 1924 Tour of Japan 229
Appendix D: Nisei League vs. Negro League 230
Appendix E: Butte Baseball League Statistics, 1943–1945 231
Appendix F: Zenimura Legacy Timeline 233
Appendix G: Japanese American Glossary of Terms 240

Notes 245
Bibliography 259
Index 263

Acknowledgments

Kenso Howard Zenimura, the son of Kenichi Zenimura, was kind enough to invite me into his home in Fresno, California, to interview him and his family at length. Together we spent hours talking baseball, and sorting through articles, photographs and memories. Before and after the trip he was always willing to answer my emails and take my calls.

Mike Okihiro is a retired doctor in Honolulu, Hawaii, and author of *AJA Baseball in Hawaii: Ethnic Pride and Tradition.* He shared his time, knowledge and photocopied articles from the early 1910s featuring Zenimura with the Honolulu Asahi.

Tets Furukawa is a former player of Zenimura's teams and a historian. He too was generous with his time to answer questions about life before, during and after Japanese American internment. He is active in preserving and telling the history of the San Maria Valley in California.

Kyoko Yoshida is a professor of writing at Keio University in Japan. She kindly exchanged research related to Zenimura's 1924 tour to Japan, the 1927 Philadelphia Royal Giants tour to Japan, and Zenimura's contacts in Asia.

Yoichi Nagata is a SABR member in Japan who answered questions about the 1927 lineup of the Philadelphia Royal Giants.

Wayne Stivers, Negro League historian, answered numerous questions about the Negro League teams and players that Zenimura and his Nisei peers played against during the 1920s, 30s and 40s.

Baseball historians and authors William McNeil and Ralph Pearce answered several questions about teams and players in California whose careers intersected with Zenimura's.

Several members of the Arizona community helped in my research of baseball at the Gila River Japanese American internment camp. This list includes: former internees Mas Inoshita, James "Step" Tomooka and Midori Hall; Karen Leong, professor of Asian Studies at Arizona State University; Ted Namba of the Arizona JACL chapter; Mary Thomas and Jeri Thomas of the Gila River Indian Community; Lowell Bailey and Carl "Scooter" Lopez of the 1945 Tucson High Badgers; Gary and Larry Wolf of the Phoenix Thunderbirds; Martin "Pug" Marich; the Bill Kajikawa family; the Cornell Fisher family; and Richard McCleve of the 1945–47 Mesa High Jackrabbits.

Tom Ikeda and the team at Denshō in Seattle, created an invaluable archive of camp newspapers on densho.org that was key in helping reconstruct Zenimura's time at Gila River.

Jim Gates and Pat Kelly of the National Baseball Hall of Fame library helped research rare photos of Pacific Coast League, Negro League and Major League pitchers who once played against Zenimura and his Nisei peers.

Don Wakamatsu, the first Asian American manager in Major League Baseball history, graciously signed on to write the foreword.

Terri Boekhoff, editor extraordinaire, offered objective criticism and invaluable recommendations to help "remove clutter and create clarity" and stay laser-focused in my attempt to tell Zenimura's life story.

Kerry Yo Nakagawa is the authority on Japanese American baseball history. Throughout the research and writing of this book, he spent countless hours serving as a mentor to me and an invaluable source of information. Without his previous scholarship in the area of Nisei baseball history — and his friendship — this book would not have been written.

Foreword

by Don Wakamatsu

When Hall of Famer Frank Robinson was named the Cleveland Indians manager in 1975, he said that he wished Jackie Robinson was there with him to appreciate the significance of the moment. Jackie had died just three years before Frank became the first African American manager in MLB history.

In January 2009, I earned the distinction of becoming the first Asian American manager in MLB history when I was asked to lead the Seattle Mariners. Unlike Frank Robinson, there was not one person who I wished could be with me to appreciate the moment — there were thousands.

I often talk about "those who came before me." These people include my family, the thousands who were sent into internment camps during World War II, the men who served bravely in the 442nd, and the pioneers of the early Japanese American baseball leagues.

With the exception of my family, none of the others were with me physically when I joined the Mariners. They were with me in spirit though.

I am a fourth generation Japanese American, also known as a Yonsei. I was born in Hood River, Oregon, in 1963, and as a child I had no idea of what my family had endured during World War II. In actuality, they kept a lot of that from me. It wasn't until college that I started to learn more about the past and that dark chapter of American history.

The implications of my heritage first struck me when a government check arrived in the mail in the late 1980s. It was my father's share of reparations for the internment of Japanese Americans in the 1940s. My dad was born in the Tule Lake camp in California, just south of the Oregon border. I didn't quite understand what the check was for. All I remember was my dad's reaction: "it was all too little, too late."[1]

Over the years, my curiosity about my heritage has grown. From a friendship with baseball historian Kerry Yo Nakagawa I learned in great detail about Japanese Americans and baseball in the internment camps. I imagined the game I loved played behind coils of barbed wire and realized just how little I knew about my past.

Since then, I have discovered that the internment camp chapter is just the tip of the iceberg when it comes to Japanese American baseball history. There is so much more underneath. For example, few people know that

- in 1897 the first person of Japanese ancestry attempted to play in the majors;
- the first Japanese American baseball team was organized in 1903;

- a major league "color-line" drawn against Japanese players was publicly acknowledged in 1905;
- the first Japanese American baseball league was founded in 1910; and
- between 1922 and 1931, Nisei and Negro League teams did more to export the American game to Japan than their major league counterparts.

All proof that there is still so much of the fascinating Japanese American baseball history that has yet to be told.

One of my goals as a player was to bring recognition to my heritage. Since that didn't come to fruition, I'm especially fortunate to be where I am now as a manager. Thus, it is an honor to introduce you to *Kenichi Zenimura, Japanese American Baseball Pioneer*, the biography by baseball historian Bill Staples. As a member of the Nisei Baseball Research Project board of directors, Staples shares my passion for preserving and sharing the legacy of Japanese American baseball.

In the same spirit that Kerry Yo Nakagawa provided a broad scope of "100 Years of Japanese American Baseball," Staples delivers a thorough and fascinating account of Zenimura's life. Zeni's exciting career crossed paths with Hall of Fame players like Babe Ruth, Lou Gehrig and Joe DiMaggio; Negro League stars Biz Mackey and Andy Cooper; and dozens of Hall of Fame players from the Nippon Professional Baseball League. Throughout, Staples demonstrates that Zeni was more than just a great player and manager; he was an important baseball ambassador between the United States and Japan as well.

Zenimura was a Hall of Famer in every sense of the word. Yet, because of the place and time in which he lived, he never received the opportunity to play at the highest level.

I am fortunate in that I was born in the right place at the right time. Yes, a lot of hard work and long hours got me to where I am today. Still, I know that am indebted to pioneers like Zenimura who paved the way during the first half of the 20th century to make it all possible.

After being named the Mariners' manager, one of the first gifts I received was a framed copy of the famous photo of Zenimura and his Nisei teammates John Nakagawa, Fred Yoshikawa and Harvey Iwata, posing with Ruth and Gehrig in Fresno, in 1927. That picture now hangs in my office, serving as a daily reminder of "those who came before" and what they did to break down barriers for future generations.

Kenichi Zenimura, Japanese American Baseball Pioneer is a wonderful book that does more than just tell the life story of the man; hopefully it helps transform a long-neglected chapter of baseball history — Nisei baseball history — into a well-chronicled saga for all fans of all races, creeds and colors to appreciate.

Don Wakamatsu

Preface

"There are numerous parallels between my father's story and that of Japanese Americans."
— Sharon Robinson, Jackie Robinson's daughter

Much like Jackie Robinson and his peers in the Negro Leagues, Japanese Americans were forced to play in their own leagues from the 1900s to the 1940s because of bigotry and discrimination in white America. Today (early 21st century), virtually all baseball fans know Robinson's story and how he courageously broke the color line in 1947 to become the first African American to play in the modern game. One need only attend a major-league game and see his retired uniform number 42 displayed in every ballpark as a reminder of his legacy.

Few baseball fans know the story of early 20th century Japanese American baseball—also known as the Nisei Leagues.[1] Despite this lack of awareness, the impact of their leagues is still visible in today's game. It's subtle though, only visible to the well-informed. The legacy is not a retired uniform number, but the *names* on the back of the uniforms—Ichiro, Matsui, Matsuzaka, Okajima, Suzuki and Wakamatsu. The national pastime has unofficially become the international pastime, and perhaps this is the enduring legacy of Nisei baseball and pioneers like Kenichi Zenimura.

During his lifetime Zenimura was known for his great strategic sense of the game and a passion for exporting the American style of play to Japan, Korea and China. After watching Zeni compete on the diamond during the 1924 barnstorming tour, a *Japanese Times* reporter declared, "Zenimura is one of the smartest and most colorful players the writer had ever seen. He was the terror of the diamond, a man who played every position in baseball. He was tricky, shrewd and positive poison to every opponent."[2]

His reputation grew over the years and during his 1937 barnstorming tour to Japan, Zenimura was prevented from playing because the games were for amateur players and, based on the skills displayed in previous tours, it was widely believed that he was a professional player back in the United States.

Between the years 1923 and 1931, no MLB goodwill tour barnstormed Japan. (Ty Cobb toured Japan by himself in '28, but not as part of an organized team.) The highest caliber of competition from the U.S. during this time came in the form of Nisei and Negro League teams like Zenimura's Fresno Athletic Club and Hall of Famer Biz Mackey's Philadelphia Royal Giants. During this eight-year MLB void, Nisei and Negro Leaguers helped elevate the level of play in Japan and set the stage for the 1931 and 1934 MLB tour of stars like Lou

Gehrig and Babe Ruth. The Nippon Professional Baseball League was officially founded in 1936.

In 1962, Zenimura was crowned the "Dean of Nisei Baseball" by veteran *Fresno Bee* sports reporter Tom Meehan. Shortly after Zeni's death in 1968, the same sentiment was echoed by *Bee* reporter Ed Orman. Approximately a quarter-century later, baseball historian Kerry Yo Nakagawa refined Meehan and Orman's tribute for a new audience and called Zenimura "The Father of Japanese American Baseball." Nakagawa argues that Zeni deserves this title for his unparalleled career as a player, manager and international and multicultural ambassador of the game.

There are some critics who say that Zenimura is not worthy of this accolade. Interestingly, much of the opposition comes from within the Japanese American community. For some Nikkei, they point out that Zeni was neither the first nor the best player in Japanese American baseball.[3] Others with a limited knowledge of the game's history have sarcastically remarked that "the only thing Zenimura ever did was take a picture with Babe Ruth and Lou Gehrig."[4] Still others feel that a disproportionate amount of credit is given to Zenimura for organizing baseball behind barbed wire during the World War II internment. They say, "there was a 'Zeni' in every camp."[5]

The parallels between the Japanese Americans and Jackie Robinson are helpful in responding to this criticism. In the Negro League baseball community — especially among former players and historians — there are grumblings that Jackie Robinson also receives a disproportionate amount of credit. Sports broadcaster Bob Costas says in response, "Jackie wasn't the first, there were others who came before him. He wasn't the best, there were others who put up better numbers. That said though, can you think of anyone more important?"

This sentiment applies to Zenimura, too. He is the most important figure in the story of Japanese American baseball. Yes, there were others who came before him. And yes, some players probably had better numbers (or might have; statistics for the Nisei Leagues are sketchy). However, when you look at the defining characteristics and enduring legacy of Nisei baseball, Zenimura has had the greatest impact.

The defining characteristics of the Nisei baseball legacy are:

Formal League and Team Development: Japanese Americans started their own teams as early as 1903; established their own league as early as 1910; and in West Coast cities like Seattle, San Francisco, Oakland, San Jose, Fresno, Los Angeles and smaller towns in between, the Nisei Leagues offered a highly competitive and financially successful form of ball and entertainment for fans until World War II.

Zeni's impact: Between 1918 and 1955, he worked tirelessly to create, maintain and elevate formal Japanese American baseball teams, leagues, or both.

Games Against High-Caliber Competition: Zenimura believed that to be the best you had to compete against the best. For this reason, he and his Nisei peers scheduled games against talent from the Pacific Coast League, California Winter League, major leagues and Negro League barnstormers, and visiting teams from Japan. In games against each level, Nisei players not only proved they were worthy of being on the same field, on many occasions they were the victors. A study of Nisei Leagues box scores and games summaries between 1920 and 1940 reveals that the caliber of play closely reflects the common assessment of the Negro Leagues: not every player in the league was talented enough to play in the majors, but the stars of the league proved time and time again that, if given the opportunity, they could have competed with their white counterparts at the highest level.

Zeni's impact: No other Japanese American player or manager can claim as many games—or victories—against PCL, CWL, Negro Leagues and Japanese players or teams as Zenimura.

Pre-War Goodwill Ambassadors: For Issei and Nisei ballplayers, "putting on a baseball uniform was like putting on the American flag."[6] Through their adoption of, and love for, the game of baseball, Japanese Americans believed they were demonstrating their loyalty to the United States. At the same time, they still maintained connections with their culture, family and friends in Japan. One way to stay connected was through a shared love of baseball. Baseball was introduced to Japan in 1872 and by the turn of the 20th century it had grown to become the country's most popular team sport. Nisei teams embarked on goodwill tours as early as 1914, and during the early 1920s to the late 1930s, they played a key role in exporting the great American game to Japan and welcoming dozens of visiting Japanese teams to the U.S. In both cases, the competitive interactions helped the Japanese improve their skill level, elevate the overall level of play, and eventually empower them to start their professional baseball league in 1936.

When Japanese Americans were not involved directly on the field, they were often involved off the field and behind the scenes. Because they knew the language and cultural customs of both countries, Japanese Americans often played a significant role in facilitating the outbound tours of Caucasian and African American teams, and U.S.–inbound tours of Japanese teams.

Zeni's impact: As a tireless ambassador, baseball entrepreneur, and diplomat, he led the first tour to Japan by a California-based Nisei team and participated in many subsequent tours to and from his home country.

World War II Incarceration Camp Baseball: Perhaps one of the most unique, fascinating and tragic chapters in all of U.S. baseball history is World War II internment baseball. The national pastime behind barbed wire started shortly after President Franklin Roosevelt wrote his famous "Green Light Letter" to Judge Landis encouraging him to continue the 1942 baseball season. Weeks later Roosevelt signed Executive Order 9066 and set the stage for the removal and incarceration of more than 120,000 West Coast Issei and Nisei.[7] Families were forced to sell their personal belongings and pack only what could fit in two suitcases. In each of the ten camps scattered across the American West and Arkansas, baseball was key to survival. It helped boost morale for everyone, players and spectators alike. Each camp had at least one baseball field and competitive league. In camps where the skill levels were more advanced, games were scheduled against top high school, college and semipro teams from surrounding cities. In the end, the outcome of these games mattered far less than the relationship mending that occurred between incarcerated Japanese Americans and the free Americans living beyond the barbed wire of the camps.

Zeni's impact: Within weeks of arriving in the camp he began to build a baseball field. Between 1943 and 1945, Zenimura arranged approximately 40 games with outside teams. He participated in each as either a player or manager. His team won more than 75 percent of these contests, including games against the top Caucasian and Negro semipro clubs in Arizona.

Post-War Goodwill Ambassadors: Just as it was important to improve post-war relations on the local level with Caucasians, Japanese Americans knew it would be critical to do the same on the global level with Japan. Unfortunately, participation in the Nisei leagues after 1945 never returned to their pre-war levels. For those Nisei who still loved the game and wanted to compete at the highest levels, they had few options. American players like Fibber Hirayama, Kenshi Zenimura and Wally Yonamine were ready for the big leagues, but the big leagues weren't ready for them. So instead they went to Japan to play in the Nippon Professional Baseball League.

Zeni's impact: After the war Zenimura continued to work as a baseball ambassador between the U.S. and Japan. In addition to welcoming Japanese teams, players and officials visiting Fresno, he also served as a scout and facilitated the signing of several players from the U.S. mainland and Hawaii to central California colleges and professional teams in Japan.

* * *

The research behind this book and the works of other Nisei baseball historians has identified many important "founding fathers" of Japanese American baseball. Nonetheless, Zenimura still emerges as one of the top performers in the above considerations. He is not always the most accomplished in each category, but when the collective body of his work is considered, his career is by far the most impressive. It is because of his remarkable legacy that the author agrees with Nakagawa's position: Kenichi Zenimura is *the* "Father of Japanese American Baseball."

Chapter 3 of this book is titled "Only the Ball Was Small." It was selected for several reasons: (1) as a tribute to historian Robert W. Peterson, whose pioneering book, *Only the Ball Was White,* helped recapture the lost era of Negro baseball; (2) to further reinforce Sharon Robinson's comparison between Japanese Americans and her father's story; and (3) to emphasize the idea that while the Nisei style of playing ball was small, their enduring legacy was anything but.

In the epilogue of *Only the Ball Was White,* Peterson wrote, "At this point the writer intends to shed his mantle as an objective historian and assume the role of propagandist." He then calls for giving full honors at Cooperstown to Negro leagues stars. "And so long as the Hall of Fame is without a few of the great stars of Negro baseball," he wrote, "the notion that it represents the best in baseball is nonsense."[8]

At the time of Peterson's death in February 2006, I was preparing a paper on Zenimura titled, "From Internment to Hope: Arizona Celebrates a Japanese American Baseball Legend." A few months later I traveled to the National Baseball Hall of Fame to present at the 18th Annual Cooperstown Symposium on Baseball and American Culture and made a similar argument to Peterson's for Nisei baseball.

In the spirit of Peterson, I said: "In the 1970s and '80s recognition was raised for the Negro league ballplayers. And in the '90s, we did it for the female ballplayers. Now, hopefully, in the early 2000s, we can do the same for Japanese American ballplayers."

I must confess that when Peterson died I knew little of his work. I do now. I also know that in the same spirit in which he called for greater attention to the accomplishments of Negro League players, Kerry Yo Nakagawa has done the same for the Nisei Leagues in his seminal book *Through a Diamond: 100 Years of Japanese American Baseball.* Following the trail that Nakagawa blazed, the goal of this book is to help transform a long-neglected chapter of baseball history into a well-chronicled saga.

Peterson inspired a generation of historians to seek out the unknown Cy Young, Babe Ruth, Ty Cobb and Honus Wagner of black baseball. With the growing presence of Asian players in major league baseball, perhaps future historians will now be inspired to identify the Japanese American equivalent to Satchel Paige, Josh Gibson and other Negro Leagues stars? Here are my picks:

Negro and Nisei Leagues Star Player Comparisons

Negro Leagues Star	*Famous for*	*Comparable Nisei Leagues Star*
Sol White	Early pioneer	Y.K. Nakamura, Spokane, WA
Bud Fowler	Early league founder	Tokugoro Ito, Seattle, WA
Moses Fleetwood Walker	First to play on white teams	Andy Yamashiro, Honolulu, HI
Satchel Paige	Longevity, success & personality	Kenichi Zenimura, Fresno, CA (the player)
Rube Foster	League founder & promoter	Kenichi Zenimura, Fresno, CA (the manager & ambassador)
Smokey Joe Williams	Fierce competitor on the mound	Kenso Nushida, Stockton, CA
Josh Gibson	Power hitter	John Nakagawa, Fresno, CA
Martin Dihigo	All-star at any position	Russ Hinaga, San Jose, CA
James "Cool Papa" Bell	Speedy outfielder & base runner	Harvey Iwata, Fresno, CA
Jackie Robinson	Integration pioneer	Wally Yonamine, Honolulu, HI

Why the Hall of Fame Oversight?

There are several reasons why baseball historians and Cooperstown have yet to give Japanese American baseball the attention and credit it deserves.

The first is "yellow peril," a sociological concept that first manifested itself in government policy with the U.S. Chinese Exclusion Act of 1882. Initially the act focused on reducing Chinese immigration, but eventually it expanded to include all non-citizens of Asian ancestry. In the 1920s, a book called *The Rising Tide of Color Against White World-Supremacy* claimed immigrants, especially Asians, threatened American society. In the early 1900s, there were lynchings of Asian immigrants by vigilante groups, and California politicians ran on the campaign promise of "Keeping California White." Like their African American brothers and sisters, Asians in America were viewed as second-class citizens. More often than not they were relegated to their own leagues, and the mainstream press seldom covered the games of "the other." As a result, because the games and their players were rarely documented, it is as though they did not even exist.

Another pragmatic reason for the lack of attention given to Japanese American baseball pioneers is the language barrier, specifically the difficulties the majority of Caucasians (this author included) have in reading and saying Japanese names and words. The vast majority of Japanese Americans in the first half of the 20th century were bilingual, speaking Japanese at home and English outside the home. As a result we saw an attempt to "Americanize" by adopting more English-sounding first names like: Ken, Harvey, Johnny and Fred. These were much more familiar to the white English ear than Kenichiro, Satoru, Junichi and Shinichi, the given first names of Zenimura, Iwata, Nakagawa and Yoshikawa.

The third reason for a lack of attention given to Japanese American baseball is a simple matter of geography. The Nisei Leagues flourished on the West Coast in California, Washington and Oregon between 1900 and 1940. From the perspective of mainstream America, baseball did not exist on the West Coast until 1958 when the New York Giants moved to San Francisco. Because of this East Coast bias, little is known about those who played ball west of the Mississippi between 1900 and 1950, especially outside of white, so-called "organized baseball"—the players of West Coast Negro Leagues teams, Nisei Leagues or the California Winter League, for instance. It is hoped that as more and more newspapers become digitized, a more accurate picture and greater appreciation of these West Coast leagues and players will emerge.

The lack of appreciation for Japanese American baseball can also be attributed to the dearth of Japanese players in the big leagues. There are two reasons for this: (1) before World War II there was the "other color line" that systematically kept Japanese out of the big leagues; and (2) Nisei Leagues were decimated by World War II relocation and, afterward, by hostility toward people of Japanese ancestry.

Baseball is a reflection of America, and in the years immediately following World War Two, America simply wasn't ready for players of Japanese ancestry. The few Nisei who did want to compete followed the path of least resistance and went to Japan to play professionally (e.g., Wally Yonamine, Fibber Hirayama, Harvey and Howard Zenimura). Those who did not want to move to Japan instead moved on to other professions, primarily in white-collar careers as medical doctors, dentists, engineers and teachers. They were educated, had options, and exercised those options.

The final reason for a lack of appreciation for the Nisei Leagues is the "small-ball factor." Hall of Fame second baseman Joe Morgan explains the concept of "small ball" well in his instructional book *Baseball My Way*. He confesses, "I think the single item I enjoy above all others is our scoring a run without the team getting a base hit or being charged with an at-bat—as when, for example, I walk, steal second, get bunted over to third, and score on a sacrifice fly."[9]

If the Major Leagues are a towering home run into the outfield seats, then the Nisei Leagues were a walk, stolen base, bunt and sacrifice fly to score a run.

For the uninitiated, the home run is easy to see and applaud. The serious and patient students of baseball like Morgan appreciate brains over brawn, strategy over strength, and individual sacrifice for the greater good of the team. Someone of this mindset can truly appreciate the greatness of the early 20th century Nisei Leagues, and the legacy of Kenichi Zenimura, the Father of Japanese American baseball.

Following typical trends of the performance of aging superstars from the past, projections still have Ichiro Suzuki on pace to surpass Pete Rose's all-time career record of 4,256 hits. This creates the possible scenario of a 42-year-old Ichiro stepping up to the plate sometime at the end of the 2015 season and slapping career hit 4,257 (1,278 hits in Japan, 2,979 hits in MLB) to surpass Rose and become baseball's "Global All-Time Hit King." If he retires after that season, he would then be eligible for induction into the Baseball Hall of Fame in 2020.

It would only be fitting that the Hall of Fame, or even Major League Baseball, properly recognize the contributions of Zenimura and other Japanese American baseball pioneers before Ichiro delivers his historic acceptance speech in Cooperstown.

To paraphrase historian Robert Peterson: So long as the Hall of Fame is without a few great stars of Nisei Baseball, the notion that it represents the best of baseball is nonsense.

A Note on Terminology*

At present there is no clear agreement about the most appropriate terminology for what Japanese Americans underwent during World War II. In the 1940s, officials of the federal government and U.S. military used euphemisms to describe their actions against people of Japanese ancestry in the United States. The deceptiveness of the language can now be judged according to evidence from many sources, notably the government's own investigation, as documented in "Personal Justice Denied" (1982–83) the report of the U.S. Congressional Commission on Wartime Relocation and Internment of Civilians (CWRIC).

In early 1942, Japanese Americans were forcibly removed from the West Coast and forbidden to return. The government called this an "evacuation," which implies the forced move was done as a precaution for Japanese Americans' own safety, as in a natural disaster. In fact the CWRIC found that the true motivations were "race prejudice, war hysteria, and a failure of political leadership." An additional factor was a desire for economic gain. "Exclusion" and "mass removal" are more apt terms, because Japanese Americans were expelled from the West Coast and subject to arrest if they returned.

The commonly used term "internment" is misleading when describing the detention camps that held 120,000 people of Japanese descent during the war. "Internment" refers to the legally permissible detention of enemy aliens in time of war. It is problematic when applied to American citizens; yet two-thirds of the Japanese Americans incarcerated were U.S. citizens. Although "internment" is a recognized and generally used term, Denshō prefers "incarceration" as more accurate except in the specific case of aliens. "Detention" is used interchangeably, although some scholars argue that the word denotes a shorter time of confinement than the nearly four years the Japanese American camps were in operation.

The Nisei ("second generation") were U.S. citizens born to Japanese immigrant parents in the United States. The accurate term for them is "Japanese American," rather than "Japanese." In public documents, the government referred to the Nisei as "non-aliens" rather than "citizens." Their parents, the Issei ("first generation") were forbidden by discriminatory law from becoming naturalized American citizens. By the 1940s, most Issei had lived in the United States for decades and raised their families here. Many had no plans for returning to Japan, and would have become naturalized citizens if allowed. (They remained aliens until 1952, when immigration law was changed.) To reflect this condition, Denshō and other sources use the term "Japanese American" to refer to the Issei as well as the Nisei.

At first, Japanese Americans were held in temporary camps that the government called "Assembly Centers," facilities surrounded by fences and guarded by military sentries. For purposes of identification, Denshō uses this euphemistic term as part of a proper noun, for example, "Puyallup Assembly Center," and in quotation marks when referring to this type of facility.

Japanese Americans were later confined within permanent camps that the government called "Relocation Centers." In fact, they were prisons — compounds of barracks surrounded by barbed wire fences and patrolled by armed guards — which Japanese Americans could not leave without permission. "Relocation center" inadequately describes the harsh conditions and forced confinement of the camps; terms such as "incarceration camp" or "prison camp" are more accurate. As prison camps outside the normal criminal justice system, designed to confine civilians for military or political purposes on the basis of race and ethnicity, these so-called relocation centers also fit the definition of "concentration camps."

**Reprinted with permission from Densho.org.*

Should euphemistic language from an earlier era be used today? This is an important question for students, teachers, and all people concerned with historical accuracy. Many Japanese Americans, some scholars, and other credible sources use the terminology of the past, which they believe is true to that era and unlikely to invite controversy. In contrast, many Japanese Americans, historians, educators, and others use terminology that they feel more accurately represents the historical events. Denshō encourages individuals to think critically about the language used during the 1940s by the U.S. government in its punitive treatment of American citizens and legal resident immigrants based on their ancestry.

Denshō's terminology conforms with the "Resolution on Terminology" adopted by the Civil Liberties Public Education Fund (see http://www.momomedia.com/CLPEF/backgrnd.html).

For examples of these linguistic questions found in the Densho Digital Archive, see: http://densho.org/archive/fromthearchive/200902-fromthearchive.asp.

See also: Roger Daniels, "Words Do Matter," a 5-part article on the Discover Nikkei website: http://www.discovernikkei.org/en/journal/2008/2/1/words-do-matter.

Introduction

"No Japs Wanted!" These were the words displayed on billboards in 1923 Livingston, California. In May of that same year, the players of the Fresno Athletic Club, one of the top Japanese American semipro baseball teams in Central California, courageously drove into Livingston to do what they did best — play baseball.

Years later, team captain Kenichi Zenimura described the events surrounding that contest. "Someone, somehow, arranged a game between the Fresno Japanese Baseball Club and a team owned by the big shot of that town," he told the *Gila News Courier*. "The Japanese nine put together enough guts and made the trip — trying especially hard to play clean ball," he added. Despite the 8–2 loss to the Merced Cubs, Zenimura and his club continued to battle.[10] He explained, "Soon there were return games and soon — sure enough — the signs disappeared."[11]

Zeni, as he was known by those close to him, could field, hit, run the bases, and out-think the competition on the field. He also had a gift for using the game of baseball to transcend the ignorance and intolerance of his era. Some 20 years after his successful struggle to open up the hearts and minds of Merced County, California, he confronted similar challenges while incarcerated behind barbed wire of a World War II Japanese American Internment Camp located in the middle of the Arizona desert.[12]

Tets Furukawa, pitcher for the 1945 Butte High Eagles, the baseball team of one of the two Japanese American Internment high schools at Gila River, Arizona, summed up the essence of Zenimura best when he said, "Coach Zeni ... indeed possessed a tremendous knowledge of baseball savvy, but above all, he wanted every player to become a better human being by realizing his responsibility and compassion for his fellow man."[13]

Zenimura had a Hall of Fame career because of his collective body of work as a player, manager and international and cross-cultural ambassador of baseball. Those who knew him best would say that Zeni was also a Hall of Fame human being. Despite his small stature (five feet tall, 110 lbs) and modest means, he was a larger than life figure who enriched thousands of lives by teaching others — either with words or by example — how to be a tougher-than-nails competitor on the field and a compassionate, caring human being off the field.

He was a dedicated husband, father, friend and coach. He loved the promise of American democracy even though he was denied certain freedoms and the opportunity to participate in the democratic process most of his adult life. He loved America, but he also loved his personal connections to the Hawaiian Territory and Japan. The experiences in those locales made him who he was.

Zeni could speak the language of his mother and father, but he also spoke perfect

English — with no hint of an accent. In fact, those who knew him said he spoke with a bit of a western twang. He was well versed in the customs of the Japanese culture, but when in America he preferred American cultural practices, offering a handshake instead of a Japanese bow.

He prepared himself and his team with all the mental discipline one would find on a baseball team in Japan, yet his aggressive style of play was purely American. Zeni also enjoyed a cold beer and a cigar after a victory in a well-played ballgame. He was Japanese American, in every sense.

His life and legacy offer valuable lessons for everyone, regardless of their ethnicity or cultural background. Zenimura's story might be that of a 20th century Japanese American experience, however it truly reflects the timeless human condition. It is everyone's story too.

Although he possessed the talent to do so, Zeni never played professional baseball at the major league level. The opportunity never materialized, at least in part because of the bigotry and systematic racism of 1920s and '30s America. So instead of breaking into the pros, he helped break down those barriers and paved the way for others to achieve their dreams. These players include Masonori Murakami in the 1960s; Lenn Sakata in the 1970s; Atlee Hammaker in the 1980s; Hideo Nomo in the 1990s; Ichiro Suzuki, Hideki Matsui and others in the 1990s; and Daisuke Matsuzaka and manager Don Wakamatsu in the 2000s.

Each one of these individuals, in some small way, is indebted to the life's work of all Nisei baseball pioneers, and especially the man recognized as the Father of Japanese American Baseball — Kenichi Zenimura.

1

Athlete in the Making (1900–1920)

"Mark my prediction. Some star ball players will come out of Japan within the next ten years."[1]
—John McGraw, NY Giants manager, 1914

In 1903, a series of events began to unfold that would set the stage for the national pastime to become the international pastime a century later. The Boston Americans defeated the Pittsburgh Pirates, five games to three, behind the pitching of Cy Young to win the first modern World Series, weeks after pitcher Andrew "Rube" Foster and his Cuban X Giants became the first (and unofficial) "World's Colored Champions," winning five of seven games from the Philadelphia Giants. Out west, the Pacific Coast League saw its inaugural season with teams in Seattle, Portland, Los Angeles, Oakland, Sacramento, and San Francisco where the first Japanese American baseball team, the Fuji Athletic Club, was founded by artist Chiura Obata.[2] And in Japan, the first championship game was played between Waseda and Keio Universities (a.k.a. the Sōkeisen).

That same year, a young 23-year-old woman named Waka Zenimura left Hiroshima, Japan, for the Hawaiian Islands. Her husband, Masakichi Zenimura, 33, was already in Hawaii trying to secure work in the sugar cane fields of Honolulu.[3] In the early 1900s it was commonplace in the Japanese culture for grandparents to help raise a child during the early years of development. Presumably, this is what Waka did when she left her three-year-old son, Kenichiro Zenimura, behind in Hiroshima. Four years later, little Kenichi and his aunt Hisa Hirokawa boarded the S.S. *Manchuria* in Yokohama and set sail to join his parents in Honolulu.[4] The ship left Japan on Thursday, December 12, 1907, and exactly two weeks later Kenichi Zenimura first stepped foot on the baseball paradise known as Honolulu, Hawaii.

Unfortunately for Zenimura and other ballplayers of Japanese ancestry with big league dreams in early 20th century America, the cards were stacked against them. In fact, the animosity towards Japanese in the U.S. mainland and its territories began to rise long before Kenichiro's birth.

In 1863, President Abraham Lincoln signed the Emancipation Proclamation, ending slavery in the United States. A dozen years later, Congress amended the Naturalization Act to grant citizenship to free blacks, but not Asians.[5] In 1882, Congress passed the Chinese Exclusion Act, ending Chinese immigration for the next sixty years. The enforcement of

From 1915 to 1920, Kenichi Zenimura honed his playing and leadership skills as a member of the all-Japanese Hawaiian Asahi, one of the top teams of the semipro Oahu-Service League in Honolulu (Nisei Baseball Research Project).

the Act unexpectedly created a labor shortage, which in turn led to an increase of Japanese immigrant laborers to the U.S. mainland and Hawaii. By 1887, the first group of Japanese immigrants founded an agricultural colony outside San Francisco.[6]

As each cultural milestone passed, Caucasian resentment towards Asians in the U.S. increased. This animosity was reflected in 1894, when U.S. district courts denied Japanese immigrants the right to vote. The courts' rationale? Persons of Japanese ancestry were not "free white" persons as required by the Naturalization Act. This decision was soon followed by the first anti–Japanese protest in California in 1900.

Kenichiro Zenimura was born in Hiroshima, Japan, on January 25, 1900. He was one of 45 million citizens living in the islands of Japan during the heart of the Meiji Period (1868–1912). The era reflected a Japan eager to adopt western cultural practices, such as a European-style constitution and a western-based education system.[7]

Sixty-five percent of the population, however, still relied on their bodies for work. Among these was Kenichiro's father, Masakachi. The elder Zenimura was a farmer and veteran of the Sino-Japanese war (1894–95), which saw Japan defeat China and claim Taiwan as its own territory. But following the war, relations between Japan and some European countries became strained over territorial disputes. As a result, Japan intensified its military and relations became strained with Russia, France and Germany. With a wife and newborn son to support, Masakichi decided to leave Japan and seek a better life for his family in Honolulu.[8] By 1904, tensions climaxed between Russia and Japan over Manchuria and Korea, and the Russo-Japanese War began. Papa Zenimura got out of Japan just in time.

In 1900, baseball was Japan's most popular team sport. It is commonly believed among historians that American schoolteacher Horace Wilson first introduced baseball to Japan in 1872.[9] However, a recent argument has been raised that Leroy Lansing Janes, also a teacher from the U.S., arrived a year earlier and introduced the game to his students at Kumamoto. Regardless of its origins, it is well documented that the game of baseball became the most popular team sport in Japan by the end of the 19th century.

In the early 1890s the American press began to report on the national pastimes' popularity in Japan. In 1891, one reporter observed that baseball has "gained a very promising foothold in Japan, and the 'Japs' can now steal the second bag, line out into center field, abuse the umpire and cut third base when he is looking in the opposite direction in true American style. The colleges have taken up the sport, and it is rapidly becoming popular throughout the kingdom."[10]

Drawing the "Yellow Color Line"

Back in the U.S., mainland players of Japanese ancestry began to make their mark on the national pastime. In June 1897, Cleveland Spiders manager Oliver Petruchio (Patsy) Tebeau attempted to sign a five-foot-three outfielder known only as "a relative of Sorakichi, the Japanese wrestler, who died a few years ago." Sorakichi was an amateur player in Chicago prior to catching Tebeau's interest.[11] According to the *Sporting Life* magazine, Tebeau thought that Sorakichi would be "the marvel of the diamond and the greatest player of the century."[12] No reason was reported as to why the Japanese outfielder never played with Cleveland. Eight years later an incident would occur that offered one plausible explanation.

In 1905, the *New York Times* announced that a Japanese ballplayer would get a major league tryout with manager John McGraw's New York Giants baseball club. Shumza Sugimoto, 23-year-old outfielder was invited to join the team in Hot Springs, Arkansas. Sugimoto was described as a 118-pound "jiu jitsu expert" who successfully took down Giants' outfielder Mike Donlin, a man who tipped the scales at 175.[13] McGraw said Sugimoto had "all the goods" as a player and described him as "extraordinarily alert, a splendid batter and base runner and unusually quick and accurate picking up flies and grounders."[14] Impressive talent was not enough. Sugimoto was not signed by McGraw for the 1905 season, and it appears that race was indeed the reason. Organized baseball was not comfortable with the idea of a Japanese player crossing the color line. Towards the end of spring training this uneasiness was expressed in a debate in the press. "Should the color line be extended to include Japanese players?" According to the *Sporting News*, the general consensus was "yes." Sugimoto told the press that he "did not like the drawing of the color line in his case" and decided to instead join the semipro Creole Stars, an integrated team in New Orleans.[15] The cases of Sorakichi (1897) and Sugimoto (1905) clearly demonstrate that there was "a yellow color line" drawn in the major leagues that would prevent Zenimura and his Japanese American peers from receiving the opportunity to compete at the highest level.

Hawaii — A Baseball Paradise

When young Zeni arrived in Honolulu in 1907, it offered a fascinating blend of people and cultures to spark the imagination of a young boy like Kenichi. In 1910, the population of Honolulu's 52,183 inhabitants reflected the following:

Population of Honolulu by Race and Gender, 1910[16]

Race	*Male*	*Female*	*Total*	*% of Total*
Japanese	7,659	4,434	12,093	23.17%
Chinese	6,948	2,626	9,574	18.35%
Other Caucasian	5,627	3,573	9,200	17.63%
Hawaiian	3,969	3,941	7,910	15.16%
Portuguese	3,042	3,105	6,147	11.78%
Caucasian-Hawaiian	2,000	2,233	4,233	8.11%
Asiatic-Hawaiian	653	727	1,380	2.64%
Korean	352	108	460	0.88%
Porto Rican	210	177	387	0.74%
Negro	179	148	327	0.63%
Spanish	141	117	258	0.49%
All other	66	61	127	0.24%
Filipino	68	19	87	0.17%
Total	30,914	21,269	52,183	100.00%

And, baseball was already the most popular sport in the islands. For that matter, the game was played in Hawaii long before it was introduced to Japan or to most of the continental U.S. In 1849, Alexander Cartwright — the man recognized as the father of the modern game — moved to Honolulu after a failed attempt at life in California. Upon arrival he quickly became one of the Hawaii's leading citizens by founding the first fire department, library, and baseball field. In 1852, he organized several teams and began to teach the game across the islands.[17] In the mid–1880s, Japanese plantation laborers played baseball to escape the tedious work of the sugarcane fields. As the rivalries between the plantation camp and company teams grew, so did the competition.[18]

Pitcher Kenso Nushida (standing left) and Zenimura (standing right) hang out with unidentified teammates at a local pool hall in Honolulu (Nisei Baseball Research Project).

The first Japanese American baseball team — the Excelsior — was founded in Hawaii in 1899 by the Rev. Takie Okumura. "I formed a baseball team, made up mostly of boys in my home," Okumura said. "Being the only team among the Japanese, its competitors were Hawaiian, Portuguese and Chinese." The Excelsiors were a successful baseball club and considered one of the pioneering Japanese baseball teams in Hawaii.[19]

Another early all–Japanese team in Hawaii was the Asahi ("Rising Sun") club, organized by Gikaku "Steere" Noda. The Asahi started off as a group of teenagers honing their skills on the sandlots of Iwilei in 1905. Within a few years they were playing in multi-ethnic leagues competing against the All-Chinese, the Braves (all Portuguese) and the Wanderers (all Caucasians). The diversity of the leagues inspired Noda to say "that through the world of sports, we can promote goodwill and fellowship."[20] Zeni joined the Hawaiian Asahi ball-club in 1915, and it appears that he gleaned Noda's wisdom and applied it throughout his career on goodwill tours.

The Early Influences of Champions

The passion for baseball in Hawaii was strong and was further elevated by visits from U.S. mainland teams. The first professional team from the U.S. to visit the Hawaiian Islands arrived in 1888 when sporting goods magnate Albert G. Spalding led a team of baseball tourists around the world. Unfortunately for both Hawaiians and the tourists, circumstances prevented the team from playing on the Islands. Their ship was delayed by bad weather and once they arrived, they found that the only possible day for them to play was Sunday. In 1888, Hawaii had a Blue Law (as did most of the U.S. states) which prohibited Sunday

Zenimura's Hawaiian Asahi teammates proudly display their 1918 league championship pennant (Nisei Baseball Research Project).

baseball. Spalding's tourists never played a single game in Hawaii. The Blue Laws were eventually changed in 1903, allowing Sunday baseball (but only after 1 P.M.).[21]

In 1908, a new generation of American tourists and sporting goods marketers set their sights on the Pacific. The Reach Sporting Goods Company announced that it was sending a team of "All-American" stars to tour China, Japan, the Philippines and Hawaii. Led by manager Mike Fisher of the Tacoma Tigers and Honolulu promoter Jesse Woods, who both had successfully led a tour to Hawaii the previous year, the proposed roster of the Reach All-Americans included an impressive list of major league and Pacific Coast League stars such as Frank Chance, Ty Cobb, Hal Chase and Joe Delahanty.[22]

But, to the fans' surprise, when the ship pulled away from the docks none of the marquee players were on board. Ty Cobb had opted for Winter League ball in New Orleans, and Frank Chance remained in California after leading his 1908 Cubs to its second World Series title in as many years. Furthermore, while in route to Japan, Joe Delahanty was notified by Washington to return home immediately for fear that he would be punished for playing with a team from an "Outlaw League"— that is, any league other than the National or American.[23]

Even without the top stars on the bill, the All-Americans drew crowds by the thousands and defeated local clubs at almost every stop. In 60 days, the team traveled approximately 10,000 miles, barnstormed China, Japan and the Philippines, and finished with an 18–2 record.[24]

Finishing their tour of Japan, the All-Americans journeyed to the Philippines, through China, and a final stop in Honolulu.[25] During this stretch of the tour they lost only three times, including two games to service teams in Manila.[26] The touring team was then scheduled to arrive in Honolulu on January 30, 1909. They were not due to return home to San Francisco until February 15, so the men had plenty of time to play three games and see the sites on the Island. The All-Americans played four games against an All-Hawaii team in Honolulu, losing only once, 4–3, when they loaned their own pitcher Bill Burns to the local club.[27] There are no documented reports of nine-year-old Kenichi Zenimura attending the games of the All-Americans in Honolulu. However, by 1912, young Zeni began to make his mark on the diamond as a budding 12-year-old star, and it seems unlikely that all the major league excitement could have escaped his attention.

In the fall of 1914, John McGraw of the New York Giants and Charles Comiskey and his White Sox embarked on a tour of the world. Joining McGraw and Comiskey was Ted Sullivan, one of the game's early pioneers and a visionary for baseball's global potential.[28] Three years after he managed the trip of the White Sox and Giants around the world, he went to South America to prepare for the invasion of two big league teams. The press remarked in 1917 that "Sullivan has probably done as much if not more, to further the best interest of baseball, than any other man." To that, Sullivan responded, "I appreciate that I have done a whole lot for the game, but I want to do more. I will make baseball as popular in South America as it is now in Cuba."[29] Through his goodwill efforts years later in Japan, Zenimura would try to match Sullivan's passion for exporting the American style of baseball to Asia.

In addition to exposure to major league players during this formative time in Zenimura's life, his early influences included Negro Leagues ballplayers as well. The 25th Infantry first arrived in Hawaii on January 15, 1913. The teams quickly organized, and after claiming the championship at Schofield Barracks against the 1st Infantry, 4th Calvary and the 1st Field Artillery teams, the 25th Infantry sought competition from civilian teams. The team joined the Honolulu City League, consisting of "the All Chinese, Portuguese, All-Japanese Asahi and the 25th Infantry." The all-black team was crowned the champions of the island of Ohau in 1913. Winning the league title in 1915, the Wreckers' roster proudly claimed several future Negro League stars, including Wilber "Bullet Joe" Rogan, Lem Hawkins, Dobie Moore, Bob Fagan and Oscar "Heavy" Johnson.[30] From the time it arrived, until 1918 when the team left for Nogales, Arizona, "the 25th regimental baseball team continued its winning streak and defeated practically every team that it played in the Hawaiian Islands."[31] That is, every team except the All-Japanese ballplayers.

Box scores between Zenimura's ballclubs — either the Hawaiian Asahi or Mills High — and the 25th Infantry have yet to surface. However, one first-hand report from a Hawaii native visiting the U.S. suggests the likelihood of him competing against the Wreckers is strong. "There is nothing but the best of feelings between the Japanese and the Americans on the islands," said Philip McKeg, a pineapple plantation owner in Hawaii. He also observed that "the national game of the island is baseball. The Hawaiian is a great lover of applause and he is keen for the game. On the Fourth of July I bobbled down on crutches to see a game between the Twenty-fifth Infantry, the negro regiment stationed in the Islands, and a team from one of the schools. The negroes were no match of the natives."[32]

Taking the Lead — High School and Semipro Ball

A tragic event from 1916 offers a rare glimpse into Zenimura's home life as a teenager. On October 21, 1916, Dr. William Levi Moore died shortly before his 53rd birthday. Moore lived at 916 Green Street in Honolulu. According to Kenichi's high school and military-draft records, the Zenimura family also lived at 916 Green Street. Closer inspection of the 1920 U.S. Census reveals that the head of the household was Nell L. Moore, a 52-year-old widow. Mr. and Mrs. Zenimura were listed as "servants" and their 15-year-old daughter Masako as a "lodger."[33] It is undetermined if the Zenimuras joined the Moore household before the doctor's passing in 1916. Nonetheless, the description of Moore's character provides a sense of the atmosphere and creative energy offered on Green Street in Honolulu.

Kenichi was the only boy in a house with four young females: his own sister Masaka and the three Moore daughters, Alice, Caroline, and Eloise. Dr. Moore was born in Michigan in 1863 and graduated with his M.D. from the University of Michigan in 1890. He moved to the islands in 1893 and was appointed to the position of government physician for Kohala, Hawaii. Four years later he was appointed superintendent of the Hilo Hospital, and during the bubonic plague in early 1900 was instrumental in setting up a quarantine to keep the disease from spreading across Hawaii. After his first wife died in 1895, he married Nell Lowry, the sister of a medical colleague, Frederick Lowry.[34]

Moore moved to Honolulu in 1901 and opened a private practice office on Beretania Street. For years he was connected with the Hawaii National Guard, serving as surgeon and holding the rank of captain. He was active in the Honolulu community, especially as an artist. As early as 1896, he was a member of the Kilohana Art League, exhibiting his own paintings at shows. Also a musician, Moore played the violin and was a member of the Honolulu Symphony Society. Upon his death, the following tribute was published by the Medical Society of Hawaii:

> Doctor Moore was a man of more than unusual ability. His purely technical qualifications were excellent, but greater than these were his artistic susceptibility and his culture. He loved beauty

> sincerely, was uplifted by harmonious sights and sounds, felt life his blood. Such men are lovers of women. He should have been an artist, pure and simple. Such work would have satisfied him better, joyed his soul, ministered to his fancy and imagination, and been better for him and the people he served than any other work whatever.... He paints! He is a poet! He writes for the newspapers! He is a great reader of fiction! He likes to work in the garden!... Doctor Moore was not an orthodox physician."[35]

Considering the creative sensibilities of Dr. Moore, it seems unlikely that the atmosphere was oppressive for the Zenimura parents working as domestic servants in the household. In

Kenichi Zenimura was a talented athlete and artist who enjoyed photography and music as a young man. Here he poses with a ukulele in this circa-1917 photograph (Nisei Baseball Research Project).

fact, during his teenage years with the Hawaiian Asahi, Kenichi displayed a passion for music and photography. It is quite possible that this creative expression was fostered by his time living with the Moore family on 916 Green Street.

Zenimura family legend has it that Kenichi's parents forbade him from playing baseball with the other boys, fearing that he would get hurt because of his diminutive stature. They would hide his equipment to keep him from playing, but sure enough little Zeni would find the hidden equipment and sneak away to the ball field to keep playing.

In a 1943 interview with the *Gila River Courier*, Zeni stated that as a 12 year old he was a member of the seventh grade champions of a grammar school league. With pride he described how his "club defeated all high schools except (one) on the isle of Oahu, Hawaii" that season.[36]

In January 1915, Honolulu witnessed the development of a formal league comprised of four and sometimes six teams, including a native team, a Japanese team, an American team, and an army team.[37] Over time the league developed senior and junior leagues based on skill level. After touring Japan in 1915, the Hawaiian Asahi competed in the junior league in 1916. That same year, Zenimura joined the Asahi.[38]

Between 1916 and 1919, Kenichi dedicated his playing time to two baseball teams, the semipro Hawaiian Asahi and the Mills High School ball club. Mills, which later changed its name to the Mid-Pacific Institute, was a perennial baseball powerhouse in the late 1910s. In his 1943 *Gila River Courier* interview, Zeni proudly shared that his Mills High school nine "played the Hilo All-Stars for Hawaii's Inter-Island Championship after defeating prep and semi-pro clubs."[39]

Mills High opened in the early 1890s when a group of Chinese boys knocked on the door of school founder Frank Damon and asked if he could teach them English and Christianity. Damon converted his home into a dormitory for 15 boarders, and by 1897 constructed a new building on Chaplain Lane in Honolulu. He called his school Chum Chun Shu Shat, which translates to "the Searching for Truth Institute." By 1910, the school was renamed as the Mills School.[40]

John McGraw observed in 1914 that with the proper coaching the Japanese could be turned into "star ball players."[41] Four years later Zenimura and his Mills teammates, Kenso Nushida, Fred Tsuda, and others, became the beneficiaries of "proper coaching" when Allison Bryce Given arrived on the scene. Given was from Covina, California, and a 1917 graduate of Pomona College. Nicknamed "Banty" for his diminutive, yet scrappy play in baseball and football, at Pomona he was described as "one of the South's most sensational back field men."[42] Despite his small size, he played big, and in 1914 he contributed to an unimaginable victory when tiny Pomona College defeated the mighty Trojans of the University of Southern California, 10–6.[43] In 1916, Given himself became the beneficiary of great coaching when legendary football coach Eugene W. Nixon took over the helm at Pomona College.[44] Nixon had previously coached Elmer Layden, one of the legendary "Four Horsemen of Notre Dame" in high school at Davenport, Iowa, and later in 1932 he co-authored the book *The Athlete in the Making*, which detailed the rise to fame of sports stars like Babe Ruth, Christy Mathewson, Bobby Jones and others.

The 1918 Season

The earliest game summary and box score located from Zenimura's playing career is dated May 31, 1918, when Mills High School defeated Punahou High (the future alma mater of U.S. President Barack Obama). Mills defeated Punahou, 4–3, and "a neat double play by Wah Han, Zenimura and Young Yuen saved the game for Mills." In addition to the glove, Zeni's quickness on the base paths was key to the Mills victory. "Punahou's pilikia* began in the sixth.... Nushida was on third — when Zenimura hit a grounder to Lydgate and the latter instead of tagging the base started in chasing Zenimura, who fooled around half way to the first base and finally landed safely there but only after Nushida had come home from third."[45]

Mills High School baseball coach Alison "Banty" Given (right), a native of Pomona, California, called Kenichi Zenimura (left) the best second baseman he coached in Hawaii (Nisei Baseball Research Project).

On June 11, 1918, Mills High defeated McKinley High in the final game of the Interscholastic Series to win the Island Championship. Nushida was the star of the day on the mound and with his bat:

> Nushida pitched a stellar game, allowing but six hits, walking two and striking out six men, while with the stick the little "Boy Wonder" was a power getting two hits, one of which went for three bags.[46]
>
> The attendance numbered some eight hundred fans, mostly school boys and girls. Mills of course, was on the job in the rooting line. At the close of the game the Mills lads danced their serpentine with Pitcher Nushida and Coach Given on their shoulders.[47]

It's worth noting that had McKinley's Wilfred Tsukiyama been available to play in the 1918 championship game against Zenimura and Mills, the outcome might have been different. In 1916, Tsukiyama was named the top athlete and scholar on the Island. He would later be named chief justice of the Hawaii Supreme Court and play a key role in Hawaii's statehood throughout the 1950s.[48]

After the 1918 summer break, Zeni returned to Mills School in September. His school enrollment form confirms his address at 916 Green Street and indicates that he was paying his own tuition through a partial scholarship and on-campus job as a building captain of the C8 dormitory. The form also provides some insight into the educational progress of Japanese students in early 20th-century Hawaii. It is unknown if Zenimura started school at a later age or if his high school education was somehow delayed. Nonetheless, the form

**Pronounced pee-lee-key-ah, meaning "trouble" in the Hawaiian language*

reveals that at the age of 18, Zeni had just completed his freshman year and was returning for his sophomore year of high school.[49]

Despite the fact that he was not yet allowed to become a citizen of the United States, Zenimura fulfilled his patriotic duty by registering for the World War I draft a month after returning to Mills. His registration card also reveals another fascinating insight — his full legal name: Jacob Kenichi Zenimura.[50] "Jacob was his 'American' name, although he never used it," explained his son Kenso Zenimura. "He always went by Kenichi, Ken, or Zeni."[51]

Fortunately for Zeni, the Allied powers signed a cease-fire agreement with Germany at Rethondes, France, bringing World War I to a close on November 11, 1918 — just 16 days after he registered for the draft.

The 1919 Season

The Mills High ballclub continued its winning ways in the 1919 season. On May 3 the *Honolulu Star Bulletin* announced that Mills defeated Punahou 9 to 7 at Alexander Field, and that McKinley did the same to St. Louis College with a 12–10 victory on Damon field. "With Zenimura on third, Sera poked a skyscraper to deep left and when the apple was grabbed Zenimura romped home for another tally, the last of the day."[52] The McKinley battery of Tani and Yoshikawa were the same as the 1918 championship game against Mills, and although in 1918 the catcher's name was misspelled as "Yoshigawa," it was in fact Fred

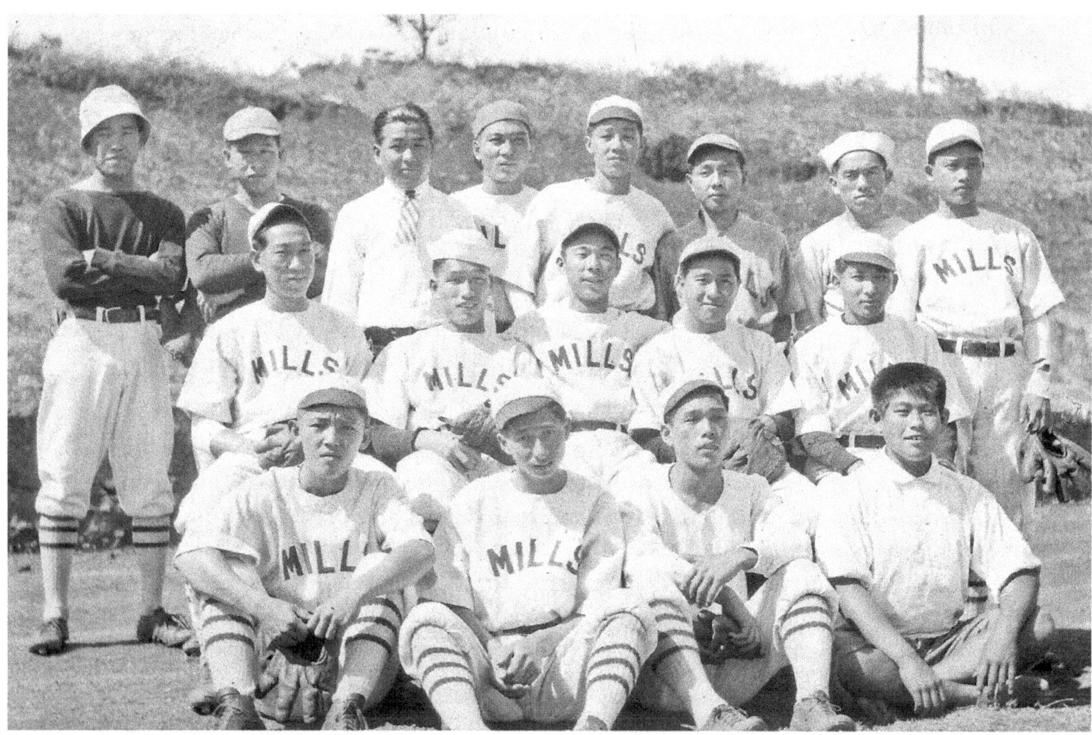

The Mills High baseball team won back-to-back Island Championships in 1918 and 1919 behind the play of Kenichi Zenimura and Kenso Nushida (second row, last two players at right) and Fred Tsuda (top row, fourth from left) (Nisei Baseball Research Project).

Yoshikawa, Zenimura's teammate on the Hawaiian Asahi and future teammate on many semipro teams throughout California. A week later Mills took on the college boys of St. Louis and defeated them 8–3 behind the battery of "Wonder Boy" Nushida and his favorite backstop, Zenimura.[53]

By late May, the Mills nine had secured its second Interscholastic Island Champi-

For the 1919 season Kenichi Zenimura moved to the catcher position, serving as on-field leader with Mills High battery-mates Ed Low (back, left) and Kenso Nushida (back, right) (Nisei Baseball Research Project).

onship.[54] A month later the school team continued to play, taking on semipro and military teams after the semester season ended. The *Honolulu Star-Bulletin* was there on May 27 covering the action: "Behind Low, the Mills school ball club overwhelmed the Fort Kamehameha team yesterday afternoon at the army post by a score of 14 to 3.... Zenimura with three hits ... and Tsuda of Mills with another circuit swat (home run) were the hitting stars of the day."[55]

After the Mills season ended, Zenimura and several of his school teammates found themselves competing against some of the best semipro and service teams on the island as members of the Hawaiian Asahi.[56] As a result of their strong showing on the diamond, the Asahi club earned an invitation to compete in the "A" league of the Oahu-Service League. The *Star-Bulletin* reported the team's promotion: "The Asahis number in their team some of the speediest of amateurs in the territory. Time was when their opponents did not consider them of championship [caliber] because they were so young and so small, but bitter experience over a period of two years has taught Honolulu balldom that the Asahis are a dangerous ball club at any time."[57]

Officials voted unanimously to admit two new clubs to the senior division of the Oahu-Service League — the Ashais and the Braves. To be the best you have to play the best. This is what Zenimura emphasized as a coach later in life, so it's no surprise that as a young player he and his teammates courageously took their lumps as rookies in the "A" league of the Oahu-Service League. "Without a dissenting voice the Asahis and Braves were promoted from the junior section to the higher leagues," reported the *Star-Bulletin*. "J.K. Zenimura and T. Miyahara, the Asahi representatives, gave the assurance in regard to the Asahi combination."[58] Zeni is already showing leadership on the team.

The Hawaiian Asahi lineup included:

Yoshikawa, 2b
Zenimura, c
Yamaguchi, 3b
Y. Kozuki, cf-rf
Tokuda, lf
Tsuda, rf
Yamashiro, 1b
Tominaza, ss
S. Kozuki, p
Matsuda, cf

The two Kozukis in the lineup were brothers Sinchi (b. 1895) and Sindo (b. 1902).[59]

In the fall of 1919, the Cincinnati Reds defeated Charles Comiskey's White Sox to win the World Series. Shortly after the series ended, suspicions surfaced that Chicago's South Side boys lost intentionally. As a result of this infamous "Black Sox" scandal, the officials decided that the league needed a commissioner. In 1920, Judge Kenesaw Mountain Landis was named the first commissioner of Major League Baseball. He ruled with an iron fist, and one of the unfortunate results was his quiet and unmovable position against blacks playing in organized ball. Landis's tenure as commissioner also hindered the multicultural and global expansion of the game. In addition to his unwavering position against blacks in the game, he also placed restrictions against players participating in exhibition games after October 30 — a direct attack against the California Winter League and international tours.

Kenichi Zenimura (front row, far left) and Ty Miyahara (back row, far right, wearing scarf) were instrumental in the negotiations to have the Hawaiian Asahi move up from the junior to the senior division of the Oahu-Service League in 1919 (Nisei Baseball Research Project).

The Early 1920 Season

On January 31, 1920, a baby boy in Cairo, Georgia, named Jack Roosevelt Robinson celebrated his first birthday. On that same day, more than 2000 miles away in Honolulu, Hawaii, twenty-year-old Kenichi entered the Mills High administration building and announced he was withdrawing from school. According to the Mills records department, the reason for his early departure was because he was "going to the States." It appears that Zenimura left Mills High without earning a high school diploma.[60]

He used the month of February to get things in order, and by March he was on his way to the U.S. mainland aboard the S.S. *Lurline*.[61] (The *Lurline* was the same passenger ship that sent a radio signal after sighting the Japanese war fleet on their way toward Pearl Harbor on November 29, 1941.)

The record reveals some interesting facts about Zenimura. According to this document, he was married when he left for America. It is unknown if this is accurate or simply a documentation error, for it is widely believed that Kiyoko Lillian Yamasaki, whom he married in 1924 and with whom he had three boys together (Kenji, 1925; Kenso, 1927; and Kenshi, 1928), was his first and only wife.

His occupation is listed as student, and the designation of his final destination and purpose raises even more questions. Zeni told ship officials that his final destination was Dubuque, Iowa, where he was "going to school." Handwritten notes above that entry seem to suggest that Zeni's school destination was "Dubuque, IA, High School."

Was he going to Dubuque High School to finish his high school education, perhaps with the plan of joining a state college, similar to his on-field rival Wilfred Tsukiyuma at Coe College? According to son Kenso Zenimura, his father mentioned a few times throughout his life that he received a scholarship to play ball in Iowa, but that ultimately "it didn't work out."[62]

Zeni never made it to Dubuque. It seems that he was either sidetracked or persuaded

Zenimura (far left) was a meticulous chronicler of his early life. In his personal archive of photographs from Hawaii, he identified this image as his 20th birthday celebration, January 25, 1920 (Nisei Baseball Research Project).

to stay in Fresno, California. How and why did Zeni select Dubuque as the destination to begin his American dream? There are a few hypotheses:

- The Dubuque Legacy—During the 1919–20 seasons, Dubuque was recognized as *the* baseball mecca of the U.S. It was where Charles Comiskey and Ted Sullivan first teamed up together in 1879 on Dubuque's ballclub in the Northwestern League, which would later evolve into the American League in 1900.[63] Zenimura approached the global and multicultural expansion of the game with the same passion as Sullivan, so perhaps he admired Sullivan and wanted to experience the baseball mecca of Dubuque first hand.
- The Wilfred Tsukiyama precedent—perhaps community leaders or school officials selected Zeni as the top athlete and wanted to send him to an Iowa College, but because of his incomplete high-school career, he needed to first earn his diploma in Dubuque.
- The Banty Given connection—perhaps Mills High coach Banty Givens leveraged his relationship with Eugene Nixon, of Iowa football coaching fame, to network and secure a spot for Zeni in Dubuque.

While unconfirmed it seems that a combination of the second and third options is the strongest possibility. First of all, Banty respected the talent of Zenimura. We know this from a 1923 *Los Angeles Times* editorial, in which he described Zeni as the best second baseman he ever coached in Hawaii.[64] Secondly, it is documented that Nixon maintained his Iowa connections after he arrived on the West coast. A contemporary of Eugene Nixon's was powerful district judge Matthew C. Matthews (1862–1921). In 1920, Judge Matthews had a son employed by Dubuque High School, a young World War I veteran named Blaney F. Matthews. The younger Matthews served as the school's baseball coach.[65]

It is unknown exactly how Zeni came to select Dubuque as his final American destination. All we know for sure is that he didn't end up there. The years in Hawaii had provided Zenimura exposure to major league ballplayers, interaction with diverse cultural and ethnic groups, a sound philosophy of sportsmanship and goodwill, and, of course, the opportunity to play ball. On March 30, 1920, Zenimura left Hawaii with his head and heart full of dreams of playing professional ball in Iowa. Instead, destiny would keep him in California as his fate already appeared to be intertwined with the future events of building baseball, serving as its ambassador, and keeping it alive behind barbed wire.

2

Breaking Down Barriers (1920–1924)

"The fight of the Japanese for equal rights is similar to the fight of the Negroes are making for their rights. Educated people of all races recognize that the color line is artificial."[1]
—W.E.B. DuBois, Atlanta University professor

On April 4, 1920, the world was in a state of transition. It was Easter Sunday and President Woodrow Wilson had just helped to create the League of Nations, an effort that would later win him the Nobel Peace Prize. Mohandas K. Gandhi emerged as the leader of India's movement towards independence from Britain. Congress passed the 18th amendment prohibiting the sale of alcohol and was just months away from passing the 19th amendment granting women the right to vote. It was an election year with the Republican ticket of Warren G. Harding preparing to take on the Democratic ticket of Cox and Roosevelt.

On the diamond, major league baseball was wrapping up spring training to begin a new season. During the winter break Boston owner Harry Frazee sold Babe Ruth to the New York Yankees, calling the slugger "the most selfish and inconsiderate man ever to put on a baseball uniform." On the West Coast, the major league Chicago Cubs lost their last spring training game to the San Francisco Seals of the Pacific Coast League. The Shasta Limited, formerly the colored Oakland Oaks, battled the Perfection Ice Creamers across the bay with Jimmy Claxton and Bullet Meadows on the mound. And just miles away at San Francisco's wharf, the S.S. *Lurline* docked at Pier 30 after completing its 2,097 mile journey from Honolulu. On this same day, 20-year-old Kenichi Zenimura exited the steamship, taking his first step on American soil and embarking on a journey to make his American dreams a reality.

When he arrived in California, Zeni was just one of 72,000 people of Japanese ancestry living in the state. The racial and ethnic composition of California was not particularly diverse. In 1920, the state's 3.4 million residents reflected the following makeup:

Population of California by Race, 1920[2]

Race	*Total*	*Percent*
White	3,264,711	95.3
Black	38,763	1.1
American Indian	17,360	0.5
Asian & Pacific Islander	106,027	3.1
Total population	3,426,861	100.0

After traveling to Fresno to visit his cousin and former teammate Katsuo "Jimmy" Hirokawa, young Zeni was encouraged to stay in Fresno. It appears that he found a more attractive offer than whatever awaited him in Iowa. He never made it to Dubuque. Instead he made central California his home and joined the fledgling all–Japanese baseball team, the Fresno Athletic Club (FAC).

The earliest known record of the FAC team is dated November 20, 1919, when it was scheduled to take on the Friends Educational Society at the Fink-Smith Playground.[3] The FAC founders were pitcher Ben Shintaku and catcher Frank Narushima, both student-athletes at Fresno High School. The two prepared for the new fall league as members of the Santos Pirates, a local semipro team led by Mike Santos, one of the top players in the Central Valley area.[4] The early box scores of the FAC reflected a team with talent, and yet a lot of room for improvement. After a 10–0 loss, the press observed that "the losers are unfortunate in that they have only been organized a short time and furthermore, because their players are not able to show up at all times."[5]

The Fresno Winter League of 1919 was comprised of five local teams: Cartwright's Pruners, Fresno Reds, Santos Pirates, Southern Pacific and the Fresno Athletic Club.[6] The *Fresno Morning Republican* praised the new ballclub's potential. "The Japanese boys of the F.A.C. who have made marked improvement in the base ball world of Fresno ... will come out for their game tomorrow ready to give a first-class battle."[7]

Off the diamond, the Caucasian farming community of central California began to feel threatened by the growing Japanese population. Shortly before Christmas of 1919, local farmers gathered in the neighboring town of Porterville for "further discussion of the Japanese question" and its impact on the raisin industry. The meeting included reports shared by officials of the Anti-Japanese League and a recruitment drive to grow their membership.[8]

Zeni arrived in Fresno to a newly formed FAC and neighborhood tensions. Once here, he not only bolstered the club's play on the field, he developed important relationships off the field as well. One of the most important relationships was with FAC co-founder Frank Narushima. He and Zeni had many things in common. Both were born in Hiroshima, Japan, both loved sports, and both possessed the charisma and drive to become winners in anything they did.

Narushima was born in Japan in 1901 with the birth name of Takizo Matsumoto. His name was changed when his family moved to Fresno when he was a toddler. Shortly after their arrival in the U.S., Matsumoto's father passed away. His widowed mother, Kiyo Matsumoto, remarried restaurant owner Hichiza Narushima, a man 14 years her senior.[9] Afterwards, young Takizo took on both an American first name and his stepfather's surname and became known as Frank Narushima. Young Frank eventually became a star athlete at Fresno High School, excelling in football (halfback and end), baseball (outfielder and catcher), and track (sprinter) between 1916 and 1919.

When Zenimura arrived in Honolulu in late 1907 with his aunt Hisa Hirokawa, she listed their closest relative in Japan as a sister with the last name Matsumoto who lived in the Takeya-cho section of Hiroshima. When the Zenimura family traveled to Japan during the late 1910s, they indicated that their closest relative in Japan was Sutosaburo Matsumoto, an uncle who also lived in Takeya-cho, Hiroshima.[10] These facts point to the strong possibility that the maiden name of Kenichi's mother Waka was Hirokawa, and that she had a third sister who married into the Matsumoto family. This being the case, there is a strong possibility, although unconfirmed at this time, that Kenichi Zenimura and Frank Narushima (aka Takizo Matsumoto) were in fact distant cousins.

The 1920 Season — Common Bonds

The summer of 1920 witnessed a heat wave and drought in Fresno, with temperatures reaching the 115 degree mark and two months without rain. The local press gave considerable ink to the extreme weather, but offered few box scores and game summaries of the Fresno Athletic Club.

Despite the lack of local baseball coverage, several significant events unfolded in 1920 that would impact Zeni and his Japanese American baseball peers. The first occurred in south Los Angeles when prominent black businessman Doc Anderson constructed a baseball stadium known as White Sox Park exclusively for West Coast Negro League teams and players.[11] The White Sox negotiated a deal for the L.A. Nippons, the local Japanese American ballclub, to also play at the new ballpark. Furthermore, they invited the Nippons' second baseman, Sanji Sakamoto, to play with their ballclub in June.[12] Known as "Sanji, the Japanese Wonder," Sakamoto was once a star pitcher with Los Angeles High School, where he was a teammate of White Sox pitcher Ajay Johnson. Sakamoto's tenure with the all-black White Sox was cut short with the arrival of second baseman Bob Fagan, Zenimura's old rival from the 25th Infantry team, formerly of Hawaii and now based in Arizona. Zeni and the FAC would play an important game in White Sox ballpark years later.

Another key event unfolding in the late summer of 1920 was the news from Atlanta that a Japanese outfielder named Satsumma, a player with the Atlanta Southern League Club, had been sold to the Pittsburgh Nationals.[13] Unfortunately the "yellow color line"— which surfaced publicly in 1905 when John McGraw gave Japanese outfielder Shumza Sugimoto a tryout with the New York Giants — was still firmly in place.[14] Satsumma, like Sugimoto and other players of Japanese ancestry before him, never saw the light of day in the major leagues.

For the Japanese American stars in Fresno, color lines were nonexistent at the semipro level. Pitcher Ben Shintaku impressed everyone with his arm as member of the 1920 Fresno Twilight League All-Star team, an interracial squad of Caucasians, Hispanics and Japanese Americans.[15]

Approximately six months after Zeni's arrival in the U.S., the FAC scheduled its first game against a black ball club — the Fresno Colored Giants. The *Fresno Bee* announced the game:

> A splendid contest is assured for the Fink-Smith playground when the Colored Giants meet the Fresno Athletic Club. The Colored Giants have got together their suits and other paraphernalia and will have practically the same personnel as represented in the City League three years ago. In addition to the splendid baseball played by the Giants, the good-natured comedy which they put on is highly entertaining to the crowd.[16]

The Colored Giants defeated the FAC by the score of 8–2, piling up eight runs in the first inning.[17]

The loss to the Colored Giants serves as a valuable assessment of the FAC's ability to play baseball, as the Giants were considered one of the top black ball clubs on the West Coast. This reputation was earned just four years earlier when the Colored Giants played as the Fresno Shadow Giants. The *Fresno Bee* reported:

> The Fresno fans are being furnished with some real live baseball now that the city league is on in full sway.... The real dark horse of the league are the Shadow Giants who are putting up the best baseball of any of the clubs. This club of fast players is lead by our old friend "Chet" Bost,

> who captained the Oak Leafs and also the Oakland Giants.... "Chet" has rounded together an all-star club and is getting good baseball out of them.[18]

In West Coast Negro league circles, Bost was considered one of the top players and managers around. The Fresno captain was renowned for having hit two home runs in one inning while playing in the Utah State League.[19] And despite his teams' numerous sponsors and location changes, their caliber of talent remained among the best in black baseball across the nation. Over the years, Bost's teams would play under many names, including the Colored Giants, Shadow Giants, Lynne Stanley Giants, Weilheimer Giants, Pierce Giants, Oakland Giants, Oaks, and Oak Leafs. As the Oak Leafs in 1916, Bost and his men received a visit from Rube Foster and the Chicago American Giants. Foster's club was on its way to Honolulu and had arranged to play the Oak Leafs as it passed though California. The *Oakland Tribune* captured the expectations of fans and players alike: "This will be some series, as the Oak Leafs can boast of the best colored team in the West, while the Chicago Giants rank as the best east of the Rockies.[20] The pregame comparison to the top Negro club in the East speaks highly of the caliber of Bost's team.[21]

While Japanese Americans and African Americans found a common bond on and off the field, tensions among the white population towards people of Japanese ancestry continued to rise. Presidential candidate Warren G. Harding declared during his campaign in 1920 that there was a greater need to protect the West from Japan.[22] And in November, just after Harding won the election, the state of California passed a stronger Alien Land Law, making it even more difficult for Japanese-born residents to own land in California. At the time, Japanese American farmers produced $67 million worth of crops, more than 10 percent of California's total crop value.[23]

The 1921 Season — First Japanese American Championship

According to historian William F. McNeil, the California Winter League (CWL) experienced an increase in talent during the 1920-21 season. McNeil called it a "breakthrough" year with competition playing at the AA and AAA level.[24] The CWL rise in talent was attributed to the participation of Negro Leagues caliber players with the L.A. White Sox, Lincoln Giants and Alexander Giants. They played all of their games at the newly constructed Anderson Park (aka White Sox Park), named after local black businessman Doc Anderson, and their rosters boasted future Hall of Famers Andy Cooper and Biz Mackey, and a host of local black athletes, including University of Southern California star running back Johnny Riddle. Zenimura and his FAC team would get their chance four years later to test their mettle against these great ballplayers.

In February 1921 in New York, a group of Japanese representatives from Waseda, Tokyo, Yokohama and Kobe universities announced that they were eager to take "an all-star baseball team made up of members of the Race," also known as Negro League players, to Japan. Spokesmen for the delegation told reporters that they were eager to see a first-class team of Negro Leaguers play Waseda University, with the goal of helping to foster interest in the pastime in Japan.[25]

Waseda University would have to wait another six years to play a first-class team of Negro League players in Japan. Yet, they only needed to wait three weeks to compete against a first-class team of Japanese American players in Hawaii. On May 9, 1921, the college boys from Waseda battled the Hawaiian Asahi, featuring many of Zeni's former Island teammates and future FAC teammates. The visiting ballclub was walloped by the Asahis to the tune of 8 to 2.[26]

But U.S.–Japanese baseball relations flourished in the later part of 1921. The *Los Angeles Times* reported that nine clubs from the Pacific Coast and Hawaii had either made the trip or were making plans to tour Japan. The list of teams invading Japan included a PCL all-star team led by Seattle baseball man Frank Miya; semipro players from Canada and Hawaii; the Seattle Asahi, the top Nisei team of the West Coast; college teams, including the University of California and University of Washington; and the Sherman Indian School of Southern California.[27]

On September 26, 1921, the *Los Angeles Times* reported that pitcher Frank "Breezy" Brindza of the Vancouver Beavers of the Pacific International League tossed a no-hit, no-run game in an exhibition contest against Fresno's Japanese Athletic Club. Brindza was in Stockton pitching for the semipro Sperry Flours. The final score was 13 to 0.[28] Brindza had a connection to Zenimura's Hawaiian past. The lean, right-handed pitcher started playing baseball in 1914 in the Hawaiian Islands while in the army. For four-and-a-half years he pitched for the All-Stars and averaged 28 victories a season. After being discharged from the army in 1921, Brindza went to Vancouver where he joined the Beavers.[29] He acquired the nickname of "Breezy" in Honolulu where he set numerous strikeout records with his army team.[30]

On October 29–30, 1921, the FAC traveled to San Jose for a weekend tournament to compete for the Japanese Baseball Championship of California. "The Fresno athletic club nine meet various Japanese nines from the northern part of the state for the Pacific coast championship," reported the *Fresno Bee.* The FAC represented the southern and central part of the state armed with the solid roster of Manager Kakebe, Captain Zenimura, Shintaku, Nakagawa, Kawamura, Sakata, Hasaki, Nakamura, Iwata, Mizote and Henmi.[31] Once again Zenimura had stepped up to the plate, showing leadership as the captain of the team. Just weeks after the New York Giants defeated the New York Yankees 5 games to 3 in a best of nine series and Babe Ruth hit the first World Series home run of his career, Zenimura and the FAC claimed the crown as the champion Japanese American baseball team in the state of California.[32]

The 1922 Season — Groundwork in Japan

Japanese American baseball teams began to solidify across the West Coast in the early 1920s. Contradicting reports surfaced in 1922 as to which team held the Japanese baseball state championship in California. According to the *Los Angeles Times*, the Los Angeles Nippons defeated Zenimura's boys in Fresno for the right to the title.[33] But, according to the *Fresno Bee*, the FAC defeated the southern all-stars for the championship in June 1922.[34] An early photograph of the Fresno Japanese team, circa 1923, features a banner displaying the words "Champion, Season 1922, Fresno vs. Los Angeles," which supports the claim that Fresno was indeed the top team in California for the season. Despite the confusion, it appears that neither team from the Golden State was strong enough to defeat the squad from Washington, the Seattle Asahi. The boys from Seattle won the 1922 West Coast Japanese baseball championship and the right to represent the U.S. during a tour of Japan in 1923. Zeni would later devise a plan to bolster the talent of his club to claim this championship from Seattle. His plan would require yet another trip back to Japan and Hawaii.

During a 1943 interview with the *Gila News-Courier*, Zenimura stated that after spending time in Fresno he moved back to Japan to coach Japan's Koryo High baseball team for two months. He reported that the Koryo team roster included his cousin Tatsumi Zenimura, outfielder and future Meiji University team captain, and Kisaku Kato, future player and manager for Nankai of the Nippon Professional Baseball League.[35] Cousin Tatsumi was born in 1905, placing Zenimura's coaching stint at Koryo sometime between July and October 1922. Joining Zenimura at Koryo High School was another cousin, Frank Narushima. According to historian Kyoko Yoshida, Narushima enrolled at Koryo at age 22 and later attended Meiji University to study economics and the Japanese language.[36] While Captain Zenimura was away in Japan, other Fresno athletic club players such as Miyahara and Mori traveled south to temporarily join the L.A. Nippons.[37]

Passenger ship records confirm Kenichi returning from Japan in late October 1922, traveling with his mother and sister. Their return passenger record on the S.S. *President Taft* featured a misspelling of the Zenimura surname: "Zinamura." This 1922 ship record indicates that Zeni was 22 and single, and that his closest friend was Mr. Torjiro Yamasaki of 1432 Tulare St., Fresno, California.[38] Torjiro was the father of Sam and Bob Yamasaki, both baseball teammates and friends of Zeni. It was through this relationship that Zeni would later meet and fall in love with their sister, Kiyoko Lillian Yamasaki. In fact, after Zeni and Kiyoko's marriage in 1924, the newlywed Zenimuras continued to live with the in-laws at 1432 Tulare St.

Earlier in the year major league baseball had announced that it would send a team of all-stars to tour Japan. The tour was the brainchild of American League President Ban Johnson, who said, "Perhaps someday we will have the Champions of America meeting the winners of the Japanese series in a real world's series. This may be my dream, but it is a dream I shall cherish until it materializes."[39] The Zenimura family and the major league tourists were literally ships passing in the night across the Pacific. Herb Hunter's boys sailed for Japan on October 14, 1922, and among the stars were Waite Hoyt, George Kelley, Irish Meusel, Luke Sewell and Casey Stengel.[40] Once they arrived in Japan, the big leaguers defeated every college, industrial, and amateur team the country had to offer — except one. On November 23, Hunter's All-Stars lost 9 to 3 to the amateur Mita Club, led by future Japanese Baseball Hall of Fame pitcher Michimaro Ono.[41] On the surface, one would think that the Mita Club and fans would be happy with the victory over the Americans, but they weren't. Reports out of Japan explained why:

> America's reputation for sportsmanship suffered a severe blow when the American baseballers threw away Sunday's game to the Mita local nine, which is strong nationally, but obviously no match for the American professionals.... The general opinion was frankly expressed that the Americans dropped the frame for advertising purposes, anticipating increased gate receipts later at Osaka and other parts.... The *Tokio Asahi* expressed the disappointment, "We welcomed the American team because we thought they were gentlemanly and sportsmanlike. They have now shown themselves to be full of the mean professional spirit. Japanese baseball followers are not foolish enough to believe they tried to beat Mita.... They disappointed our hopes and left an unpleasant impression upon us."[42]

Losing pitcher Waite Hoyte would later explain that he and his teammates were just "clowning around" on the field and meant no disrespect to their Japanese hosts.[43] Nonetheless, the damage was done. As a result of several factors — including the 1922 Herb Hunter All-Star thrown game fiasco, the 1923 Great Kanto earthquake in Japan, and restrictive post-season play policies established by Commissioner Landis — no major league team would tour Japan for another eight years. This major league void would proudly be filled by Zenimura and his West Coast Nisei and Negro League peers. Ironically, just as Zenimura and his teammates were about to enter the role of goodwill baseball ambassadors to Japan, on November 13, 1922, the U.S. Supreme Court ruled in *Ozawa v. U.S.* to reaffirm the ban on Japanese immigrants becoming naturalized American citizens.[44] First-generation Japanese Americans, or Issei, would have to wait another 30 years for the opportunity to call the United States of America their true home.

A week after the Ozawa ruling the Fresno Winter League season prepared for another exciting round of competition. The Winter League was comprised of the best amateur and semipro teams in Fresno, which included Billings and Meyering, Fraternal Brotherhood, Standard Oil, Fresno Morning Republican, Fresno Bee and the Fresno Athletic Club. Just before the season started, a "slight objection was advanced against the Japanese on the grounds that once before they entered a playground league and then dropped out." It's unknown why the FAC pulled out of a previous season. Regardless, the Fresno Japanese nine gave league officials their word that they would play the entire schedule. The FAC response to this concern also shed some light on Zenimura's secret plans to bolster the talent of the club. "Manager Shintaku stated that a pitcher would be here soon from Hawaii and that his team would be prepared to fight for every game."[45]

Even without Zenimura and the new talent source on the roster, the FAC defeated the Fresno Republican squad in its first Winter League game by the score of 6 to 4. The press called the contest "one of the best games that has been played this season.... The Japanese players ... are a bunch of hustling ball players who will give the other teams in the league a run for the flag."[46] A week before Christmas 1922, the Fresno press observed that all FAC competitors would "have a tough proposition on its hands in the tough Japanese players. This bunch has been strengthened by the addition of some fine pitching talent and will make the rest of the teams step up."[47]

The 1923 Season—The Recruiter and Organizer Emerges

Zenimura holds the distinction of being the first to organize and bring a Hawaiian All-Star nine to the U.S. mainland.[48] This claim is supported by the *Oakland Tribune* in 1923. "The first all Japanese baseball team to visit the mainland will start from here in February and make a tour of California, according to an announcement made here today. The All-Hawaiian Japanese is the name of the team."[49] Zenimura's plan to improve his team began to unfold in the press. He would encourage the top talent in Hawaii to tour the U.S. and, once the tour ended, convince the best players to stay in Central California and help expand Japanese American baseball throughout the region.

The FAC's need for more on-field support was reflected in box scores from the early 1923 season. "The Japanese players representing the FAC ... are in and outers," declared the *Fresno Bee.* "One day they put on a great exhibition and the next week look terrible, as was the case last Sunday when the Brotherhood team won 15 to 0."[50] The following week the FAC defeated the Fresno Republican nine 6 to 2,[51] and then weeks later lost to the Fraternal Brotherhood 18 to 9.[52] The team, while talented, was inconsistent and needed help. Help was on the way.

On February 5, 1923, Zenimura departed Honolulu on the passenger ship *President Cleveland.* A few days later he arrived in San Francisco with a final destination of Fresno.

It's worthwhile to note that Zeni also listed his contact in the U.S. as James Hirokawa, his FAC teammate and cousin, and his occupation as "student."[53] According to Zenimura's son Howard, his father attended school to become a mechanic. Most likely, this passenger ship record entry reflects Kenichi's time as a mechanic in training.

Zenimura wasted no time in putting his recruitment plan into place. He scheduled a contest on February 23 between the existing FAC squad and his newly formed Hawaiian All-Stars. With Zeni on the team of Hawaiian Stars, they defeated the FAC 9 to 5 and the San Joaquin Valley Japanese All-Stars 12 to 3." The *Fresno Bee* reported, "The touring Japanese (Hawaiian All-Stars) will play in Stockton Sunday, after which the club will be disbanded, six of the players coming to Fresno to remain." The six players joining Zeni from the Hawaiian All-Stars were the "Boy Wonder" Kenso Nushida, 23; William Nakamura, 22; and two sets of brothers: Takeo "Tom" Hirano, 21, and Jenichi "John" Hirano, 19, from Honolulu; and Hisashi Okino, 23, and Yoshi Okino, 25, from Hilo.[54]

The arrival of the All-Hawaiian Japanese ballplayers generated a lot of buzz among the fans and press. It even helped open the eyes, ears and minds of those with prejudices towards Japanese. According to the *Fresno Bee*, stereotypes of Japanese were quickly challenged. "The All-Hawaiian Japanese Ball tossers ... showed snappy fielding ability ... all of the players are American born, having first seen the light of day in the Hawaiian Islands. They all speak the American language without an accent. The Orientals are all larger than the average Japanese and one of them weighs nearly 200 pounds."[55]

The presence of the All-Hawaiian Japanese ballplayers also revealed the racial stereotype of the times. In early 1923, *Los Angeles Times* sports reporter Harry A. Williams featured a letter from Zenimura's high school coach Banty Given in his editorial "Sport Shrapnel." In the letter, Given reveals "certain athletic characteristics of the Chinese and Japanese contrary to the general conception of the little brown men." Zeni's former coach shared his views:

> Here in Honolulu we have good opportunity of seeing the evolution of the player of oriental parentage.... Four years of baseball and other coaching in a school exclusively oriental, has taught this [sic] writer many things and suggests several generalities ... the best hitter I had in four years was a Japanese ... the best pitcher a Japanese; height 5 feet even, weight 104 lbs ... best second baseman Japanese; weight 100 lbs; hardly any height....[56]

While not named directly, the pitcher appears to be Kenso Nushida, and the second baseman is Zenimura, both Mills High players for Given. Their former coach concluded: "World series between Oriental and Occidental never a possibility, I think, as the Chinese and Japanese lack the sheer physical strength to battle America's best. Don't think that nine little men could ever be good enough to trim nine big men on a baseball field or any other field."[57]

Early March 1923 saw the addition of the recruited Hawaiian-All Stars to the FAC roster. The press was in awe of Nushida's pitching prowess. "[T]he Orientals (FAC) have a new flinger that has been standing the Valley semipros on their collective ears," they declared.[58]

With a loss in a close game for the season finale, the FAC failed to make the Winter League playoffs. In the heated contest against the Biola nine, the FAC held the 1–0 lead until the seventh inning. "Bunched hits in the fatal seventh inning gave the Biola baseball team a 2 to 1 victory yesterday over the FAC. Unto this time Nushida, the Japanese twirler, had the Biola swingers helpless but he wobbled slightly in this frame and the game was lost."[59]

The FAC might have lost the final Winter League game, but they won the respect

Kenso "The Boy Wonder" Nushida, star pitcher and teammate of Zenimura's in Hawaii and California, became the first Japanese American to play in the Pacific Coast League when he was signed by the Sacramento Solons in 1932 (Zenimura Family Archive).

of the local press and baseball peers. Impressed with the performance and potential of the semipro FAC, the Salt Lake City Bees — a Pacific Coast League team that recently made Fresno its spring training home — agreed to meet the Japanese ballclub in an exhibition game.[60]

Well aware of the FAC reputation, Bee manager Duffy Lewis announced he would use his first string players against the Japanese ballclub.[61] And he would need them. The *Fresno Bee* reported that "the contest Sunday between the FAC, the snappy Japanese aggregation, and the Salt Lake Club, is attracting a lot of attention among the Orientals of the Valley. Nushida, the Japanese mound man, has been hurling great ball this season and will appear on the firing line."[62]

On Saturday, March 16, the anticipation for the contest was captured by *the Bee*:

> The big Sunday game will be with the FAC, a Japanese team, that has defeated some of the best of the local Winter leaguers. The club team will be strengthened by the addition of the best talent from the Hawaiian Stars, the barnstorming Island team that recently won a double-header here from the Valley Orientals. Nushida, the lad who came over from Honolulu with the Stars, will do the hurling for the Athletic Club. This little fellow has a world of stuff and in the warm weather he should give the Coast Leaguers some nice shoots to look over.[63]

On Sunday, March 17, 1923, a crowd of 3,000 fans, more than half of them Japanese residents of the San Joaquin Valley, gathered to watch the first game ever between an All-Japanese team and a Pacific Coast League ballclub. According to the *Fresno Bee,* "the crowd yesterday saw a bunch of fancy fielding on the part of the Orientals who looked like a bunch of grammar school boys when stacked against the Salt Lake club. Iwata, the left fielder, was the star of the afternoon." The Bees trimmed the FAC by the score of 3 to 0. Nushida held the Bees to three runs and 12 hits, however the real challenge for the FAC was not the fielding, but hitting. In all, just four FAC batters reached base, and all were stranded.[64]

In his first game against PCL-caliber pitching, Zenimura recorded six plate appearances and reached base twice, once on a walk and the other an error. Defensively he had a solid day at the shortstop position with 3 putouts and 4 assists. In fact, his glove work matched his counterpart on Bees, shortstop Tony Lazzeri, who recorded 1 putout and 4 assists.

After the historic Bee-FAC matchup, each team went their respective ways. The Bees jumped back into their spring training routine to prepare for two contests with the Chicago Cubs, and the FAC geared up to take on local semipros teams like the Medera Coyotes, Sun Maids, Pierce Lumber Company and Murphy Motor Company in the new Twilight League season.[65]

The spring of 1923 also saw the inaugural San Joaquin Valley Japanese track meet, held in early April to honor the birthday of the historic Buddha. Billed as the biggest attraction of the year for the local Japanese, the nine-event track meet was held at the Fresno Buddhist Church Athletic Grounds, and featured teams from Bakersfield, Hanford, Visalia, Parlier and Fresno. The hometown featured two teams, the Japanese Young Men's Christian Association (YMCA) and the Young Men's Buddhist Association (YMBA). Several FAC ballplayers were members of the Fresno YMBA, such as Henmi, Yoshikawa, Tsukimura, Sako, Yamasaki, Nakagawa, Matsuda, and Iwasaki. Zenimura most likely was also a participant, as one name in the Japanese lineup is "Zeusmian," probably a typo by the local press.[66]

The spring of 1923 brought a lot of rain in the Fresno area. In late March, the FAC had a game "scheduled in the semi-finals for the Japanese championship but this was postponed. They asked Lewis for a chance so the Salt Lake skipper put them on the Sunday morning time."[67] In the second game ever between a Japanese ballclub and PCL team, the boys from Salt Lake were victorious once again, defeating the FAC 7 to 0 in the spring training exhibition game.[68]

Shortly after the FAC-Salt Lake contest, the Fresno City Baseball League announced a game between Zenimura's team and the Fresno Tigers. "The FAC is a worthy opponent for any bunch of ball tossers. The fans that take in the contest tomorrow will see some remarkable fielding. The Japanese are weak with the hickory but, Oh Man, how they can snare the drives and every one of the outfielders can cover more ground than a circus tent."[69] The results of the Tigers-FAC contest were not published.

In late April 1923, the FAC team won the state Japanese baseball championship for the third consecutive year by defeating the San Jose Asahi club, 6 to 3, at Ewing Field in San Francisco. Members of the championship Fresno team were Captain Zenimura, Nushida, Yoshikawa, Kawamura, Sakai, T. Hirano, Sasaki, Iwata, Tsukimura, Mizote, Iwasaki, J. Hirano and Tomiyama.[70]

An announcement was also made in April that a formal All-Japanese Baseball League would soon be organized in California. According to the *Oakland Tribune*, "the cities which would be represented are San Francisco, Oakland, Alameda, San Jose, Stockton, Sacramento, Isleton, Florin and Fresno, and possibly Lodi." The Stockton Japanese were the envy of the league with their own ball park.[71]

Another new ballpark appeared in California in May 1923, this time in Livingston in Merced County. The new ball park was named Hammett Park and the field was dedicated with the opening game of the season between the Merced Cubs and the Fresno Athletic Club.[72] The Cubs defeated the FAC 8 to 2, but a greater opponent confronted Zenimura and his ballclub when they rolled into town that day — racism.

As the team drove into Livingston they saw signs that read "Go Home Japs," and "No Japs Allowed." Years later Zenimura reflected on how he used the game of baseball to transcend the anti–Japanese sentiment in Livingston. He achieved this by playing clean ball and asking for return games. With each visit into Merced County by the FAC, the signs of big-

Outfielder and pitcher Junichi "John" Nakagawa was known as the Nisei "Babe Ruth." Partial stats from 1923 to 1935 have him batting .377, with 119 hits, 10 doubles, 24 triples, and 8 home runs in 316 at-bats in 76 games (Nisei Baseball Research Project).

otry, both literally and figuratively, slowly began to disappear. This valuable lesson of using the game of baseball to transcend ignorance and racism would prove to be a necessary survival skill 20 years later behind barbed wire in the Arizona desert during World War II.[73]

The summer of 1923 saw the addition of new talent to Zenimura's ballclub, but this time the talent was homegrown, not imported from Hawaii or Japan. The Fresno High School baseball squad was one of the strongest prep teams in the area. Much of their success was due to pitchers Al Sako and Johnny Nakagawa.[74] Sako was a FAC veteran, but fortunately for them Nakagawa joined at the right time. After a strong summer of defeating all of the Japanese teams in California, the FAC were scheduled to take on the perennial powerhouse from Washington, the Seattle Asahi.

In preparation for the battle against the Seattle Asahi, Zenimura worked his Fresno contacts and scheduled a meeting with Chet Bost's Negro League west coast powerhouse, the Pierce Giants of Oakland. A social event between the Japanese and black players was scheduled in advance of the baseball contest and reveals that the relationship between the Japanese and black team included both competition and camaraderie.[75] Zeni's invitation for both clubs to mix at a social and dance offers a rare insight into race relations in 1920s California. During a time when Japanese and blacks were both marginalized by white America, this pregame social suggests that they found common ground in their shared struggle for respect and equal opportunity as both ballplayers and human beings.

After the social and dance, there was a baseball game to be played, and it proved to be a good one. More than 2,000 fans gathered at the Policemen's and Firemen's Ballpark to watch the FAC defeat the Pierce Giants by a count of 11 to 7 to become the semipro champions of California.[76] The Nisei victory over the Pierce Giants is a testament to the strong caliber of talent they possessed as well. Much like their black counterparts, the Japanese Americans had the passion and talent to play at the highest level — they simply lacked the opportunity.

With their confidence and skill level lifted as a result of the victory over the Oakland Pierce Giants, the FAC set their sights on the Seattle Asahi. The

Top: **On July 2, 1923, Zenimura's ballclub won 11 to 7 over the Oakland Pearce Giants, one of the top Negro League teams in California. The Giants roster included player/manager Chet Bost, star shortstop Hillary "Bullet" Meadows and pitcher Harold "Yellowhorse" Morris. (Richmond History Collection, Richmond Public Library).** ***Bottom:*** **Zenimura's Fresno Athletic Club won the right to tour Japan in 1924 by defeating the Seattle Asahi in a best-of-three game series on Independence Day weekend 1923 (Nisei Baseball Research Project).**

Seattle nine had earned the respect of the Japanese baseball world by winning the majority of their games against college and university clubs during several tours to Japan between 1915 and 1923.[77]

The Asahi arrived in Fresno after a 1,171 mile journey from Seattle. Perhaps it was fatigue from travel, truth to the rumors that Zenimura strategically placed the Asahi on the

Pitcher Hideo "Alfred" Sako was one of the founding members of the Fresno Athletic Club in late 1919. He was a member of the Goodwill Tour to Asia in 1924, and Hollywood Japanese All-Stars during the 1930s. Sako was relocated to Jerome, Arkansas, during World War II (Zenimura Family Archive).

sunny side of the field, or just plain talent; but whatever the reason, the Fresno Japanese defeated the Asahi in a best-of-three game series and became the undisputed Japanese champions of the Pacific Coast. By defeating the Seattle Asahi for the 1923 Independence Day Championship, the FAC also won the right to tour Japan the following year.[78] Zenimura immediately began to make his plans for a tour to Japan in 1924.

By late 1923, Zenimura and the FAC had established a reputation as one of the strongest clubs in the San Joaquin Valley. In December the Japanese nine defeated the semipro Bingham-Wenks (BW) club and Aristo Cubs to become Fresno City Winter League champions.[79] "In the final game of the season, the FAC defeated the BW team by a score of 8 to 2."[80]

To cap off the end of a successful year, Zenimura announced that his club would play a team of PCL and independent all-stars from Oakland on Christmas day 1923.[81] And, to everyone's surprise except Zenimura and his teammates, the FAC defeated the PCL stars 10–9 by running the bases with "considerable speed and cleverness," coupled with a solid mound performance from righty Al Sako.

The relief pitcher for the PCL stars on Christmas day was at his least talented on the mound. His name was Earl McNeely and he was an outfielder with the Sacramento Senators. He would make his major league debut in 1924 with the Washington Senators, who faced the New York Giants in the World Series that same year. McNeely is remembered for bringing home the game winning RBI in the 10th inning of game 7 to help the Senators defeat the Giants. McNeely enjoyed a seven-year career in the majors before returning to the PCL in 1932. He made history again that year when his Sacramento ballclub became the first team in PCL history to sign a Japanese player. The player was Zenimura's long-time teammate, Kenso "The Boy Wonder" Nushida.[82]

The 1923 Christmas day contest was the FAC's third battle against a team with PCL-level talent. The fact that some of the PCL position players did not appear should not take anything away from their victory, as they faced some proven competitors in Bill Butler, Mike Dolan and Earl McNeely. From their first spring training exhibition game against the Salt Lake Bees in March, to their victories over the West

Coast Negro League Oakland Pierce Giants, the Seattle Asahi, and the PCL Oakland All-Star aggregation, 1923 proved to be a milestone year for the FAC. Through hard work and sheer dedication to improve game after game, the Fresno Athletic Club increased the level of respect others held for them as a team and for the caliber of Japanese American baseball in general.

The 1924 Season—The Respect of Their Peers

Zenimura and the FAC started the 1924 season off strong with a series of games scheduled against the Fresno Bee All-Stars. The Bees were reinforced by local legend "Mighty Joe" Cartwright. He was a former first baseman who hit .252 in three minor-league seasons: two seasons in the Class AA PCL with the San Francisco Seals in '21, and Salt Lake City Bees in '22; and one season in the class A Western League, splitting his time between the Des Moines Boosters and Lincoln Links in '24.

With the slugging first sacker in the lineup, the first game was close and hotly contested. Cartwright hit a triple and two doubles, and helped the All-Stars edge the FAC 7 to 6. "The work of Zenimura, FAC second baseman bordered on the sensational," declared the *Fresno Bee*. "The little second sacker almost completed a triple play in the eighth." In addition to a solid glove, Zeni recorded three hits, a double and two singles, in six at-bats.[83] In the second of the three-game series, the Bee Stars defeated the FAC 7 to 5.[84] With two consecutive victories secured by the Bee Stars, a third game was unnecessary.

Immediately following the series between the FAC and Fresno Bee All-Stars it was announced that a new semipro league was in development, called the San Joaquin Valley Baseball League (SJVBL). In the kickoff meeting in Selma, five other teams joining the discussion were Hanford, Dinuba, Porterville, Fresno and Zenimura's Fresno Athletic Club. Of the proposed teams, Zenimura's was the only Japanese ballclub.[85]

Led by businessman S.A. Seawright, president of the SJVBL, the teams met and drafted the by-laws. "A salary limit of $1,250 a month was adopted. The number of professionals each club may use was limited to four, four men who have had 60 days experience in organized baseball. Each city agreed to post a forfeit of $500 thirty days before the season opened."[86]

Days after the announcement of the new SJVBL, the unexpected occurred. Porterville said that they would not join in the new league if Zenimura's FAC was allowed to participate. "We don't want the Japanese to play in Porterville," declared Leighroy Miller, commander of the Porterville American Legion Post. "We have kept them out in other lines and if we let them come in baseball, they will bring a following and this we don't want," he added. "This is a white man's town and we intend to keep it as such.... If the Japanese team is excluded, Porterville is ready to come into the valley league. Otherwise Porterville will affiliate with the proposed Tulare County League."[87] After much debate, SJVBL officials announced the clubs for the inaugural 1924 season. The selected teams were: the Fresno Tigers, Dinuba, Hanford and Selma.[88] Zenimura and his Japanese Americans ballclub were excluded from the new league. And despite the ruling, Porterville still opted to play in the Tulare County League after all.

Porterville was not alone in its hostility towards people of Japanese ancestry. Unfortunately for Zeni and his Nisei teammates, there was an unofficial color line for Japanese Americans in California, and there were many Portervilles to defend it. So the resilient Zenimura was forced to find high-caliber competition in others places, which he did.

On March 4, 1924, a series of three games with the Salt Lake City Bees — the Utah representative in the Pacific Coast League — was announced. The Bees were kicking off their second spring training season in Fresno. The press observed that "[t]he Japanese club has been playing greatly since playing the Bees here last year, and should put up a good battle against the Salt Lake aggregation. In anticipation of this, (Duffy) Lewis will send a strong crew into the game next Sunday."[89]

Fresno Bee reporter F. H. Vore attended the much anticipated March 9th game:

> Duffy Lewis sent his Salt Lake recruits against the Fresno Athletic Club (Japanese) here yesterday in the initial ball game for the year for the Bees, and when the smoke and dust had cleared away at the ball park the record shows the Bees had been trimmed by a score of 6 to 4 by the speedy Oriental aggregation, who surprised not only the Salt Lake players but the goodly crowds of fans by the speed displayed at running the bases and in the field.[90]

Salt Lake pitcher Phil Mulcahy went the full nine innings, allowing six hits and three bases on balls to the Japanese nine. One of those walks was awarded to second baseman and captain Zenimura, who scored one run and drove in another with a sacrifice hit. The defensive star of the day for the FAC was Harvey Iwata, the speedy left fielder who made several amazing catches on ball that would normally have fallen in for base hits. Right-hander Hideo "Al" Sako, one of the original members of the FAC, was the winning pitching of record.[91]

In addition to the outcome of the game, Vore reported that the Salt Lake City management had just secured the services of pitcher/outfielder Frank "Lefty" O'Doul from San Francisco. Vore added that the night before the game Manager Lewis, the Salt Lake City Bees owner, and a *Salt Lake Tribune* reporter were guests at a banquet given by the Fresno Athletic Club.

With its first victory over a complete PCL quad, the FAC prepared for its second game against the Bees. The Salt Lake club was eager to avenge its stunning loss and made some necessary adjustments. "If the FAC Japanese team wins from the Salt Lake Bees in the game scheduled for Sunday afternoon, it will be quite an achievement," declared the *Fresno Bee.* Duffy Lewis announced that he was going to "send a strong outfit against the Japanese who have won a lot of respect as a ball club by the good showing made last Sunday."[92]

The boys from Salt Lake did indeed step it up. "While the Japanese boys played their sensational ball in the field, the Bee moundsmen were a little too much for them, and six hits were all they chalked up."[93] Offensively for the Bees, shortstop Tony Lazzeri, a future major league Hall of Famer, belted a two-run homer in the eighth. According to the *Los Angeles Times,* it was the first time a ball was hit out of Fireman's ballpark.[94]

The last of the three-game series was scheduled for Sunday, March 30. The Fresno Athletic Club was swamped under a flood of base hits and the score was 15 to 2. Performing well at the plate for the FAC were Iwata and Tsukimura with two hits a piece, and captain Zenimura and Sako who recorded singles on the day. The heavy sticks were swung by the Bees, with pitcher Fred ("Fritz") Coumbe going 3 for 3, second baseman Knight going 3 for 5, and left fielder Lefty O'Doul also going 3 for 5. O'Doul was a home run short of the cycle, with a single, double and triple recorded in the contest.[95]

More important than O'Doul's performance at the plate is the historical significance of his presence in the lineup. The gregarious southpaw would later go on to lead several tours to Asia and serve as a major baseball ambassador between the U.S. and Japan after World War II. For his role as an international ambassador, O'Doul would later be elected into the Japanese Baseball Hall of Fame in 2002. All of that said, it appears that the March

On March 4, 1924, the Fresno Athletic Club defeated the Salt Lake City Bees of the Pacific Coast League, 6 to 4. Featured above are (left to right) player/manager Duffy Lewis, Fred Yoshikawa, unknown, Kenichi Zenimura, Frank "Lefty" O'Doul, and Al Sako. For O'Doul, who was honored by the Japanese Baseball Hall of Fame in 1998 for his post-war diplomacy, this Bee-FAC series was his first interaction with ballplayers of Japanese ancestry (Nisei Baseball Research Project).

30, 1924, game between the Salt Lake Bees and the Fresno Athletic Club was O'Doul's first documented interaction with a team consisting of ballplayers of Japanese ancestry.

Captain Zenimura and his boys lost two of the three games against the Salt Lake Bees in the spring of 1924, but ultimately they — and to some degree, Japanese American baseball itself— won the respect of their Caucasian peers in the Pacific Coast League.

After the series with Salt Lake, the FAC looked forward to some heated contests against Japanese American ball clubs. In April they welcomed the Stockton Yamato to the Firemen and Policemen's ballpark and defeated them, 5 to 4. The *Fresno Bee* also announced that Zenimura's club "will play a two game series with the Meiji University team here on May 10th and 11th, after which they will plan an invasion of the Orient."[96]

The Meiji University team — the college champions of Japan — planned to tour the East and Midwest, in addition to its games against West Coast clubs including Zenimura's, and then return home on June 29.[97] As it turned out, the San Jose Asahi would be the only

Japanese American team to defeat the 1924 Meiji ballclub on its tour in the U.S.[98] Ironically, while the Meiji University ballclub was in the United States touring, President Calvin Coolidge signed into law the Immigration Act of 1924 which effectively ended all Japanese immigration to the U.S.[99]

During the months of June and July, Zenimura was busy making plans for the upcoming tour to Japan. Once all the details were addressed and players secured, Zeni distributed the following information on the *Associated Press* night wire:

> *Fresno Japs Will Invade the Orient*
>
> FRESNO, July 17.—The Fresno Athletic Club will sail from San Francisco September 2 on board the *President Pierce* for a tour of the Hawaiian Islands and Japan, it was announced today. The regular team will be reinforced by Pitcher Miyahara of Centre College, Kentucky; Outfielder Tsuda of Whitman College, Washington, Pitcher Nushida of Stockton and a couple of Fresno players yet to be selected. The Fresno Athletic Club claims the Japanese baseball championship of America."[100]

In preparation for the tour, Zenimura had the club increase workouts from three to four times a week. In addition, he scheduled a best-of-three-game series against the tough Fresno Tigers, an independent team led by new manager Art Ramage. The Tigers' new skipper competed at Santa Clara College and enjoyed brief stints in professional baseball with the New York Americans (1916) and Sacramento Senators (1918).

Zeni also announced that a "mystery player" would be added to his roster. "The management of the Japanese Club is combing California for two or three all-star players and hinted mysteriously that likely one of these players, who is considered one of the best players in the state may be here tomorrow."[101]

In the first game against the Fresno Tigers, Zenimura's boys were leading 8 to 7 going into the bottom of the ninth inning. The Tigers tied the game 8–8, and with Jackie Kohl on second and in scoring position, Delozier, a lanky red-headed policeman who played outfield, drove in the winning run with a sharp single to left field. The defensive highlight of the day was recorded in the fifth inning when the FAC turned a 5–3–4 triple play. According to all records on file with the *Fresno Bee*, this was the first triple play ever made at the Firemen and Policemen's Baseball Park.[102]

The game against the Tigers was a tough one for the FAC to lose. As a result they worked out every day of the week "under the watchful eye of Captain Zenimura" who was determined to take the next game. Zeni was going to fix the problem: "[he] left for the north last night where he hopes to be able to secure the services of a high-class pitcher for the game tomorrow afternoon." The second game was a close one as well, with the Fresno Tigers finishing the game on top 7 to 5. The star of the day for the FAC was Captain Zenimura, who got two hits and accepted 13 chances with no errors at second base.[103]

On August 23, just a few weeks before the FAC was to sail for Japan, the team achieved a new level of fame when they were immortalized by *Fresno Bee* cartoonist Bob Buel. Six players were depicted by name, position and some noteworthy description. They were: K. Zenimura, captain and shortstop; Fred Yoshikawa, catcher; H.S. "Hornsby" Iwata, left fielder who batted .325; "Rabbit Maranville" T. Hirano, the diminutive second base man "who would be playing big league ball if he weighed 40 pounds more"; T. Miyahara, third baseman; and Fred Tsuda, right fielder who batted .350.

Buel added two notes—a hand holding a spy glass over a miniature base runner which read: "One needs a magnifying glass to see 'em on the diamond," as a reference to the size of the Japanese players; and a bat in Fred Tsuda's hand, accompanied by a caption reading,

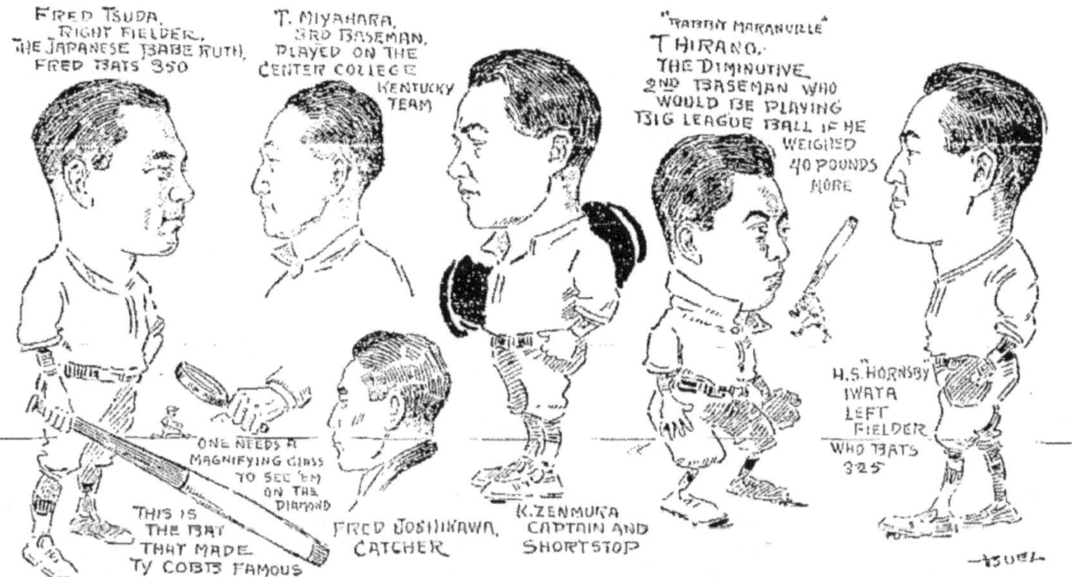

Zenimura and other stars of the Fresno Athletic Club were featured in a *Fresno Bee* cartoon prior to their 1924 Goodwill tour of Asia (The Fresno Bee).

"This is the bat that made Ty Cobb famous."[104] An accompanying article in the *Fresno Bee* explained the rationale behind the Cobb-bat reference.

> *Fresno Nipponese are Given Baseball Bat Autographed by Cobb*
>
> When the Fresno Athletic Club's baseball team packs its paraphernalia to depart on a tour of the orient September 2nd, it will safely tuck away in its bat bag a highly prized bludgeon with which the local Nipponese stars hope to pound out many victories. The bat is the one Ty Cobb, manager of the Detroit Tigers, used when he played in an exhibition game in Fresno four years ago (1920). Cobb socked out a homer, a couple triplets and a two bagger in the contest which was staged at Holmes Field. Cobb was up four times. Homan and Company, local sporting goods house, has presented the bat to the Japanese boys. The bat was autographed by Cobb and presented to Homan's after the exhibition. It has not been used since.[105]

According to Kenso Zenimura, Homan Sporting Goods was the store of choice for his father. Zeni purchased all of his baseball equipment from Homan's, and it appears that the gift Cobb bat was a token of appreciation to return the favor and wish the FAC well during its first tour to Japan. The relationship between Zenimura and Homan lasted decades, and would play a key role in providing equipment to Zeni while he and his fellow Japanese Americans were incarcerated at Gila River, Arizona, during World War II.

With roughly a week remaining until the trip to Japan, the FAC battled the Army nine from the Presidio. The FAC easily defeated their opponents 9 to 3 at the Firemen and Policemen's park. Nushida worked on the mound for six innings, allowing three runs and nine hits. Zenimura led the hitting attack with two singles and a double. Defensively, the Presidio offense was cut short by three double plays by the FAC.[106]

Stung by the close defeats in the series against the Fresno Tigers, Zenimura issued a challenge for another contest, and Art Ramage, the Tiger skipper, accepted.[107] It appears that Zenimura's club was out for revenge, and fine-tuned for its tour to Japan. The FAC defeated the Fresno Tigers 5 to 1 behind Nushida's pitching and the fancy defensive work of outfielders Nakagawa and Iwata.

After its defeat of the Fresno Tigers, Zenimura's club boarded the S.S. *President Pierce* on September 2 for its first journey to Japan. According to passenger ship records, the team was joined by family members during their first leg to Hawaii. The members of the traveling party included:

Family Name	*Given Name*	*Age*	*Occupation*	*Height*	*Residence*
Furubayashi	Kenichi	24	Rancher	5'3"	Danuba, CA
Hirano	Takeo	23	Student	5'1"	Los Angeles, CA
Iwata	Satoru	21	Rancher	5'3"	Fresno, CA
Yoshikawa	Fred S.	24	Bookkeeper	5'2"	Fresno, CA
Miyahara	Taijiro	28	Student	5'3"	Fresno, CA
Nakagawa	Junichi	19	Student	5'6"	Fresno, CA
Nagao	Jasotaro	28	Rancher	5'7"	San Francisco, CA
Nushida	Kenso	24	Clerk	5'1"	Stockton, CA
Sakata	James	24	Student	5'4"	Fresno, CA
Sako	Hideo	21	Student	5'5"	Fresno, CA
Tomiyama	Isamu	19	Student	5'5"	Walla Walla, WA
Tsuda	Fred K.	25	Student	5'7"	Walla Walla, WA
Tsukimura	Hideichi	19	Student	5'2"	Fresno, CA
Zenimura	Kenichi	24	Student	5'2"	Fresno, CA

Non-players joining the team included:

Zenimura	Lilian	18	Housewife
Zenimura	Masako	20	None

Additional information from the record suggests that the destination for all in the party was the home of Masakichi Zenimura at 916 Green Street in Honolulu, and that the party was planning on staying in Hawaii for three weeks. The ship arrived in the Port of Honolulu on September 8, approximately one month before the first scheduled game in Japan.[108] Zeni and Kiyoko were married March 18th in Fresno by a justice of the peace. But the one-month stay in Honolulu provided the ideal opportunity for Kenichi and Kiyoko to hold a more formal Japanese-style wedding so the Zenimura family could participate.[109]

While in Hawaii, Zenimura recruited additional players from Hawaii to help bolster the lineup. Joining the FAC from Hawaii were eight players: Hirata, James Hirokawa (20), Iwano, Noboru Kawamura (22), Shimamura, Masaru, Takahara and Tomita.

The FAC players demonstrated their skills with a 20–8 overall record in the Orient (Japan, China and Hawaii), a .714 winning percentage. Zeni would also form professional and personal relationships in Japan that would prove valuable for planning future tours.[110] After watching the Fresno captain compete in Japan, a reporter with the *Times* wrote, "Zen-

Opposite, top: **Kenichi and Kiyoko Zenimura (far left, back row) were married on March 18, 1924, in Fresno, by a justice of the peace. The 1924 tour provided the ideal opportunity to hold a more formal Japanese-style wedding in Hawaii so teammates and the extended–Zenimura family could attend.** ***Bottom: Left to right:*** **Kenichi Zenimura, Johnny Nakagawa, Jimmy Hirokawa and an unidentified teammate enjoy some rest and relaxation in Japan during the 1924 tour (Nisei Baseball Research Project).**

imura is one of the smartest and most colorful players the writer has ever seen. He was the terror of the diamond, a man who played every position in baseball. He was tricky, shrewd and positive poison to every opponent."[111]

The FAC was the third mainland team to compete in Japan, with the Seattle Asahi and Vancouver Asahi (Canada) preceding them. Chujun Tobita, manager of the Waseda University team they played in November, praised the Fresno club's baseball skills by saying they were "amazing" in their demonstration of technique and power.[112] The November 9 contest against the Meiji University squad at Komaba Ground ballpark in Japan is noteworthy for two reasons. First, it was the first time since Zenimura's return to California that he reunited with his cousin Takizo Matsumoto, who was now a student in Meiji and manager for the university ballclub. Second, the 8 to 3 loss was delivered courtesy of three future Japanese Hall of Fame members, Shunichi Amachi, Nobuaki Nidegawa and Saburo Yokozawa.

The FAC players returned to the U.S. in December and immediately picked up where they left off, battling the Fresno Tigers. On December 21, 1924, the Japanese club defeated the Fresno Tigers 6 to 3. The *Bee* then announced some unexpected news: "Due to a number of the Japanese players leaving Fresno temporarily, the third game scheduled for next Sunday has been postponed until a later date."[113]

The members of the FAC "leaving Fresno temporarily" were Zenimura, Hirokawa and Furubyashi. They were called for an emergency in Honolulu, Hawaii.[114] It appears that Zeni put baseball on hold to be with his wife Lilian Kiyoko, who was about to deliver their first child. Well versed in the role of baseball player, manager and international ambassador, Zenimura was about to take on a new title — father.

3

Only the Ball Was Small (1925–1929)

"In our baseball, if you walked to first base, you stole second, they'd bunt you over to third and you stole home.... Actually scored runs without a hit. This was our baseball."[1]
— Buck O'Neil, Negro Leagues baseball patriarch

The 1925 Season — Build It and They Will Come

Just days before his 25th birthday, Zenimura was again on the passenger ship *President Taft*. After making arrangements for his wife Kiyoko and newborn son Kenji to stay in Honolulu with his parents, Zeni and teammates Jimmy Hirokawa and Kenichi Furubayashi left Honolulu for Fresno, California.[2]

Winter was giving way to spring and baseball clubs everywhere began to look towards the new season. Fresno State College (FSC) reported its pleasure in knowing that third baseman Jimmy Hirokawa was no longer touring Japan with the Fresno Japanese baseball team. The FSC Bulldogs were also depending on the pitching of Eldridge Hunt, the sensation of the conference in previous seasons, and Charlie Hendsch, the veteran southpaw.[3] Captain Zenimura would later use his connections through Hirokawa to land the services of Hunt and Hendsch for yet another tour of Japan with the Fresno Athletic Club. As for the FAC itself, Zeni acted as a leader, usually serving as its business manager in addition to captain. Regardless of his official title he was always the leader on the field and its salesman off the field.

There was still a lot of work to do in preparation for the 1925 season. Zeni worked out the team and scheduled its customary preseason games against local semipro clubs. He also tackled his biggest project by completing the construction of his first stadium, the Fresno Japanese Ballpark, which was scheduled to open with new bleachers and fence for the new season.

While Zenimura was busy putting the final touches on his dream ballpark, the team's long-standing rivals, the Fresno Tigers, welcomed a new brand of baseball into Fresno — a black baseball team from the California Winter League comprised of the top Negro League talent from the East. On March 22, 1924, the St. Louis Colored Giants rolled into town to do battle with the Tigers. The club had just completed its Winter League season in southern California with a 27–3–1 record for the championship.[4]

In the first contest between the Giants and the Tigers, the St. Louis club trimmed the local team by a 7 to 2 score. The Tigers starting lineup was essentially the same that lost 6–3 to the FAC at the end of the 1924 season.[5] In the second game at the Firemen and Policemen's Baseball Park, the St. Louis Colored Giants showed plenty of class and nosed out the Fresno Tigers by a score of 3 to 2.

Kenichi Zenimura's wife Kiyoko posses with son Kenji in Hawaii circa late 1925. Kenji moved to Japan with the Zenimura grandparents in the late 1930s and became a star soccer player at Keio University (Zenimura Family Archive).

The St. Louis Lineup included James "Cool Papa" Bell, cf; Joe Goodrich, 2b; Hurley McNair, lf; Willie Bobo, 1b; Dewey Creacy, 3b; Willie Wells, ss; O'Neal Pullen, c; Bill Foote, p; John Reece, rf; and Spencer Butcher, c.[6] The composition of the Colored Giants lineup is important for several reasons. First, it features two future Hall of Famers in James Bell and Willie Wells. Secondly, it includes several players — Pullen, Foote and Butcher — who are also members of Lon Goodwin's Los Angeles White Sox, the sole black team participating in the semipro Greater Southern California Baseball League. And finally, it serves as a great yardstick to measure the level of talent on both the Fresno Tigers and its rival the Japanese Fresno Athletic Club.

In the spring of '25, the *Fresno Bee* announced that former Pacific Coast League pitcher Harry Morton was hired to take over the managerial duties of the Fresno Cubs in the San Joaquin Valley League. Morton's first game as skipper of the Cubs was a contest against Zenimura's Fresno Athletic Club at the newly constructed Japanese Ball Park on Memorial Day.[7] Located at the intersection of California and Fresno, the stadium now featured a wooden grandstand.

Zenimura's son Kenso later recalled how every spring his father dedicated a considerable amount of time at the ballpark just to make repairs and fix the grandstand.[8] The opening of the Japanese Ball Park marked the beginning of a new era. It was both the pride of Fresno's Japanese American community, and would later serve as a welcoming home ballpark for other minority ballplayers throughout Central California as well.

In a pitching duel between two left-handed hurlers — Tomiyama for the FAC outfit and Makel for the Cubs — the Fresno Cubs of the San Joaquin Valley League trimmed the FAC nine 5 to 4, in a ten-inning contest at the new baseball park. For eight frames the FAC boys had the lead, but the Cubs tied the score, 4–4, in the ninth, and came back in the tenth and scored the winning run. "The Japanese boys made a desperate effort to tie the count in the tenth.... After Yamasaki grounded out to Stockholm, Tsukimura tripled and went to third, while Shintaku was being retired at first. Furubyashi walked and Hirokawa rifled the ball into right field. Cartwright happened to be playing close and managed to throw Hirokawa out at first. The ball beat the stocky second baseman by a fraction of an inch."[9]

In June 1925, Zenimura's friend and worthy baseball opponent from San Jose, Russ Hinaga, was in Japan for the first and only tour of the San Jose Asahi. During the tour an exciting announcement hit the wire: "30,000 Yen Offered to Ruth for Baseball Tour of Japan." The *New York Times* provided the details. "A telegram was sent today by Jack Graham, *Mercury-Herald* sport writer, to Babe Ruth, offering his guarantee of 30,000 yen, approximately $15,000, by the Waseda College of Tokio for an exhibition tour of Japan after the close of the 1925 season. Graham was authorized to make the offer by 'Duke' Sera, Stanford student and member of the San Jose-Japanese Asahi ball club, which is touring the Far East."[10] The offer from Sera and the San Jose Asahi was the first time Ruth was offered, and declined, the opportunity to tour Japan.

Zenimura had a tradition for scheduling big games on the fourth of July, and an even greater reputation for spectacular performances in those contests. On Independence Day 1925, the Fresno Athletic Club welcomed the Daimai nine to the Japanese Ball Park. Also known as the Osaka Mainichi nine, the team began its journey to the U.S. in late March and arrived on the mainland in April.[11] The team was comprised of former college baseball stars who were now employed "in an editorial capacity" by the *Osaka Mainichi* newspaper. The visiting Japanese nine boasted an impressive .812 winning percentage over the previous four years with 212 victories, 44 losses and 5 ties.[12] The Fresno Athletic Club defeated the Daimai nine, 6 to 2.[13]

The next day the nine from Osaka played the Fresno Tigers. In the pregame summary, the *Bee* declared, "Damai lost a close game to the FAC, rated as probably the best Japanese ball club in the world."[14] The Tigers, powered by the battery of McKenry and Ramage, defeated the Osaka club by the same score as the FAC victory the previous day, 6 to 2.[15]

Zenimura's club finished the 1925 summer season with a 7–6 win over the strong Fowler Firemen ballclub,[16] and a 6 to 4 loss against the Post Office club.[17] That same summer it was also announced that Zenimura's formidable opponent and shortstop-peer with the Salt Lake Bees, Tony Lazzeri, was sold to the New York Yankees for cash and five players. At the time of his signing, Lazzeri was leading the PCL in home runs, triples and stolen bases.[18]

On Sunday September 6, 1925, the FAC traveled to Los Angeles to play a doubleheader, first starting with a contest against the Diamond Japs, an L.A.-based Japanese club, and then an afternoon contest with the all-black semipro Los Angeles White Sox, led by manager

Lon Goodwin. All of the games were to be played at the White Sox Park, located on the corner of Compton and 35th in Los Angeles.[19] Coming off of a dominating four-game win streak, the Los Angeles White Sox were ready to tackle the Fresno Athletic Club.

The White Sox had developed a reputation as one of the fastest semipro teams in Los Angeles. Armed with his longtime friend and teammate from Hawaii, Kenso "The Boy Wonder" Nushida, Zenimura felt good about his chances against Goodwin's White Sox. Fresno defeated the White Sox on the Los Angeles diamond, 5 to 4. Three thousand fans witnessed the contest.[20] In addition to his 2 for 5 day at the plate, Zenimura recorded a stolen base. The Fresno Athletic Club's victory over the White Sox stunned everyone. The victory marked the second time in baseball history for an all–Japanese team to defeat an all-black team — the first was the FAC over the Oakland Pierce Giants in 1923.[21] Virtually all the members of the White Sox had some experience playing in organized black baseball in the east or in the California Winter League against major league and PCL-level talent.

Leading off for the White Sox was pitcher/outfielder Bill Foote, long-time member of the club and former player on the California Winter League (CWL) Alexander Giants in 1920. Outfielder Azel Savage was a member of the 1924–25 CWL White Sox who once recorded a 2–4 day at the plate against Detroit Tigers pitcher Pug Cavet.

Catcher O'Neal Pullen was a Negro-League journeyman from Texas who spent time with the Brooklyn Royal Giants, the New York Lincolns, and Hilldale, in 1920. After the '20 season, he accompanied Bill Pettus to the West Coast to play in the CWL. He fell in love with California and decided to stay and play with the L.A. White Sox during the regular season and in the CWL during the winter months. This encounter marked the beginning of a lifelong professional relationship between Pullen and Zenimura.

Third baseman John Riddle joined the L.A. White Sox in 1920 as a high school student. He later attended the University of Southern California (USC) and studied to become an architect. Considered an all-round athlete, he played football for the Trojans as well. His nickname was "Up the Middle Riddle" and he was described in 1921 as "Trojan Fullback, a dark, handsome gentleman of power and skill." Riddle became the first African American from USC to play in the Rose Bowl when the Trojans defeated Penn State 14–3 in 1923.

Second baseman Robert Fagan was a familiar face to Zenimura. Fagan was a member of the 25th Infantry Wreckers stationed at Scholfield Barracks in Hawaii up until 1918. He was also one of the players signed by the Kansas City Monarchs during the charter year of the Negro National League in 1920. Fagan participated in several CWL clubs, including the LA White Sox in 1920, Colored All-Stars in 1921, St. Louis All-Stars in 1922–23 and St. Louis Stars in 1923–24.

Like Goodwin and Pullen, pitcher Ajay Deforest Johnson was a native Texan. Described as a lanky right hander (6'0", 165 lbs), he attended L.A. High School where he pitched and played outfield. After completing school it's believed that he traveled east to join the Peoria Black Devils in 1920. And when that team folded he spent a brief stint with the Dayton Marcos club, led by Candy Jim Taylor. Johnson's mother passed away in the early 1920s, and it's believed that he returned home to California to help his father raise his younger siblings. He would eventually join the Los Angeles Police Department (LAPD) as a beat patrol officer and continue to pitch for Goodwin's semipro White Sox. Johnson would eventually join the Philadelphia Royal Giants in the 1927 California Winter League season and accompany the club on its tour to Japan, Korea and Hawaii. He became the number-two ace behind lefty Andy Cooper and helped lead the Royal Giants to a phenomenal 25–0–1 record against competition in Japan and Korea. Once out of baseball, Johnson dedicated himself to his career as a police officer, and in 1943 earned the distinction of becoming one of the first black uniformed patrol lieutenants and sergeants in LAPD history.[22]

Manager Lon Goodwin shifted his focus from the semipro GSCBL season to another CWL season with the addition of some of the top talent in the Negro Leagues from the east. Historically Goodwin carried his GSCBL team name of L.A. White Sox into the winter league season. Perhaps the timing is coincidental, but immediately after his loss to Zenimura's FAC in September 1925, he changed the name of his CWL team to the Philadelphia Royal Giants.[23] Joining Goodwin for the '25-'26 Winter League season were Crush Holloway, Tank Carr, Jess Hubbard, Biz Mackey, Joe Rogan, Connie Day, Rap Dixon, O'Neal Pullen, Newt Allen, Bob Hudspeth, Rube Currie and George Britton. Mackey, Dixon and Pullen, along with Los Angeles White Sox teammates Fagan, Riddle and Johnson, would all later join Goodwin for a tour of Japan in 1927.

In addition to the competition on the field, the ballpark configuration of the momentous FAC-White Sox game was also a challenge for Zenimura and his ballclub. Often compared in structure to Sulpher Dell Field, the "Improbable Ball Park" located in Nashville, Tennessee, White Sox Ball Park could be described as a field "where the second baseman and the right fielder play the same position." The fence in right field was approximately 270 feet from the home plate. Those familiar with Sulpher Dell said that right field was so close that the outfielder backed up first for overthrows on a grounder with no men on base, instead of the catcher. To further convey the odd dimensions of the field, it was said that the "right fielder ordinarily plays so close to the second baseman that he's virtually breathing down his neck and they have been known to throw out men at first on balls through that side of the infield."[24]

After the historic defeat of the White Sox, the FAC returned home to the Fresno Japanese Ballpark to take on local white semipro and visiting West Coast Japanese teams. The final noteworthy baseball news of 1925 occurred in late 1925 after a 21-game schedule in which the University of Chicago won 13, lost 3 and tied 5 while touring Japan. According to Dr. R. W. Webster, who accompanied the college ballclub during the tour, "the Japanese will monopolize the field of professional baseball when they learn how to improve their batting average."[25]

The 1926 Season—The Scout Shows Up

The new season kicked off with a match between Zenimura's FAC and Shan Kilburn's Hazlewood Service Station baseball team in the early spring. Kilburn's lineup included several Valley stars and future major leaguers including Alex Metzler, a 22-year-old center fielder and rookie with the Chicago Cubs. For the 1926 season, the left-handed hitter was traded to the Philadelphia Athletics for the legendary Jimmie Foxx. During his six-year major league career Metzler hit a solid .285.[26] Kilburn's Hazelwood club defeated FAC, 7 to 2, in a game described as a fast contest.[27]

On March 5, the Associated Press announced that "a Japanese baseball league for California, the first of its kind to permanently organize, has been formed for a schedule of Sunday afternoon games. Fresno, Stockton, Alameda and Sacramento are represented on the circuit. The players are all Japanese, and the games will be played in private parks owned by the Japanese baseball associations in the respective cities on the circuit. The Stockton team has incurred considerable expense in importing a number of players from the Hawaiian islands, while Fresno has gathered in star athletes from various parts of the United States.

The schedule starts next Sunday and closes November 3, with an intermission during the summer months."[28]

In the first game of the season for the California Japanese Baseball League (CJBL), the Fresno Athletic Club blanked the Yamato Club of Stockton, 4 to 0, at the Japanese Ballpark in Fresno. Nitta held the Stockton lineup to two hits, while Nushida and Munishi were touched for 11 hits by the Fresno crew. The big sticks for the Japanese were carried by Nakagawa, who drove in two runs — base runners Zenimura and Sukita — with a long single in the fifth. Yoshikawa, Kunitomo, and Iwata all got wood on the ball to drive in the other two runs.[29]

On April 15, the *New Castle News* in Pennsylvania announced that "the crack Japanese baseball team of Fresno, Calif., will sail early in May for a tour of Japan."[30] This report, however, appears to have been premature or simply wrong. Zenimura was making plans for a tour to Japan, but it wasn't scheduled to take place for another year.

In early May 1926, the FAC were at home in the Japanese Ball Park battling against Kenso Nushida and his Stockton Yamato ballclub again. The "Boy Wonder" Nushida sought and gained his revenge against Zenimura with an 8 to 6 victory over the FAC battery of Furubyashi, Nitta and Yoshikawa.[31] The following week the FAC traveled to Stockton and returned the favor when the same Fresno battery won 5 to 2 over the Yamato battery of Aruki and Higashi.[32] On May 23, the FAC kicked off a two-game series against Lew Marley's Sciot ball club. The clash was described as a heavy-hitting contest in which the pitching of Jeffries and Simons outlasted the FAC hurlers Sako and Nitta, 11 to 9. Nakagawa and Iwata swung the big sticks for Fresno, each with a double. In a rare start at the hot corner, third base, Zenimura recorded a 3-for-5 day at the plate and scored 3 runs.[33]

The month of June brought the mid-season break of the CJBL. With a gap in the schedule, Zenimura and his club battled with independent teams. In late June the FAC completed their series with Lew Marley's Sciot lodge team. The FAC avenged their first game loss with an 8 to 3 victory over the Sciots in game two. The *Fresno Bee* reported, "Zenimura of the Fresno Athletic Club played a fine game, handling seven chances in a spectacular manner. Yoshikawa was the heaviest sticker for the Japs, gathering three singles in four times up. It was announced at the game that the Fresno Athletic Club would play the White Sox colored team of Los Angeles next Sunday on the Japanese Ball Park."[34]

Zenimura and Goodwin scheduled a rematch of their 1925 meeting to take place in Fresno. It was decided that if the L.A. White Sox were going to travel over 200 miles north for baseball, they should make it worth their while and play two. So a two-game rematch was scheduled for the Fourth of July weekend, except this time Goodwin's men would not to play against the All-Japanese FAC, but against a Fresno all-star team comprised of the top stars from the Japanese, Police and Fire Department teams and managed by Johnny Steinhauer.

The Fresno All-Stars defeated the Los Angeles White Sox, 9 to 4. The game was "featured by heavy hitting and spectacular fielding on the part of the local aggregation.... The colored boys outhit the locals, but their batting rallies were repeatedly halted by flashy fielding stunts. The All Stars played through without making an error, while the visitors turned in four."[35] An unexpected highlight then followed: "Zenimura hit a home run with one man on in the fourth inning. The boss of the Fresno Athletic Club's baseball outfit was the star of the day, getting three hits and playing a fine game at short."[36] The man best known for playing "small ball" had surprisingly belted a home run. Years later Zenimura's son Howard commented that he thought his dad's 1926 Fourth of July home run must have been an inside-the-parker. "I don't think he could hit the ball that far," said Zeni's son. "It must have gone over somebody's head or landed inside the baseline. And he's so fast that he just ran around the bases."[37]

The next day the Fresno All-Stars defeated the L.A. team again by the score of 4 to 3. "A single in the ninth inning by Iwata with Hill on base, followed by an error by Fagen (sic), gave the Fresno All-Stars a victory."[38] With the exception of Evans pitching for Los Angeles and Sako pitching for Fresno, the lineups remained unchanged from the previous day.[39]

Based on the precedent of inviting the Oakland Pierce Giants to a social and dance during their weekend visit back in 1923, this Fourth of July weekend visit to Fresno by the L.A. White Sox provides the greatest scenario as the time and place when Zenimura and Goodwin first discussed a joint tour to Japan for 1927. The tour to Japan was still more than eight months away and there was still a lot of baseball to be played — and still more barriers to break.

After the fireworks displayed during the Independence Day weekend victories with the Fresno All-Stars, three members of the FAC — K. Zenimura, Al Sako and F. Yoshikawa — were asked to join an all Caucasian Fresno Twilight League team. The Post Office team won the City League Championship, 6–5, in the final game. The *Bee* reported, "Zenimura, FAC captain, proved himself a valuable addition to the Post Office roster yesterday when he collected two singles in two trips to the plate, scored twice, and greatly pleased the grandstand by stealing two bases with apparent ease. Yoshikawa, also an FAC man, knocked out a triple and a sacrifice hit in four times at bat."[40]

The FAC stars continued to shine in more games after helping the Twilight League Post Office club win the city title. The 1926 summer highlights included: Al Sako pitching a two-hit shutout over the Printers, winning 3 to 0 for the P.O.;[41] Fred Yoshikawa collecting two home runs, a double, and a single against Little Lake at the Frank H. Ball field;[42] and Zenimura hitting 3 for 3 at the plate with 3 stolen bases, as the FAC defeated the Firemen's team in a slugfest, 14–11.[43] In fact, during his time of playing side by side with the white Twilight leaguers, Zenimura earned the nickname "Thief" for repeatedly stealing multiple bases in a game.[44]

Shinichi "Fred" Yoshikawa was considered by Zenimura to be the greatest Nisei catcher of the 1920s–30s. He joined Zeni as a Hawaiian All-Star and moved to the U.S. mainland in 1922. As a member of the FAC, he participated in the 1924 and 1927 Goodwill Tours to Japan. Upon retirement, he pursued a career as a professional golfer (Zenimura Family Archive).

The fall brought a return to the scheduled games in the CJBL. On October 3, the FAC lost a close game to the Alameda Japanese pastimers by a 5–4 count. "A bunch of errors at the critical moment caused the Fresno athletic club to lose their nine inning encounter," reported *the Bee.*[45] The following week the FAC went down in defeat again, this time at the hands of the Sacramento Japanese club by a score of 6 to 4. "Poor support and slack pitching in the first two innings proved to be the downfall of the Fresno Athletic Club."[46] When you lose, don't lose the lesson. This is the philosophy of winning athletes, and it was these late-season losses that opened Zenimura's eyes to the fact that the team needed to bolster its pitching staff if it was to have any success in Japan during the 1927 tour.

A solution for stronger pitching presented itself to Zenimura when a contest was scheduled between the stars of the PCL and Fresno Twilight league in October 1926. "Fresno fans will get a long-wished-for opportunity to see some genuine Coast League stars in action this afternoon at the ball park when the coast team meets the All-Star Twilight League aggregation. With Howard Craghead, former Fresno High School pitcher and popular local boy, on the mound for the coast team, the stands should be packed for there have been many who wished to see Craghead share his debut into Coast League baseball."[47]

Besides Craghead, a lot of interest was focused on Lyn Lary, the sensational shortstop from Visalia High School who signed with Oakland in the PCL; outfielder Alex Metzler, Philadelphia Athletics; and Buzz Arlett, another popular Oakland player, who played left field. "Under the managership of Joe Cartwright, a snappy bunch of all-star players from the Twilight League have been brought together and will endeavor to do their stuff. Cartwright will play first base, Doc Jacobson third, Jackie Kohl second, and Donnie Hunt shortstop. Jud Simons will take the offerings of both Eldridge Hunt and Jimmy Hansen. Coffman and Zenimura will be used as utility men."[48]

On October 31, 1926, the Oakland Coast Leaguers defeated the Fresno Twilight All-Stars 5 to 4. The starting pitchers were Howard Craghead for Oakland and Al Hunt of neighboring Fowler for the Twilighters. Zenimura did not play in the two-hour contest. Instead, he quietly observed as a scout and evaluated the talent of three players — pitchers Craghead and Hunt and catcher Jud Simons — for possible inclusion in his upcoming tour to Japan.[49]

The FAC wrapped up the CJBL season with a series of games against Kenso Nushida and the Stockton Yamato in November. Stockton took the first game by the score of 12 to 5. Stockton also won the second game, and with it, their claim to the championship and the right to tour Japan in 1928.[50]

The 1927 Season — International Goodwill

In January, the FAC announced its arrangements to make a second tour of Asia in March with 40 games in Japan scheduled and plans to take the team to China and Korea with a stop in Honolulu on the way home. There were a number of new players on the team.[51] Not included in the initial news wire was the fact that the FAC were visiting Japan at the invitation of Meiji University, or more specifically, Zenimura's cousin, friend and colleague, Takizo Matsumoto, the man formerly known as Frank Narushima, one of the co-founders of the FAC.

In February, the Japanese American newspaper *Rafu Shimpo* announced similar news about Lon Goodwin and his Philadelphia Royal Giants.[52] According to historian Kazuo

Sayama, the Philadelphia Royal Giants traveled to Japan on its own budget and "on recommendation by a certain Japanese American entrepreneur in California."[53] Although he is never mentioned by name, historians believe that the entrepreneurial Californian is Zenimura based on his previous interactions with Goodwin and their teams throughout the 1925–26 seasons.

Records in Japan indicate that Goodwin attempted to bring his entire winter league roster on the tour. However, because of their contractual obligations to teams with Negro League clubs back east, the majority of the players declined the offer. When Goodwin's men arrived in Yokohama on March 28, the local press reported the incoming guests as the complete Philadelphia Royal Giants 1926-27 California Winter League roster.

According to Kyoko Yoshida, baseball historian and professor at Keio University, the roster was telegraphed by Royal Giants interpreter George Irie to the Japanese media and promoters prior to their arrival. It is unknown why Irie did not modify the roster before leaving Los Angeles.[54] What is known is that Goodwin became persona non grata with the Negro Leagues for taking their stars Mackey, Cooper and Dixon away for part of the regular season.[55]

Zenimura and the FAC all-stars almost didn't make it to Japan. On March 31, the Yokohama press reported that "after careful examination for symptoms of smallpox, the Fresno, California baseball team was permitted to land here from the liner *Korea Maru* which is now in quarantine. On arrival, two cases of smallpox were found in the steerage. After an examination all steerage passengers were held for observation but cabin passengers including the team, were permitted to go ashore."[56] Five days later, the Tokyo press reported the official arrival of Zenimura's team:

> The Fresno Japanese baseball team augmented by three American players reached Japan a few days ago and will make their first public appearance in Tokyo at the Meiji Shrine Field Tuesday afternoon when they lineup against the fast Meiji University nine. The visitors had a couple of nice workouts already and are raring to go. They are rapidly recovering from their long trip across the Ocean and should provide plenty of opposition against the local teams. One of their proudest records is that of defeating the Royal Giants who are now in Japan and cleaning up on the Japanese nine.
>
> The Fresno team carries with them seventeen members including half a dozen pitchers so they are well supplied with plenty of reserve players in case of emergency. Hunt and Hendsch are two of their leading hurlers while Simons, the other American entry will carry the bulk of the catching burden.
>
> Manager Zenimura will probably handle the shortpatch himself and he needs no introduction to the Japanese sporting public for he made his initial bow a few years ago when the Fresno squad made their first trip here. The other infielders are Miyahara, a former varsity star, Nakano, Kunitomo, Hirokawa, and Yamasaki. The gardeners include Iwata, Nakagawa, and Furubayashi while Mamiya, Kawasaki, Aoki and Yoshikawa make up the rest of the squad.[57]

The FAC received generous press coverage during their 1927 tour. Fans were provided with detailed information to get to know the Fresno pastimers. One paper provided the following summaries of the FAC team:

> Ken Zenimura, manager and shortstop is the mainstay of the Fresno team. He has steered the team for the past several years through 14 successful seasons. Upon graduation from Mills High School in Honolulu in 1919, where he was captain, he went over to the mainland to join the Fresno Club and continue his higher education. While in Honolulu he was captain of the Asahi Ball Club. This is his second trip to Japan.

Captain Fred Yoshikawa, catcher, played for four years on the McKinley High School team in Honolulu. He captained the team through a series of games with Mills High which was headed by Manager Zenimura. He is a graduate of the Technical College of Kansas. This is his second trip to Japan.

Harvey Iwata, the left fielder, is a graduate of Fresno High, and is now making a special study of agricultural science. He was captain of the Fresno High team that won the Pacific Coast Championship in 1920. This is his second trip to Japan.

Ty Miyahara, third baseman, proud of the fact that he was received at the White House by President Coolidge last year. He made his first trip to Japan with the Honolulu Asahi team (in 1920). He also made a trip with the Fresno team in 1924. He studied at Center College, at Danville, Kentucky, where he played Center Varsity as a third baseman. At present he is a student at Columbia University.

Anthony Kunitomo, second baseman, joined the Fresno Club last year. He is attending Regis College at Denver, where he also played second baseman on the Varsity team. He has made his college team for the past three years.

Michael Nakano, first baseman, is attending college in Alameda, California. He was considered the best first baseman in the Japanese baseball league in 1926 on the coast.

John Nakagawa, centerfielder, is known in the states and here in Japan as the Japanese "Babe Ruth." He pitched and played outfield for Fresno High, finishing there in 1926. This is his second trip to Japan.

Tandy Mimura, third baseman, is still in high school, attending Dinuba High. He made the highest batting average on his high school team last season.

Ken Furubayashi, outfielder, made his first trip to Japan in 1924. He pitched on his high school team Orosi High. On his last trip to Japan he was a Fresno pitcher but is now in the outfield, owing to his heavy hitting.

Samuel Yamasaki is the team's leading batter and a third baseman, playing the same position now on the Fresno High School team. He will finish high school next year and he is the youngest member of the aggregation.

Richard Kawasaki, pitched for both Los Angeles High School and a Japanese team in that city. He joined Fresno in 1926 as a member of the pitching staff.

James Hirokawa is on his second trip to Japan with Fresno, Playing second base also for the Fresno State College.

Thomas Mamiya finished McKinley High School and has now joined Fresno to take up higher education in the states. He pitched for his high school and for the Asahi team and has the reputation of being the best Japanese pitcher in Hawaii.[58]

A separate report described catcher Jud Simon as "one of the snappiest receivers in the valley.... His presence behind the plate always gives the opposition something to think about before they attempt to steal."[59]

The FAC won its first five games in Japan: two games against Keio, both by the score of 6 to 2, featuring future Japanese hall of famer Shinji Hamazaki; two games against Meiji, 10 to 5 and 6 to 0, against hall of famers Fujio and Nakazawa; and a thrilling 10-inning victory over Hosei University by the score of 3 to 2. While no protests or controversy was ever reported, it is worthwhile to note that the umpires of the tight Fresno-Hosei game were two representatives from the Meiji club: Tatsumi Zenimura and Takezo Matsumoto, both relatives and close friends of player-manager Ken Zenimura.[60]

Zenimura and the boys also displayed their athletic versatility by meeting the strongest local basketball teams in a series of games against quintets of the Tokyo Intercollegiate League. The press reported that "Peppery Yoshikawa who is captain of the ball squad is also captain of the basketball team and is one of the leading forwards while there are six other cage stars to help him out in their attempt to down the local collegians. The basketball

In April 1927, Zenimura and the Fresno Athletic Club embarked on their second Goodwill Tour of Asia. Competing against the best semipro, industrial and college teams in Japan, China, Korea and Hawaii, the FAC finished with a 40–8–2 record, an .800 winning percentage (Nisei Baseball Research Project).

players on the squad are — Forwards, Zenimura, Hirokawa, Yoshikawa; Center, Yamasaki; Guards, Iawata, Miura, Nakagawa."[61]

Although the FAC lost its basketball game against Rikkyo University, the team scored a victory in the area of international goodwill. According to Rikkyo University officials, it was during this interaction that the FAC ballclub was invited to a party with Rikkyo missionary and professor Dr. Paul Rusch, in which both teams exchanged fight songs. Zenimura and his men sang "Rikkyo Will Shine Tonight" for the host team, and afterward Rusch adjusted it to reflect the English name for their school, St. Paul's University. "St. Paul's Will Shine Tonight" has been Rikkyo's official fight song ever since.[62]

On April 20, 1927, the FAC and Philadelphia Royal Giants met head-to-head in the newly constructed Meiji Shrine Stadium in Tokyo. Captain Zenimura shared with reporters his eagerness and excitement to play the upcoming game with Goodwin's club. "The Fresno players, who have defeated the invading Royal Giants in America in baseball, will have the opportunity of demonstrating their superiority over the same nine when they cross bats in their first game in Japan on Friday afternoon at the Meiji Shrine Field. This match ought to attract a huge attendance as both teams have shown great strength in their contests against the local nines."[63]

According to Japanese historian Kazuo Sayama, Zenimura's comments about previously defeating the Royal Giants caused quite a stir with several of the black players, especially Mackey, Dixon and Cooper. They openly expressed their disappointment with the FAC and wondered why the Japanese players from Fresno would lie about beating the Royal Giants, when they knew for a fact that they had never played one another.[64] More than 80 years later, we now see the historic misunderstanding that unfolded between Zenimura and Mackey.

Based on his comments to the Japanese press, it appears that Zenimura was under the impression that the Negro League team he was scheduled to play in Tokyo was comprised of players from the 1925–26 L.A. White Sox, the squad he had help defeat three times prior to the tour. Zeni had no idea that the Royal Giants team that boarded the ship in April was actually comprised of two different rosters: Cooper, Dixon, Duncan, Pullen and Mackey from Goodwin's 1926–27 CWL team, and select members of Goodwin's 1926 L.A. White Sox of the semipro GSCBL.

While the misunderstanding was unfortunate, it worked in favor of the Royal Giants. Who knows, perhaps Goodwin was a mastermind when it came to motivating his players? Either way, Biz Mackey channeled his anger into his bat and more than 10,000 baseball fans at Meiji Shrine Field witnessed the future hall of famer singlehandedly defeat Fresno 9–1.[65] "Mackey, the star shortstop of his team, was the heaviest slugger of the day, getting three safeties on four official trips to the diamond, one being a four-ply wallop, and the other two, a three sacker and a double." He was a single shy of hitting for the cycle.[66]

Future Hall of Famer Biz Mackey handed the FAC a 9-to-1 defeat during the 1927 tour of Japan. A single shy of hitting for the cycle, Mackey's home run was the first-ever in the newly constructed Meiji Shrine Stadium. In this Japanese cartoon depicting the historic blast, FAC outfielders John Nakagawa and Harvey Iwata are depicted chasing the historic blast (Nisei Baseball Research Project).

His historic home run, the first ever hit at Meiji Shrine Stadium, whistled through the air and landed in the center field bleachers.[67] The ball then rolled out of sight some hundred feet into a clump of trees, setting a record for the first and longest home run since the stadium opened.[68]

According to reports, the game was actually much closer than reflected by the final 9–1 score. It was still anyone's ball game after the sixth inning with a 2 to 0 score, but the Royal Giants "blew the lid off" the game by scoring four runs in the seventh and then adding three more runs in the eighth. The Fresno club was able to get on the board in the ninth inning on a double by Jud Simons and a run batted in by pinch-hitter Sam Yamasaki.[69]

After the game it was reported that the Fresno Japanese would have a chance to "wreak their sweet revenge upon the boastful Colored nine" in a follow-up game scheduled for Friday.[70] Unfortunately, the game was rained out and never rescheduled. For the majority of players on both teams, they would have to wait until they returned to the U.S. for a rematch.

After the rained-out contest, each team went their separate ways to play the best semi-pro, industrial and college teams in the Japan, China, Korea and Hawaii. Both squads completed their respective tours with impressive winning records. The FAC finished with a 40–8–2 record, a solid .800 winning percentage. Playing against the same competition, the Philadelphia Royal Giants finished with a 35–2–1 record, an amazing .921 winning percentage.[71]

Perhaps more important than the wins and losses was the positive cross-cultural impact made by the tour. The Japanese players and fans were enamored with the Philadelphia Royal Giants, and the feeling was mutual. In Japan, both the Nisei and Negro players found sanctuary from the racism they faced back in America. And in the end, both teams were recognized by their Japanese hosts as true sportsmen and gracious ambassadors for the U.S. during the tour.[72]

In his book *Gentle Black Giants*, Japanese author and historian Kazuo Sayama credits the 1927 tour, especially Mackey and his Philadelphia Royal Giants teammates, as the inspiration for the start of professional baseball in Japan in 1936.[73] Sayama states that Japanese players and spectators knew about the racial segregation in professional sports in America and understood that, although they could not play in the Major Leagues, they were as good as, or even better than, the major league players. Sabur Yokozawa, a Japanese player, later described how the Royal Giants played each game gentlemanly, with warm pedagogical thoughtfulness toward the inexperienced Japanese players, while the All-American team (of 1934) sometimes treated the Japanese players with entertaining contempt during the actual games.[74]

This mutual respect is best exemplified in an exchange between Biz Mackey and a Japanese pitcher. Mackey was accidentally beaned with an inside pitch by a young Japanese player. The pitcher bowed to the burly switch-hitting catcher as a form of apology. Before taking his base, Mackey bowed back.[75]

On May 16, 1927, the Fresno Athletic Club defeated the Damai nine by the score of 4 to 0 at Koshien Stadium.[76] This game is significant for two reasons. First, the Damai lineup consisted of three future members of the Japanese Baseball Hall of Fame: Kirihara, Ono, and Yokozawa. The second reason is because on the same day while Zenimura was busy defeating Daimai, his second son Kenso ("Howard") was born in Fresno, California.

This joy for the Zenimura family occurred just days after an unfortunate sorrow. Kenichi's sister, Masako Zenimura Sakata, passed away. At the time she was married to James Sakata, FAC first baseman who accompanied Zeni on the 1924 tour to Japan. But for this tour Sakata had fortunately stayed home. He lost his wife on May 14 and a few days later he signed the hospital birth certificate for the newborn Kenso on behalf of his brother-in-law traveling in Japan.

After their April and May games near Tokyo, the FAC team barnstormed a series of games in June against Hiroshima prefecture, Shikoku island, Hokaido, Chosen (the Japanese name for Korea) and Manchuria (NE China). In all, the FAC played 50 games in Japan, Korea and China, and recorded a 40–8–2 record.[77]

In early August Zenimura and his men journeyed towards the Hawaii islands for an 11-game series. Highlights from Hawaii included:

Philadelphia Royal Giants catcher O'Neal Pullen greets Keio University's Shinji Hamazaki during the 1927 Japan Tour. Decades later as the manager of Hankyu Braves, Hamazaki was instrumental in the signing of the first Negro Leaguers to play in Japan (Negro Leagues Baseball Museum).

Upon Kenichi Zenimura's recommendation, manager Lon Goodwin (far right) took his ballclub on a tour of Asia in April 1927. Behind catcher O'Neal Pullen, pitcher Ajay Johnson and shortstop Biz Mackey, the Philadelphia Royal Giants finished with a 35–2–1 record, a .921 winning percentage playing against the best semipro, industrial and college teams in the Japan, China, Korea and Hawaii (Negro Leagues Baseball Museum).

- A 4–2 victory over the All-Hawaiians, the undisputed leaders of the Hawaii league, at Honolulu Stadium, in which Zenimura stole home for the first run of the game.
- A 5–4 victory over the Honolulu Asahi. Kawasaki belted a home run, while Nakagawa closed the game to defeat future Japanese Hall of Famer Bozo Wakabayashi.
- Against the All-Navy squad at Pearl Harbor, Johnny Nakagawa hit a home run to help secure a 4–3 victory.
- In the 7–3 victory over the All-Chinese squad, each of Fresno's first 7 batters scored a run.

Satoru "Harvey" Iwata was a speedy outfielder for Zenimura's FAC during the 1920s and early 30s. Known as the Nisei "Rogers Hornsby," Iwata batted .370, with 134 hits in 362 at-bats in 91 documented games between 1923 and 1934 (Nisei Baseball Research Project).

- In a 10–4 victory over the Maui All-Japanese at Wailuku, Iwata went 3–4 with a home run, triple, single and sacrifice hit. Defensively he recorded four putouts, one assist, and kept a home run from clearing the fence with his bare hand, holding the runner to a double.
- Back in Honolulu, the FAC defeated the All-Navy club of Pearl Harbor, again by the score of 3–2, in a 12 inning game. Tied two-all in the last frame, Zenimura reached on an error, Yoshikawa sacrificed, and Nakagawa's single scored Zeni as the winning run.

It appears that in its final game in Hawaii against the Braves on August 29, the FAC lost steam and suffered its first and only defeat on the island. At Honolulu Stadium, leftfielder Henry "Hank" Oana, was the batting star of the Braves, going two for four at the plate and helping to secure the 2–0 victory for local pitching star Sam Guerrero, who also held the Fresno lineup to three hits.[78] Oana would later earn the nickname "The Hawaiian Prince" as a major league pitcher with the Detroit Tigers and veteran player-manager in the Texas League with Dallas and Fort Worth.

On September 6, 1927, Zenimura and his FAC teammates departed Honolulu and set sail for America on the passenger ship *Taiyo Maru*. Not on the return ship with the team were the three Caucasian ringers, Hunt, Hendsch and Simons. All three had returned home early in June. According to Kenso Zenimura, he recalls his father saying that the three players said they couldn't take the living conditions, wanted more money for their efforts once they saw the large crowds flocking to the games, and overall were unhappy during their time in Japan.[79]

While Zenimura and the A-team FAC players were barnstorming Japan, the junior squad that stayed behind established some important relationships. The first was with the Fresno Monarchs, the all-black team formerly known as the Fresno Colored Giants. Led by star first-baseman Gene Hinds, the brother-in-law of legendary West Coast black-baseball star Chet Bost, the Monarchs adopted the Japanese Ballpark as their home park in West Fresno. The Monarchs would eventually go on to win the championship of the Cosmopolitan League of the Twilight circuit in 1927.

The other important relationship was with visiting guests from Japan, 20 individuals representing a baseball team, city council members and reporters from Wakahama, Japan. After a visit to Yosemite park, the tourists arrived in Fresno in August to play the FAC junior squad. Although the championship high school team defeated the FAC junior club, it was the diplomatic exchange of goodwill that left the lasting impression on everyone involved.

On Thursday September 8, the *Fresno Bee* announced the return home of the FAC. After spending six months touring Japan, Korea, China and Hawaii, and playing 60 games, many of the team members opted to stay in San Francisco for some rest and relaxation. Captain Zenimura announced "that many offers for games again in the Orient were received by the club, and another trip probably will be made next year."[80]

The Bambino and Iron Horse

Just weeks after their return to the U.S., it was announced that Babe Ruth and Lou Gehrig had their sights set on a tour of the West Coast. The tour was to consist of a series of 15 games that would begin as soon as the World Series ended, and conclude on October 31, as dictated under the rules of Major League Baseball and Commissioner Judge Landis.[81]

Preparations for the exhibition baseball game on October 29 featuring Babe Ruth and Lou Gehrig were moving along rapidly under direction of the Fresno Post of the American Legion, under whose auspices the game would be played.

Gene Jewett and Pete Shepherd, members of the committee on arrangements, were responsible for lining up the two teams for the game. Ruth and Gehrig would start at first base on their respective teams, with the possibility of pitching late in the game.

Alex Metzler of Fresno, the sensational outfielder of the Chicago White Sox, and Lyn Lary of Visalia, crack shortstop for the Oakland Pacific Coast League Club, were among the first players signed to play. Four members of the Fresno Athletic Club's baseball team were also selected. They were Captain Zenimura, shortstop; Iwata, center field; Nakagawa, left field, and Yoshikawa, catcher. The original plan called for splitting up the Japanese players, placing two on Ruth's club and two with Gehrig's team.[82]

In preparation for the big game with the Yankee legends, Zenimura arranged for a game between his FAC and an all-star club representing the local Veterans of Foreign Wars (VFW). The *Fresno Bee* called the contest "the best game seen in Fresno in many years." About 1,000 fans viewed the game which proved to be a hurling duel between Howard Craghead and George Hollerson, both pitchers in the PCL. Alex Metzler was the center of attention as an established MLB star, but "Craghead, sharing honors with Metzler, looked mighty sweet on the hill for the FAC." Slugger John Nakagawa was also heralded as a star of the day along with Zenimura, who had a 3-for-5 day at the plate. Despite the efforts of the FAC stars they were defeated 4–3, but "now everyone was warmed up and ready for the Ruth-Gehrig show to arrive in Fresno."[83]

Following the close of the World Series, Ruth and Gehrig had traveled the nation on a barnstorming tour. Ruth's team — the Bustin' Babes — was renamed the Sun Maids to give a local flavor. Gehrig's team — the Larrupin' Lous — was renamed the American Legion All-Stars. Fresno native, Alex Metzler, who was now playing with the Chicago White Sox and had played against Ruth and Gehrig in the previous season, increased local interest.

With Pete Shepherd managing the Sun Maids, his starting lineup was: Adams, lf; Kohl, 2b; Ruth, 1b; Larry, ss; Stephens, rf; Baker, cf; Broderson, 3b; Mitchell, c; Hollerson, p. Reserves included: Armstrong, c; Kilner, 1b; Bier, ss; Curry, 3b; Miller, outfielder, Bidwell, outfielder; Hunt, p; Crawford, p.[84]

Gene Jewett managed the Legion All-Stars. His lineup for the start was: Metzler, cf; Frazier, rf; Gehrig, 1b; Ramage, c; Cartwright, 2b; Parret, lf; Ostenberg, 3b; Zenimura, ss; Craghead, p. Reserves, including the other Japanese players were: Simons, c; Yoshikawa, c; McKenry, p; Cano, p; Fries, 2b; Santos, ss; D. Jacobsen, 3b; Iwata, outfielder; Nakagawa, outfielder; Coffman, outfielder; I. Jacobsen, outfielder.

Before the game the two sluggers gave an exhibition in hitting and autographed a bunch of baseballs. When asked to give advice on how to hit the long ball, they gave their same old answers, "Just keep your eye on the ball and give it everything you have when you meet it," Ruth explained. "Of course, sometimes I connect when I don't even see the ball. It's in the swing and eye," Gehrig added. Prior to their arrival to Fresno, Ruth knocked nineteen home runs in that many games on the barnstorming tour. Gehrig hit eleven round-trippers.[85]

On Saturday, October 29, 1927, at 3 P.M., a crowd of roughly 5,000 fans packed Firemen's Park in Fresno, California, to watch two of the game's greatest icons play ball with their local heroes. Ed Orman reported that "the Bustin' Babe satisfied the appetite of the fans by lifting one of Howard Craghead's fast ones over the right-field fence in the first inning. Ruth's long drive cleared the fence by a big margin. The distance to the right-field wall from home plate is 410 feet. Despite the mammoth home run, Ruth's club took a 13-to-3 licking at the hands of the Laraupin' Lous."[86]

"Columbia" Lou did not connect for a home run in the game, but he did sock one over the left center field fence in batting practice and also drove two to the fence in deep center. Ruth matched Gehrig's feat in practice. Lou also rattled the boards in the third inning of the game with a triple to right center, and also made a two-base hit out of a high fly into center in the sixth. Ruth got a single to left in the seventh. The ball game went on the rocks at the start of the ninth. Hundreds of kids flocked into the infield and surrounded Gehrig and Ruth and forced the sluggers to autograph baseballs for them. The crowd got so big on the field that the game had to be called with two down in the ninth inning.[87]

Ruth disappointed the fans in the ninth when he struck out. Moose Cano, a Fresno youngster who was signed by Hollywood of the Coast League for the 1928 season, was on the mound when the mighty Babe whiffed. In addition to his hitting feat, Ruth showed signs of his early-career pitching prowess. When his pitcher went to pieces in the third, allowing five runs to trickle down, Ruth strolled over to the mound. He pitched four balls and got credit for pitching a full inning. Jackie Kohl, second baseman for the Bustin' Babes, aided Ruth in the effort. He snagged a line drive over second, touched second base and tossed to third for a triple play, ending the inning.[88]

Zeni was walked twice in two plate appearances. Some 35 years later Zenimura recalled his few at bats during the big game a little differently. "The first time I up I got a single. I was very fast and took my usual lead off first. Ruth glanced at me and said 'Hey, son, aren't you taking too much of a lead?' I said no. He called for the pitcher (Hollerson) to pick me off. The pitcher threw and I slid behind Ruth. He was looking around to tag me and I already was on the sack. I think this made him mad. He called for the ball again. This time he was blocking the base and he swung his arm around thinking I would slide the same way. But this time I slid through his legs, and he was looking behind. The fans cheered. Ruth said 'if you do that to me again I'll pick you up and use you as a bat, you runt.'"

More memories from the game were shared by Babe Ruth's bat boy. In 1927, 15-year-old Al Bier of Fresno was the lucky lad who helped Ruth with his bats. His brother, Dick, played second base for the Babes. Bier recalled that "Babe played first base, and Gehrig

(Left to right) Johnny Nakagawa, Lou Gehrig, Kenichi Zenimura, Babe Ruth, Fred Yoshikawa and Harvey Iwata after an exhibition game at Fresno's Firemen's Ballpark on October 29, 1927. This encounter marked Zeni's first with the Babe which laid the foundation for Zenimura to later extend an offer of $40,000 to Ruth to play in Japan (Nisei Baseball Research Project).

played first, too." Bier added, "There was this little guy named Kenny Zenimura on the Larrupin' Lous, and he made it to first base. Stood about 4 feet 11. The Babe was two or three ax handles wide, big butt. Legs that looked like a canary bird. He had a pug face that looked like he'd been hit with an iron. Now, Gehrig was handsome. But not the Babe. Well, Babe went over and talked to the pitcher and when Zenimura got a big lead, Babe just put himself between him and first base and Zenimura couldn't get around him to get back to the bag. They threw him out."[89] With two different versions of the same situation, clearly the facts of the game were a bit fuzzy for everyone to remember decades later.

Bier left the ball game that day with two memories and a keepsake from the game. As the batboy for Ruth's team, he received a baseball signed by Ruth and Gehrig. The style of play he witnessed by Zenimura and the other Japanese players also left a deep impression on him. Some 70 years after the game, Bier recalled that "pound-for-pound the Japanese players were as good as major leaguers."[90]

After the game, photographer Frank Kamiyama captured Zenimura, Nakagawa, Yoshikawa and Iwata posing with Ruth and Gehrig. Also in the stands was 48-year-old Taizo "Howard" Toshiyuki, the proprietor of the West Fresno Drug Company. Zenimura and Toshiyuki became close friends over the years. In fact, Zeni named his son Howard

After helping Lou Gehrig defeat Babe Ruth 11 to 3, Zeni secured autographs on his official PCL ball from both Yankee sluggers, Fresno star and MLB outfielder Alex Metzler and PCL President Harry Williams (Zenimura Family Archive).

after Toshiyuki. While the five ballplayers were posing for photographer Frank Kamiyana, Toshiyuki captured the action on his 8mm movie camera. Toshiyuki took the film home and placed it in his attic. In 2009, almost 82 years after this historic game, the 21 seconds of game footage resurfaced and were donated to the Nisei Baseball Research Project. As of the publication of this book (2011), the rare footage of Ruth and Gerhig with Zenimura, Nakagawa, Yoshikawa and Iwata has yet to be seen by the public.

Several months after the game Zenimura sent a copy of the Kamiyana picture to his sources with the Japanese press. "I got a call from Japan to see if I could get Ruth to go to the Island and play for a $40,000 guarantee," said Zenimura. "I contacted Ruth and he said he would go for $60,000. It was too much but a few years later [1934] he went [to Japan] and made a big hit."

The day after the Ruth-Gehrig game, Zenimura was at it again, taking on many of the same all-stars with his FAC squad. Zeni's men defeated the Fresno All-Stars, 5 to 4. According to the *Fresno Bee*, "Ostenberg broke into the limelight again with a home run to deep center.... Only fast fielding work on the part of the Japanese boys in the ninth inning saved the day for their club. Zenimura, Iwata and Nakagawa led the club with two hits apiece, accounting for 6 of the team's 11 hits."[91]

The 1927 season proved to be the most important season, to date, of Zenimura's career. The goodwill tour to Japan with the Philadelphia Royal Giants, combined with the opportunity to play with and against Babe Ruth and Lou Gehrig during their barnstorming tour in California, made the season something special. Off the field, life brought its joys and sorrows as well with the passing of his sister Masaka, and the birth of his second son Howard.

Knowing what we know now, we see that at age 27 Zenimura had only reached the halfway point in his long and exciting career. There was still plenty of baseball to be played.

The 1928 Season — Fresno Focus

Zenimura kicked off the year with more international goodwill efforts by welcoming Waseda University to Fresno. Except this time, it was not a baseball team, but basketball.[92] This speaks to the multitalented abilities of the FAC and the respect other teams held for Zenimura as a competitor. Joining Zeni on the court were Tachino, Murashinta, M. Nakamura, Sako, Nakagawa, Tsukimura, Matsui, Nakamura and Yoshikawa. Basketball also served as a great way to stay in shape during the off-season and train for the upcoming baseball season.

In late February the *Fresno Bee* announced that Zenimura was also busy coordinating plans for another incoming team, the Keio University baseball team. Zeni attempted to schedule games for the squad against some of the top college teams in the area, including Fresno State College, Stanford and the University of Southern California.[93]

By mid–March, spring had arrived. The FAC were ready to take on the top clubs in the area and, to their surprise, they found it again in the Philadelphia Hilldale Royal Giants. The Giants — rated as one of the strongest black teams in the U.S.— had just completed their 1927-28 California Winter League season, and many of the team's stars traveled north to Fresno on their way east for the 1928 Negro League season.

No explanation was given as to why the Royal Giants' star of the CWL, Biz Mackey, did not make the trip to Fresno. In 18 winter league games he hit a whopping .385 (65 AB/ 25 H).[94] Perhaps he still harbored bad feelings about the media incident in Japan? We may never know. It was later reported that Mackey loved the West Coast and playing in the California Winter League. So much so that eventually he made California his home.[95] Even without Mackey in the lineup, the FAC still had difficulty containing the bats of the visiting squad. Behind the pitching of Elvis "Bill" Holland and lefty Jesse "Pud" Flournoy, the Philadelphia Hilldale Royal Giants defeated Zenimura's club, 12–7. Despite the loss, the shining light for the FAC was the hitting of John Nakagawa, who went 5 for 5 on the day, recording 2 triples and 3 singles.[96]

April 1928 brought more heated contests on the diamond and lots of rain. Mother Nature prevented the FAC from playing with a series of showers. After a scheduled game against the Iron Boys was rained out, the *Fresno Bee* announced that the next game on the books for the FAC was Keio University, scheduled to arrive in San Francisco on April 13 on a barnstorming tour of California.[97]

In addition to the much anticipated arrival of Keio, April also brought the annual Japanese Central California track meet held in honor of the historic Buddha's birthday. This year's event was moved from the Fresno Buddhist Church to the Japanese Ball Park. Thirteen teams entered the event with the hope of winning and representing Central California at the statewide meet. As the host of the event, Zenimura served as the spokesperson for the annual track and field event.[98] On Sunday, April 8, more than 2,000 fans turned out to watch the Fresno YMBA defeat Bakersfield, Parlier, Visalia, Del Rey, Sanger, Dinuba, Fowler and Bowles to secure the right to represent their region at the state level.[99]

Mid-April saw a tough contest between the FAC and the Tollhouse Cubs, an undefeated semipro team led by local brothers, pitcher Ed McMurtry and catcher Orville McMurtry.[100] In their home ballpark, and behind the stellar pitching of Tomiyama, the FAC slammed out a 5 to 3 victory over Tollhouse. Coach Zenimura proved to be the difference in the game gathering two hits and scoring three of the FAC runs.[101]

Immediately after the upset of the semipro Cubs, the *Bee* announced that Fresno would be the scene of a baseball tourney for the Japanese championship of California. Scheduled for April 27 and 28 at the Japanese Ball Park, the tournament included the FAC and clubs from Sacramento, San Jose and Alameda.[102]

The San Joaquin Valley was a hotbed of barnstorming baseball activity in the spring of 1928. The Fresno Tigers, led by Art Ramage, welcomed the House of David nine in late April and the returning Hilldale Colored Giants of Philadelphia in early May.[103]

As the game day with Hilldale approached, the media reported that the club coming to town was indeed the same group of Hilldale players who defeated the FAC weeks ago and, led by manager Lon Goodwin, was in fact now called the Los Angeles Colored Tigers.[104] However, when the L.A. Tigers' lineup was announced, none of the familiar Negro League stars were present. Instead the lineup reflected a team of lesser status. The Fresno Tigers walloped the L.A. Tigers 18 to 1.[105]

By early May many of the barnstorming Hilldale players had returned to Pennsylvania for the regular 1928 season. On May 12, the *Afro-American* announced, "Philly fans will get a chance to judge the last five years of baseball development in the Orient when ... the Keio University of Japan ball team, composed of all Japanese, will be the opponents of Hilldale at Hilldale Park."[106] Hilldale defeated the diminutive Shinji Hamazaki by the score of 10 to 5.[107] Keio would then head west for more games in California, including one against the FAC.

The FAC continued its winning ways against local semipro clubs. In late April, Zenimura and the boys defeated the Merced Bears by the score of 9 to 3 at the Japanese Ball Park. *The Bee* reported that "the local pastimers found the delivery of Piggozzi, Merced pitcher, for a total of eleven safeties during the nine innings while the battery of Murishima and Nakagawa limited the invaders to six swats while on the hill for the athletic clubbers. Zenimura ... gathered a three bagger to score Murishima in the eighth frame to furnish the batting thrill of the afternoon."[108] Weeks later FAC traveled to Merced for a return series and found themselves on the short end of a close 3 to 2 ballgame.[109]

On June 3, the FAC defeated Alameda, 9 to 3, and Florin, 15 to 8, to win the district title and the opportunity to play for the CJBL championship in San Jose.[110] In preparation for the upcoming series with both Keio and San Jose, Zenimura scheduled a contest against a collection of Twilight League all-stars led by Shan Kilburn. Behind the battery of Murishima and Yoshikawa, the FAC defeated the all-stars 11 to 5.[111]

On Flag Day, June 14, the *Bee* announced that the Keio Japanese baseball team was finally on its way to Fresno for a series of games with the FAC. Scouts identified the stars of the incoming Keio club as Hamazaki, southpaw pitcher; and Miyatake, pitcher, home run slugger and utility man. Both would eventually be elected into the Japanese Baseball Hall of Fame. The *Bee* also heralded the "local nine [FAC] is the claimant of the Japanese Club title of the United States.... Led by Manager K. Zenimura, the athletic clubbers are a fast and scrappy outfit which depends largely on speed and smart baseball for success."[112]

The outcome of the first game between Keio and the FAC resulted in a 10 to 6 victory over the Fresno Athletic Club. Local sports writer Tut Jackson reported, "Johnny Nakagawa led the Fresno club in hitting with two hits out of five tries while Hamasaki finished in front of his outfit, Captain Zenimura of the Fresno outfit had a busy day around the short patch, accepting eleven chances without a bungle."[113]

In game two of the series, the Fresno boys came out punching. For the first four innings it was a tight ball game. However, with the score 5–3 in the fifth, the wheels came off the bus for the FAC pitching and defense, allowing Keio to score 13 runs in the fatal inning. "In the fifth affairs took on the appearance of a batting practice for Keio and continued from bad to worse from then on," for the FAC. The *Bee* declared that the victory gave Keio the Japanese Championship title for both the United States and Japan. In the drubbing, the highlights for the FAC included a home run from Nakagawa. The *Bee* also added that "Zenimura and Yoshikawa seemed to be the only part of the Fresno lineup that was able to keep its feet on the ground. The rest soared far and wide to chalk up a total of nine errors." Zenimura finished the day with two hits, including a triple, in four plate appearances.[114]

Still licking their wounds from the shellacking by Keio, the FAC battled Art Ramage's Fresno Tigers at Fireman's Park. Zeni bolstered his lineup with pitcher Jimmy Hansen and third baseman and long-time friend Mike Santos. Zenimura's snappy fielding, timely hitting by Yoshikawa and six costly errors committed by the Tigers led to a 6 to 4 FAC victory.[115]

Game two between the FAC and Fresno Tigers was billed as a contest between "two of the best teams in the San Joaquin Valley" and as a "battle for the independent baseball championship of Fresno." The *Bee* added, "should the Tigers win today the playoff that would be necessary to decide the championship will have to be done away with as the Fresno Athletic Club manager, K. Zenimura, is leaving this week for the Orient."[116]

With the score tied 0 to 0 in the ninth inning:

> The FAC tossers had the fans falling in the aisles when they launched swats, walked and did everything in general but score. With two out the bases were bulging and Zenimura, who hits them usually when he doesn't walk, decided he could do away with a step-ladder and hit one of Templeton's high ones. He didn't, and the West Side threat was over. Zenimura had three balls and two strikes already counted and another ball would have walked in what then would have been the winning run, was floating towards him when he heard the urge to get things over with and swung wildly to pull down the curtain on his club's last stand.[117]

The Tigers scored two runs in the 10th inning, including an RBI single by Cam Templeton, to secure the victory. And there was no joy in Fresno, for the mighty Zeni had struck out.

After the disappointing loss to the Tigers, Zenimura shifted his focus to an anticipated pleasure and business tour of Hawaii. On July 14, 1928, Kenichi boarded the *S.S. City of Los Angeles* bound for Honolulu. Joining him were his expecting wife Kiyoko (due in December with Kenshi) and 15-month-old son Kenso (Howard).[118] Zeni was taking the family back to Hawaii to prepare for the birth of their third son, to visit grandparents Masakichi and Waka, and to see their first-born son, Kenji (Harry), who was still living in Hawaii. That was the pleasure part of the trip.

Grandmother Waka Zenimura (back, center) and Kenji (front, center) pose with Kenichi Zenimura's FAC teammate Ken Furubayashi (left) and sister Masako Zenimura (right). Kenichi and Kiyoko returned to the U.S. in 1929, leaving Kenji behind to be raised by the Zenimura grandparents (Zenimura Family Archive).

The business side of the trip consisted of baseball games to be played throughout the islands. The touring team was not the Fresno Athletic Club, but the all-black Los Angeles White Sox. According to the passenger ship records of the S.S. *City of Los Angeles*, joining the Zenimura family were the following players: Joe Cade, Sam Cooper, Connie Day, Alexander Evans, Robert Fagen, Julius Green, Harold "Yellowhorse" Morris, Henry Moore, O'Neal Pullen, Azel Savage and Jesse Walker.[119] Pullen, Morris, Cooper and Day had recently competed with the Philadelphia Royal Giants and Cleveland Stars in the 1927-28 California Winter League in southern California.[120]

With Zenimura away in Hawaii, more noteworthy events were unfolding in the area of cross-cultural and international baseball relations. In September, the headlines declared news unimaginable for the times, "Negro and Jap to Umpire Ball Game." In Marysville, California, the Negro Woodland Giants were scheduled to play the Sacramento All Star Japanese ballclub. As a compromise, the two agreed that the umpires for the game would include a representative from each race.[121]

On October 7, the FAC pastimers, led by Yoshikawa as interim manager in Zeni's absence, took on Shan Kilburn's All-Stars comprised of local Twilight Leaguers and professional ballplayers from the leagues in the West. The all-stars defeated the FAC 7 to 4, behind pitcher John "Moose" Cano and other stars, including: Phil Funkner, Jack Stewart, Les Malone, Martin Bonzagni, George LaRoux, Foy Frazier, Connie Busch, Jack Kohl, Pete Shepherd, Leo Ostenberg, Johnny Coffman, Para, Mike Ferriera and Pete Berdoy.[122] In 1928, Cano compiled a 6–3 record with the Boise Senators of the class C Utah-Idaho League; Ostenberg hit .335, including 13 home runs in 55 games, for the same club; and Foy Frazier hit .257 in 63 games with the Oakland Oaks of the AA Pacific Coast League. In short, the caliber of competition, even without Zeni in the lineup, serves a gauge to measure the level of talent for the FAC squad.

Meanwhile, in Honolulu Zeni welcomed his third son, Kenshi "Harvey" Zenimura, to the world on December 1, 1928. He also found time for networking and negotiating tours for both Hawaiian and teams back on the U.S. mainland. Upon his return to Fresno, Zeni stated that he "signed up a number of teams from the islands to play a series" with ball clubs back on the mainland.[123] Although unconfirmed at this time, Zenimura's 1928–29 stay in Hawaii might have also been foundation for O'Neal Pullen's return tour of Hawaii in 1929, and Asahi team owner Steere Noda's financial support of the Philadelphia Royal Giants' second tour of Japan in 1931–1932.

Also in Hawaii in December 1928 was the great Ty Cobb, who had just completed his own tour of Japan. Four years after Zenimura and his FAC brought a Ty Cobb-autographed bat as a gift for their Japanese hosts, the "Georgia Peach" finally paid a visit to Japan. The future hall of famer was a huge hit with the Japanese fans, as he not only attempted to learn the language of his hosts, he even donned the uniforms of the big four universities.[124] For a day, the great Ty Cobb was an honorary member of the Meiji University squad and teammate of Zeni's cousins, Captain Tatsumi Zenimura and manager Takizo Matsumoto.

The 1929 Season: An International Baseball Entrepreneur

The Fresno Athletic Club started 1929 with two decisive victories: a football game at the Japanese Ball Park against the Sacramento Japanese eleven in January, winning by a score of 19 to 0; and their first baseball game of the season by a similar score. Still without the assistance of Captain Zenimura, the FAC nine — behind the battery of Murishima and Yoshikawa — jumped all over the Firemen for a 20 to 3 win at Firemen's Park on March 3.[125]

On March 12, 1929, the *Fresno Bee* reported the return of Captain Zenimura. "The baseball game between the FAC and Fresno Sciots, halted last Sunday by rain, will be staged next Sunday at the Firemen's Ball Park. Captain Zenimura, flashy shortstop of the FAC nine, who has been in the Hawaiian Islands for several months, will return home Saturday and will perform with his club. Zenimura has signed a number of teams from the island to appear in a series with the local Japanese pastimers."[126]

Back on the diamond, it appears that Zenimura did more than set up games with teams just from the Hawaiian islands. The Meiji University baseball team which had won the intercollegiate championship of Japan the previous year was now coming to Fresno too. Frank Narushima was the business manager and Tatsumi Zenimura, Zeni's cousin, served as the captain and right fielder of the club. Zeni had signed Meiji as well as other leading university teams of Japan for games in California.[127]

In his first game back with the FAC, the club suffered an 8 to 3 loss to the Sciots. Zenimura's pitchers, Phil Funkner and Yosh Murishima, gave up 9 hits and 8 runs, while Lew Marley's pitchers, Eldridge Hunt and Em Brandon, gave up 5 hits and 3 runs. Joe Cartwright and Johnny Coffman were the batting stars of the day.[128]

With a 7 to 1 victory over the Stockton Yamato ball club under their belt, the Meiji nine were ready to take on Zenimura and the FAC. The game ended in a 4–3 victory over Meiji.[129]

The following day, April 14, the Meiji nine were scheduled to play Lew Marley's Sciots, but "a shift was made at the eleventh hour and a combined team tossed on the field because the Meiji pastimers declared that they had had too much baseball and some of them wanted to take it easy." As a result, four Meiji players joined nine FAC players and the combined squad took on the Sciots. Calling themselves "an all-star Japanese baseball club," the combined Meiji University and FAC team had little difficulty administering a 10–3 drubbing to the Fresno Sciots. The Japanese All-Stars were comprised of: T. Zenimura, cf; Sumida, ss; Okada, c; Iwata, lf; Tsukimura, cf; Yamasaki, 3b; Washio, 1b; Tachino, 2b; Yasuda, p; K. Zenimura, 3b; and Kmano, rf. This 1929 lineup appears to be the first time ever that a visiting Japanese squad combined with a Japanese American team.[130]

In late April 1929, more international and multicultural baseball arrived. The Chinese Association of Fresno hosted a Sports and Dancing celebration, which included baseball games at the Japanese Ball Park between the Fresno Colored Cubs and the Wah Sung Chinese nine from Oakland on Saturday, and the Wah Sung club and FAC on Sunday.[131] The results of both games were not reported. However, a few days later Zenimura and the FAC hosted the L.A. Nippons, hammering out a 9 to 4 victory over Los Angeles. Fresno's longer hits prevailed for the win.[132]

The international baseball bug began to spread in Fresno and clearly Zeni was to be found at the center of it. On May 3, the *Oakland Tribune* announced that the Fresno Sciots were heading to Hawaii. Lew Marley, manager of the Sciots, said they would make the trip in the coming year and that Captain Ken Zenimura would make the booking. The plans were for Zeni to go to Hawaii around June 1 and to act as business manager.[133]

By May 1929, Kenichi Zenimura had established an impressive resume and reputation as an entrepreneur and business negotiator on the diamond. He could not only close a deal, but turn a profit as well. At least one Fresno resident took issue with the price of admission

On April 14, 1929, members of the Meiji University squad teamed up with Zenimura's FAC to defeat the Fresno Sciots. This rare photo from the Japanese Ballpark features (left to right) Torajiro Yamasaki, Zeni's father-in-law; cousin and Meiji captain Tatsumi Zenimura; Kenichi Zenimura; cousin and Meiji manager Frank Narushima; unidentified man; and Tad Yamada (front row), FAC bat boy (Zenimura Family Archive).

Zenimura charged for a ball game. It seems that $1.00 was just way too much.[134] (Author's note: Adjusted for inflation, $1.00 in 1929 is equal to $7.50 in 2010.)[135]

Zenimura left again for Hawaii in June 1929 and stayed until October 30. While he was in the islands, he continued to promote and book games for local teams like the Fresno Sciots lodge club.[136] Another baseball promoter and ambassador made headlines, and sadly, for the final time in his life. The world said goodbye to baseball pioneer Ted Sullivan on July 5. In many ways, Zenimura and Sullivan lived similar lives and had equally important impacts on the game as international ambassadors.

After six months in the Hawaiian Islands, Zenimura and his family returned to Fresno. On the passenger ship *President Grant* the manifest listed Howard, age 2; Harvey, 10 months-old; Kiyoko, 22; and Kenichi, 29. Zenimura listed his occupation as "mechanic" and his address as 1560 Kearny Street, in Fresno, California, the home of his father-in-law Torajiro Yamasaki.[137]

According to the 1930 U.S. Census, the Zenimura family in Hawaii no longer lived on Green Street with the Moore household. Instead, father Masakichi was now the head of the household at 1552 Kassati Lane, Honolulu, and was working as a janitor in a public school. Included in the Zenimura home was mother Waka, 50; Kenichi's first-born son Harry, 5; and a widow, Murata Gekitaro. The same document confirms that father Masakichi Zenimura arrived in Hawaii in 1902 and mother Waka Zenimura arrived in Hawaii in 1903.[138]

Years later Howard Zenimura would say that this return to the United States marked one of the most difficult chapters in his father's life. Zeni's wife Kiyoko wanted to move back to California, but grandmother Zenimura wanted the family to stay in Hawaii. Perhaps as a compromise, the oldest brother Kenji (Harry), age 4, stayed behind in Honolulu and lived with his grandparents. Years later Howard says that "mother never forgave grandmother for making them leave Kenji in Hawaii."[139]

Just two days before Zeni and his family's departure for the mainland, the U.S. experienced "Black Friday," the day when the stock market collapsed, causing a global economic crisis. The Zenimura family, and baseball in Fresno in general, would not be immune to the hardships caused by the resulting "Great Depression" of the 1930s.

Kenichi Zenimura's sons (left to right) Kenji, 3, and Kenso, 1, were exposed to baseball and barnstorming early in life. The Zenimura family traveled to Hawaii in July 1928 for six months. While in the islands, Kenichi booked games for teams back in California as the family reunited with first-born son Kenji and the Zenimura grandparents (Zenimura Family Archive).

4

The Twilight Era (1930–1941)

"It [the Twilight League] was comparable to a Class D minor league. We had minor leaguers, guys who would go on to the majors and the best talent to come out of the high schools and colleges around here."[1]
—Earl "Hands" Maloney, 1930s Twilight League Hall of Famer, father of MLB pitcher Jim Maloney

The 1930 Season—Hard Times Create Opportunity

In late February 1930 the *Fresno Bee* announced the start of a new season in the San Joaquin Valley Japanese Baseball League. Fresno, Fowler, Dinuba and Parlier made up the four Class-A teams, while the six Class-B teams were Kings YMBA, Visalia, Bowles, Selma, Fresno YMCA and Hanford. Roy Mizote, a mechanic from Hanford and good friend of Zenimura, took on the role of manager for the Fresno Japanese team. Another new addition to the FAC was Bill Ishida, star player from Fresno High School.[2] The spring season was scheduled to open March 2 and last until May 4.[3]

Early April saw Zenimura's Japanese Baseball Park as the host of the annual Valley Japanese track meet. Commemorating the birthday of Buddha, the meet was sponsored by the Fresno Young Men's Buddhist Association (YMBA), and featured the 75- and 200-yard dashes, 440- and 850-yard runs, high jump, broad jump, shot put, mile run and relay.[4]

On April 16, the *Fresno Bee* reported that the FAC was starting workouts in preparation for a two-game series against the Stockton Japanese Club for the local Japanese Baseball Park Raisin Day celebration on April 26–27. Manager Mizote reported the lineup as Fred Murashima on the slab with H. Yoshikawa behind the plate; Ryo Ino, 1b; B. Yoshikawa, 2b; George Kebo, 3b; Bob Yamasaki, ss; L. Yamasaki, lf; M. Doi, cf; and Johnson Kebo, rf.[5]

After a series of games with teams in the area and throughout the state, the Fresno Athletic Club captured the 1930 pennant of the Central California Japanese League when it secured an 8 to 4 victory from Parlier. The win gave Zenimura's boys their fourth consecutive title. According to the *Bee*, "George Kebo's pitching was too much for the Parlier tossers, who used two hurlers, J. Mouye and B. Shimzu. Henry Yoshikawa was behind the bat for the victors, while Chimori caught for Parlier." The final standings of the 1930 CCJL were:[6]

Teams	*Won*	*Lost*
Fresno	4	0
Dinuba	3	1
Parlier	0	4

Due to the hardships created by the Great Depression, the senior members of the FAC found themselves working longer hours on the farms or additional jobs, and doing whatever it took to make ends meet. As a result, the FAC evolved into a junior pick-up team of high school players by the spring.

For Zenimura and other veteran stars of the team still wanting to play competitive ball, they turned the negative into a positive and joined their all-white peers in the Fresno Twilight leagues.On April 19, the *Fresno Bee* reported that the Twilight League "Jaynes and Sons nine is richer by a total of three new men this year: Funkner, from the Sun Maids; Bill Stoker, who played with the Zellerbach team here two years ago, and K. Zenimura, leading Japanese player of Fresno." The report added, "Zenimura makes one of the most interesting figures on the garage-men's team. Outstanding in athletics among his countrymen here, he at one time captained a team of coast all-stars to tour the Orient. Captain of the FAC for many years, Zenimura was without a berth this season when the club decided not to organize so the Jaynes club secured him. Fast and shifty, the little short-stop chases balls with agility and when he gets on base he worries a pitcher a lot, being able to maintain a good distance from the bag and always beating out the ball when he is threatened."[7]

In his first game with the Jaynes & Sons nine, Zenimura helped the club with his bat and glove for a 3–2 victory over the Sugar Pine nine. "Little Zenimura, Japanese flash, got a hit, got to second on a passed ball. Cropsy got a walk. Then pitcher Funkner came up and did nothing less than slap out an aerial message to the clouds which landed over the left field fence and produced three runs."[8]

Jaynes & Sons which now also included Fred Yoshikawa traveled to Hanford on July 13 to take on the all-stars of that town. Among the Hanford all-star squad were some strong

The Depression prevented the Fresno Athletic Club from organizing in 1930. Kenichi Zenimura and Fred Yoshikawa turned this negative into a positive and joined the all-white Jaynes and Sons ballclub of the semipro Fresno Twilight League (Nisei Baseball Research Project).

Japanese ballplayers, including Al Tamayo, described as a "heavy sticking chucker." Tamaya held his opponents to 8 hits and 8 runs, while the Jaynes & Sons club couldn't find a pitcher. The club started Koch, then went to relief in the fourth inning with Draklich, Lauderdale and Patsy Castro, a high-school pitching star. When none of those four could keep men off the bases, Zenimura took the mound in a rare relief appearance. The Jaynes pitchers gave up a ridiculous 46 hits for 21 runs in the loss.[9]

Years later Don Jorgensen, former Jaynes & Sons player, reflected on Zenimura as a teammate: "He was a little small, but real smart in baseball, real smart. He knew all the tricks of the trade in baseball. He was a fair hitter, but he was hard to pitch to, so there were lots of walks in there. He never swung at a bad pitch." Jorgensen added that as a captain, "Kenny didn't hesitate to chew you out if you made a bonehead play. He had my respect and he had the respect of all the ballplayers on his team."[10]

Despite the fact that Zeni and Yoshikawa became trusted teammates of the Caucasian Jaynes & Sons in the Twilight League of Fresno, off-the-diamond racial tensions between whites and Japanese on the West Coast continued to escalate in 1930. Seeing that an organized political voice was needed to advance the rights of Japanese Americans, the first convention of the Japanese American Citizens League (JACL) was held on August 29 in Seattle, Washington. The JACL would grow to become the largest Japanese American political organization during and after World War II.

For Zenimura, baseball was the best way to break down barriers, and in September he marshaled his latest effort to do so by organizing a doubleheader between an all-star team chosen by Big Jake Jacobsen and Ray Obenchain and a group of Japanese players that he considered the best ever to play in the state. For pitcher he imported Morio Matsuno, captain of the Guadalupe Aratani nine on the coast, who had quite a reputation as one of the best Japanese pitchers in California. Another addition to the team was Kenso Nushida, second baseman from Stockton who was kept in reserve as a pitcher. And, he brought Tsuda from San Jose to play first base.

The all-stars were a lineup of Twilight League favorites, several of whom had been playing semipro ball post season. The lineups of the two teams were: for the Fresno Japanese: Tsuda, 1b; Nushida, 2b; Yamasaki, 3b; Zenimura, ss; Iwata, lf; Tsukimura, cf; Nakagawa, rf; Yoshikawa, c; and Matsuno, p.; and for the All Stars: Funkner, 1b; Berdoy or Kohl, 2b; Doc Jacobsen, 3b; Earl Jacobsen, ss; Bidwell, lf; Tocher, rf; Big Jake Jacobsen, rf; Rogers and Stoker, p; Windell, c; and LaRoux, utility.[11]

For the second game of the advertised doubleheader, Zenimura tapped the best talent from his opponents in the first contest. The hybrid team won 6 to 5 in an exciting and close 10-inning game. Aratani's lineup included Ryan, Walker, Tsuda, A. Montez, Alexander, Maglia, D. Brown, G. Brown, Matsuno, P. Montez and Nushida. The Fresno blended squad featured Tsukimura, Iwata, Funkner, L. Jacobsen, J. Jacobsen, Berdoy, Zenimura, Yoshikawa, Stoker and Tamaki. Zenimura recorded four plate appearances, walked twice, stole one base, and scored what appears to be the decisive run.[12]

The fall of 1930 saw another group of barnstorming major leaguers visiting Fresno. Baseball fans in the Raisin City were treated with a game at the Firemen's Baseball Park between the American and National League All-Stars against a team of Fresno All-Stars. The big leaguers, led by Earl Mack, son of Connie Mack, included stars like Lefty Grove, Rube Walberg, Bing Miller, Earl Whitehill, Lefty O'Doul, Harry Heilmann, Charley Gehringer, Bill Sweeny and Ralph Kress. The Fresno All-Stars were led by manager Jake Jacobsen, who selected brothers I. and D. Jacobsen, Jud Simons, Howard Craghead, Monte Pearson,

Player/coach Kenichi Zenimura quickly gained the respect of his Caucasian peers with the Jaynes & Sons nine. Partial stats show that Zenimura held a .346 career batting average against semipro or amateur competition between 1923 and 1936 (Nisei Baseball Research Project).

Bill Phebus, Charley Moncrief, Johnny Coffman, and Alex Metzler for his squad. The big leaguers were passing through Fresno on their way to Los Angeles where they would depart for a tour of Japan.[13]

More than 2,250 fans witnessed the Big Leaguers defeat the local all-stars by the score of 8 to 4, behind the sensational pitching of Lefty Grove. They also witnessed for the first time in many years, a local-all star game that did not feature a single all-star Japanese American baseball player.[14] With Zenimura, Yoshikawa, Iwata and Nakagawa in the prime of their playing careers in 1930, they were inexplicably excluded as among "the best local baseball talent" in Fresno.

Was racism the reason? According to a study conducted by Stewart Tolnay and E. M. Beck in 1995, there is an identifiable correlation between decreased economic prosperity and increased tension among social and ethnic groups. For example, during the late 1800s an inverse relationship was identified between the price of cotton and the frequency of lynching in the south. When cotton prices were strong, the lynching decreased. When the prices dropped, the farmers and those in other related industries felt the economic pinch and took their frustrations and anger out on innocent African Americans.[15] The study called this phenomenon "scapegoating" and it is quite possible that the start of the Great Depression in 1930 also marked the beginning of a new level of hostilities towards Japanese Americans in California. For the first time in many years, the greatest Japanese American baseball players in Fresno were excluded from a high profile barnstorming game against accomplished pro players.

The 1931 Season—Tours to and from Japan

The new season brought the continuation of Zeni's plans to host more teams from Japan. During his earlier tours to Japan, Zeni had befriended Nubuo Fujita, the head of Hosei University baseball and the Big Six university system. This resulted in Hosei's four-month tour beginning in April to the U.S. that included a visit to Fresno. As the 1930 Tokyo Big Six university baseball champions, Hosei was scheduled to play Fresno in late June or early July.[16] Howard Zenimura said of his father's relationship with the Big-Six executive: "If Fujita knew that my dad was coming to town, they would always eat and drink together."[17]

Zenimura also introduced another colleague in Japan, Frank Narushima, to Harry Kono, manager of the Nisei Alameda ballclub. As a result, Narushima extended an invitation to Kono and his club to visit Japan for a series of games.[18] Thanks to the networking of Zenimura, the Alameda ballclub departed on March 5 for its Goodwill Tour of Japan. And if that wasn't enough, Zeni also served as a mentor/coach to the Alameda ballclub prior to the 1931 tour as well.[19]

The spring of 1931 saw the annual observance of the Buddha's birthday with festivities and a track meet at Zenimura's Japanese Baseball Park. Several thousand Japanese Americans from the San Joaquin Valley traveled to Fresno for the annual two-day observance on April 11–12. The Rev. I. Kyogoku, minister of the Fresno Buddhist church, officiated services each morning of the contest. More than 2,000 school children, representing valley YMCA's and YMBA's, participated in athletic contests on the church grounds and at Zenimura's ball park.[20] Years later Howard Zenimura said, "The church had a track, tennis court, and a baseball field.... I think they even played a few ballgames there too."[21]

By late May, the Alameda club returned to the States from its Japanese tour, just in time for the "Diamond Tourney" in Sacramento, California. The tournament included Japanese ball clubs from the host city, Alameda, San Jose, Stockton, San Francisco and Fresno. The 1931 Fresno Athletic Club roster included Zenimura, ss; Yoshikawa, c; Tsukimura, cf; Iwata, lf; Kebo, 3b; Yamasaka, 1b; Tachino, 2b; Kumano, rf; Murashima and Saiki, p; Utility: B. Yamasaki, Saito, B. Yoshikawa.[22]

The FAC performed well in the tournament, but failed to secure the state championship crown after a 9–9 tie with Sacramento. A tiebreaker was originally scheduled for July 4 in Fresno, however it appears that the game was delayed for several months and not resumed until late September.[23]

Just before the scheduled play off game against Sacramento, Zenimura received word from his colleague Nubuo Fujita that the game with the Hosei University baseball team would be cancelled. Due to a shortage of time on their trip, the squad was unable to make it to Fresno as originally planned.[24] Hosei did, however, have time for a contest with Kensho Nushida and his Stockton Yamato ballclub. Hosei defeated Stockton in an exciting 13-inning game.

On July 10, the Yamato team headed to Fresno to take on the FAC. For this particular game, Zenimura was not serving as the manager of the Fresno club. Instead, the team was now managed by veteran catcher Fred Yoshikawa.[25] The difficulty of the times would occasionally shift responsibilities for all the players. In the game, "[t]he FAC trounced Stockton, 14–6, collecting 21 hits off the combined offering of Mirikitani and Nushida, Stockton hurlers. Murishima, the Fresno hurler, got two three-baggers to lead the long distance hitters for the day while Kumano, Fresno right fielder, got four hits out of four time at bat."[26]

In late summer, Hiroshima High School — championship high school baseball team of Japan — was on tour in the United States and scheduled a game with the FAC. The Hiroshima High School team from Shogyo were a reputable star outfit. Shoygo launched their tour in the Northwest and started with a 2–1–1 record. Starring for the visitors was Haiyama, a right-handed pitcher promoted as "the best prospect in Japan."[27] To everyone's surprise, the Shogyo nine squeaked by the FAC squad, winning the contest 4 to 3. Played at the Japanese Ball Park, "the game early developed into a pitching duel between Murashima of the local club and Haiyama.... The visitors tallied once in the second frame and three time in the fourth for their total while the FAC scored in the first, eighth and ninth innings. An attempted rally in the last frame fell one run short of tying the score."[28]

Weeks later Zenimura finally welcomed the Sacramento Japanese nine to Fresno for the Northern California Japanese Baseball League championship. The *Fresno Bee* reported the results: "The Wakaba Club of Sacramento this week won the ... championship, defeating the Fresno Taiiku Club by a score of 5 to 4. A three-run rally in the eighth won the contest for Sacramento."[29] *Taiiku* is the Japanese word for athletic club. *Wakaba* is a Japanese word meaning "young leaf," signifying a new beginning. The 1931 season marked the first time that the team historically known as the "Fresno Athletic Club" referred to themselves by a Japanese name. This change is important because it represents a shift in the cultural identity of Japanese American baseball in Fresno. For years putting on a baseball uniform was like putting on the American flag. But now, as Japanese Americans, it also meant expressing pride in their heritage as well. The term *taiiku* would begin to find its way into press coverage of the games as a synonym for the Fresno Athletic Club.

Over time, Zenimura's Japanese Ball Park became known as a welcoming home for those marginalized by white society: Japanese Americans and other Asian groups, African Americans and political outsiders. In late September, the *L.A. Times* reported that "after being refused the civic auditorium, the courthouse park and the Firemen's baseball park as a location for the address of former senator Heflin here Tuesday night, A.W. Drew today announced that he has engaged the Japanese Baseball Park in West Fresno."[30]

This is noteworthy because Senator James Thomas Heflin was a segregationist and Ku Klux Klan–supported U.S. senator from Alabama during the 1920s. Legend has it that in 1908, while a member of the U.S. House of Representatives, Heflin shot and seriously wounded a black man who confronted him on a Washington streetcar. Heflin had the charges dismissed and throughout his life often bragged of the shooting as one of his major career accomplishments. Furthermore, in 1930, James Heflin officially protested against the New York state permission of racial intermarriage between a black man and a white woman. In one speech Heflin declared the white race as "the climax and crowning glory of God's creation."[31]

On September 22, 1931, approximately 2,500 persons filled the Japanese Baseball Park to hear Heflin speak. In his address he denounced members of the city commission and board of supervisors for their refusal to allow the use of public buildings or grounds for his speech. "They talk of this not being a bar to free speech. What is it when your councilmen and your supervisors set themselves as censors of what you are to hear? It is nothing more than a bar to free speech and peaceful assembly, rights guaranteed you in the constitution."[32]

Critics expected Heflin to preach religious bigotry, but instead he devoted less than five minutes to religion, mentioning it then as a warning that church and state must be separated. Instead his speech was devoted to a discussion of immigration. "America for Americans is my doctrine. We should be God's right arm in saving the world from oppression and persecution. We came here to establish a model government, free from intolerance. We have established it, let's keep it." Heflin added, "Aliens are swarming in here by the millions.... We should line up every last one of those aliens and, if they have not applied for citizenship, deport them."[33]

This tale from Zenimura's life story is one of the most paradoxical scenarios, to say the least. Why would a Japanese immigrant who's been denied a right to become an American citizen allow a politician with white supremacist views to use his ballpark to deliver a right-wing, anti-immigrant speech? Was Zeni's decision a public gesture in support of the first amendment right to freedom of speech? Did he share some of the same conservative views as Heflin? Or did it come down to a more practical issue that 1931 was the midst of the depression and for the right price, anyone was welcome to use the Japanese Baseball Park in Fresno?

In early October Zenimura joined forces at Frank Chance Field with other Twilight League players for "the old timers benefit baseball game" created to raise funds to aid injured Twilight League players. Game committee member Phil Koerner announced that more than 100 players were invited to participate and given a chance to play. The list of participants resembled a list of future Twilight League Hall of Famers.

The starting lineup of the Professional Old-Timers featured: Art Ramage, c; Pete Shepherd, p; Joe Cartwright, 1b; Gene Jewett, 2b; Ollie Pickering, 3b; Connie Bush, ss; Rube Gardner, lf; Neal Cullen, cf; Beals Becker, rf; Jack Savory, p; and Dutch Leonard, p. The Twilight League Old-Timers starting lineup included: Shan Kilburn, c; Jim Hansen, p; Pop Barton, 1b; Dick Bier, 2b; Augie Fries, 3b; Dave Beard, ss; Doc Tocher, lf; Johnny Coffman, cf; and Roscoe Ford, rf. Among the other stars on the Twilight roster were Ken Zenimura, Fred Yoshikawa, Ivan and Ed McMurtry, Ty Lawson, and Hasty Bidwell.[34]

Two weeks later another fund-raising exhibition game was scheduled in Fresno. This time the cause was the American Legion, and the guest of honor was none other than George Herman "Babe" Ruth. Making his second appearance in the last four years, Babe gave a ten-minute hitting exhibition and then joined the Fresno Sciots to take on the Fresno Auto Wreckers to raise money for the American Legion. Babe was slated to play first base and pitch as well. The Fresno stars included the usual list of Caucasian local talent like Monte Pearson, Jack Savory, Jud Simons, Augie Fries, Jack Heizenrader, Johnny Coffman, Hasty Bidwell, Big Jake Jacobsen and Alex Metzler.[35] For the second time during the 1931 season, the all-stars of Zenimura's Japanese American ballclub were not invited to participate in an exhibition game featuring barnstorming professional players.

Approximately 2,500 fans witnessed the Bambino, "clad in a sparkling maroon and white uniform and looking in the best of shape," give the hitting demonstration before the game, and then, during the night-time game, continue the exhibition by swatting a home run over the center field fence off Merle Anderson. Ruth's team, the Fresno Sciots, was defeated 4 to 2 by Shan Kilburn's Fresno Auto Wreckers. Ruth also singled and walked in four trips to the plate. Defensively the Yankee great was charged with two errors, both infield throws.[36]

Perhaps offering excuses for his two errors in the infield, Ruth talked at length after the game about his disdain for night baseball. "It just isn't natural," said Ruth, "for you can't see as well as in the day time and you just can't muster up that old pep that you get under the bright sunshine. And it's hazardous. When you get up to the old plate the ball is hard to follow.... In the field you can't follow the ball as you can in the day time." The *Fresno Bee* commented that "the home run king thinks night baseball is all right for circuits that need the cash badly and have to figure out some way to get the fans into the gates. 'But you bet the big leagues never will play night ball,' Ruth added."[37]

In Tokyo the 1931 tour of the Big League stars drew between 55,000 and 60,000 fans at games. The Japanese not only saw future American Hall of Famers like Lefty Grove, Rabbit Maranville, Mickey Cochrane and Frankie Frisch in action, they also witnessed future Japanese Hall of Famers like Bozo Wakabayashi and Takeo Tabe. Although they were considered semipro players at the times, Gehrig's prediction about Japanese baseball proved to be more on the money than Ruth's about night baseball. "I haven't a doubt that within another couple of years they will be playing baseball all over the country [Japan]," he predicted.[38]

During the 1931 MLB tour, future parliamentary Vice Minister Takizo Matsumoto of the House of Representatives of Japan (aka Frank Narushima of Fresno) served as an interpreter for the American all-stars. As a result of this role, he became close friends of Lefty O'Doul, San Francisco Seal manager, Connie Mack, manager of the Philadelphia Athletics, and the Yankees' Lou Gehrig.[39]

This was an important year for U.S. and Japanese baseball relations. Historians today seem only to recognize the contributions of the MLB tour that occurred late in 1931, but there were many other important and influential relationships forged by teams both in Japan and in the U.S. One such noteworthy team was the visiting Hosei University, led by Zenimura's colleague Nubuo Fujita and his accomplished coach H. Takata. In an interview with *Oakland Tribune* reporter Ann Anderson Lacy, Hosei coach Takata offered a psychological snapshot of the differences between U.S. and Japanese baseball in 1931. Lacy asked "What is a coach's most difficult duty?" Takata responded:

> The great task of a coach is to adapt himself to the personalities of his athletes. The hardest struggle I ever had was in training an America-born Japanese boy to subject himself to Japanese discipline. I have but one such on my team (Bozo Wakabayashi). All his training has been different from ours.
>
> I must respect this personality or he will never develop into a great player. At the same time he must learn our ways or our team can never co-operate as a unit. For example we frown upon dancing. It is beneath an athlete in Japan. Now comes my most promising pitcher who takes dancing for granted. He cannot conceive of my right to control him to that extent. I grant him the right to dance because he is of American heritage, but if you notice he is the only member of our team granted this privilege.
>
> And then I ask him his attitude regarding students smoking and drinking. Sake, Japanese spirits, is forbidden, but smoking is permitted in moderation. Because it is better to permit it than to have our boys practice deception ... I will cooperate with my boys rather than have them deceive me and themselves.
>
> For example, I will sacrifice a little bit of my principles in order to make a winning team of them and to prevent them lying to me. As a consequence they come to me before the game when we are tense with strain, we will relax with a pull and play better. And so I permit it although I do not approve of it."
>
> What qualities do you look for in your young players? "Fleetness, accurate vision, coordination and adaptability,"

Takizo Matsumoto (aka Frank Narushima) was one of the original founders of the Fresno Athletic Club in 1919. He moved to Japan in the early 1920s to attend Meiji University and there became one of Zenimura's key figures in arranging tours to and from Japan (Zenimura Family Archive).

he replied. "And our boys must have character and personality. They must get along with their teammates, and that is often harder to master than the technique of the game."[40]

The 1932 Season — Reorganization Is the Rule

Sometime during the 1932 season Zenimura received a phone call from one of his contacts in Japan asking him to help negotiate a $40,000 offer for Babe Ruth to play in Japan. Zeni told the *Fresno Bee* in 1962, "I contacted Ruth and he said he would go for $60,000. It was too much but a few years later he went and made a big hit."[41]

Another slugger who also stayed in contact with Zenimura was Negro Leaguer O'Neal Pullen, catcher for the 1927 Philadelphia Royal Giants. Five years after his initial tour of Japan and Hawaii, Pullen continued to rely on Zenimura to use the Japanese Baseball Park in Fresno. On May 16, the same day as little Kenso Zenimura's fifth birthday, Pullen and his Bakersfield Cubs traveled to Fresno to battle the Fresno Colored Athletic Club at the Japanese Baseball Park. Pullen's Cubs lost 4–3 in a closely contested game.[42]

In late June Zeni made Twilight League news when he and Fred Yoshikawa joined the Schneider Aviation Club of the American League. Zenimura was a contribution to the team as he "has led a Japanese team from Fresno to Japan two or three times and is considered an A-1 shortstop. He will take Vernon Bandy's place.... The two Japanese pastimers are small, with the result that they are hard to pitch to. A walk for them is as good as a hit, as they are both good base stealers."[43]

Late June also marked the first time that Shig Tokumoto, star pitcher from Hanford, joined Zenimura's Japanese American team. The *Bee* detailed one of his first starts: "The FAC scored one more run than the DePrima's All-Stars in the fifth inning barrage to win a 9-to-8 victory yesterday at the Japanese Ball Park. The batteries were: J. Renna, T. Renna and Christian; Tokumoto, Saiki and Yoshikawa.... The athletic club will make a holiday tour July 2nd, 3rd, and 4th, meeting the Los Angeles Nippons and the Guadalupe YMBA in a series of games."[44]

In late June the *Rafu Shimpo*, the Japanese American newspaper in Los Angeles, announced that the Fresno-L.A. series was set and would take place at White Sox Park. Prior to the game the managers of the two clubs agreed that the rosters of both teams should contain only Japanese players. In preparing for what they considered to be the toughest lineup they would face all year, the Nippons enlisted the services of the best talent from teams that had already completed the Japanese League season play.[45]

Before the contests Fresno was billed as the strongest team in Central California, and was predicted to give the Nippons a close battle and perhaps win both games.[46]

The 1932 Fresno All-Stars lineup featured: Kenichi Zenimura, ss; Yushio Murashima, p; Fred Murashima, p; George Kebo, p; Tai Saiki, p; Bob Yamasaki, p; Fred Yoshikawa, c; Jiro Omata, 1b; Sam Yamasaki, 1b; Yosh Tachino, 2b; Saito, 2b; Matsui, 3b; Yukio Kawakami, 3b; Hy Takano, ss; Kono, ss; Iwata, lf ; Ed Tsukimura, cf; and Kats Kumano, rf. The L.A. Nippon lineup included: George Matsuura, p; Clyde Ishii, p; Jimmy Tajini, p; Bucky Harris, c; "Butch" Tamura, c; Min Watanabe, 1b; Saturo "Half-pint" Sugi, 2b; Pete Kondo, 3b; Sam Takahashi, ss, captain; Jimmy Horio, lf; Zuke Tanaka, cf; Harry Okida, rf; Masa Igasaki, of; Yoshio Nakamura, of; and Doi, utility.

The L.A. Nippons made a clean sweep of the two-game series against Fresno by taking both night games at White Sox Park, 14–5 and 17–1 respectively. Both teams played under handicaps. Fresno was playing together for the first time as a team and it was evident, as reflected by the 20 errors committed in total for the two games. Even the steady presence of the veterans, Yoshikawa and Zenimura, in the lineup failed to help the Fresno All-Stars live up to their reputation. The psychological handicap for the L.A. club was received just before game time when, in compliance with the pre-game agreement, the Fresno club asked Nippon player-president Igasaki to bar Bucky Harris, the Caucasian catcher, from participation in the series. The announcement was a bombshell in the Nippon dugout. Kondo stepped in at the backstop position and filled in just fine. It appears that the request to remove Harris from the game served to key the local club morale to a finer and more effective pitch, as the lopsided scores testified.

The *Rafu Shimpo* observed that the games between Fresno and L.A. were "poorly played and uninteresting." At one point during the series, one sarcastic fan was overheard during a particularly long and uneventful inning to say that "the game would go down in the books as the first night tilt to be called on account of daylight."[47]

After suffering a double defeat at the hands of the L.A. Nippons in Los Angeles, the Fresno Japanese traveled to Guadalupe to take on the Y.M.B.A. nine. Scoring five runs in the opening inning Guadalupe celebrated the Fourth of July by slugging their way to a 12–1 victory over Fresno. Aratani, E. Matsuno and Tsuda were the "big guns" in the hitting department. Aratani's homer over the left field wall was the highlight of the game. According to the *Rafu Shimpo*, Aratani's home run was the first time that a Japanese had ever hit one over the left field wall. Tsuda and Matsumo collected three hits apiece.[48]

After the series against L.A. and Guadalupe, Zenimura scheduled a contest between his own Japanese club and his new Twilight League teammates, the Aviators. Having won the Central California Japanese baseball championship by defeating several San Joaquin Valley teams as well as the Fresno Colored Giants and the Italian Athletic Club, Fresno was confident. The FAC lineup consisted of: Murishima, p; Yoshikawa, c; Yamasaki, lb; Tachino, 2b; Zenimura, 3b; Tahano, ss; Saiki, lf; Tsukimura, cf; Kunano, rf; and Tokumoto, relief pitcher.[49]

The Aviators won the first game, 15 to 10. A return game was to be played the following weekend but was prevented by the destruction of the Firemen's Ball Park by fire.[50] The game location was moved to the Japanese Ball Park. Despite the location change, the outcome remained the same. The Aviators trimmed Zenimura's Japanese Fresno Athletics, 19–11. Ed Lung and Yamasaki were the hitting aces during the contest, getting five hits out of five times at bat.[51] (In the spring of 1935 a 12-year-old boy confessed to setting nearly a score of fires on the outskirts of the city. One of these included the Japanese baseball park.[52])

Zenimura would not make his next trip to Japan until 1937. And this tour almost didn't take place because of an unfortunate accident that occurred in the fall of 1932. According to the *Hayward Review*, Alameda baseball manager Harry Kono was in critical condition after his car dove 300 feet over a cliff. Kono was badly burned and injured when his auto plunged through the guard rail, struck a pole and catapulted end over end to the creek bed below. The reports said "it was only by a miracle ... that Kono was not killed instantly."[53] Fortunately for the international baseball world, Kono made a full recovery. Five years later he funded the important Kono-Alameda tour to Japan that included both Zenimura and Nushida.

The 1933 Season — Zeni's Ballpark Is Home to Many

In the spring of 1933, the newest baseball star in the San Joaquin Valley was 17-year-old pitcher/infielder Shig Tokumoto of Hanford High School.[54] The lefty submarine pitcher was just as strong with the bat as he was with the fastball and his change-up. Always on the lookout for budding talent, Zenimura wasted no time adding Tokumoto to his roster of Japanese all-stars once school came to a close.

The first recorded game of Tokumoto pitching on Zeni's squad in 1933 occurred on Sunday, July 16, at the Japanese Ball Park. This is the same day that 18-year-old Joe DiMaggio hit in his 53rd consecutive game on his march to a 69-game hitting streak in the PCL. Tokumoto and DiMaggio would face one another in the near future. Tokumoto and Zenimura were the winning battery of the day, defeating the Fresno Tigers 15 to 13.[55]

The arrival of Tokumoto also marked the first time since his high school playing days at Mills in Honolulu that Zenimua returned to the catcher position. The switch was facilitated by aging knees, the need for better communication with his rookie pitcher, or both.

Tokumoto said this about his senior manager and battery-mate: "I remember every time I pitched good, he wouldn't give you credit. But if you didn't throw the pitch where he wanted, that ball came back faster than I could throw it. He gets up closer and throws hard, six feet in front of the plate. I would never argue." Shig added, "his [Zenimura's] theory was we've got to play American ball, not Japanese ball. We've got to hit, run, field, everything's got to be just right. He was a good manager."[56]

Articles on Zenimura and the Japanese All-Stars were scarce for 1933. Of those that surfaced, there appeared to be an increased frequency of games involving all-black teams playing at the Japanese Ball Park. The Fresno Colored Athletic Club called the Japanese Baseball Park their home field this season, and it served them well. Led by local star athlete Gene Hinds, the brother-in-law of West Coast Negro League legend Chet Bost, the Colored Athletic Club finished with a winning record and secured the pennant of the Fresno Twilight League.[57]

In early September a familiar name from Zenimura's past appeared at the Japanese Baseball Park. Former Philadelphia Royal Giants catcher O'Neal Pullen was the captain of the Bakersfield Cubs during the early 1930s, and each year his club went head-to-head with the Fresno Colored Athletic Club for the Labor Day dance and Colored Baseball Championship of Central California.[58] Pullen wasn't satisfied with the holiday contest alone, and afterwards was quite active in recruiting more games against Fresno clubs. He offered a financial incentive of a 50–50 or 60–40 split of the gate receipts.[59]

Zenimura's Japanese Ball Park was also a welcome home for Fresno's Mexican-American community. September 15 marked the 123rd anniversary of Mexico's Independence from Spain, and as part of the local celebration the Mexican All-Stars baseball club battled against the Fresno Colored Athletic Club at the Japanese Ball Park.[60] The outcome of the contest is unknown, but a month later the battery of Gonzales and Rodriguez joined the lineup of the Fresno Colored Athletic Club.[61]

With the Firemen's ballpark destroyed due to fire, even the barnstorming major leaguers found a home in Zenimura's Japanese Ballpark. On October 15, Jackie Heizenrader's All-Stars with Monte Pearson of the Cleveland Indians and Alex Metzler with the Milwaukee club "batted out a 14-to-8 victory over the Sciots in the Japanese Ball Park.... The Sciots had the Dean brothers, Dizzy and Paul, and Pepper Martin on their nine.... The clowning antics of the Dean combination at shortstop and the mound livened the game up considerably, while Martin made some fast plays off first base."[62] The complete rosters of the teams were not available, so it is unknown if Zenimura was invited to participate in the local all-star contest held on his own diamond.

The 1934 Season—New Competitors

In the spring of 1934 the *Fresno Bee* published only a handful of articles on Zenimura's club. However, when the first series of the year occurred in May, a gold mine of rosters began to surface. Week after week the *Bee* provided the names of virtually every Japanese ballplayer who visited Fresno. For Japanese American baseball historians, this is an important addition to the untold chapters of their leagues.

Opening day of the 1934 California Japanese Baseball League occurred on May 6 when Fresno battled the defending CJBL champions, the Stockton Yamato. The lineup for Stockton included: Tanaka, c; Shironaka, p; Nushida, p; Kawasaki, 1b; Mujanishi, 2b; Mirikstani, 3b; Tsukinkawa, lf; Okino, cf; Okada, rf; and Omura, ss. The 1934 Fresno ballclub featured: Zenimura, 2b; Yoshikawa, c; Tsukimura, cf; Saiki, rf; Yano, 3b; Yamasaki, 1b, p; Takagi, ss; Kasakami, ss; Iwata, lf; Ishida, lf; Tokumoto, p; and Murayama, p.[63]

Stockton continued its winning ways with a 12 to 9 victory over Fresno. Zenimura's men enjoyed batting sprees in the sixth and seventh innings which netted them three and four runs respectively, but they could not overcome the substantial lead gained earlier by the northerners. Kawasaki of Stockton hit a home run in the seventh with one man on base.

A week later Zenimura's club traveled to Salinas to take on the Japanese ball club of that town. The Fresno Japanese "administered a 25-to-4 shellacking to the Salinas Japanese. Every member of the Fresno team got at least one hit. Yoshikawa hit a home run."

On May 20, Zenimura welcomed the Alameda Japanese Club to Fresno. New additions to the Fresno Japanese lineup included Takagi and Kumano. The roster of the Alameda Japanese featured: Sadamune, lf; Iwahashi, c; Rakutani, p; Nogami, 3b; Utsumi; L. Nakano, ss; M. Nakano, 1b; Nanba; Takokura, rf; Tanizawa, p; Nakagawa, 2b; Nakagawa, rf; Takeda, cf; and Madokora, 2b.[64] The game was a real "slugfest" as the Fresno Athletic Club defeated Alameda 11 to 5. Yano, Iwata, Tsukimura and Kawakami were the heavy hitters for the locals. Yano got a home run and the others each a three-bagger.[65]

The following Sunday (May 27th) the Fresno Japanese had an open date. Zeni placed an open call in the *Fresno Bee* asking any team mangers interested in playing to contact him. Gene Hinds of the Fresno Colored Athletic Club answered the call. Zenimura's club continued its winning streak by defeating the Fresno Colored Athletic Club 14 to 1 in a free-hitting baseball game. Iwata and Tsukimura got five hits apiece to lead the slugging Japanese. Moriyama and Tokumoto limited the Colored Athletic Club batters to five hits, one a three-bagger by Turry.[66] Years later Howard Zenimura recalled this game. "When I was about seven or eight years old I remember my dad's team playing a Negro team at the Japanese ball park in west Fresno. The team was very good. After watching the team take infield and outfield warm up many people wondered how the Fresno Japanese team was going to beat them. Well, what my dad's team did was play small ball. They must of laid down about four or five bunts, hit and run and stole bases whenever they could. This is the reason if you wanted to play ball for my dad you'd better know how to bunt and run."[67]

With a winning streak intact, the Fresno Japanese welcomed the San Jose Asahi to the Japanese Baseball Park on June 3. The *Fresno Bee* reported that "two double plays by the San Jose Japanese, coming in each instance when the bases were loaded, nipped a pair of ambitious batting rallies by the Fresno Athletic Club ... and the San Jose nine eked out a 5-to-4 victory over the locals. The double killings came in the seventh and ninth innings, with one out and the sacks bulging with Fresnans each time. The locals outhit the visitors, 14 to 13, but failed to bunch their hits effectively. G. Ikeda of San Jose was the heavy hitter of the day, getting a home run, a triple and a double in four trips to the plate." For Fresno, Zenimura reached base three times in five at-bats, while Shig Tokumoto had a 2-for-4 day at the plate and scored two runs in the losing effort.[68]

Zenimura and his Fresno nine bounced back from their close loss to San Jose by defeating Kenso Nushida and his Stockton Yamato 5-to-2. The young pitching ace Shig Tokumoto limited Stockton to six hits, and nipped a threatening rally in the fifth by performing his best Satchel Paige imitation. He fanned two batters in succession when the bases were full with only one out.[69]

It is worthwhile to note that while the *Fresno Bee* detailed the sensational pitching of Japanese ballplayers in California like Tokumoto in Fresno, the Hinaga brothers in San Jose, and for that matter, Paige in the Negro Leagues, they also reported a tragic irony of the times: "[D]istressed over the big shortage of pitching talent, the major leagues are conducting an unprecedented raid for college baseball talent this year."[70]

The dog days of summer witnessed the Fresno Japanese defeat Salinas again, this time by the score of 10 to 4, behind the pitching of Tokumoto.[71] Zenimura's club then traveled to Guadalupe, near Santa Maria, to take on the local Japanese club. Despite five errors by Fresno, the club edged Guadalupe 10 to 7. Down in the fourth inning, Zenimura's club scored five runs and secured the victory. The battery for Guadalupe included Tomooka, Kawada and Tamura; while Tokumoto and Yoshikawa worked for Fresno.[72]

In early July Zenimura took a break from playing his Japanese baseball peers to participate in a baseball benefit for the family of Taky Amata, pioneer Elks Club employee and prominent member of the Japanese American community, who passed away a few days earlier.

At the same time when major leaguers from the National and American Leagues were preparing for battle at the New York Polo Grounds in the second-annual All-Star game, Zenimura's Japanese All-Stars battled the Elks Club at the Japanese Ball Park. In front of a large crowd, the Elks lodgemen eked out a win over the Fresno Japanese, 14 to 12. "The Japanese had tied the score by the end of the third stanza ... and had a one-run lead at the beginning of the sixth, when four hits and an error were responsible for four runs, putting the game on the ice for the Elks."[73]

The Fourth of July holiday also brought news of a long-desired visit to Japan by Babe Ruth. The *New York Times* reported: "Babe Ruth admitted last night that he will take a world tour after the world series in October ... with a team of American League players under the direction of John Shibe, vice president and secretary of the Athletics."[74] The third time was the charm. In 1925, Ruth was offered $15,000 by Duke Sera of the San Jose Asahi; in 1932, he was offered $40,000 by Zenimura; and in 1934, he was offered $60,000 by Matsutaro Shoriki in Japan. U.S.–Japanese baseball relations would never be the same after Ruth's visit to the Land of the Rising Sun.

In Fresno in July 1934, Zenimura and Yoshikawa next joined the Fresno All-Stars in a game with the Detroit Colored Giants who were on a nationwide barnstorming tour. With two winning seasons behind them, the Detroit team was also known for its comedic performances.[75]

The Detroit Colored Giants had just completed games in Stockton, Oakland and Martinez, California. The full lineup of the Colored Giants for this particular game was not provided; however, articles published before and after the team's game in Fresno indicate that the 1934 Detroit Colored Giants ballclub was comprised of: Peter Lorenzo, 3b-1b; Albert Morehead, c-1b-3b; A.J. Smith, 1b; Allen Moore, ss; Clifford Larkins, c; Arthur

Parks, rf; Mose Britton, rf; David Whitney, lf; Johnson Hill, 2b; "Dypper" Knight, p; and Big Bill Smith, p-of.[76]

Knight was described as a spitball artist, catcher Morehead as a baseball comedian, shortstop Moore as "Dobie's little brother," and Bill Smith as "King Kong," a 6'4" slugger who had hit over 35 home runs prior to the game in Fresno. Second baseman Johnson Hill was a Negro Leagues veteran who got his start in Texas prior to 1920. Hill enjoyed a seven-year career with the St. Louis Giants, New York Lincoln Giants, Detroit Stars and Brooklyn Royal Giants. Several players in the Detroit Colored Giants' lineup also toured with Abe Saperstein's All-Americans in 1933.

A small crowd of 300 people watched the Fresno All-Star team defeat the visiting Detroit Giants, 17 to 16, at the Fresno Japanese Baseball Park. The turnout was poor due to bad weather, which also negatively impacted playing conditions. Moose Cano and Hal Windell worked as the Fresno battery for three innings and were relieved by the battery of Ty Saiki and Ken Zenimura for the remaining four innings.[77]

The second half of July saw the Fresno Japanese ballclub involved in a series against the Mexican All-Stars of Hanford. In the first game Fresno pounded the offerings of three pitchers and defeated the Mexican All-Stars 15 to 5. Described as a loosely played game, ten runs were scored by Fresno in the first inning when the Hanford hurlers gave up six bases on balls and two hits. Moriyama hit the only homer of the game.[78] In game two of the series, played a few weeks later in Hanford, Zenimura's boys won again, 8 to 4. Moriyama, Zenimura and Tokumoto each got three hits for Fresno. Moriyama hit for the circuit (a home run) in the first inning.[79]

While Zeni's club was on the road in Hanford, a portion of the Japanese Ball Park was damaged by fire. The fire destroyed a dugout and a portion of the fence.[80]

Despite the fire, the games played on at the Japanese Ball Park. A week later Zenimura welcomed the Kerman nine, led by Twilight stars Lefty Fuchs, p; Frank Homan, 1b; Leo Ostenberg, 3b; and Jacobsen, of. The game itself proved to be a bizarre one for the books when "everybody but the pitchers had a field day at the Japanese Baseball Park ... including the spectators.... After the two teams had run up a total of more than forty runs between them, the scoreboard showed the Japanese were leading, 22 to 21, when the Kerman outfit finished its half at bat in the first of the ninth inning. The Japanese had gathered up their bats and gloves preparatory to leaving when the Kerman players protested they were swindled out of a run somewhere, that the score was tied and that the Japanese batters had take their licks. The Japanese however were satisfied with the scoreboard's figures and refused to play longer, which resulted in a heated argument. A later check by the scorekeeper showed that each team had made twenty-two tallies, so the official result was a 22–22 tie."[81]

More than 50 years after this controversial contest was played, Zenimura's son Howard said, "I remember this game. There was a big argument about the runs. I think it was my brother and me hanging the numbers on the scoreboard.... I guess I lost count, the score was just too high."[82] Mystery solved.

The opening game of the Northern California Japanese Baseball championships occurred on August 18. Zenimura's Fresno squad was slated to tangle against the Hinaga brothers and the San Jose Asahi.[83] "The Fresno Japanese Athletic Club got off to a fast start in the first inning ... at the Japanese Baseball Park and trounced the visitors, 13 to 6. It was the opening game of the second half of the state Japanese League. San Jose won the first half and Fresno finished in third place. Ichishita, who started on the mound for the visitors, was wild, and Fresno scored five runs in the first stanza on three walks, an error and a home run by Saiki. They added three more tallies in the second inning to put the game on ice."[84]

In early September Zenimura crossed a new multicultural baseball barrier when he welcomed the Filipino All-Stars from San Francisco. The Fresno Athletic Club defeated the visitors in a close game, 12 to 11. Fresno was outhit 16 to 13 and trailed by five runs at the end of the eighth. Moto was relieved by Vasquez for the visitors and Fresno rallied with six runs. Kawakami hit a home run with the bases full during the melee. The visiting team punched out two runs in the first of the ninth but Fresno staged another rally to earn a one run advantage.[85]

After the victory over the Filipino nine, Fresno welcomed the Japanese All-Stars of Seattle in a night ballgame at the Frank Chance Field. Twelve members of the squad made the 927 mile journey (approximately 15 hours by car) from Seattle. The 1934 Seattle Japanese All-Stars included: Okazaki; Sakagami, p; B. Yoshida, p, 1b; N. Yoshida, p; Sasaki, 2b; Tanaki, 3b; Itan, ss; Yamanaka, lf; Kawasaki, cf; Terao, rf; T. Nakamura, manager; and George Nakahara, coach. The Fresno lineup had several new players including: Yamato, p; Kebo, 2b; Shibata, 3b; Takagi, ss; and Doi and Aburamen as reserves. The outcome of the Fresno-Seattle game was not reported in the *Fresno Bee*.[86]

Five days later Fresno made the journey to San Jose to battle Russ Hinaga's ballclub. Zenimura's boys made three errors in the seventh inning of a game with the Asahi, enough to allow four runs to be scored and give San Jose the victory, 7 to 6. With the exception of poor fielding, the game was a good one and close throughout. Yoshinga and Onitsuka of San Jose were the batting stars, each getting two hits.[87]

Early October 1934 found the Fresno club in a doubleheader with the Hollywood Japanese All-Stars at the Japanese Baseball Park. "The invaders will have some former Fresno players in the lineup such as Al Sako ... and Tomiyama. The Matsui brothers are also from this locality and played at Parlier High. Saiki will probably start for the locals while Hirata may pitch for the All-Stars. Hirata is considered one of the best twirlers among the southland Japanese." The 1934 Hollywood Japanese All-Stars roster included: Sako, 1b; K. Yamasaki, 2b; Matsui. 3b; R. Matsui, ss; Hirata, lf, p; C. Nishikawa, cf; Usil, rf; B. Yamasaki, rf; Mori, c; Tomiyama, c; Kurumatsu, p; Komai, p; and DeVinno, ss.[88]

In a loosely-played baseball game, Fresno defeated Hollywood 14 to 10. The visitors "started out with a bang in the first inning, scoring six runs on four hits and two errors. Hirata, pitcher, hit a home run during the parade of Hollywood batters to the plate. The locals, however, turned the tables in the eighth inning to grab the lead and put the game on ice. A total of eleven errors was made during the game." During the ballgame, Zenimura again proved to be the difference maker in scoring four runs in five plate appearances, with a hit, two walks and a stolen base.[89]

The 1934 season witnessed the Fresno Japanese playing a wide-range of multi-cultural competitors: the Colored Athletic Club, Mexican All-Stars, Filipino All-Stars and, of course, Japanese teams from the entire West Coast. So it was only fitting that the club finish the year by playing a competitor they had never faced before — themselves. On October 14, the *Fresno Bee* reported that Zenimura's 1934 ballclub would play former members of the Fresno Athletic Club at the Japanese Baseball Park. For the first time in many years, Zenimura, Yoshikawa, Nakagawa and Iwata were together again in an FAC lineup.[90]

Just months away from turning 35 years old, Zenimura was officially labeled an "old-timer" by the press. "The Fresno Japanese Athletic Club baseball team defeated a team of local Japanese old-timers, 12 to 6," reported the *Fresno Bee*. "Leading 6 to 3 as they came to bat in their half of the eighth inning, the regulars added six more tallies on five hits and two errors by the players of former years. The old-timers retaliated with three scores in the ninth, but their rally was not sufficient to overcome the lead."[91]

The FAC Old Timers included: Zenimura, ss; Yoshikawa, c; Tsukimura, cf; Iwata, lf; Nakagawa, rf; S. Yamasaki, 3b; Tokumoto, p; Nakamura, 1b; and Tachino, 2b. The Fresno Japanese included: W. Ishida, cf; B. Yamasaki, 1b; Fujita, c; Saiki, p; Yano, 3b; Y. Kawakami, ss; Wada, lf; B. Ishida, lf; Yamato, 2b; Kumano, rf; and S. Kawakami, rf.

On October 20, 1934, "a group of baseball missionaries, headed by Connie Mack and Babe Ruth, left for a two month tour of the Orient." The schedule of the MLB all-stars called for one game in Honolulu, eighteen games in Japan, one in Shanghai and three in Manila. Joining Mack and Ruth were Charley Gehringer, Moe Berg, Frank Hayes, Eric McNair, Bing Miller, Lou Gehrig, Jimmie Foxx, Rabbit Warstler, Earl Averill, Earl Whitehill, Clint Brown, Lefty Gomez, Joe Cascarella and Frank "Lefty" O'Doul.[92]

After the tour was completed, Connie Mack called the 1934 tour to Japan "one of the greatest peace measures in the history of nations." When the big leaguers arrived in Japan they sensed "strong anti–American feelings throughout Japan over this country's stand," said Mack. "Things didn't look good at all. And then Babe Ruth smacked a home run, and all the ill feeling and underground war sentiment vanished just like that."[93] All of this was a nice sentiment, but perhaps Mack spoke too soon.

A month after his comments about improved relations, the underground war movement in Japan surfaced in an ugly way. "Babe Ruth found himself ... a cause for political violence," declared the *New York Times*. "In Tokyo, Matsutaro Shoriki, publisher of the Japanese capital's third largest newspaper, was stabbed and dangerously wounded by Katsuke Nagasaki, 28, member of the Warlike Gods Society and fanatical patriot." The motive for the stabbing? The attacker believed that the "publisher had been disloyal to Japan by sponsoring Ruth's recent baseball barnstorming tour."[94]

News of the attack reached New York two days after Ruth returned home from his 21,000-mile trip around the world. During the tour he had put on considerable weight. His trainer estimated that he was up to 240. The Japanese fans had warmly welcomed Ruth, he said, and as for the caliber of baseball played in Japan, Ruth said, "They are pretty good in the field, but they haven't got the arm and they can't hit that onion." Exactly seventy years after Ruth's comment, in 2004, Seattle Mariners outfielder Ichiro Suzuki recorded 262 hits in a single season, surpassing an 84-year-old major league record held by hall of famer George Sisler.[95]

The 1935 Season—First Professional Team from Japan

Kenichi Zenimura turned 35 years old on January 25, 1935. At this point in his life he was a dedicated father to his sons Kenso (Howard), 8, and Kenshi (Harvey), 7, teaching them the finer points of the game. "I can remember him telling us to learn baseball, because we weren't going to be too big when we grew up. Football and basketball weren't going to be options for us," said Howard. His oldest son Kenji (Harry), 11, was still living in Honolulu with grandparents Masakichi and Waka Zenimura. Sometime between 1935 and 1937 grandfather Masakichi quit his job as a janitor at the YMBA in Honolulu and moved the family back to Japan.[96] In doing so, they took little Harry with them. Kenichi would not see his oldest son again until 1937 when he made his third and final tour to Japan.

When Zeni was not at home in the role of father or on the diamond playing ball, he was working as a mechanic at the Robinson Studebaker garage. Wife Kiyoko Zenimura worked for the Robinson family as well.

The New Year also brought new baseball opportunities. On January 8, the *Fresno Bee* reported that the Pacific Coast League was exploring the creation of a new Central Valley Baseball league, and that Ty Cobb would preside over the groundbreaking of Fresno's new 5,000-seat baseball park.[97] Of course, these new opportunities were not available for Zenimura and his Japanese baseball peers. Instead, they would continue to be relegated to playing against each other, semipro teams of all creeds and colors, and exhibition games with barnstorming teams visiting Fresno.

In the spring of 1935 one such barnstorming team was the Dai-Nippon Tokyo Professional Club of Japan, the first Japanese professional baseball team to visit the U.S. They came at the invitation of the San Francisco Seals' Lefty O'Doul. The team included Victor Starffin who, although Russian, had spent seventeen years in Japan. Four members of the team did not make the trip due to service commitments with the Japanese army.[98]

In 1935, O'Doul was a rookie manager with Seals, and with the arrival of a young outfielder named Joe DiMaggio, his club was a formidable opponent for any team. The Seals lost their first game against the Tokyo ballclub, 9 to 1, despite DiMaggio's two-run home run and two doubles.[99] In the second game the boys from Japan again defeated the Seals by the score of 8–1.

The Dai-Nippon journeyed south to Mexico for a game, followed by a stop in San Jose, and then headed to Fresno for a two-game series against the FAC and a combined multi-ethnic team led by Zenimura. The 1935 FAC roster included: Bob Yamasaki, p; Yano, p; Ty Saiki, p; Shig Tokumoto, p; Maruyama, p; Tom Fujita, c; Fred Yoshikawa, c; Sam Yamasaki, inf; Tamura, 1b; Zenimura, 2b; Yamato, 2b; Kawakami, 3b; Yano, 3b; Takagi, ss; Hirasuna, ss; Bill Ishida, of; Kumano, of; Wilson Ishida, of; Ed Tsukimura, of; and Harvey Iwata, of.[100]

The combined multi-ethnic Fresno team included: Lefty Fuchs and Alvarez, pitchers; Jud Simons, c; Heizenrader, 1b; Bechtold, 2b; Holley, 3b; Zenimura, ss; Eli Parret, cf; Iwata and Tsukimura, lf; Saiki and W. Ishida, rf; Storms, utility outfielder.[101]

After suffering a 3–2 defeat to the San Jose Asahi on March 27, made possible by a thrilling game-ending RBI by captain Russell Hinaga in the ninth inning, the Dai-Nippon arrived in Fresno.[102]

Prior to the game it was announced that several members of the Tokyo ballclub were offered major and minor league contracts to play ball in the United States. The coveted stars included pitchers Eiji Sawamura and Victor Starffin, outfielder Jimmy Horio, and infielder Takeo Tabe. All of them except Horio were unable to accept the offers because they were not U.S. citizens. Horio on the other hand was born in Hawaii, and accepted an offer from the Sacramento Salons.[103]

Overcoming a three-run lead the Tokyo Giants scored five runs in the fifth and seventh innings to defeat the Fresno Japanese All-Stars, 6 to 4. The second game with the Fresno multi-ethnic nine was stopped in the first inning due to rain.[104]

The Tokyo All-Stars included: Kumeyasu Yajima, rf; Takeo Tabe, 2b; Hisanori Karita, ss; Usaburo Shintomi, lf; Jimmy Horio, cf; Fujio Nagasawa, 1b; Shigeru Mizuhara, 3b; Tamotsu Uchibori, c; Kenichi Aoshiba, p. The FAC included the regular roster of the 1935 season plus the addition of Takagi, ss, and Moriyama, p. The All-Stars squad included future Japanese Baseball Hall of Fame members second baseman Tabe and third

In April 1935, the Dai-Nippon arrived from Japan to battle Zenimura's ballclub. Behind future Hall of Famers Eiji Sawamura, Victor Starffin, Takeo Tabe and Shigeru Mizuhara, the boys from Tokyo overcame a three-run lead in the seventh inning to defeat the Fresno Japanese All-Stars, 6 to 4 (Densho Digital Archives).

baseman Mizuhara. The starting pitcher for Tokyo was Aoshiba who was drafted into the Japanese military in 1938 and died in a military hospital in 1945.

A week after the Tokyo contest, Zenimura and his club returned to their home field to play the Fresno Colored Cubs. Perhaps in response to their previous defeat to the Tokyo nine, Zenimura's boys came out swinging and trounced them 20–2.[105]

In the Fresno City baseball league, Zenimura's FAC entered the clip with confidence after recording a solid 10–8 victory over the LeGrand Baseball team, champion of the Yosemite League.[106] The team started off strong, impressing the opposition with their unique brand of small ball. In a 2–1, ten-inning defeat of the Rialto Recreation Club, Zenimura's ballclub put on a fine display of strategic hitting, fielding and pitching from submariner Shig Tokumoto.[107]

Five weeks into the new league season, the FAC (3–2, .600) were in second place behind the Mount Whitney Brewers (3–1, .750).[108] The league standings made the next contest on July 31 between the Japanese and Brewers even more meaningful. But, in a game that had the crowd on the edge of their seats, they lost 5 to 4.[109]

In August, Zenimura and other stars of the Japanese club made headlines by being named to an all-star aggregation to take on Lefty O'Doul, Joe DiMaggio and the rest of the San Francisco Seals. This all-star team included Okada, a new pitcher from Japan; Saiki, pitcher and outfielder; S. Kawakami, first baseman; Moriyama, pitcher; and Zenimura, catcher.[110]

On August 5, approximately 2,000 fans watched the San Francisco Seals defeat the Fresno all-star club, 17 to 10, at Frank Chance Field. Joe DiMaggio, right fielder, played five innings and got two hits, one a rousing triple to left center in the third and a double in the fifth. Other noteworthy performances included O'Doul, 1–6; Saiki, 1–1; Tokumoto, 0–1; Zenimura 1–2, 1 run. According to Howard Zenimura, this contest could have been the first time for the Seals to see a submarine pitcher in Shig Tokumoto. He faced DiMaggio once and forced the future hall of famer to pop-up for an out.[111]

The FAC continued their winning ways in the City League. Against the last-place Sera club, Ishida and Zenimura each recorded three singles in a 13–8 victory.[112] In their next game against the Sun-Maids at Chance Field, pitcher Lefty Alvarez, Hanford's fast curveball artist, struck out twenty men, but amazingly the Fresno Athletic Club still managed a 6-to-2 victory.[113]

With all cylinders firing, Zenimura's club took on the mighty Brewers again, and this time gave the boys from Mt. Whitney a 10–2 drubbing to take over first place. Playing at the Japanese Baseball Park, "for five and one-half innings the two clubs waged a nip and tuck battle to have the Brewers turn sour and boot the ball hither and yon. Mt. Whitney had difficulties seeing Moriyama's easy southpaw curve for five innings. They began connecting in the sixth so Captain Ken Zenimura sent in big Ty Saiki to take the club the rest of the way in."[114] But like two boxers going toe-to-toe in the ring, the Brewers battled back the following week and defeated the Japanese boys in a high-scoring affair, 17 to 13.[115] The Fresno Japanese team finished third in the second half of the Fresno City League but only a little behind the top position team.

Early September brought a new round of contests in the California Japanese Baseball League with a championship series matching the Los Angeles Nippons with Fresno and playing at both the Fresno Japanese Baseball Park and Frank Chance Field. Lineups for Los Angeles were: G. Matsura, T. Kigomura, F. Matsurra and L. Toyama, pitchers; S. Kodama, catcher; Y. Nakamura, first base; M. Iriye and Fukuyama, second base; S. Takahashi, shortstop; S. Sugi, third base; J. Suski, left field; S. Tanaka, center field; M. Watanabe and Nishikawa, right field. The Los Angeles team had experience to the man, on school and college teams in the vicinity of Los Angeles. Sugi, Takahashi, Matsuura, Nakamura and M. Watanabe made a trip to Japan in 1931 with the Nippons. B. Harris, one time catcher for Sacramento in the Coast League, coached the Nippons.[116]

Fresno and L.A. split the first two games of the series. The Nippons won a free-hitting opener 19 to 18, and Fresno took the closing game at Frank Chance Field, 8 to 7. Ty Saiki hit a home run in the fifth inning of the afternoon game with the bases loaded. Yano also belted a homer with one man on in the sixth. Saiki pitched the Fresno victory, allowing only three hits after the fifth inning, as Fresno rallied with three runs in the ninth to steal away the victory.[117] Behind the plate the entire game, Zenimura received the tosses of Tokumoto, Okuda and Saiki.

A third game was played at the Japanese Baseball Park, and feeling comfortable at home, Zenimura's nine defeated the Southerners 14 to 9. Captain Zenimura and Yano hit triples, with Wilson Ishida, Shiro and Yukio Kawakami and Saiki all hitting two-baggers. The next two games for the state championship of Japanese players headed to Los Angeles for games on September 21st and 22nd.[118] Unfortunately the results of these game were not located.

After the three-game series against the Nippons, the Fresno City League released the official averages from the previous season. Elbert McMurtry, of McMurtry brothers fame, led the league in batting with a .533 clip, slapping 16 hits in 30 at-bats. Brother Del batted an impressive .396 with 19 hits in 49 at-bats. Left-fielder Wilson Ishida was the sole Japanese player in the league top-ten batting list with a .364 average, securing 16 safeties in 44 at-bats. The top three batters for the Japanese club in the 1935 Fresno City League were:[119]

Batting Leaders, Fresno Japanese

	AB	*H*	*.Pct*
Ishida, lf	44	16	.364
Saiki, of	39	14	.350
Zenimura, c	35	12	.343
Team Avg.	338	93	.250

In late September the champions of the Central Coast Japanese League, the Watsonville Japanese nine, made the trek to the San Joaquin Valley to take on the Fresno Japanese Athletic Club. The Fresno lineup featured all of the regulars with the addition of Hitsuna, a new second baseman.[120] Fresno had an 8-to-3 triumph over the Watsonville team. The defeat over Watsonville was quite an accomplishment. The boys from Watsonville had proved their mettle when they defeated the "Tokyo Giant-Killers" San Jose Asahi, 4 to 3, in an eleven-inning thriller in the state playoffs.[121]

Zenimura finished the 1935 season by scheduling his usual contest against an all-star team comprised of the top local talent. The Fresno Athletic Club — now champions of the Japanese in California — were scheduled to play Lew Marley's All-Star baseball team at the Japanese Baseball Park. Zenimura announced that arrangements were under way to get Monte Pearson, Bill Phebus and Leo Ostenberg, all players in major league baseball, to join Marley's team. Their other players were drawn from the Rialto Recreation team. Tokumoto and Saiki were to pitch for the Japanese, and Yoshikawa, now considered an old-timer, was to catch."[122] Unfortunately the results of this game were not published.

The 1935 season was a successful year for Zenimura, Nisei baseball, and Japanese baseball in general. The Dai-Nippon Professional Baseball Club arrived in the U.S. and returned to Japan as the "Tokyo Giants." Just months after their return, the second professional baseball team in Japan was formed, the Osaka Tigers. More professional baseball teams would be formed in Japan, and by 1936 the Nippon Professional Baseball League would become a reality.

The 1936 Season — National Japanese Baseball Championship

Prior to the start of the first season of professional baseball in Japan, the Tokyo Giants returned to the United States for another visit. In their first games back in California, the Giants defeated the San Francisco Seals 5 to 0 behind the golden arm of Sawamura. The boys from Tokyo then defeated the Seal Rookies 6 to 2 with Hatafuku whiffing eight batters. The stands were practically empty for the March 12 ballgame. Putting the low turnout behind them, the Tokyo Giants headed south to take on the Japanese baseball champions of California — the Fresno Athletic Club. It was announced that the game would be the last appearance of the champions from Japan in Fresno. Zenimura was to put together a veteran lineup in an attempt to defeat the professionals. "Takagi and Yanod (sp) will come from

Delano to play shortstop and right field, respectively. Tokumoto, southpaw pitcher, will report to Zenimura from Hanford. Yoshikawa, one of the oldest Japanese catchers still playing baseball, and Zenimura, second baseman, will strengthen the team."[123]

The bolstered Fresno lineup was still not strong enough for the Tokyo Giants. The Japanese professionals ganged up on the Fresno club in the fourth and seventh innings to score a 10-to-3 victory at Frank Chance Field. Tabe, Giants pitcher, started the Tokyo onslaught in each inning. His single in the fourth was the spark for the seven-run deluge as Nakayama followed with a double. The Giants gathered six hits in this inning. Again in the seventh, the Tokyo team got to Saiki, Fresno pitcher, and converted four singles and a pair of walks into three runs. Saiki struck out eleven men and Tabe whiffed eight.[124] Captain Zenimura called in submariner Shig Tokumoto to salvage the game for Fresno. With Zenimura serving as his battery mate, Shig held the boys from Tokyo scoreless for the final two innings, but the Giants' lead was just too large to overcome.

Featured in this Tokyo Giants lineup was future Japanese Baseball Hall of Famer, Takeo Tabe, the winning pitcher of record. Normally a shortstop, he was known as a versatile baseball genius who could excel at any position. "He was an all-rounder at Meiji University, playing every position except behind the plate. He stole 109 bases in 105 games when the Tokyo Giants made an American tour in 1934, which was prophetic of his potential greatness in pro baseball." Tabe was enshrined in 1969.[125]

April brought a benefit game between the Fresno Athletic Club and the Fresno Police team. Sporting new uniforms and playing in a newly fenced park, it was to be start of a prosperous baseball season. Receipts were to go to the policemen's relief fund. Zenimura was to play catcher. The FAC regulars from the previous season were joined by newcomers Emoto and Aburamen, both utility players.

Out of the league for three years, the police department assembled a strong club. Joe Renna, former Fresno State College and Twilight League pitcher, handled the mound duties. Ernie Ford, team captain, played shortstop. Les Malone, the only man on the team not connected with the department, was catcher. Other familiar faces to Zeni included: Ty Lawson, first base; I.M. Baylis, right field; Leo Ostenberg, third base; Foy Frazier, left field; Walter Komosky, second base; Mike Kleim, Dan Lung and Harry Ebell, utility.[126] The Fresno Athletic Club defeated the Fresno Police Department baseball team, 7 to 5.[127]

Zenimura's next guests on the schedule were Buck Lai's Hawaiian All-Stars, direct from Honolulu. Lai, who played with Jersey City in the International League, Bridgeport, New York Bushwicks, East Orange, South Phillies, and once tried out with the New York Giants in 1928, was to bring a team of the best players of the islands. His club was composed of Chinese, Japanese, and Hawaiian players. Lai was a member of the original Hawaiian Merchant team which came to the United States in 1913 and toured the country, playing to large crowds. The Chinese and Japanese players were noted for their fielding ability, and Lai included a number of six footers to do the hitting. The team was declared by Babe Ruth to be the best club the All-Americans played on their trip to Japan. The Hawaiian All-Stars also boasted Lee Kunihisa, star second baseman from the islands.[128]

Unfortunately Buck Lai and the Hawaiian team did not arrive in the U.S. on time because of a boat delay. Coach Zeni was quick to find a substitute team for the Sunday game, the Wa Sungs Chinese team from Oakland.[129] While the Fresno Police Department baseball team won the first game 6-to-4 in a Wa Sung doubleheader on Sunday, Zenimura's club took on the Chinese nine in the second game, Fresno winning 10 to 3 behind the battery of Saiki and Zenimura. Wong, center fielder, played a bangup game for the losers, getting a triple and a double in four times at bat and cutting the competition with sensational catches. B. Chang, catcher, hit three for four to lead the Wa Sung batters. Yukio Kawakami, Fresno shortstop, also hit three times in four chances to top the Japanese sluggers.[130]

May 1936 brought the opening of another summer Fresno City Twilight League. It was announced by the *Fresno Bee*, "With Ken Zenimura, veteran catcher and infielder for the Fresno Japanese Club, as manager, the Fresno City Twilight League will see some fast baseball from the Robinson Motor Company team this season. Zenimura will play many of the same players which have performed for him on the Japanese team."[131]

This season marked the first time in Zenimura's career when he managed and played for two separate teams simultaneously. Just a week after starting the new season with the Robinson Motor Company, Zenimura kicked off another season in the California Japanese Baseball League. The Fresno Japanese nine welcomed the Sacramento Mikado club for the first time in years at the Japanese Baseball Park. Sacramento won its last state Japanese championships in 1920 and 1921. Fresno won from 1922 to 1927 without a break and won again in 1935.

The FAC defeated the Sacramento club 20 to 8. Other than the score, no details of the game were reported. Shortly afterwards an announcement was made of a proposed Japanese Baseball tournament between Watsonville, Delano, Guadalupe and Fresno. Zenimura's boys were the favored team.[132] And indeed that was the case. "Fresno dominated the state series of eliminations for the Japanese teams at the Japanese Ball Park, winning games on both days. Fresno defeated Watsonville, 17 to 4, in the first game Saturday, then edged out Guadalupe, 8 to 7. Tokumoto and S. Yamasaki pitched for Fresno Saturday, while Saiki hung up yesterday's victory."[133] At age 36, Captain Zenimura turned in an impressive display of physical strength and stamina by catching all games for Fresno in the tournament.

Zenimura's Fresno Japanese baseball team continued its march toward the state Japanese championship by defeating Sacramento the following week, 17 to 4, the same score as the Guadalupe game the previous week. Fresno was held scoreless until the fifth when they went on a rampage and scored seven runs. They tallied five more runs in the fifth, and Saiki held Sacramento to seven hits. Zenimura had a stellar day offensively, recording three hits in four at-bats, a sacrifice hit, two stolen bases and scoring three runs.[134]

Shifting his focus back to the Twilight League and his managerial duties with the Robinson Studebaker team, Zenimura found himself a player short and on the mound against the Dickey Unlimited nine. Robinson-Studebaker lost 9 to 2 despite Zenimura's five-hit performance from the hill. The difference was the lineup and the fact that the Zeni had only eight players to suit up. According to the box score, Zenimura opted for two outfielders, Kawakami in right field, Ishida in centerfield, while left field remained vacant.[135]

On Flag Day, June 14, the world was buzzing with excitement for the upcoming Joe Louis-Max Schmeling fight. Closer to home the Merced Merchants paid a visit to the Japanese Baseball Park. They defeated Fresno, 6–3, with three hits and an error in the ninth inning. Zenimura, playing catcher, hit two for three, including a triple.[136] Next up was a game with Waseda University of Japan, scheduled to take place on June 28.[137]

By late June 1936, the Fresno Athletic Club boasted an 18–3 (.857) record in 21 games.[138] Zenimura's strong record was about to be tested with the arrival of Waseda University. Regarded as the "champions of Japan" for winning the national college tournament, the visiting team was guided by Professor Chimaki Kageyama of the Waseda University faculty and Tadashi Hushino, team manager. The visiting squad included Kenichi Oshita, Shoza Wakahara, Kanemitsu Kondo and Jiro Kawamura, pitchers; Masao Murakata, catcher; Taichi

Satake, Kiyoshi Takasu, Katsutaka Shirakawa, and Meisho Go, infielders; and Kiyoshi Suzuki, Toshiatsu Tsuruzaki and Saburo Nagata, outfielders.[139]

At this point Zenimura's team had won every game against California Japanese opposition in the season.[140] Having shut out Harvard and Yale, Waseda pitcher Shoza Wakahara was a main attraction. In the Yale game he struck out twelve and scored a no-hit, no-run contest.[141] But Wakahara, who entered the game in the sixth inning, could not duplicate his former no-hit, no-run performances, partly due to errors on the field. The first men to face him, however — Zenimura and Tsukimura — were strikeout victims when a vicious drop caught both for the third strike. With the score tied 4 to 4 as the fifth inning opened, Waseda University staged a five-run rally which enabled the visitors to win, 10 to 6.

The next game at the Japanese Baseball Park was not played by the Fresno Japanese or a visiting team from Japan, but instead two African American teams. The Fresno Colored Athletic Club matched up with the Bakersfield Cubs in a Fourth of July celebration by West Fresno's black community. Nine years after his participation in the tour to Japan with the Philadelphia Royal Giants, Bakersfield Cubs manager-catcher O'Neal Pullen was still an active ambassador in the brotherhood of the Negro and Nisei Leagues.[142] And the park that Zeni built provided a venue for all kinds of teams to play.

The summer of 1936 provided Zenimura with plenty of opportunities to play ball throughout the work week. He continued to put in double duty between the California Japanese Baseball League games and Fresno Twilight League games. For example, during one week in mid–July, Zenimura hit four-for-four in a perfect day at the plate during a 15-to-3 victory for the Robinson-Studebaker team, and two days later took on Kenso Nushida and the Stockton Yamato.[143] At an age when most ballplayers begin to decrease the frequency of play, Zenimura doubled his.[144]

On July 31, the Fresno Tigers of the California State League defeated Zenimura's Fresno Athletic Club, 11–10, at Frank Chance Field.[145] Zeni would have preferred a victory, but the big news of the day was the 1936 Summer Olympic Games that were about to start in Berlin, Germany. The day before the opening ceremonies, the International Olympic Committee announced that it had awarded the 1940 Summer Games to Tokyo, Japan. The American members of the IOC, William May Garland of Los Angeles and Avery Brundage of Chicago, both voted for Japan. Brundage said, "We'll be delighted to go to Japan because we know the Japanese are fine sportsmen." Garland, the Californian who had pledged to support the Japanese four years before, was influential during the entire debate.[146] The selection of Tokyo for the 1940 games would later have a direct impact on Zenimura's close friend and colleague Takizo Matsumoto, arguably his most important contact for organizing baseball tours to and from Japan.

Just as the '36 summer games were heating up in Berlin with Jesse Owens winning four gold medals, the Fresno Twilight League pennant race was heating up as well. It came down to a final game between the Fresno Japanese and the Mt. Whitney Brewers to determine the league champion. Despite Zenimura's 3 for 4 day at the plate, and Tokumoto's no-hitter through four innings, the Robinson-Studebaker nine couldn't hold their lead and lost the contest 6 to 3.[147]

Following the game, *Fresno Bee* sports reporter Burt Leifer delivered some critical comments about Coach Zeni: " 'Ole man' Zenimura pulled a fast one on the fans and the Mt. Whitney club by importing pitcher Tokumoto from Hanford, but it made for a sweet battle anyhow. The side-winging Tokumoto plays with Zenimura's Japanese state league team, but according to reliable reports, last evening was the first time he worked with the Studebaker club. Tokumoto's curves which start from the hip were a mystery to the Brewers ... until the fourth. Had Zeni won yesterday, he would have had another surprise twirler brought in from Delano today."[148]

Leifer's commentary makes for good banter and barroom debates, unfortunately for him the facts suggest that his reliable source was wrong and accusations misguided. At the beginning of the Twilight League season, Zeni clearly announced that he would "play many of the same players which have performed for him on the Japanese team."[149] What's more, just two days after Leifer's editorial, the official averages of the 1936 Little World Series were published, indicating that with 13 official at-bats, Tokumoto had indeed participated in games other than the final contest against Mt. Whitney.[150] According to those official stats, the leading hitters for the Robinson Studebaker nine during the championship series were:

	AB	*H*	*AVG*
Zenimura, c	18	7	.389
Tokumoto, p	13	5	.385
Yamamoto, 2b	20	7	.350
Ishida, cf	19	6	.316
Team	170	45	.264

On August 29, the Fresno Japanese Athletic Club defeated Monterey, 13 to 7, in a California State Japanese League game. Fresno pitcher Ty Saiki aided his own effort with a homer. A week later the Fresno Athletic Club again defeated the Monterey Japanese champions, 5 to 2, in Monterey. The game was tied until the fifth inning when Fresno scored its first run. Fresno came back with four runs in the sixth. Monterey opened up in the seventh when K. Muyamoto put a ball over the center field fence. Saiki, Fresno center fielder, hit a home run and Ishida a triple for Fresno. Shibata doubled for the Fresnans.[151] With the defeat Monterey was eliminated in the state race for the California Japanese Baseball Championship.

After a 24–11 drubbing of the Caucasian team from LeGrand, Zenimura's boys welcomed the Northern California Japanese Baseball champions from Alameda to the Japanese Baseball Park. The game would determine who would continue in the playoffs and the quest to wear the state crown. "Pitcher Tanizawa of the visitors is a star left-hander and will give the Fresno pitchers, Tokumoto and a good workout. Five Japanese stars have been picked up by the Alameda club to strengthen it this season."[152]

Relief pitching by Tokumoto earned the Fresno Japanese baseball team a 9-to-4 victory over Alameda at the Japanese Ball Park—and put them within one game of the California Japanese championship.[153]

The Fresno defeat of Alameda in the second game earned them the right to wear the crown as California Japanese Baseball Champions of 1936, and to meet the Seattle Japanese team for the National Japanese Baseball Championship.[154] While the exact outcome of the Fresno-Seattle game is unknown, the fact that Zenimura, Nushida and Kono began plans for a tour of Japan to unfold in 1937 suggests that the Fresno Japanese were indeed the victors.

The 1936-37 California Winter League season saw the return of pitching sensation Satchel Paige to the West Coast. His prowess on the diamond stirred debate on the entry of Negro League ballplayers in the Pacific Coast League. One supporter of the effort was *Los Angeles Evening News* sports editor Gene Coughlin, who wrote: "[PCL] Players have never had any objections to meeting Negro teams in the winter league and only clubs in organized baseball have opposed the Negro clubs. With the Japanese making great strides in baseball it will be only a few years before international competition will be a reality with the Japanese on one side and the Americans on the other." Coughlin then added, "Negro players in the United States are far superior to anything the Japanese have to offer or will offer for many years."[155]

Coughlin's views are not surprising given the lack of historical information available about Nisei-Negro league contests. Based on the research behind this book, we now know that Zenimura and his Japanese teammates were not inferior to Negro league talent. On the contrary, they held their own and, in the majority of the games, demonstrated the superiority of small ball.

The 1937 Season — Fresno's Greatest Exporter of Baseball

On February 12, the *Hayward Daily Review* announced that Harry Kono, Alameda baseball enthusiast, was making the final plans to take a ball club to Japan to play professional and exhibition games. The team had already received financial guarantees from Tokyo managers and sailing was set for March. The first athlete named to the tour was Nobuyashi "Ben" Tanisawa, star pitcher with the Alameda Japanese Athletic Club. According to this report, Tanisawa once turned down an offer to pitch in the Pacific Coast League.[156]

Eight Fresno ball players were included in the Kono Alameda All-Star team which set sail in March on the *Chichibu Maru* from San Francisco, bound for Honolulu to begin a 42-game schedule. Zenimura, as coach and business manager of the team, took twenty players, including Shigeo Tokumoto, Masa Yano, Paul Allison (Caucasian), and Marion Alleruzo (Italian-American), pitchers; Shiro Kawakami, first base; Noboru Takagi, shortstop; and Wilson Ishida, center field. Other players included Norman Riggs, Ty Shirachi, George Davis, Tut Iwahashi, Frank Mirikitani, Charles Hiramatsu, Kiyo Nogami, Ky Miyamoto, Al Sadamune and Frank Yamada. Harry Kono of Alameda served as manager, Zenimura was head coach, and Kenso Nushida, of Stockton, joined them as assistant coach. Zenimura alternated as catcher and second baseman.[157]

With plenty of time to pass during the 18-day journey from California to Japan, Zenimura wrote the following letter, dated March 17, 1937, to *Fresno Bee* sports editor Ed Orman:

> Tomorrow we will arrive in the Land of the Rising Sun — Japan. It is reported that on the same day as our arrival, Prince Chichibu is sailing for Seattle and later will pass through Canada en route to attend the coronation in England. The entire battle fleet will guard the ship on which Prince Chichibu is sailing and I can imagine that the sendoff will be a great one. We are lucky to be on hand to witness the sight from the Yokohama Bay on *Chichibu Maru*.
>
> I cannot write about Japan yet so I will drop you a line to let the Fresno fans know about Honolulu. The ship was delayed in reaching the islands due to a heavy storm that lasted for two days. Instead of arriving around 8 A.M. we finally reached port at 11:30 A.M. When the ship made headway toward the pier, the famous Hawaiian Band played "California, Here I Come" and many other popular songs. The sports editors of various papers met us and placed leis of flowers around our necks, meaning Welcome to the Paradise.
>
> After taking several pictures of the team we were all invited for a short sightseeing trip. Jimmy Hirokawa, one-time Fresno State baseball player who played with the college in 1922 and 1923, was there and arranged for five automobiles for the players to drive on the sightseeing trip. We visited the famous Waikiki Beach and there saw real Hawaiian girls doing the hula hula dance.

In late 1937 Kenichi Zenimura served as a player-coach for the Kono Alameda All-Stars. While in Japan the team finished with a record of 40 wins and 20 losses. Many of the club's defeats occurred when Zeni was barred from playing on the pretense that he was a professional ballplayer back in the U.S. (Nisei Baseball Research Project).

It was wonderful, seeing the real movements and not imitations like we usually see in America. After passing Waikiki we came around the Diamond Head and later visited the Pall. From here we saw one of the sights that I cannot express in words.

At 1:30 P.M. the Honolulu Asahi invited the entire squad to a Chinese dinner and you should have seen them eat. The players ate so much that they could hardly move. We ate one dish cooked from a frog leg in Chinese style and the food was delicious. Of course, the players, and even myself, thought all the time that we were eating chicken. After the party one of the Honolulu players asked us "how did you like the frog legs cooked in Chinese style?" You could imagine what our players thought after hearing this. It was the first time that they had tasted frog legs. The dinner was perfect just the same.

We came back to the ship and dressed in baseball uniforms and rushed to the park to play against the Asahi. For four innings we played a swell game, but after Kunishisa scored by stealing home the players became excited and blew up. Our team made eight errors during six innings, The final score was 10 to 0. It was a good workout for the players. We will win most of our games in Japan. If I should fail in Tokyo, I will be taking the next ship back to the states.

Paul Allison and Marion Alleruzo both are enjoying the voyage but I expect to see them make good in Japan. Both are working out every morning and they seem to be in shape. I probably will start Alleruzo in the first game in Japan. In Honolulu I signed another pitcher, Ed Suzuki, the best Japanese pitcher in the islands. This boy no doubt will win most of the games with his speed. I made a quick decision to take the pitcher and I believe that I made a wise move.

This morning I received a wire from Manila stating they want us to play eight games there. The Warner & Barnes Company, Ltd., is trying to promote the games. I have written to them stating my terms. If they are suitable I probably will divide the team into two squads and take twelve players to Manila.

I will let you know later about this. If we do go we probably will play one game in Shanghai and another in Hong Kong in China before arriving in Manila. I will ask Paul Allison to write to you about his ideas on the voyage and if he does kindly publish it in your paper. I will write to you from Yokohama, giving you the results of the four games we play there.

Thanks for the space given us in your sports page. Please extend our best regards to all the American baseball fans in Fresno.

Sincerely yours,
KEN ZENIMURA
Coach, Kono All-Stars[158]

In Zenimura's absence during the 1937 tour, the Fresno Athletic Club proceeded to elect new officers. Among those elected included a new baseball manager in Sam Yamasaki and assistant manager Ed Tsukimura.[159]

The Alameda All-Stars returned home from Japan on July 15. Although no additional letters from Zenimura were published by the *Fresno Bee* during the tour, Zeni's tour experi-

Left: **Kenichi Zenimura's tour to Japan in 1937 provided an opportunity to reunite with his son Kenji, age 12. *Right:* Within five years Kenji Zenimura was serving in the Japanese Air Force as a pilot during World War II (Zenimura Family Archive).**

ences and perspectives on baseball in Japan were detailed by Ed Orman in his column *Sport Thinks*:

> Kenny Zenimura, Fresno's leading Japanese exponent of the great American national pastime of baseball, is back home after a sojourn in his native land, and the popular little baseball man has a bag full of interesting tales about Japan.
>
> Being sports minded, Kenny paid more attention to things athletic in the land of the rising sun, and particularly his sport — baseball. The Nipponese, believes Zenimura, have improved in baseball proficiency at least 100 percent within the last decade. It was in 1927 that Zenimura took a squad of ball players, American and Japanese, to Japan for a barnstorming trip. Baseball then was just beginning to sprout wings in that country, but today it is vastly different.
>
> "Baseball has blossomed into THE sport in Japan now and the Japanese can play ball which compares favorably with the brand played in America," related Zenimura. "I was agreeably surprised. Ten years ago the Japanese did not know the scientific points of playing. Today they know as much as we do in this country, or just about, at the least. Where they used to be weak hitters, the Japanese now can hit them hard and far. I saw many home runs inside of parks with fences some 420 feet from the plate."
>
> Zenny, now a West Fresno automobile dealer, noted the new generation of Japanese people is larger in stature and for that reason the young ball players get more power at the plate. Always noted as fancy and fast fielders and base runners, the Japanese are only coming into their own as distance hitters.

Although engaged as coach for the tour, when he reached Japan he found he was barred on the diamond on the pretense of being a professional and it was a month before Zeni could help out his squad. As result, the team lost games until Zeni could participate, winning forty in sixty some played.

Wasting no time in Japan, he was also engaged as a scout for teams playing in a professional league around Tokyo and for a Honolulu team. Any talent he found in California could be exported to Honolulu and Japan.

With plans to return to Japan in 1938 and 1940 for the Olympics, Zeni had reserved more than sixty rooms in a Tokyo hotel to accommodate the party that he intended to bring to the amateur baseball competition associated with the 1940 Olympic games. Zenimura had become a major conduit between baseball in the U.S. and Japan.

Zenimura scheduled a contest in September for the Fresno Athletic Club to entertain the Seattle All-Stars. On September 14, with the Japanese Ball Park in less-than-ideal conditions from the lack of attention due to the recent tour to Japan, the two teams met at Frank Chance Field. Zenimura's boys faced their toughest competitors since their return from Japan. The game was tied 7–7 in the top of the eighth inning. Zenimura, as catcher, walked and scored on a double by Tsukimura. Saiki then received another free pass and with a single George Kebo drove in Tsukimura. The Fresno Japanese Athletic Club pushed across two runs to defeat the Seattle All-Stars, 9 to 7.

No other box scores or articles for the 1937 Fresno Japanese baseball club were uncovered. Two big headlines regarding baseball in Japan did hit the newspapers at the end of the season though. First, officials in the Japanese Baseball Association voted to abolish admission fees to all games because of declining attendance as a result of the war. In the Japanese Professional Baseball League, catcher Bucky Harris (full name Andrew "Bucky" Harris McGalliard) was named most valuable player. A former player with the Sacramento PCL team, Harris had served as catcher for Nagoya Kinko in 1936 prior to joining the Tokyo Eagles in 1937. He was arguably the best of the few American playing professional baseball in Japan during the league's first two seasons. The MVP award provided Harris the opportunity to joke about the language barrier he faced in Japan. "The only trouble I have is when I want to bawl out an umpire," said Harris. "I have to call an interpreter and it cools me down."[160]

The 1938 Season — Attention to Business

On January 25, 1938, Kenichi Zenimura turned 38 years old. For the past 15 to 20 years he could have been called a baseball player who dabbled in cars on the side. This year was different. It marked the first time in his life that he could be called an auto dealer who played baseball on the side. The game was still his passion, but the practical financial responsibilities of depression-era life forced him shift his priorities.

Over the years Zenimura worked his way up from a mechanic's assistant to become lead mechanic, garage manager, and then business owner. In early 1938, Zenimura partnered with Louis Pimental to open the Pimental & Zenimura Studebaker dealership located on 1342 Tulare in Fresno. Between his duties as a father, business owner at the car dealership, and baseball tour organizer preparing for the 1940 Olympic Games in Tokyo, Zeni had little time for play.

Off the field, Kenichi Zenimura worked his way up from a mechanic's assistant to become lead mechanic, garage manager, and then business owner. In early 1938, Zenimura partnered with Louis Pimental to open the Pimental & Zenimura Studebaker dealership. This photograph of Zeni was used in local print ads for the Studebaker business (Zenimura Family Archive).

The summer brought the start of the new California Japanese Baseball League and Fresno City Baseball League seasons. Zeni and his club traveled north to San Jose to take on the Asahi for the fourth of July holiday series on July 3rd and 4th. The *Nichi Bei Shimbun* [Japanese American News] covered the games. "In a three game series over the weekend, the strong San Jose Asahi bested the Fresno Yaiiko nine two out of three games. The first game was won by Fresno in a slugfest by a 13–10 count, while San Jose copped the last two games in a fine style," 12–6 and 15–13. Before the three-game series commenced, both teams commemorated the holiday weekend by posing together in a joint team photo.

If the *Fresno Bee* is a reliable reflection of Zenimura's on-field activity, then the lack of articles and box scores suggests that he did not play much ball in the spring of 1938. By the summer months it became apparent that he would not be playing ball in Japan anytime soon either. Tensions between China and Japan flared up in June, and on July 15, Japanese Welfare Minister Koichi Kido cancelled the 1940 Olympic Games. "In a time when the whole nation is preparing for war," he said, "I think that it cannot host the [Olympics] and it cannot be helped."[161] Given the level of enthusiasm Zenimura expressed in his letters to Ed Orman for his upcoming goodwill tour to Japan during the Olympics, there is little doubt that this news was extremely disappointing for him and colleague Frank Narushima.

Months would pass before the *Fresno Bee* would publish anything on Zenimura's baseball activities. On October 9, approximately 100 former professional and Twilight League

In the summer of 1938, Zenimura split his time between work, playing ball, and arranging plans for a tour to Japan for the 1940 Summer Olympic Games in Tokyo. Shortly after this Fourth of July weekend tournament in San Jose, the Tokyo games were cancelled due to the escalating war between China and Japan. The news was a disappointment to Zeni and foreshadowed things to come with World War II (Ralph Pearce).

baseball players, including Zeni, donned their spikes and baseball uniforms at the Frank Chance Field for a benefit game to raise money for injured Twilight League players. "Every former player in the San Joaquin Valley has been extended an open invitation to come here and participate in the game." It was the second annual "old timers" game from which it was hoped to raise enough money to maintain the "relief fund." Phil Koerner, one of the founders of the contest, announced the lineups of the old-timer Twilight Leaguers: Shan Kilburn, c; Joe Cartwright, p; Dick Bier, lf; Dave Beard, ss; Augie Fries, 3b; Ken Zenimura, 2b; Pat Miller, cf; Frank Kelly, rf; Roscoe Ford, 1b. The old-timer Professionals featured: George Sporer, c; Pete Shepherd, p; Gene Jewett, McFarland, cf; Connie Bush, ss; Harry Cassidy, rf; Cline McCann, 3b; C.E. (Tiny) Turner, lf; C.M. (Pop) Barton, 1b. Other pro players participating were: Monte Pfyl, Orval Overall, Phil Koerner, Dutch Leonard, Walter Schmidt, Buck Wheat and George Brandt.[162]

The ex–Twilight Leaguers handed the pros an 8 to 4 defeat. The former pros drew first blood in the game with two runs in the first inning, but the Twilight players came right back in the second to even the count and then chalked up six runs in the third and final inning for the victory. The pros scoring efforts ended with two runs in the first half of the final frame. Joe Cartwright of Visalia (age 43) went the route on the mound for the winners while Pete Shepherd (age 49) and Cline McCann (age 45) held down duties for the losers. A girl's softball game and wrestling exhibition were also part of the festivities.[163]

The 1939 Season — Closer to Home

Thirty-nine-year-old Zenimura increased his baseball-playing frequency in 1939. Perhaps he was inspired by a flash from the past who rolled into Fresno that same spring. After completing another successful run in the California Winter League in southern California, the Philadelphia Royal Giants traveled north on March 19 to take on the Fresno Brewing Company. Zenimura did not play in the contest, however two familiar names from the 1927 Japan tour who did were Jud Simons, the one-time catcher with the Fresno Athletic Club, and Biz Mackey, the man who hit the first home run ever at Meiji Shrine Stadium in Tokyo.

The Philadelphia Royal Giants defeated the Fresno Brewing Company nine of the California State League at the Frank Chance Field by the score of 4 to 3. The star of the game for the Royal Giants was Pepper "Rocking Chair" Bassett, a 220-pound catcher who "provided most of the entertainment during the nine inning affair. Bassett got credit for two doubles and two runs scored. Mackey, the 42-year-old third baseman in this game, reached base twice, on a double and walk, and recorded a sacrifice hit which proved to be the difference in the close ball game."[164]

In late July, Zenimura was again behind the plate as catcher for the FAC. His club lost 8–3 to the Laton Oaks of the San Joaquin Baseball League (SJBL) behind the pitching of Nishi, a new twirler for Fresno.[165] Weeks later the same battery of Nishi and Zenimura battled the SJBL Central Indians. In a close 5 to 3 loss, the hitting star of the day for Fresno was Juichi "George" Miyake, who went two for four at the plate against the Indians.[166]

With Zenimura at the helm, the Japanese baseball club shifted their home base to Bowles, a neighboring community to Fresno. The Bowles Japanese baseball team played the Santa Barbara Japanese All Stars at the Holmes playground on September 2. Taking position at first base for the Bowles outfit was Shiro Kawakami, who recently returned from Asia, where he had played baseball for the past two years with the Dairen Gitsugyo team of Manchuria.[167] Kawakami was one of the players from the 1937 Kono Alameda All-Stars who decided to stay in Asia to play professional baseball. The 1939 Santa Barbara Japanese All-Stars included: Tokyo Takeuchi, p, captain; Joe Watanabe, c; Hiroshi Goto, 1b; Nobu Tamura, 2b; Tomochi Tamura, 3b; Suyeo Hirashima, ss; Caesar Uyesaka, lf; Tadashi Matsumoto, cf; George Iwasaki, rf; Takeo Kodomi, coach; and reserve players Tadashi Yamamoto, Yoshite Inouye, Shoji Morihisa, Hideo Uyesaka and Henry Seki. Zenimura's 1939 Bowles Japanese ballclub featured: Tokumoto, p; Yano, p; Zenimura, c; Kawakami, 1b; Miyamato, 1b; S. Shibata, 2b; Miyake, 2b; Takagi, 3b; K. Shibata, ss; Ishida, lf; Tanaguchi, rf; S. Omata, cf; and Arakawa, cf.

The 1939 local baseball season ended much as it began — with a member of the 1927 Japan Tour paying a visit to Fresno. On September 7, former Philadelphia Royal Giants catcher O'Neal Pullen joined the Fresno Colored Monarchs in a "grudge" match against the Augie Fries Service nine. Led by manager Big Jake Jacobsen, the Fries team was the recent Fresno Twilight League champion and was preparing to enter the National American Baseball Congress playoffs in Battlecreek, Michigan. The Colored Monarchs had lost to the Fries nine the week before and requested a rematch.[168]

The 1940 Season — The End of an Era

The Studebaker Champion was billed as the most successful new car in 10 years. "The lowest price car leads in style and money-savings" by averaging 29 miles per gallon. Priced at $660, it was available at the local Pimentel & Zenimura Studebaker distributor on Tulare Street in Fresno. The car dealership, wife Kiyoko, and sons Howard, 13, and Harvey, 12, were Kenichi's primary focus in 1940.

The spring saw a return of Negro League veterans from the Philadelphia Royal Giants. Charles Lawrence, manager of the Bakersfield Colored Cubs baseball team, placed an open call to independent nines in the Fresno area. Among the players in the Bakersfield lineup were O'Neal Pullen, A.D. Daniels and James Brown, formerly of the Philadelphia Royal Giants. Pitcher Art "Nooky" Demery had struck out 141 batters in fifteen games last year as Bakersfield's leading flinger.[169]

In March Zenimura appeared on a local diamond playing in a sanctioned Central California Japanese League game. On Sunday, March 31, Zeni played catcher with the Bowles Japanese baseball team in a contest against the Hanford Blue Sox. Bowles staged a three-run rally in the tenth inning and defeated the Blue Sox, 9 to 8. The Bowles team was charged with seven errors, four of them by M. Shibata, third sacker, but the winners outhit the Hanford team, 14 to 10, and Noburu Sasaki, the winning pitcher, bore down in the tenth to retire the side for the victory. Sasaki fanned eight and walked two while Shig Tokumoto, Hanford loser, struck out six and walked three. At the time Bowles was leading the loop with a 2–0 record.[170]

Independence Day 1940 marked the end of an era in Fresno Japanese baseball history. Starting with the Fourth of July contest between the Fresno Athletic Club and the visiting Los Angeles White Sox in 1926, the holiday had brought the most exciting games at Zenimura's Japanese Baseball Park. The fireworks officially came to an end in 1940. The *Fresno Bee* announced that the city donated approximately 60 acres of land to the National Guard to be used for a new armory and military field, including facilities for police arms practice. The desired sixty acre site was located south of California Avenue near the end of West Fresno Street, part of which was occupied by the unused Japanese Baseball Park.[171] There is a Buddhist saying that "everything made of parts, falls apart." This includes baseball diamonds. No ball field was made to last forever, and the Japanese Baseball Park in Fresno was no exception to this rule.

Clearly, the most enduring aspect of Zenimura's legacy was his tireless efforts to strengthen U.S.–Japanese baseball relations. He began his global baseball journey in 1920, and the 1940 Olympics in Tokyo were to be the pinnacle of his role as an international baseball ambassador. Instead, at a time when the Summer Games should have been coming to an end in Tokyo, officials announced that America's baseball influence was being erased in Japan. In October 1940, the *Fresno Bee* reported that Japanese officials voted to eliminate English-inspired expressions and foreign players from the professional leagues. The directors of the collegiate circuit Tokyo Six University Baseball League, voted to retain the American baseball expressions and other aspects of the games as introduced from America. The head of the Big Six University Baseball League at the time was Nubuo Fujita, Zenimura's close friend and colleague in Japan.

In the fall of 1940, Zenimura scheduled a weekend series against the San Pedro Skippers, a strong Japanese ball club from the southern Los Angeles area. Instead of taking his Bowles lineup, Zeni created a Central Valley Japanese All-Star club. Among the players he selected was Fumio Ikeda, a speedy outfielder with the neighboring Clovis Commodores, a ballclub that always seemed to have an edge against the Bowles Japanese team. Years later, Ikeda recalled the events around the trip to San Pedro. "Zenimura was among the all-time greats.... I remember he drove several of us down to L.A. in a new Studebaker.... Playing for Clovis we competed against him a lot, but this was the first time for us to be on the same team."[172] Ikeda was impressed with Zenimura as a player. "For his size, pound for pound, I think it's pretty hard to beat him. He could play so many positions. He could bunt, he could hit. He wasn't that fast, but he could steal bases on you ... he was so fiery and competitive. Very competitive. Just absolutely hated to lose."[173]

Ikeda was also moved by Zenimura as a human being, too. He shares this account from the game against San Pedro. "Just before Zeni got to the plate, Suds [Kodama, the catcher] stuck his knee out and tripped Zeni. And Zeni went up in the air, and I think it really hurt. But showing his 'dokyo' [true character], he got right up and the only thing he said was, 'why did you do that?,' and just walked away. To me this was one of the most courageous acts. Real '*Yamato-Damashii*,' meaning 'brave' or 'the way of the samurai.'"[174] Zenimura's *yamato-damashii* would be put to the test in 1941.

The 1941 Season—A New and Dark Era

Everyone in the U.S. had a difficult time making ends meet during the depression years. This was especially true for the Zenimura family. Prior to the 1937 tour to Japan, Zeni could not afford to own a home. At one point between 1937 and 1940, they couldn't even afford to pay their rent and were forced to move in with the Yamasaki family, the in-laws. The Pimental & Zenimura Studebaker dealership continued to be a top priority for Zenimura. As for baseball, he did not play much in 1941. When he did manage to play with the Japanese team out of Bowles, he would take Howard, 14, and Harvey, 13, to watch the games. Howard recalls how "five to six players on that team were pretty good." The top team in the Central Valley now was the Clovis Commodores, who defeated Shig Tokumoto and the Hanford YMBA ballclub for the championship in the spring of 1941.[175]

Zenimura's sons started to play organized baseball as well. At the time there were no Little League or Babe Ruth teams, so they played against other teams around Fresno. Father Kenichi was now also coach to his sons for their youth team.

The summer of 1941 was an exciting time for baseball fans, especially those with California connections. At the highest level, two West Coast boys were thrilling the nation and the world with their accomplishments at the plate. The first was former San Francisco Seal Joe DiMaggio, the master batsman whom Tokumoto and Zenimura forced into a pop out back in 1935. He was on his way to a 56-game hitting streak with the New York Yankees. The other was a skinny kid from San Diego named Ted Williams, who batted an amazing .401 for the season with the Boston Red Sox.

In the midst of their record-setting seasons, Zenimura's former teammate for a day, Lou Gehrig, passed away. The world said goodbye to the Iron Horse on June 2, 1941. The entire nation mourned his passing.

That same month in Fresno, the status quo was being challenged in white organized baseball when the Western Compress baseball team, an all-black team from Fresno took their case to the superior court, asking for an injunction to prevent the Fresno City Recreation Department from refusing to schedule their club in Twilight League games. In their complaint, the Compress team claimed the league was engaging in "discrimination, un-American and unsportsmanlike conduct" by denying the team the opportunity to play. Compress players claimed there was a secret agreement among the members of the league teams to boycott their club by refusing to play baseball games against them. They contended that the discrimination was not only depriving them of their rights, but also disturbed the "unity among the United States' citizens so much desired in the present state of unlimited emergency."[176]

Down south in Los Angeles the 1941-1942 California Winter League saw just four exhibition games. A few of those participating included major league stars Ted Williams and Jimmie Foxx and Negro Leagues legend Biz Mackey with the Royal Giants.[177]

The young Zenimura boys were coming into their own by the fall of 1941. Fourteen-year-old Howard Zenimura was elected class president of the Edison Tech School eighth-grade class.[178] On Monday, December 1, Harvey Zenimura celebrated his 13th birthday. As

"K. Zenimura's Family, 3/12/41." ***Left to right:*** **Kenshi, 13; Kiyoko, 35; Kenichi, 41; and Kenso, 14. Nine months before the bombing of Pearl Harbor, and less than a year away from Executive Order 9066 (Zenimura Family Archive).**

a seventh grader he was recognized as a young boy who loved baseball, basketball, and the school-age girls. His birthday week started off well. Unfortunately, his life, and the lives of his family and friends and the rest of the world, would drastically change by the weekend.

On Sunday morning, December 7, 1941, the Zenimura family went to the Frank H. Ball Recreation Center to watch a youth basketball game. The Pimentel-Zenimura dealership had sponsored a team in the minor division of the city basketball league.[179] With hundreds of fans enjoying a basketball game in the recreation center, the news began to spread like wildfire. The United States had just been bombed by Japan. The naval station base in Pearl Harbor, Hawaii, was under attack. More than 2,000 American soldiers, many aboard the battleship U.S.S. *Arizona*, had been killed.

The news was devastating for Zeni. His birth country, Japan, attacked the country he loved, the U.S., by bombing the city in which he was raised, Honolulu. To say all of this hit close to home would be an understatement. It literally hit his home and his heart. But he was not alone, for many California Issei still had family in both Hawaii and Japan.

The next day the world woke up to the start of a new and dark era in American history. On Monday, December 8, at 9:00 A.M. Fresno time, President Roosevelt addressed the nation via radio broadcast with his famous "Day of Infamy" speech to Congress.

Roughly 500 miles to the east on the campus of the University of Arizona (U of A) in Tucson, more shocking events unfolded. That morning U of A students and faculty were "humiliated and embarrassed" to discover a Japanese flag flying from the flagpole in front of Old Main administration building instead of the familiar Stars and Stripes. To make matters worse, the perpetrator cut the halyards to make it impossible to easily remove the enemy flag.

Closer inspection showed it to be a replica of a Japanese merchant flag made from a white pillowcase with a red crayon circle drawn in the center of it. Night watchman C. S. Hoffman discovered the flag at 7 A.M. and called in Herb Miller, a local painter with previous experience at ascending the 110-foot pole. Miller climbed up a Tucson Fire Department ladder most of the way, but slowly shimmied up the last few feet to the top to remove the flag. When he finally brought the flag down about 10:20 A.M., a crowd of students had gathered at the base of the flagpole. Photographers got hold of it for a few minutes and then a sailor on leave from San Diego ripped it apart, with the help of some patriotic students. Many on campus that day seem to agree that it is likely that this was not just a college prank.

University of Arizona President Alfred Atkinson later wrote an editorial, stating, "Whoever placed this enemy flag on the university's flagpole must be classed as an enemy of the country.... He also brings down upon himself the universal condemnation of all loyal citizens." Although it may be the only Japanese flag ever to be flown over a campus in the United States after the bombing of Pearl Harbor, the incident was quickly buried deep in the University of Arizona's past.[180] Little did anyone know but this incident in Tucson would impact the Japanese American baseball community years later in 1945 as internees at the Gila River Relocation Center in Arizona. Tensions were so high, and attitudes towards people of Japanese ancestry so strong, that the Tucson officials would not welcome the Gila River relocation camp baseball team into their town.

Back in Fresno, teenagers Howard and Harvey Zenimura did not return to school on Monday morning, December 8. In fact, several days passed before they felt comfortable enough to face their classmates again. When they did they were confronted by both supportive and hostile Caucasian students on campus. Some students were smart enough to know that the Nisei had nothing to do with the bombing of Pearl Harbor. Unfortunately, others were not. Some white students let fear get the best of them, and this fear reached a tipping point at the national level during the next eight weeks.

In the Sunday *New York Times* an advertisement ran for a new book titled *The Spector of Sabotage* by Blayney F. Matthews. The book brought attention to possible attacks by Germany and "other enemy saboteurs," and offered tips on how American industry could prevent such attacks. Critics panned the book for its paranoia and conspiracy theories. What's more, in *The Specter of Sabotage*, Matthews wrote that even though Japanese Americans were few in number and that their "racial characteristics made it difficult for them to operate undetected as saboteurs," they could not be ignored as a potential threat to American security.[181] At the time of the book's publication, author Blayney Matthews was an FBI agent and serving as the Director of Plant Protection at Warner Brothers Studios. But twenty years earlier he was a high school teacher and coach. Specifically, he was the baseball coach at Dubuque High School in Iowa in the spring of 1920. Had Zenimura followed through with his plans to go to Dubuque when he left for the mainland two decades earlier, Matthews would have been his baseball coach.

The close of 1941 brought with it a lot of fear and uncertainty for the Zenimura family and the larger Japanese American community. The majority of white America shared the views of Matthews and believed that all persons of Japanese ancestry were "a potential threat to American security." Eight years earlier, President Roosevelt warned the nation that "the only thing we have to fear is fear itself." Unfortunately, fear would get the best of everyone, including Roosevelt, after the bombing of Pearl Harbor. Little did he know, but on New Year's Eve 1942, Kenichi Zenimura was roughly 50 days away from having his world turned upside down with the signing of Executive Order 9066 — a document that allowed for the systematic and forced relocation of 120,000 people of Japanese ancestry currently living on the West Coast. With that order, one of the darkest chapters in U.S. history was about to unfold.

5

Relocating and Rebuilding Hope (1942–1943)

"Without baseball, camp life would have been miserable. There was no torture or anything like that, but it was humiliating, demeaning being incarcerated in your own country."[1]
— George Omachi, Zenimura All-Stars, 1942

The 1942 Season — A New Vision in the Desert

On January 15, 1942, ten days before Zeni celebrated his 42nd birthday, President Roosevelt wrote a letter to baseball's Commissioner Judge Landis. In the historic memo, now referred to as "the Green Light Letter," the President declared, "I honestly feel that it would be best for the country to keep baseball going. There will be fewer people unemployed and everybody will work longer hours and harder than ever before. And that means that they ought to have a chance for recreation and for taking their minds off their work even more than before.... Here is another way of looking at it — if 300 teams use 5,000 or 6,000 players, these players are a definite recreational asset to at least 20,000,000 of the fellow citizens — and that in my judgment is thoroughly worthwhile."[2]

Whereas Roosevelt wanted to continue baseball to uplift the morale of the American public, others contended that to abandon the game would do the same for the enemy. "The Japs so envy us for our baseball prowess and our love for the game that to call it off during wartime would be like tonic to them," said Hap O'Conner, the umpire who traveled with Lefty O'Doul to Japan back in 1931. By canceling the baseball season, O'Conner and others believed that the Japanese people "would construe it to mean we were becoming panicky or something in this country."[3]

Kenichi Zenimura would later find his own morale-lifting reasons to play ball.

Despite any hostilities that Howard and Harvey Zenimura faced in school, the boys were able to concentrate on their studies and make the honor roll for the six-week period after the bombing of Pearl Harbor.[4] But tensions continued to escalate and reached a climax on February 19, when President Roosevelt issued Executive Order 9066. The order banished all persons of Japanese ancestry on the West Coast, including native-born Americans, to incarceration camps for the duration of World War II. In the Japanese American community, February 19 would become another day that would live in infamy.

Japanese Americans began to find ways to express their patriotism and support for Uncle Sam. To the north in Alameda, baseball manager and business leader Harry Kono, along with others from the local chapter of the Japanese American Citizens League (JACL), donated $142 to the American Red Cross War Relief Fund.[5] Despite his display of patriotism, Kono was among the first 550 "enemy aliens" forced to leave their homes after the issuance of Executive Order 9066. Kono, who was considered the unofficial mayor of the Alameda Japanese, made headlines when he joined his neighbor, 70-year-old "Grandma" Firpo, on the list of enemy aliens. The absurdity of the law was highlighted by the fact that the grandmother had moved to the U.S. from Italy when she was four and also had a grandson serving in the Navy, at Pearl Harbor, when the attack occurred.[6]

By March 27, a curfew was put in place to limit the movement of enemy aliens and Japanese Americans. The new order affected 260,000 persons on the West Coast and said that no Japanese, German or Italian national or Japanese American could be more than five miles from his or her home. Exceptions were given for travel to and from work, travel to an official "alien control office" or when being evacuated under army permit.[7]

The Zenimuras were not the only baseball family impacted by the alien-travel restrictions. In San Francisco, the parents of Joe DiMaggio were placed on the enemy-alien list because they were born in Italy, just like Kono's neighbor Grandma Firpo. In addition to the curfew, the FBI began to round up persons in the San Joaquin Valley considered potentially dangerous enemy aliens. More than 130 men in Fresno, ranging in age from 40 to 66, were apprehended under the suspicion of being members of "The Black Dragon," a Japanese secret society believed to have branches outside Japan.[8]

The curfew and upcoming relocation impacted opening day of the 1942 prep baseball season in ways previously unimaginable. First was the obvious impact on players of Japanese ancestry. The 8 P.M. curfew hit Fresno Tech, Edison Tech and Fresno High, each losing one player. Edison lost right fielder Kenso Howard Zenimura; Fresno Tech lost center fielder Yashima Takemoto; and the Fresno High Warriors lost outfielder Bob Kawahara.[9]

Fresno's high school lost the services of some Caucasian baseball players too. Several boys age 18 and older were hired as temporary laborers to help construct the Fresno "reception center" for Japanese aliens. All of the boys worked eight to sixteen hour shifts in building the assembly center for Fresno's citizens of Japanese ancestry.[10]

Construction on the Fresno fairground continued through the month of April. More change was in the air for the Zenimura family when, on April 28, plans were announced for the purchase of Kenichiro Zenimura's interest in the Pimentel & Zenimura Garage at 1342 Tulare Street. His business partner, Louis Pimentel, had filed a notice of sale with the San Joaquin county recorder. Effective May 4, 1942, Zenimura was no longer part owner of the Studebaker dealership and garage.[11]

The day after the sale was announced the press coverage of a youth baseball game captured the tense atmosphere growing in the community. "Fresno High School's reshuffled baseball club and the Pimentel-Zenimura nine played to an eleven-inning 4 to 4 tie yesterday afternoon on the FHS diamond," reported the *Bee*. "The game had to be called so the Japanese members of the P-Z club could get home before curfew time."[12]

Two weeks later the entire Zenimura family was forced to leave their home and move into the assembly center located at the Fresno fairgrounds. On May 16, 1942, Kenso Howard Zenimura celebrated his 15th birthday while living in temporary barracks inside a hosed-down horse stall.

Inside the assembly centers, most families reflected with sadness and disappointment on the fact that their homes, cars, furniture, businesses, heirlooms had been sold off at a fraction of their value. They brought into the centers only what they could carry in two suitcases. According to historian Kerry Yo Nakagawa, Japanese Americans culture stressed modesty and hygiene, and placed a premium on privacy. As a result, "the indignities of assembly-center and camp life were a painful hardship."[13]

In response to this hardship, Zeni acted. "When the Fresno people were evacuated to the Fresno Assembly Center, my dad's first objective was to build a backstop and a diamond," said Howard. "In a short time he organized an A and B league. The A league were veterans or old timers and the B league were the younger group. The old timers were Shig Tokumoto, Fred Yoshikawa, Ed Tsukimura, Sam Yamisaki [*sic*] and Shiro Kawakami." Howard added, "us young guys, we sure learned a lot watching them play."[14]

"Zeni had everything for a baseball diamond in his mind," recalled Herb "Moon" Kurima, who managed and pitched for the Florin Athletic Club in the assembly center. "He lined up tractors, lumber, carpenters, and we started to work on the grounds. Within a week, everything was ready."[15]

As Japanese Americans tried to adjust to their new living quarters, the U.S. government

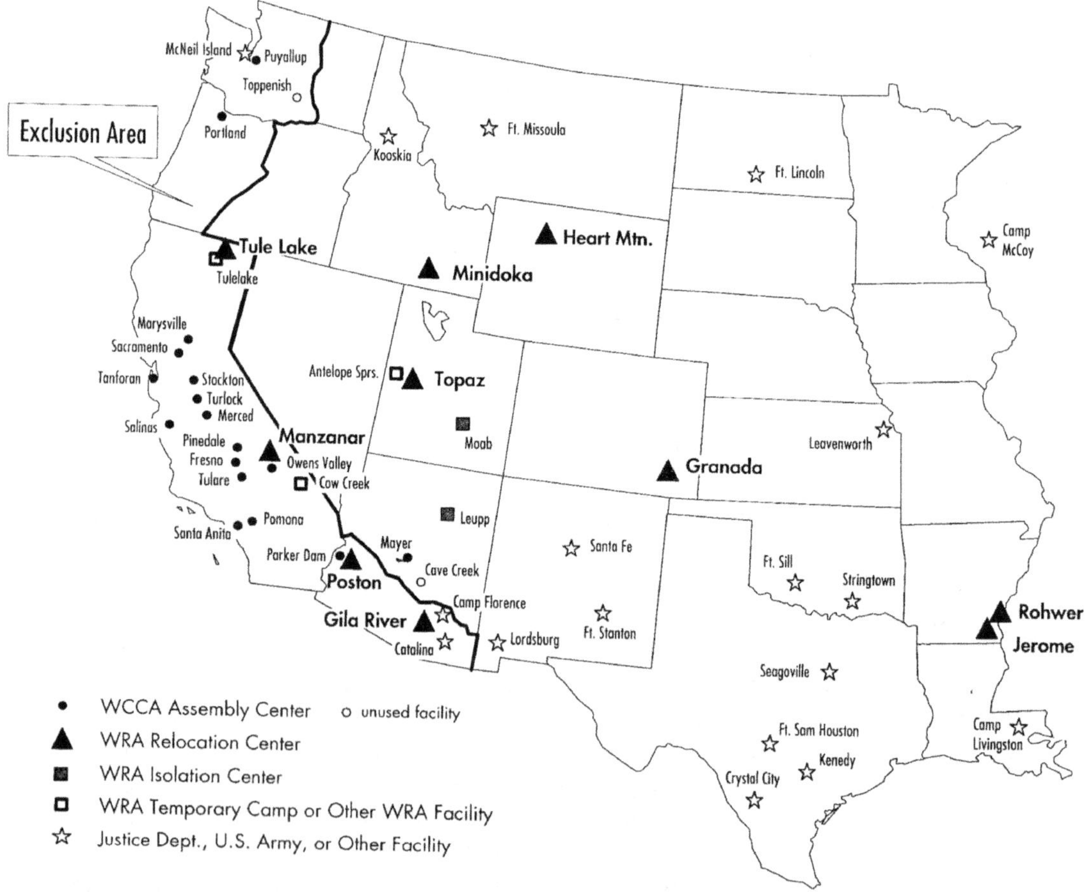

Kenichi Zenimura and his family were among the 120,000 Japanese Americans forced by the U.S. government to leave their homes during World War II. After their stay at the Fresno Assembly Center, the Zenimuras were relocated to Gila River in Arizona, while many of their friends and family members were sent to Jerome, Arkansas (National Park Service).

was preparing ten permanent camps in wastelands in California, Wyoming, Idaho, Utah, Colorado, South Dakota, Arkansas and Arizona. At Rivers, Arizona, located 25 miles south of Phoenix on the Gila River Indian Reservation, two camps were under construction: Camp 1, known as Canal; and Camp 2, known as Butte. While Japanese Americans who were forced to relocate lost much of their financial wealth, government contracts for the construction of camps helped white business owners become rich.

One such person was Del Webb, a construction company owner in Arizona. A former Fresnan, Webb once competed as a pitcher in the same Twilight Leagues with Zenimura and his peers. He would later be inducted into the Fresno Athletic Hall of Fame in 1961. Sometime around the 1930s Webb relocated to Arizona, and because he saw his father lose everything in construction during the depression, he was mindful to diversify his investments. In addition to his home building efforts, he procured War Relocation Authority (WRA) contracts to build the barracks to house the anticipated 17,000 residents in Poston, Arizona, and a portion of the homes on Gila River.[16] Financially, Webb did well during the war. As a result of his shrewd business practices, he later embarked on what he called "the best deal I ever made." With partner Al Topping he acquired the New York Yankees in January 1945. The acquisition included the major league and farm teams, for a total of 450 players. The deal also included stadiums in New York, Newark and Kansas City. Webb and his partners paid $2.8 million for the team in 1945. At the end of the 1964 season, they sold the club itself for $14 million. During Webb's co-ownership of the Yankees, the club won 15 pennants and 10 World Series.[17]

Ironically, while Zenimura was held inside the assembly center, his past baseball accomplishments were still being celebrated by the free press in Fresno. Just before Independence Day 1942, the *Fresno Bee* recalled how "[t]he Fresno Athletic Club baseball team, composed of Japanese players, defeated the Southern All Stars to capture the state championship" back in 1922.[18]

The first Japanese Americans began to arrive in Rivers, Arizona — the official name for the combined communities of the Canal and Butte Camps at Gila River — in July 1942, just in time to experience the intense 100-plus degree days of the Arizona summers.[19] The name of Rivers was selected to honor Jim Rivers, a Pima Indian who was one of the first causalities of World War I. In addition to getting adjusted to the extreme weather, Japanese Americans immediately made additions to their new homes to make the Gila River camp feel more like a community. One of their first action items was to establish the Buddhist Church.

On September 19, the Buddhist Church held its first service, led by the Rev. D. Suzuki, and Sunday school, led by 23-year-old Masaji Inoshita. A few months later Inoshita would choose to leave Gila to serve his country in the Military Intelligence Service (MIS), a unit comprised of Nisei soldiers. Some 50 years later Inoshita became the proud caretaker of a relic from the Butte camp, the recovered home plate from Kenichi Zenimura's baseball field. Through his tireless efforts to keep the history of wartime internment alive, by the late 20th century Inoshita also became the guardian of the Japanese American Memorial at Gila River.[20]

Baseball is a reflection of American society, and in late 1942 even the ugly side of American society was reflected through the prism of the game. According to the September 10 *Sporting News*, umpire Babe Pinelli, a former California resident and player in the Pacific Coast League, expressed his satisfaction in the forced relocation of Japanese Americans. "More and more people are hating the Japs, it appears, which is a source of great elation to umpire Babe Pinelli of the National League.... [E]ver since he was a little boy in San Francisco, Babe says he has hated ALL Japs and long before Pearl Harbor he tried to convert everybody he knew to the same kind of hatred."[21] Given the parallels in the struggles for both Japanese Americans and African Americans, it is worthwhile to mention that Pinelli was the home plate umpire on April 15, 1947, the day when Jackie Robinson stepped into a major league batter's box for the first time in his career. Pinelli's last game behind the plate was in game six of the 1956 World Series, when Don Larsen pitched a perfect game against Jackie Robinson and the Dodgers.

At the Fresno Assembly Center competitive baseball was underway between teams comprised of the best available talent, which at the time was mostly aging veterans and inexperienced high-school kids. Many of the better military draft age players were already in the armed forces. During the summer of '42, the Florin team, led by pitcher Moon Kurima, established itself as the team to beat by going undefeated in 13 games. In the final "A" league championship game between Florin and Fresno, approximately 3,000 fans witnessed Kurima pitch a 7-to-2 victory over Zenimura's all-stars.

The B-league title was captured by the Fresno club. This team included Howard and Harvey Zenimura, and a young player named Hatsuo "George" Omachi, also known as

Kenichi Zenimura constructed his second baseball field at the Fresno Assembly Center in 1942. In the "A" League, Zenimura's All-Stars lost the championship to Florin and star pitcher Herb "Moon" Kurima, 7 to 2. The "B" league title was captured by the Fresno club, which included both Zenimura boys and Hatsuo "George" Omachi (Nisei Baseball Research Project).

"Hats" to his friends. Years later Omachi summed up the importance of baseball during internment. "Without baseball, camp life would have been miserable. There was no torture or anything like that, but it was humiliating, demeaning being incarcerated in your own country."[22] In 1955, Omachi would later take over the coaching duties of the Fresno Japanese baseball club from Kenichi Zenimura, and as a major league scout play a pivotal role in developing several major league stars from Fresno, including Bobby Cox, Tom Seaver and Will Clark.

On October 10, it was announced that Japanese Americans held at the Fresno Assembly Center were being moved again, this time to the Jerome Relocation Camp in Arkansas.[23] The Zenimura family would not make the trip to Arkansas. Instead, they were one of the many families from the Fresno Assembly Center sent to Arizona due to a medical exemption. Wife Kiyoko suffered from tuberculosis and it was decided by WRA officials that the dry climate of Arizona would be better suited for her health condition.[24]

How would Japanese Americans be treated in post–Pearl Harbor Arizona? The following *Arizona Republic* article from October 1942 answers that question: "The University of Arizona Board of Regents voted to refuse college courses to Japanese American students inside the relocation camps."[25] U of A President Alfred Atkinson explained why. "We're considered to be in the coast war zone, and not accepting people of doubtful loyalty," he said.[26] According to Carey McWilliams, author of *Prejudice: Japanese Americans, Symbols of Racial Intolerance During World War II*, when Gila River and Poston camp administrators asked the University of Arizona to lend library books and faculty lecturers, Atkinson responded, "We are at war and these people are our enemies."[27]

Atkinson shared a similar background story with Zenimura. Both were born outside the U.S. and arrived in the country at age 20. Born in Canada in 1880, Atkinson immigrated to the U.S. in 1900. He served as president of Montana State College from 1925 to 1938, and moved to the Arizona desert in 1939 to take over the administrative reins at the University of Arizona. Unlike Zenimura and other immigrants of Japanese ancestry, Atkinson was allowed to become a citizen of the U.S. Perhaps Atkinson's hostility towards Japanese Americans in the above statement reflects an over-zealous, over-compensating sense of patriotism for his adopted country.

The first residents of Gila River had arrived from Turlock back on July 19. It is recorded that their first comments were the comical: "Gee, this is a dusty place."[28] On October 17, 1942, the population of Gila River grew when approximately 350 people from Fresno and Stockton arrived.[29]

Zenimura was not a happy man when he first stepped foot in Gila. "Kenichi was so frustrated that he did nothing for two weeks, didn't even open up his suitcase," said wife Kiyoko. "After all, his friends were sent to the Arkansas camp, and here we were in Arizona."[30]

According to his son Howard, "It got pretty cold at night in the desert, so we would gather scrap wood and build bonfires. I remember one night standing around the fire and dad starting talking about building another baseball field."[31]

In November 1942, Zeni's perspective on the situation took a turn for the positive. Where others at Gila River only saw barbed wire and miles of desert, Zeni began to see potential. He "envisioned a baseball stadium, complete with bleachers, dugouts and an outfield wall."[32] "Finally he started to walk through the desert and sagebrush, looking out over the horizon," said Kiyoko. "One day, I saw him from the mess hall cutting down the sagebrush and clearing rocks by hand. He decided that he was going to build a baseball field again."[33] The construction of Zenimura Field began in mid–November 1942. "At first it was just with our sons, then many new friends heard he was building a baseball field, so many came to help," explained Kiyoko.[34]

"Guys from the other blocks asked, 'What are you doing?'" Kenso recalled. "Pretty soon all these people were coming with shovels, helping to clear the area. We piled up the brush and burned it, and my dad somehow got a bulldozer to level the ground. Then we flooded it to pack the ground down."[35] "Using picks and shovels, the workers created two dugouts. They framed these with wood 'borrowed' from a lumberyard during night time forays. They also used the stolen wood to construct a small grandstand, which even had a reserved-seat section."[36]

On December 11, Gila River officials announced the start of fence construction around the perimeter of the camp. Director R. B. Cozzens explained that the fences "were being constructed for the purposes [of] delineating or outlining the area of the center" and not for "holding the people within the community." WRA rules, as set forth by Lt. General DeWitt, were that evacuees were free to move any place within the area from sunrise to sunset, but were required to stay within either Canal or Butte communities from sunset to sunrise, except when given a permit by the project director to allow movement outside of the communities.[37] The timing of the fence construction could not have been better. Unbeknownst to camp officials, it provided the proper materials to complete the baseball backstop. "They took every other pole from the barbed wire fence for support beams," said Kiyoko.[38]

Zeni was not the only person breaking ground at Gila for the sake of sport. In Novem-

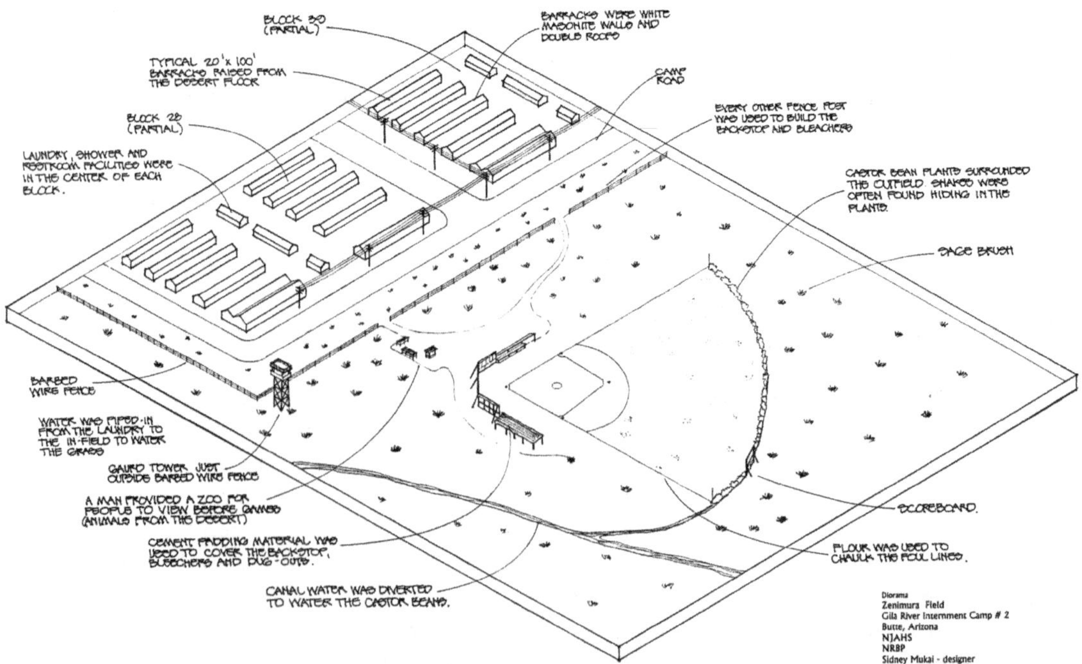

The diamond at Block 28 was the third and final baseball field constructed by Kenichi Zenimura. According to his son Kenso, the field gave all internees a sense of normalcy and hope: "Baseball was the only thing that kept us going. If we didn't play baseball, camp life would've been unbearable. Even when we didn't play, we were out there watching" (Nisei Baseball Research Project).

ber plans were announced that a golf club in Butte would be constructed by George Aratani of 57-10-B. Acting as temporary chairman of the proposed club, Aratani said "plans for the golf course are now being made and will be laid as soon as land is allotted and the proper equipment and workers are available."[39]

On December 17, shortly after the construction of the fence began, camp officials released a statement emphasizing to the evacuees that they were not prisoners of war, just "under the supervision of the WRA."[40] Tension rose in the camp with each fence post installed. Two days later acting project director Cozzens announced his resignation. New project director Leroy Bennett was scheduled to arrive and speak in person with Canal and Butte residents in the following week.[41]

Described as soft-spoken and affable, Director Leroy Bennett told the crowds, with a twinkle in his eye, that he "came to Rivers because it is a good winter resort." Then in a serious tone he spoke from the heart, "I came here because it was a challenge to do a job that will benefit the evacuees and the country." Bennett added, "I expect to continue the policies established by Mr. Cozzens, for, I believe them to be best for the community."[42] Cozzens was the third director to leave Gila, as E.R. Smith and E.R. Fryer each resigned after just a short time at the helm.

Another policy was passed for the betterment of the community in early December. New rules for student-athlete eligibility were drafted by the Athletics and Physical Education board for Canal and Butte schools, which stated:

1. No boy attending school shall be eligible to participate in any major sport as a member of any team other than teams developed under school program.
2. Major sports shall be as follows: Football of any type, baseball, softball, basketball, track and field athletics.

The new eligibility rules were established to seek and foster community support of the school activities. The board members believed that recreational leagues offering the same sports would be viewed as competition, splitting the interests in the community and ultimately preventing the development of school spirit.[43] Fortunately for Zenimura and others working together to build a new field and leagues not affiliated with the schools, this rule was debated and then eventually overruled. Had this policy remained in place for the duration of the relocation camp experience, the quality of play on Zenimura field would have been severely impacted or even non-existent.[44]

Shortly after the change in eligibility rules, efforts were underway to form new leagues. The first formal baseball meeting at Gila River was called by George Ichimoto of the Canal Athletic Society (CAS). Seven teams gathered on Sunday evening, December 22, to discuss an upcoming season. They were:

Team	*Manager*
Cards	Kango Osumi
Roughriders	Benny Matsura
Deltans	Butch Oto
Vikings	Shak Yamada
Angels	Akira Marutani
Ochi's	George Fujiwara
Rio Vistans	Tad Takeda

Harry Kono's Block 26 and Kibei clubs did not attend the meeting but were expected to join the new CAS league.[45]

In 1942, an Arizona baseball tradition came to an end. At various times between 1920 and 1941, the Sonoran desert was the site of spring training baseball for several major league teams, including the Chicago Cubs, Chicago White Sox, Detroit Tigers, Pittsburgh Pirates and New York Giants. Spring training in Arizona ceased because of wartime travel restrictions and partly because of the image it might create in the public mind. Commissioner Landis disapproved of wartime spring training camps in California and Florida as well. "I do not propose," he said, "to have athletes lolling about on the sands in some semitropical climate" while the nation was at war. "He required that teams instead train north of the Potomac and Ohio rivers and east of the Mississippi."[46]

The New York Giants settled in Lakewood, New Jersey, and the Yankees trained at Asbury Park, New Jersey, in 1943 and at Atlantic City in 1944. Universities were also favorite sites for spring training "because of the big field houses, which sheltered the athletes from the biting weather." The Washington Senators trained at the University of Maryland, the Indians chose Purdue University at Layfayette, Indiana, and the Pirates trained at Muncie, Indiana, where the high school gymnasium was available.[47]

Before the '43 season opener the American League reported a total of 144 players serving in the U.S. military. The most famous of them all was Joe DiMaggio, who made his army debut with the Santa Ana Fliers on March 27. With no big league baseball in Arizona, the highest caliber of play in the Grand Canyon state was now played in the semipro leagues of Phoenix, Tucson, and as fans would soon discover, behind barbed wire at Gila River.[48]

The semipro baseball scene in Arizona was amongst the strongest in the nation in the late 1930s and early 1940s. In 1937, a diminutive middle infielder from Tucson and former University of Arizona star, Hanley "Hank" Slagle, was named to the National Baseball Congress All-American team. Joining him for those honors was future Boston Red Sox pitcher Earl Johnson (1940–42, 46–51; 40–32; 4.30 ERA) of Tacoma, Washington; and Tommy Fine, Red Sox and St. Louis Browns pitcher.[49] Slagle, known by his Tucson semipro peers as "the toughest man in the league,"[50] was signed by Red Sox scout Ernie Johnson in May 1938.[51]

Other contenders for the Arizona semipro baseball championships were the all-black Arizona Compress ball club and the integrated (Caucasian and Hispanic) Phoenix International Thunderbirds. The Arizona Compress club was the Arizona state champion of 1940 and led by former Texas Negro League stars James Searcy, Luther "Sugar" Westbrook, pitchers "Schoolboy" Stennet and Ford Smith (Kansas City Monarchs), and catcher Tom Gee (New York Lincoln Giants). The Thunderbirds, Arizona state champion of 1941, were led by manager/shortstop Otto Wolf. In 1939, Wolf was named to the National Baseball Congress All-American team as an outfielder along with a shortstop from Oregon named Johnny Pesky (Boston Red Sox). Other players joining Wolf on the '39 All-American team were Dick Whitman (Brooklyn Dodgers), and PCL veterans Roy Hesler (Portland Beavers) and Joe Erautt (Seattle Rainiers).[52]

Three of these Arizona semipro stars — Hank Slagle, Otto Wolff and Leon Westbrook — would eventually catch the attention of Zenimura and others inside Gila River and accept invitations to play the Japanese American all-stars.

The 1943 Season — Butte Baseball Czar

The population of Rivers was 13,246 at the start of the New Year. The largest of the 10 camps was Poston with 17,107 evacuees.[53] With this tremendous population growth, Poston and Rivers became the third and fourth largest cities in Arizona overnight, just behind Phoenix and Tucson.

Camp Director Bennett issued a New Year's statement saying he believed "the most serious and difficult times have passed" and that many new and positive opportunities were in store for 1943. The WRA encouraged evacuees to relocate to other parts of the U.S. for employment, and many did. For others, staying at the camp meant working on the farms or nurseries, in the camouflage net factory, or attending school.[54] Zenimura did none of the above. He continued to refine his baseball field, and perhaps through a special agreement with Director Bennett, he was paid to focus solely on baseball. By definition, he was no longer a semipro. For the first time in his life, Zenimura was a professional baseball player-manager, albeit behind barbed wire.

Director Bennett was correct about new opportunities. A small but significant event unfolded in early January when the high school basketball team from Chandler, the neighboring farming community just north of the Gila River Indian Reservation, traveled into the internment camp to battle the Butte High Eagle basketball team. "The scrappy Butte High School basketball team handily trounced the Chandler prepsters 15–33," reported the *Gila News Courier*. "The invading Chandler aggregation, although holding a great advantage on height, failed to capitalize on it as the speedy Butte boys caught afire in the second half."[55] The game was important because it marked the first time an outside team entered the camp to play the interned Japanese Americans in any sport.

Zenimura would make sure to book many games with outside teams in the near future. One way in which he researched possible opponents was through the *Arizona Republic*, the daily Phoenix newspaper which was made available free-of-charge to evacuees in the Butte Adult Education office.[56] Through this newspaper Zenimura learned about the semipro Phoenix Thunderbirds and Victory Nine, also known as the Arizona Compress nine, the all-black ballclub also from the city. Both teams had earned the title of Arizona State Champions in semipro ball and earned the right to represent the state at the National Baseball Congress tournament in Wichita, Kansas, the previous two seasons. Zeni would take note of these teams as potential rivals for future games. He continued to seek out the highest caliber opponents he could find.

In early February it was observed by Butte High authorities that a small minority of students were engaging in "various misdemeanors, such as, using profane language, defacing property with obscene words, smoking in latrines, disorderly conduct and destroying property."[57] Howard Zenimura confessed years later that "without baseball we would have been juvenile delinquents." With an uptick in juvenile delinquency in both camps, the arrival of the first shipment of baseball supplies was perfect timing. The *Gila News Courier* announced the arrival of "a complete line of baseball supplies" at the Canal camp. Players were advised to contact George Inai at barrack 69–15 or in the Canal canteen. They could now select baseball shoes in the Canal shoe department, and arrangements were made by Inai to obtain any other equipment though large sporting goods companies Spalding and Goldsmith.[58]

It was announced in the *Gila News Courier* that "[b]aseball at Gila will commence this Sunday afternoon, as a virtually intact Guadalupe YMBA nine encounters a strong Stockton aggregation at the newly built baseball field near block 28.... The newly built field was built through the hard efforts of Ken Zenimura and supported by the CAS."[59]

On February 23, a scrimmage was scheduled between the Guadalupe club and Block 28, Zenimura's club. In the first game ever played on Zenimura Field, the Block 28 baseball squad defeated the Guadalupe "Bee" team, 8 to 0. Zenimura's starting pitcher, Masato Kinoshita, hurled a one-hit shutout. With the *Gila News Courier* coverage of the inaugural game played at Zeni's ballpark, we are introduced to the reporter's writing convention of referring to the top-tier clubs as "Aye" and the second-tier clubs the "Bee" team.

On March 2, witnessed by nearly 3,000 baseball fans, the hustling Block 30 ball club came from behind in the eighth inning to hand a surprised Guadalupe ballclub a 7 to 6 beating. The YMBA squad literally outfumbled their opponents with 10 errors, mostly at inopportune moments. Block 30 put up two runs in the second inning off Keizo Okuharo's bases-loaded line drive just past the shortstop. "Team Captain Mas Okuhara hurled masterful ball for Block 30 until the fifth and sixth frames when the aging veteran got together and push across a run in each. Brother Eiji Okuhara came from right field to pitch to start the 7th inning but was ushered out by YMBA batters in the eighth."[60] Guadalupe outfielder James Tomooka started the eighth-inning rally with a bloop single to center. The YMBA added three more runs to take a 6–3 lead, but Block 30 came back in the bottom of the eighth on a string of walks, errors and quiet singles. Yosh Hirano, the 16-year-old left fielder who pitched in relief in the eighth inning, earned the victory.

After months of construction, Kenichi Zenimura officially opened his field on Sunday, March 7, 1943. Zeni created this poster by hand to attract fans for the Opening Day twin bill. Gate receipts for the day show that the effort brought in $25.77 (adjusted for inflation, that's roughly $315 in 2009) (Nisei Baseball Research Project).

Zenimura announced that he and others builders of the block 28 baseball field needed the help of Butte residents in collecting scrap lumber to build bleachers. He asked residents to stack scrap lumber by their block manager's office where he would pick it up later.[61] The bleachers would be the key in turning Zenimura Field into a "stadium," with numbered seats and higher prices charged for those closest to the action.

On March 6, the *Gila News Courier* announced the "official opening" of the 1943 baseball season. Several administrative officials were scheduled to take part in the inauguration ceremonies of the block 28 field. "The field was planned and started on about a month ago by Ken Zenimura and boys from blocks 28, 39, 29, and 30."[62] The *Gila News Courier* sports editors declared, "That Zenimura ball diamond certainly is some humdinger. Makes us remember the good ole days back home—when Steve's faithful 'peanut wagon' was right on time with refreshments and the five cents per ball income for finding those 'over the fence' balls."[63]

Opening day promised to thrill the fans with a doubleheader. In game one Guadalupe YMBA coach Butch Tamura was eager to "emerge from the wreckage of their disastrous first exhibition game" in their battle against Canal's Parlier Cards, led by manager Harry Kono. Game one was scheduled to commence shortly after Block 28 was officially inaugurated at 1:30 P.M.[64] In the second game of the doubleheader, "Youthful block 28 squad, coached and managed by the renowned veteran, Ken Zenimura, will seek victory ... when they entertain the visiting Kingsburg Vikings, coached by Shak Yamada and managed by Irving Morishita."[65]

Prior to the ceremonial first pitch, Zenimura announced the starting hurler for Block 28 as ace Masato Kinoshita and either his brother Min Kinoshita or himself as catcher. It was speculated that Hank Okai or Ken Hamaguchi were the likely pitchers for the Kingsburg Vikings, with Juice Ikeda, as the receiver.[66]

Game one was "led by the phenomenal slugging, diminutive shortstop Mas Iriyama, who rapped out four stinging hits, Butch Tamura's Guadalupe YMBA baseball club came through with their season's first win as they broke an 8 to 8 deadlock in the last of the ninth to outpoint the Parlier Cards." The second game of the doubleheader saw 17-year-old Masato Kinoshita pitch a masterful game for Zenimura's All-Stars over a cocky Kingsburg Viking nine, while his teammates were pounding hurler Hank Okai to a 6 to 3 score.

According to historian Kerry Yo Nakagawa, the equipment the ballplayers used for the first few games was primitive. Scrap wood was crafted into home plate and the pitcher's rubber. Months later Zeni ordered a real rubber and a home plate from Homan's Sporting Goods back in Fresno. For those who did not bring their uniforms from California, camp uniforms were sewn from mattress ticking. Likewise, bases were hand-sewn bags filled with rice, and the foul lines were drawn with flour from the mess hall.[67]

Fans throughout the two camps flocked to Zenimura Field. They dropped donations into a coffee can placed at the entrance, allowing Kenichi Zenimura to subsequently purchase bats, balls, bases and uniforms by mail from Homan's. The crowds never stopped coming. The fans who couldn't find space in the bleachers would stand along the foul lines.[68]

The diamond became a social hot spot too. "The teenagers and the adults would gather every night to watch the games," remembered the late actor Pat Morita. "I had never seen a live baseball game before, so this was my introduction to baseball — sitting and cheering with a couple of thousand rabid fans."[69]

The success of Zenimura Field near Block 28 inspired the construction of even more diamonds throughout Rivers, Arizona. In the Canal camp, Ken Yorioka and a team of helpers constructed a field near Block 16.[70] Ultimately, these diamonds were more than just a place to play baseball, they represented the hopes of internees. "It was a great hardship for everyone being in the camp because nobody had anything," said Kiyoko Zenimura. "Building the ballpark really saved us. It kept the spirits of the people up and helped everyone to stay positive and not become angry and short tempered."[71]

The fields also provided a sense of aesthetic beauty in the rugged and harsh desert. "It was always so hot and dry in the desert," recalled Pat Morita. "Zeni would water the grass very early in the morning. I must say, it became a very nice ballpark."[72]

Baseball diamonds also offered a forum to overcome the barriers of prejudice. It was reported that in the Topaz, Utah, camp and other centers that "suspicious people in the nearby communities eventually accepted internees as one of their own." The reason? "Evacuees went more than half-way to extend friendliness," observed an editorial in the *Gila News Courier*. Zenimura and other leaders at Gila shared a similar sentiment. "We, too, must break down the barriers that have been raised against us through just such contacts. We, too, must go three-quarters of the way."[73] Inviting outside teams was a natural way for Zeni to go more than halfway to extend an olive branch of peace, friendship and brotherhood.

On March 20, the *Gila News Courier* announced new baseball leadership positions for two veterans of the 1937 Tour of Japan. Harry Kono was officially named the commissioner of the Canal Camp Athletic Club (2CAC) and Zenimura the head of the Butte Baseball Association. That same week, another important first occurred at Gila River. The Canal High School girls' basketball team traveled *outside* the barbed-wire fences to play the Pima Indian team in Sacaton. This marked a first for the interned Japanese Americans to leave the camp to play an outside team.[74]

Weekend ball games of the newly founded Butte Baseball Association saw Zenimura's hustling Block 28 squad win two games by knocking off Block 31, 10 to 7, on Saturday and trimming Pasadena on Sunday. The *Gila News Courier* observed, "Although Masato Kinoshita hurled effectively against the Pasadenans, veteran catcher Ken Zenimura with sons—shortstop Kenshi and second sacker Kenzo—stood out by pulling many an outstanding father and son act."[75]

On March 23, a meeting of Butte baseball managers finalized the teams in each league. Eight teams were selected to the "A," or Major League, competition, while twelve teams were selected to enter the "B," or minor league. Zenimura was nominated to serve as director of both leagues with Zuke Tanaka, Butch Tamura, Mike Nakano, Kaname Matsuno, Kaz Ikeda, Horse Inouye and Teiji Itow as members of the leagues' board of directors. Key Kobayashi was selected as secretary of the league, with Bill Kashiwagi as official scorekeeper. The Butte Baseball Board of Directors voted to start the major and minor league play on Saturday afternoon, April 3, with a doubleheader.

The 12 teams in the "Aye" or Major League were:

YMBA	Lompoc
Pasadena	Block 31
Firemen	Block 33
Giants	Block 30
Block 65	Block 28
Hinodes	Bulldogs

The Board decided that the leagues would abide by the official Spalding rule book. All "Aye" teams were limited to 15 players. "Bee" teams could not have more than 18 players. Umpires selected were Jack Kasai, Kaz Ikeda, Horse Inouye, Kiyo Sumii, Teiji Itow, Zuke Tanaka, Mas Mitani, Bob Yamasaki, Jack Nishikawa, George Sakamoto, Harry Ota, Sam Yamasaki and Ken Zenimura.

It was also agreed upon that an entrance fee of $5.00 for "Aye" teams and two dollars and $2.50 for "Bee" teams would be collected and refunded at the end of season (unless the team dropped out during the season). A policy of guarding against the "swiping" of players was also put in place.[76]

While Zenimura Field and the Butte Baseball League were all operating according to Zeni's plan, a surprising statement was issued by Project Director L.H. Bennett. All of the scrap lumber that Zenimura had requested be stored next to or underneath the barracks

Internment camp baseball provided the Zenimura men with their first opportunity to play together as teammates. Competing in the "Aye" division of the Butte Baseball Association, Zenimura's hustling Block 28 team defeated Block 31, 10 to 7. The *Gila News Courier* observed, "Veteran catcher Ken Zenimura with sons — shortstop Kenshi and second sacker Kenzo — stood out by pulling many an outstanding father and son act" (Japanese American National Museum).

were deemed a fire hazard. The Internal Security Division Camp authorities confiscated all the wood.[77] Zeni would have to patiently wait for other scrap wood alternatives.

In the meantime, Zeni further established himself as the "Baseball Czar" of Gila River by becoming a source for pastime information and strategy. He ordered 100 copies of "The Parade of Louisville Sluggers Champions, 1943 edition," an informational pamphlet which he generously shared with the Butte Baseball League managers, free of charge.[78]

On March 28, six of Butte's top ball clubs were set to square off for battle, and according to the schedule — every four hours. Teiji Itow's Pasadena squad took on the Fireman at 9:00 A.M., Lampoc battled the Giants at 1:00 P.M., Block 28 was set to take on Block 30 at 5:00 P.M. and the Block 66 Hinodes hosted the tough Guadalupe YMBA squad on the new field near Block 66 at 2:00 P.M.

The *Gila News Courier* provided a pre-game analysis of the day's games. "Hinodes was red hot from the recent win over the highly-regarded Cards, and Guadalupe was feeling strong fresh from their impressive victory over the newly disbanded Bulldogs. Pasadena, with many added faces should give manager Art Kaku's Firemen a very bad time while Arroyo Grande Giants are favored over Lampoc. Another closely contested tussle should be the battle between Zenimura's Block 28 and Block 30 club of Ted Iwasaki and Tosh Okuhara." Zenimura and Masato Kinoshita were listed as the probable battery for the Block 28 team.

In the first game, Guadalupe edged Hinodes (Block 66), 14 to 13, behind the impressive pitching of Mas Mitani and impressive slugging of James Nishino (3 for 6) and Ted Morishita (3 for 4). Maino Okazaki, stellar shortstop for Hinodes, hit 2 for 5, including a grand slam. Other stars for Hinodes included Joe Shimada, who belted two triples; Kay Komura, who enjoyed a 3 for 6 day at the plate; and Joe Watanabe, who had a perfect 4 for 4 day, including a home run.

The second game featured a closer contest with Lompoc trimming Block 65 (Arroyo Grande), 5 to 3, behind Kiyoshi Kataoba (2–3), Kay Toyo (3–4) and Hunter Doi who hit a "terrific homer to center in the second."

Pasadena squeaked by the Firemen 14 to 11 in the third game of the day, led by Horse Inouye's home run and 3-for-4 day at the plate. Other top hitters for Pasadena were Shig Kawai and Shozo Ikemura. The Firemen gave a good fight behind the bats of Louie Hayashida and Tad Nakamura.

In the grand finale on Zenimura Field, Block 28 crushed Block 30, 17 to 4, behind the three-hitter pitched by Masato Kinoshita. Block 30 pitchers Yoshi Hirano and Mas Okuhara surrendered 9 hits, including three by the veteran catcher Ken Zenimura.[79]

Plans were underway for the Butte High baseball team to play teams outside the internment camp and they were anticipating games with outside schools at the opponent's fields. Arrangements had been made with North Phoenix, Mesa, and Phoenix High School. There were also tentative plans to book games with Glendale, Scottsdale, Litchfield Park and Peoria. But they still needed approval and "if the games cannot be played at the outside schools, the contests would need to be held in the center."[80]

Sadly, camp life was starting to take its toll on the mental health of the community. The headlines of the April 3 *Gila News Courier* read: "Despondency Blamed in Suicide Case." Mrs. Misai Konya, age 26, of 34-5-B was found dead in her apartment by her husband, Megumi, on Tuesday, March 30, at 2:30 P.M.[81] While the joy of spring and the first Butte baseball league games at Zenimura Field gave hope to some internees, deep despair unfortunately got the best of others.

A few days later more positive news emerged when the demand for scrap lumber to improve the Block 28 diamond (Zenimura Field) was met from an unexpected source—the watchtower once used by the Butte camp officials.[82] It was fitting that the wooden watchtower once used to monitor and limit the freedom of the camp's residents was torn down, allowing the lumber to be used as seats and stands for watching the great game of baseball. Furthermore, it was fitting that all of this occurred during the same week that a grand symbol of American Democracy, the Jefferson Memorial was opened (April 13, 1943), Thomas Jefferson's 200th birthday.

Additional news from the camp newspaper suggested a bit more freedom was extended to the internees. "Outstanding Butte baseball figures disclosed that they are attempting to get a team or two from the Poston Center to come and compete here for possibly several days, with transportation expenses guaranteed."[83] This attempt would later be put on hold by WRA officials, either due to a reported outbreak of polio at the Poston camp, or other policy concerns.

Coached by Ken Tanaka, the Butte High Eagle baseball team played its first game outside the camp when it traveled 25 miles to the northeast to battle the Mesa Jackrabbits on April 15. Perhaps more important than the scoreboard was the taste of freedom that came with the outside trip. "The people outside sure are friendly." That was the reaction of the boys who went out to Mesa for a ball game. They stated that the Mesa students were nice to the boys from the camp. "Don't let anyone kid you. Them guys are swell," said Dave Aizawa. Though there was little in the way of candy or gum, the boys were happy because "they got their malts, hamburgers and an eyeful of 'blondes.' As Jack Kasai puts it, 'Man! You should have seen that girl named Irene.' The squad is looking forward to more outside games and who wouldn't."[84]

Desert Sentinel sports editor George Toyoda was also impressed by the significance of the Butte-Mesa contest. "In any game sportsmanship is a great element. To us who are in camp, it is vital. When the boys came home from Mesa after a ball game, the first thing they spoke of was the host's good sportsmanship. Recently the Casa Grande team came to play Butte, some rooters teased a certain player on the opposing team. What these boys said displayed the sportsmanship of the whole school. The outside teams do not have to play us. If we do not display good character, they may disband future games. All the students want outside contests. Let's keep this in mind and show good sportsmanship so that we may be complimented by the outside people."[85]

Next on the schedule for the Butte Eagle hardball squad was the North Phoenix Mustangs, but for reasons not reported in the *Gila News Courier* or *Desert Sentinel*, the game with North Phoenix was cancelled. Instead, the Butte High Eagles took on their cross-camp rivals—Canal High—and lost 8–4. Weeks later Butte sought revenge and defeated Canal 20 to 3.

Despite the cancelled game with North Phoenix, more outside games made their way onto the radar. Conversations were underway with teams from surrounding cities such as Casa Grande, Eloy and Chandler. Butte baseball officials announced that they received inquiries from the Arizona State Prison at Florence as well.[86]

For Arizonans, late April means the end of a beautiful spring and the start of warmer weather. Zenimura and the players in his league could feel the rising heat with each passing day. As a result he decided to change the majority of Butte "Aye" Major League games to twilight affairs.[87] To be on the field and ready to play a 6:00 P.M. game, Butte League players arrived at the mess hall for an early 4:00 P.M. dinner and were on the field warming up an hour later.[88] The decision to let the ballplayers eat earlier than the rest of the camp created a small controversy, bringing complaints of favoritism for the ballplayers.[89]

Late April 1943 also marked the addition of the tall castor bean plants planted by the fence near Zenimura field. Resembling tall stalks of corn, their purpose was to serve as a marker for the outfield wall, windbreaks and the overall beautification to the camp.[90] Zeni planted castor bean "seeds 10 feet apart and watered them by diverting an irrigation canal that ran alongside the camp grounds. The plants grew to be seven feet high and fanned across the outfield from foul pole to foul pole. Balls hit over the plants were home runs; balls hit through them were ground rule doubles." It was reported that "outfielders chasing balls to the wall [of castor bean stalks] learned to be wary of lurking rattlesnakes."[91]

On April 24, the *Gila News Courier* reported rumors of several beautification and home-improvement projects taking place in preparation for a special visitor to the camp, first lady Eleanor Roosevelt.[92] From the outside perspective, Gila River was considered a "comfortable" place to live. Due to this perception that the Japanese Americans were given special treatment, the first lady was paying a visit to Gila River to see conditions firsthand. Her observations were published in *Collier's Magazine* on October 10, 1943. In it, she described what she saw:

> I can well understand the bitterness of people who have lost loved ones at the hands of the Japanese military authorities, and we know that the totalitarian philosophy, whether it is in Nazi Germany or Fascist Italy or in Japan, is one of cruelty and brutality.... These understandable feelings are aggravated by the old time economic fear on the West Coast and the unreasoning racial feeling which certain people, through ignorance, have always had wherever they came in contact with people who are different from themselves.
>
> To undo a mistake is always harder than not to create one originally but we seldom have the foresight. Therefore we have no choice but to try to correct our past mistakes and I hope that the recommendations of the staff of the War Relocation Authority, who have come to know individually most of the Japanese Americans in these various camps, will be accepted.
>
> A Japanese American may be no more Japanese than a German-American is German, or an Italian-American is Italian, or of any other national background. All of these people, including the Japanese Americans, have men who are fighting today for the preservation of the democratic way of life and the ideas around which our nation was built.
>
> We have no common race in this country, but we have an ideal to which all of us are loyal: we cannot progress if we look down upon any group of people amongst us because of race or religion. Every citizen in this country has a right to our basic freedoms, to justice and to equality of opportunity. We retain the right to lead our individual lives as we please, but we can only do so if we grant to others the freedoms that we wish for ourselves.[93]

In April 1943, Secretary of Interior Harold LeClair Ickes also became personally involved in wartime relocation when he hired three U.S. citizens of Japanese ancestry to work on his farm in Olney, Maryland. He said, "We should do all we can to ease the burden that the war has placed upon this particular group of our fellow citizens." Joining them were four others from Poston, Arizona, who worked on the farm of Sam Rice, a former baseball player and neighbor of Ickes. "I do not like the idea of loyal citizens, no matter of what race or color, being kept in relocation centers any longer than need be," Ickes said. He added that the farm workers were graduates of the California State Polytechnical Institute.[94]

The plans to get a baseball team from the Poston Center to compete at Gila finally came together for Zenimura by April. The *Gila News Courier* reported, "Mr. Yano, resident of Unit 1 and manager of the strong Delano nine, is getting up a team under the name of the Delano All-Stars from Poston. Among the quite a few well-known players will be about a seven man pitching staff." A five-day stay near Memorial Day—May 29, 30, 31, June 1 and 2—was planned.

April 1943 brought the end of the first spring baseball season of the Butte Baseball League at Gila. According to stats published in the *Courier*, the top-performers were James "Step" Tomooka and Kenso Zenimura. "With a splendid average of .538, James Stephen Tomooka, league leading YMBA's hard-hitting outfielder, leads Butte Major Leaguers in four rounds of hotly-contested play. Kenso Zenimura, 28 skipper Zeni's keen-eyed 16 year old younger son second sacker, holds the coveted position of runner-up with a fine average of .529."[95]

The Butte High baseball team also completed their first clip. The 1943 Butte High yearbook provided a summary of their inaugural effort. "Because of a late start in the season and the scarcity of outside competition, the Eagle horsehiders could only muster a five-game schedule."

Despite the challenges of operating a serious baseball league behind barbed wire, Zenimura's Butte Baseball League proved to be a success in terms of both the quality of play and profitability. The big challenges were the ongoing attempts to schedule outside teams, the cancellations of these outside teams, and the growing trend of non-paying customers taking seats at the ballgames.[96]

On May 6, the directors of the Butte Major League released its first monthly financial statement which included ticket sales from the exhibition and league games held between March 7 and April 25. Recorded intakes included donations of $85.21 from three collections in six exhibition games and $195.29 collected 12 times in 16 league games. Figures include money collected in practice games as with Case Grande when collections were made with league games. Total amount collected equaled $280.50 with expenses running up to $252.12 for a balance (profit) of $23.36 up to April 25. Expenses were mostly for baseballs, equipment and various other costs. All figures are through the courtesy of Harry Komatsu, gate cashier and ground manager.

Expenses 3/7/43 to 4/25/43

1 home and pitchers' plate	$30.01
1 rope & on ami	.77
2 sign paints	2.55
1 hatchet	1.00
3 sets of bases	47.13
1 indicator	1.55
Pd. Score keeper and ball chaser 3/7/43	1.55
2 official score bks.	4.00
6 doz. balls	$114.00
1 complete chief first aid kit	19.50
12 water faucets	19.06
Printing tickets	3.40
Total Expenses	$252.13

Collections and Donations

Date	*Amount*
3/7/43	25.77
3/28/43	16.67

Date	*Amount*
4/3–4/43	42.77
4/10–11/43	45.00
4/14/43	26.50
4/17–18/43	65.35
4/24–25/43	58.44
Total Intakes	$280.50[97]

Author's note: Adjusted for inflation, $280.50 from 1943 is roughly the equivalent of $3,460 in 2010.[98]

The profits from the first six games did not go into anyone's pocket. Instead they were invested directly back into league operations. Zenimura coordinated equipment orders with all of the Butte coaches and placed one large order with Homan's Sporting Goods.[99] Sporting goods store owner Frank Homan was also the mayor of Fresno just before the war. He was a former teammate of Hall of Famer Frank Chance, and became his brother in-law when he married Chance's sister in 1900. Kenso Zenimura has fond memories of Homan Sporting Goods. He recalls that he and brother Kenshi had some "really slick baseball cleats made of kangaroo leather. The shoes were light-weight and felt really good on the feet. Dad ordered them from Homan's. He got all of his equipment from there because he had really good credit from all the previous years of dealing with him."[100]

Sixty miles south of Rivers, the University of Arizona Wildcats had just completed their spring baseball season in Tucson. Led by J.F. "Pop" McKale, the Wildcats squad embarked on a 600-mile trip to Mexico for a tournament. The *Arizona Republic* reported that the strong U of A team swept the Mexican series by defeating Culican in a double-header, 4–1 and 9–4, and Mazatlan, 8–2.[101] Upon their return to Arizona, the Wildcats were slated to close their regular season by crossing bats with Harry Kono's Canal All Stars inside the relocation camp at Gila River.[102] The game was scheduled for Saturday, May 8, 1:00 P.M., and, according to the *Tucson Daily Citizen*, the University of Arizona "horsehiders" planned on taking a tour of the center after the contest.[103] For reasons not reported in the press, the U of A baseball team decided not to play the game. Instead, the Canal All-Stars took on the Butte All-Stars. The score of the game was not provided, but it was reported that James Tomooka slapped out three triples in the Butte All-Stars loss to the Canal All-Stars.[104]

On May 8, the *News Courier* reported that Zenimura called a meeting in his home with all Butte Major League managers to decide the schedule of the coming series of games with the Poston All-Stars team.[105] The first half of the Butte Major League season was also discussed. Teams received two points for a victory and one point for a tie game, and it all added up to the YMBA as the league champion with a winning total of 11 points. Zenimura's Block 28 was right behind them with 9 points.[106]

No sooner did the Butte managers meet to discuss the upcoming Poston series than they received word that the trip could potentially be cancelled.[107] Both the Butte and Canal League managers were disappointed with the news so they decided to send a representative to Poston to dig deeper and learn more about the rationale behind the cancellation. The representative selected to make the trip was Harry Kono.[108]

The cancellation of the Poston series brought to light some perceptions held by the Caucasian community towards the interned Japanese Americans. There were some who called the internees "the best fed civilians in the world." According to the *Gila News Courier*,

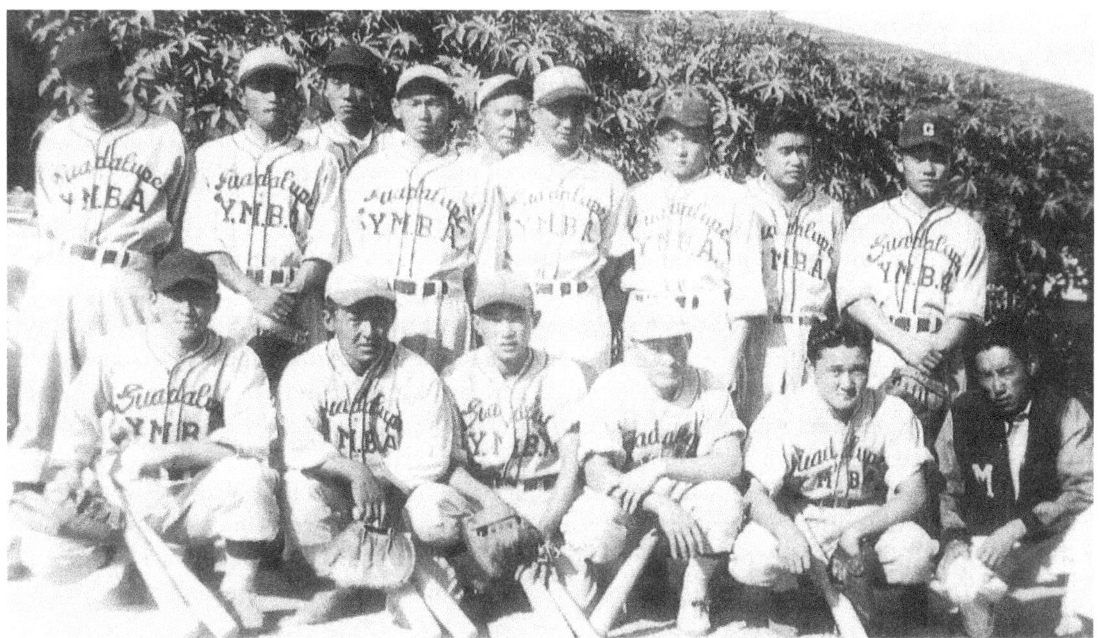

The Guadalupe YMBA ballclub was crowned the Butte Baseball Major League champions for 1943. YMBA coach Fred Tsuda (back row, center), Zenimura's lifelong friend and former teammate in Hawaii and Fresno, also taught a class on baseball strategy for all Butte Baseball League participants (Tets Furukawa Collection).

the Dyes Committee investigators said that "plentiful supplies of beef, pork, mutton, canned pork and beans, fish and chocolate bars are stocked by the ten Japanese relocation centers in the country." Some officials came to the defense of the internees. "Most of the charges are made by persons who do not understand the situation and are unable to grasp the problem in its entirety," said WRA official Keadle. "Everything the center residents eat conforms with outside ration point regulations. Everyone 15 years and older receives one pound of coffee every four weeks. Sugar is rationed at two pounds per person per month. Each person is allotted 16 points of meat, butterfat, and vegetable oil per week. Since June 1, one point per pound of canned milk has been taken off the meat points. This will lower the meat consumption per week per person. Each resident is authorized to receive 48 points of processed foods every month. As for canned pork and beans, we have never had any, because it happens to be a commodity sent overseas for the past 14 months or so."[109]

To further demonstrate that the internees at Gila were not the "best-fed civilians," *Courier* editors shared that "62 individuals, the largest single day's group, left the Gila center on season and indefinite leave on Tuesday [of] this week." The fact that internees continued to leave on their own volition was a clear sign that no one living behind barbed wire was being "pampered and coddled."[110]

Harry Kono returned from Poston with the official news of the canceled series. The reason given directly to him was that officials believed that allowing the Poston team to travel for baseball "would make the camps too attractive and would slow leaves."[111]

John C. Powell, Acting Chief of Poston Community Services, wrote a discouraging letter to Poston baseball manager Masao Yano. Yano in turn shared the letter with the Butte Baseball Association. The letter read in part:

> I am sorry to tell you that permission for the games at Gila must be refused. Relations with Gila have veered from the period in which interchange of visits was free and unrestricted to one in which only the most personal matters, or Project business can be accepted as basis of permission to visit.... Many persons with serious matters to attend to, have been refused permission to visit Gila, and it would not be fair to them or to later applicants if we sent twenty men down to play ball.... You will understand, I am sure, that this is one of those cases in which the desires of a group have to be met with the broader rules of Project policy....[112]

Zenimura and the rest of the Butte Baseball Association were disappointed with the news of the Poston series cancellation, but not discouraged. They immediately announced that holders of tickets to the Poston series could have their money refunded or use them as season passes to all Butte league games at Zenimura Field. The Butte League season consisted of 56 regular league games plus all replayed ties and a playoff series. Together the total number of games was well over 70, and all for $1. The best sections—A, B, D and E—were reserved for ticket holders of the canceled Poston series.[113]

A week after the Poston game cancellation, more tragic news unfolded at Rivers. Seventeen-year-old Fumiko Taira, formerly of Guadalupe and most recently a kindergarten teacher in Butte, took her own life. Friends and family said that she had been in a depressed mood for several days before her death. At noon, while everyone was eating in the mess hall, Fumiko hung herself.[114]

Life outside of camp was not pleasant for Japanese Americans either. Officials ceased offering passes for internees to travel outside of the camp to Phoenix due to reports of hostile attitudes towards the Japanese.[115] Perhaps in response to this civilian hostility, local sports hero and Arizona State Teachers College baseball coach Bill Kajikawa, joined the 442nd, the Japanese American battle unit being formed by the Army. He had been a football star at Phoenix Union High School and at Arizona State, where he had served as a football, basketball and track coach since 1937. Kajikawa was inducted into the service in Salt Lake City, Utah.[116]

In June, Zenimura released the second monthly financial statement for Zenimura Field. Twelve games played in the month of May 1943 generated $319.57 in revenue. Expenses were higher at $348.31, but the previous month's profits kept the operation in the black.

Immediately following the second financial statement, Zenimura announced that he was stepping down as the manager of the Block 28 baseball team because of what he called "awkwardness in being both league director and team manager." Sam Yamasaki, Zenimura's brother-in-law, was named as the replacement manager of the Block 28 team.[117]

The Butte League batting leaders were also announced at the mid-season break. Nob Oki of Lompoc led the Butte horsehiders with a hefty .520 batting average. And for the first time in their lives, 15-year-old Kenso Zenimura was outperforming his dad, with the younger Zenimura batting .446, compared to the elder's respectable .368 average.

The second half of the Butte Major League season kicked off with "Masato Kinoshita's superb 3-hit mound work giving Block 28 its first win by edging Block 30 4–2. The game was finished in a new league record of one hour and 21 minutes. Duke Tokunanga's single to center broke Masato's no-hitter until the seventh. The deciding tally came when Kenso Zenimura tripled and pinch-runner Sab Yamada ambled home on a wild pitch. Mas Okuhara met a tough loss yielding 7 hits—some after a couple of miscues on part of mates. This was the last Major League game before that circuit prepared for the July 2, 3, 4, and 5 tournament."[118]

The Fourth of July holiday also brought a welcome change in Arizona law for Japanese

Americans. It was announced that the existing law in Arizona prohibiting business transactions with Japanese and others "of restricted movement without triple publication [documentation]" was unconstitutional. The ruling by Superior Court Judge H.T. Phelps of Maricopa County meant that Japanese American business owners and farmers could conduct business as usual, and compete fairly with their white counterparts.[119]

The Independence Day tournament at Rivers presented a heated contest between Zenimura's ballclub against the Canal All-Stars. According to the *Courier*, "Zenimura's '28–'30 ... put in 3 decisive tenth canto tallies for a 6–3 victory and Rivers' Inter-Camp Tournament Championship last Tuesday night. The gathering — one of the largest in either camp — was estimated well over 2,000 — including many Canalites.... One basers by Kenshi, Ken and Kenso kept alive the rally which brought home the bacon — a banner which read Butte-Canal Tournament Champion, Rivers, Arizona, 1943."[120] A few days later the tournament trophy was presented to Zenimura's ballclub by 2CAC commissioner Harry Kono.

Perhaps in an effort to ease the tensions in the camp, Gila River's officials announced in July that they would discontinue the use of the word "Wardens" and rename the security positions as "Patrolmen."[121] Despite the downgrade in security perception at Gila River, distrust continued to grow in other camps. The *Tucson Daily Citizen* reported concerns that the Japanese Americans held at Poston were a potential threat to destroy Parker Dam.[122] Arizona's "Japanese situation was under study," announced General Petterson. Arizona congressmen sent a report to President Roosevelt expressing a concern that due to "American soldiers now being held in Japanese prison camps," there was danger of serious outbreaks in the state.[123]

In July 1943, the WRA administered a loyalty test, a short questionnaire consisting of only two questions. All internees over age 17 were required to take the test. The first question asked male internees if they would be willing to serve in the armed forces of the United States on combat duty wherever ordered. The female internees were asked if they would be willing to serve in the Army Nurse Corps or the Women's Army Corps. The second question in the loyalty test for both genders asked if the internee would defend the United States faithfully, and strongly reject allegiance and obedience to Japan's emperor and other powerful organizations in Japan. Those who "passed" the loyalty test with "Yes-Yes" answers were allowed to leave the camps for work or school. Those who "failed" the test with "No" answers were sent to the increased security of the Tule Lake Relocation Camp in California.[124] The "no-no's" were also given the opportunity to apply for repatriation back to Japan. According to the *Courier*, 77 Gilans eventually opted to leave for Japan, while 873 Gilans were sent to Tule Lake.

In late July 1943, Zenimura received a letter from his good friend Russ Hinaga of San Jose Asahi fame asking if his all-star club from Heart Mountain, Wyoming, could pay a visit to Arizona. Just as the Gila boys welcomed outside Caucasian teams, so did Hinaga's ballclub.[125]

Another old friend with whom Zeni stayed in touch was Ed Orman, sports reporter with the *Fresno Bee*. On July 29, 1943, Orman shared the highlights of a letter he received from Zenimura. "Still Play Baseball" declared the headline. "Before their interment into relocation centers, sportsminded Japanese in this sector devoted more time to baseball than any other single sport. They carried on in leagues at the Fresno County Fairgrounds until transferred. Many of them are living in the Gila River Relocation Center. In Rivers, Ariz., where Kenny Zenimura, veteran Japanese baseball [player/manager] here for years, puts it, 'baseball is played more than any other sport and it does much in helping morale.' Only a short time ago in Japan, the government banned the great American national pastime which the Nipponese adopted as probably their leading participant sport. Zenimura, by the way, played on the team which won the Intracamp tournament at Rivers. He reported most of the performers were young fellows."[126]

The summer of 1943 also brought new policies in the Butte Baseball League. It was announced that after August 5, no players would be allowed to change teams or clubs. "To protect independent 'bee' teams from unethical competition," Butte baseball Czar Ken Zenimura declared, "no 'aye' player — even if resting two games — will be permitted to play bee ball or bee player be allowed to switch from one league or club to another."[127]

The top performers of the Butte Baseball League were Nob Oki's .383 and YMBA .285 averages, pacing the major league's individual and team batting records as the circuit neared its final stretch. Coach Kenichi Zenimura led the Block 28 squad with a .333 (20 hits in 60 at-bats) average in 17 games, while his team hit an anemic .212.

The top-hitting YMBA ballclub of Guadalupe was led by James "Step" Tomooka. "The games were very competitive," recalls Tomooka. According to the outfielder/pitcher, "we had a good team because a lot of us played together before the war [in Santa Maria, California]."[128]

In early August, Zenimura's all-stars tied the Lompoc Firemen in a 6 to 6 contest. It was the second "standstill battle between the two clubs in the second half. Fireman's Shim Shimasaki replaced Junius Sakuma in the eighth and coach Ken Zenimura relieved Masato Kinoshita in the seventh. Timely singles by Ken Zenimura and Roy Nakamura in the late innings led to the tied score.[129]

The Arizona summer also brought with it the monsoon season and a handful of games in the 1943 summer season were cancelled or postponed due to severe weather. The extreme dust, heat, lightning and rain of the Sonoran desert was a dismay to housewives in the camps and brought gloom to a normally sunny Arizona. One example of how fast and furious the monsoons can be in the desert occurred one afternoon when a student choir group had to run for cover in the middle of a performance. It is reported that the children were singing "God Bless America" when the wall of wind, dust and rain hit them. The irony of the moment did not escape the internees unjustly incarcerated behind barbed wire.

Forever hopeful was Coach Ken Zenimura, who in the summer of 1943 announced that he had plans to plant Bermuda grass on the ground of Zenimura Field.[130] According to *Sports Illustrated*, Zenimura devised tactics "straight out of *Stalag 17*" to get the grass to grow. "He had a plumber cut into the laundry room's water line and extend underground pipe some 200 feet (running under the camp fence) to the pitcher's mound so that he could water the infield. Zeni also persuaded the Butte fire department to hold its drills in the ballpark so the grass would benefit."[131]

"I remember watching this little old brown guy watering down the infield with this huge hose," said actor Pat Morita, who was interned with his family at Gila River. "He used to have his kids dragging the infield and throwing out all the rocks. Jeez, I was glad I wasn't them. They worked like mules."[132]

Zenimura's sons and other young boys at Gila River also kept busy reading the new books at the Gila River Library, including the popular *Who's Who in the Major Leagues.*

Despite the fact that the director of the Heart Mountain Relocation Center was 100 percent behind the trip to Gila, it looked as though the trip would not take place after all due to the excessive costs for travel — over $1,000.[133] Fortunately plans came together at the last minute and it was announced that Heart Mountain was coming to Gila after all. Zenimura immediately began to develop an elaborate ticket system for the proposed games.

His old opponent Russell (Rusty) Noboru Hinaga, manager and oldest of the well-known three Hinaga brothers, was still going strong after 25 years of diamond warfare. Starting his brilliant career at the age of 15, Hinaga co-founded the San Jose Asahi team in 1918. He had led the Asahi to many championships and boasted a lifetime winning record of more than 200 games. In 1925, he had toured the Orient with the Asahi's, pitching against Japan's leading university teams, including Meiji and Waseda. He emerged victorious in all but two of the 29 games he worked.

His lineup of players included: Ryozo Roiso Matsui, 1b; Babe Nomura, 2b; Tom Ghosty Okagaki, ss; one of the Hinaga boys at third; Joe Jio, lf; Chi Akizuki, cf; and Tosh Asano, rf[134]—nearly all original Asahi players except Roiso Mutumi, Babe Nomura, and Tosh Asano.[135]

Hinaga humbly told the press that he did not expect to play so many games, and that the Asahi were not as prepared as they would have liked to have been. Above all, he promised their best effort for the public.[136] The Asahi would go on to win three of four games from the Canal camp. Block 28 was next on their schedule.[137]

Celebrating the end of the 1943 baseball season, a "Horsehiders" ball was to be held on Monday, September 6, Labor Day, at mess hall 60. The San Jose Asahi's were the guests of honor. Pasadena White Sox ace backstop Horse Inouye served as the emcee.[138] In addition to the farewell dance, there was a game to be played.

Manager Russ Hinaga's ballclub lost to Block 28, 6–4, then sought revenge with a 13-hit attack to defeat Lompoc, 11 to 5. Ken Zenimura, Chit Akizuki and losing hurler Jackson Tono garnered two safeties apiece. With a shortage of solid arms, Hinaga was forced to make three mound appearances in four days.

In their final game at Butte, the Asahi battled the "Aye" major league all-stars, a team selected by coaches Ken Zenimura and Fred Tsuda. The "Aye" major league all-stars included Keizo Okuharu, Massy and Step Tomooka, Masao and Noboru Iriyama, Shig Kavai, Koizo Komura, Koi Nishino, Ben Tsusimi.

In the September 8 game, the Asahi found the Butte "Aye" all-stars just too strong. "The cream of the circuit's crop worked out a 11–9 win. Russ Hinaga, in his eighth appearance on the hill, was the loser." Both teams combined for 23 hits in the final contest, but it was James "Step" Tomooka's game-winning hit in the late innings that stood out in the battle against Heart Mountain. "My dad used to talk about that game for years after the war," Tomooka says.[139]

Although they were guaranteed $500.00 of their $1,040.00 expenses, the Asahis were offered a generous $725.00 instead: $325.00 from Canal and $400.00 from Butte. And as they departed the camp for their 1,164 mile trip back to Wyoming, the Asahi ballclub delivered a note to the *Gila News Courier* which expressed their appreciation and thanks for the many acts of kindness they received, especially to Zenimura, Block 28, and the baseball associations of both camps.[140]

Hinaga's ball club wasn't the only group of Japanese American ballplayers getting a taste of freedom that summer. Nisei players in Arkansas and Utah were invited to attend a camp with the Brooklyn Dodgers. In Utah, Nisei baseballers, including former San Pedro Skippers' Ichi Hashimoto and ex–San Jose Asahi's southpaw Henry Honda, displayed their talents before Brooklyn Dodger scout George Sisler at a baseball camp.[141] And, the Nisei nine from Hunt, Idaho, were allowed to compete in the Idaho State Semipro Tourney.[142]

Shortly after the Asahi series ended, the *Gila News Courier* posted the final hitting and pitching stats for the 1943 season. Nob Oki's .397 batting average gave him the Major

League's batting championship crown, while Block 28 Coach Ken Zenimura served as a model of consistency by maintaining his .333 average from the first half of the season.[143] The Butte Major League's pitchers were led by YMBA's Ted Morishita, with a winning average of .944, eight wins and one tie game. Lefty Nishimura of the Pasadena White Sox proved to be the workhorse of the league, pitching in 17 games and recording 10 wins and 7 loses.[144]

On September 16, the *Gila News Courier* announced even more records, but this time by non-ballplayers. "Rivers packing is ready to sort, pack and ice an estimated 300 to 350 carloads of vegetables to send to the nine other relocation centers. This is double the output produced earlier in the year. To handle the tremendous load, approximately 1,700 acres have been set aside this year for shipment to other centers."[145] This high level of production would be difficult to match after the first of October. Camp officials discovered that they would need to find more than 700 workers to replace those headed to Tule Lake after answering "No-No" on their loyalty tests.[146] In all, 1,818 Gilans were scheduled to leave for Tule Lake beginning October 1, 1943.[147]

The number of No-No's at Gila River was more a reflection of family loyalty than it was of disloyalty towards the United States. In many cases the younger members of a family voted No-No to stay with a senior family member, an Issei perhaps, who out of principle alone answered negatively. This sentiment is supported by the fact that of 1,000 letters sent from Canal to Japan, only ten were sent back for inadvertently mentioning business matters pertaining to the army, place names, and gave mention of telegrams, wire and airmail.[148]

The so-called loyalty test impacted those on the diamond too. Teams in both camps were losing players, so a farewell best-of-three series was set up between the "Yes-Yes" and the "No-No" ballplayers. "The 'yes-yes' nine Coach Ken Zenimura has put together a formidable 17-man squad against Manager Tosh Komura's 21-strong Tule-bound nine," reported the *Courier*. The last series of "Aye" league games before they parted company was to be held when the all-stars of both camps met for the Rivers' Butte-Canal All-Star Championship.[149]

Butte's Yes-Yes and No-No nines split one a piece in their weekend series. The Tule-bound squad lost out on Saturday, 5–4, but came back to take the second title, 7–5, on Sunday night. It was decided not to hold the scheduled third game. The general consensus towards playing a third game was captured in the *Courier*. "All in all, the novel classic ended seemingly just right — being called with one win apiece."[150]

After the No-No's left for Tule Lake, Zenimura and Joe Hikida of the CAS announced they were trying to secure ball clubs from nearby towns to compete inside Gila River. Teams on the list included a Florence Interment Camp nine. The office of Hugo Wolter said that nothing definite could be disclosed yet, however 2CAC Baseball Commission Chairman Harry Kono revealed that "the Arizona State Semipro Champions, a team from around Phoenix, name undisclosed, may face an all-star group here."[151]

The name of the team was soon shared and the camp was buzzing with excitement about the impending games with the Phoenix Thunderbirds, one of the top semipro teams in Arizona.[152] The Phoenix Nine "Thunderbirds" were to make an appearance against both the Butte and Canal All-Stars on September 26. The games were arranged through the help of Deputy Project Director Luther T. Hoffman and Community Management Head Hugo Wolter. The *Courier* profiled the Thunderbirds, describing a team that had won its league championship for the past three years. This championship team included a pitcher — Harold "Blondey" Robbins — who was reported to average 15 strikeouts per game and had been signed by the Chicago White sox for 1944.

General admission to Butte games was 10 cents for children and 25 cents for adults. Reserved seats for sections A, B, D and E were available for the same 25 cents from Ken Zenimura, according to Ground Manager Harry Komatsu. Despite the enthusiasm displayed for the impending game, camp officials declared that more games with outside teams were "unlikely," especially with other internment baseball clubs. With the arrival of fall, many baseball teams had already disbanded and were now playing football.[153]

With the anticipated arrival of the Phoenix Thunderbirds, Zeni was encouraging the importance of displaying sportsmanship towards their high-profile guests. He recalled the long ago experience of Livingston in an editorial in the *Gila News Courier*:

> Some time ago, back in a California town called Livingston, there appeared huge signs of billboard proportion, "No Japs Wanted." It was quite some time ago; a long time ago to whom this note is directed. At any rate, someone, somehow, arranged a game between the Fresno Japanese Baseball Club and a team owned by the big shot of that town called Livingston. The Japanese nine put together enough guts and made the trip—trying especially hard to play clean ball. Soon there were return games and soon—sure enough—the signs disappeared. MORAL: The sentiment around Phoenix never was too good for us; it's worth trying here.[154]

Unfortunately, Zenimura's game against the Phoenix Thunderbirds would have to wait. Another monsoon hit the afternoon desert and the game was rained out. The Butte-Thunderbirds rescheduled game was announced for October 10, 1943.[155] In preparation for the big Thunderbirds game, the Butte baseball team scheduled a contest against a combined Cards-Viking All-Star group. The Phoenix Thunderbirds also scheduled a tough contest against the all-black Arizona Western Compress squad in preparation for their contests against the Japanese Americans at Gila River. "Staging a scoring spree, the International Thunderbirds buried the Western Compress nine under a 13–1 score in exhibition baseball game on the Phoenix Municipal Stadium diamond yesterday."[156]

Player-manager Otto Wolf posted his players for the game. The Phoenix Thunderbird roster consisted of:

Catcher—Hal Kolovare
Pitchers—Ken Cantrell, Joe Salazar and Blondey Robbins
First base—Phil Jacobs
Second base—John Tischilar
Third base—John Pock
Shortstop—Otto Wolf (manager)
Outfield—Okey Flowers, Bill Wolf, Oki Mosely
Utility—Bob Combs[157]

The Butte All-star roster included:

Catchers—Horse Inouye and Kaz Ikeda
Pitchers—Masato Kinoshita, Mits Mitani and George Kanagaki
First base—Nobu Oki, Sam Yamasaki and Mike Nakano
Second base—Kenso Zenimura
Third base—Sab Yamada
Shortstop—Seirin Ikeda and Maino Okazak
Outfield—Kenshi Zenimura, Shig Kawai, Keiza Okuhara and Noburu Iriyama

Fred Tsuda and Kenichi Zenimura would handle the coaching duties.[158]

The Thunderbirds' visit to the camp marked the first time that a Japanese American Internment Camp ballgame was covered by the *Arizona Republic*. The major paper of the Phoenix metropolitan area reported the outcome on October 10:

> The International Thunderbirds suffered a double setback in exhibition baseball games with the Japanese nines here today. The Birds dropped a 3–2 decision to the Butte Camp nine in the first game, and then took a 5–0 drubbing from the Canal Camp team.
>
> The Phoenix Club took a two-run lead in the second inning of the game on a single by Molis and four errors, but Butte got one run in the fifth on a single and two errors. The Butte team clinched the win in the sixth with two runs on a double by K. Zenimura, a walk and a triple by Iriyama. The Birds collected seven hits, while Blondey Robbins held the winners to six.
>
> The Canal nine got two runs in the third and three in the fourth to decide the second game. Lefty Salazar relived Okey Flowers in the fifth for the Birds and did not allow a hit or a walk the rest of the way. He fanned three. The Birds were held to three hits, while the winners collected five off of Flowers."[159]

In an interview years later Arizona pitching legend Lowell Bailey commented on the Gila River victories. "Blondey Robbins was a real fireballer. He had a herky-jerky motion that made him tough to hit," he said. "If the Japanese team beat Blondey, they must have really been the horse."[160]

The *Gila River Courier* also covered the Thunderbirds' visit. In doing so it marked the first time that the results of a game involving the Phoenix ballclub were reported in English and Kanji:

> *Butte Pick-ups Edge Visitors from Phoenix by 3–2 Margin*
>
> Phoenix Thunderbirds second invasion of Gila proved unsuccessful in both ends of a doubleheader last Sunday afternoon. The Caucasians were turned back in the opener by a Butte pick-up all-star group 3–2. A 2CAC all-star nine avenged itself of a previous loss by whitewashing the visitors 5–0 in the night cap.
>
> Kenshi Zenimura's first of two singles broke a 2–0 count in the fifth — hotfooting it around on a sacrifice and a pair of miscues. Kenso Zenimura's double, Maino Okazaki's walk, Horse Inouye's grounding out and Noboru Iriyama's three-baser netted the tying and winning markers in the sixth.[161]

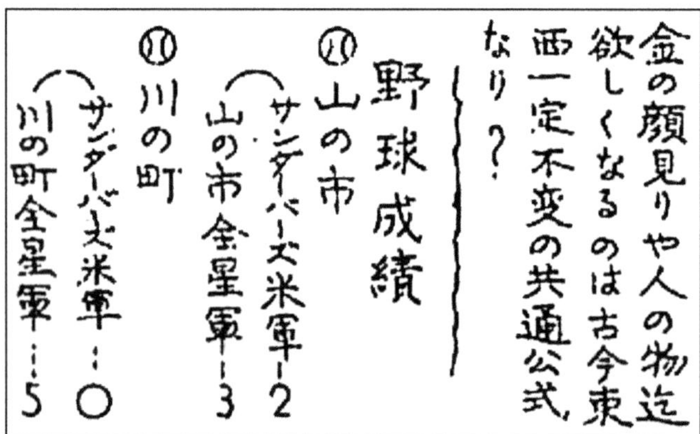
金の顔見りや人の物迄
欲しくなるのは古今東
西一定不変の共通公式、
なり？

野球成績
⑩山の市
（サンダーバーズ米軍ー2
山の市全星軍ー3
⑪川の町
（サンダーバーズ米軍：0
川の町全星軍：5

In October 1943, Kenichi Zenimura assembled an all-star squad that defeated the semipro baseball champions of Arizona, the Phoenix Thunderbirds, 3–2. Above is the Thunderbird-Butte box score from the Japanese section of the relocation camp newspaper (*Gila News Courier*).[162]

The Thunderbirds-Butte contest generated $122.53 at the gates. Zenimura was feeling generous and awarded the visitors $115. Although they played only one game against Butte, the payment reflected the fees for the previously rained-out game. According to Zeni, the two games would have totaled $130; however he and Otto Wolf compromised at $115.[163]

In the fall of 1943, President Roosevelt called for racial unity in his weekly radio announcement: "Men of all races — black, brown, white and yellow — fight beside us for freedom.... We cannot stand before the world as a champion of oppressed people unless we practice as well as preach the principles of democracy for all men.... All true Americans must be prepared to protect with life itself the inalienable rights of all men without regard to race, creed, or color...."[164] Just a few days later it was reported that some Arizonans were upset because a Japanese American teacher was given a job on the Navajo reservation in Window Rock.[165]

It was a common practice for Zeni to sweeten the pot to encourage visiting ball clubs. Shortly after the T-Bird series he placed ads in the *Arizona Republic* seeking more outside teams to play.[166] Another former Arizona state champion accepted the offer and within days Zenimura had a contest booked against a ball club that called themselves the "Phoenix Colored Nine," which appeared to be the Western Compress ballclub with some new players. The visitors' line-up included: catcher Hamilton; catcher-Manager James Searcy, first base Fisher, second base Fulice, shortstop Lewis, third base Brakeen, left-pitcher Williams, center field Westbrook, right field Harris, pitchers Meyers, Bonner, utility Harol and Coach Eli.[167]

Shortstop/manager Otto Wolf is called "The Father of Valley Baseball" for his leadership in helping to create a thriving baseball community in Phoenix during the 1930s-40s. In 1939 and 1941, his semipro Phoenix Thunderbirds won the Arizona state championship and the right to compete at the National Baseball Congress tournament in Wichita, Kansas. Wolf was named to the 1939 NBC All-American team, along with future Red Sox star Johnny Pesky (Gary Wolf).

The outcome of the October game was a trouncing of the visiting team, with Butte smashing the Phoenix Colored nine, 11–3. The all-star for Phoenix's black squad was Leon "Sugar" Westbrook, an outfielder and pitcher in the Texas Negro Leagues, Arizona semipro leagues, and the West Coast Negro Baseball Leagues. Westbrook was considered a tough out and a solid hitter who could spray the ball to all areas of the field. He was described as both a tough competitor, yet someone who made the game fun by telling jokes or performing trick catches in the outfield.[168]

Another star on the Phoenix Negro nine was 22-year-old Cornell Fisher, an all-state football and baseball player from neighboring Mesa, Arizona. With the decline of black baseball in Arizona after the breaking of the color line by Jackie Robinson, Fisher moved on to competitive softball, as did most African Americans in Arizona. According to the Arizona Softball Hall of Fame, between 1948 and 1965 Fisher was one of Arizona's finest catchers and most powerful hitters. He was named to the All-State team eight times and was always among the leaders in home runs and runs batted in. He won several batting championships in major competition in Mesa. His 17-year softball career spanned three decades and earned him recognition as one of Arizona's all-time greats.

Years later Cornell Fisher Jr., who was only age 5 at the time of the Butte All-Star vs. Negro Nine contest, recalled his father returning home from the Japanese American internment camp at Gila River with a baby pig.[169] Perhaps not too coincidental, just a week before the game the *Gila News Courier* reported the start of a new livestock class to offer students the opportunity to learn how to handle livestock. Among the animals were an estimated 100 pigs kept at a hog farm a few miles away from the Butte Camp.[170] It's quite possible that Fisher, after receiving his earnings from the game at Zenimura Field, bought a piglet on his way out of the camp. By the end of the 1943 the hog population at Rivers was an estimated 1,700.[171]

Kenso Zenimura has fond memories of the game and the comedy displayed by the black ball team. "They committed a lot of errors," recalled Kenso, "but most of them were because they were acting silly; trying to catch the ball behind their backs, making trick catches and throws."[172]

Catcher Kaz Ikeda remembers more of the strategic mind of Coach Zenimura than the comedy act of the visitors. "Even though I was the catcher, Coach Zeni called every pitch and pretty much controlled every aspect of the game from the dugout," said Ikeda. "He [Zeni] had a great knack for analyzing hitter's strengths and weaknesses in just one at-bat," said the Butte backstop. "If a player got a hit in his first at-bat, Zeni would be sure he never saw that same pitch again. He was a great coach." Ikeda then reflected on his coach's legacy. "By 1943, I never saw him play at his most competitive level, so I don't know if he could have ever played in the majors. But there's no doubt in my mind that Zeni would have made a great major league manager."[173]

The games between internees and outside semipro teams were not unique to the Gila River Relocation Center. The team at Rohwer, Arkansas, also played a Caucasian semipro nine from the nearby town of Gould, and the University of Arkansas A&M inside the camp.[174]

Zenimura had secured the top talent for his leagues which created a void in the high school baseball arena. He had both the resources and the support of his fellow internees. So in late October he got to work on refining his ballpark gem in the desert. While he was planting grass on his field, the "No-No's" at Tule Lake wrote back to Gila and told the *Gila News Courier* that the "ball diamond stinks compared to Zenimura field."[175]

There were many in the Japanese American community with torn allegiances during World War II. There were patriotic (love of country) and family allegiances, and for many the two were not the same. Zenimura loved living in America and loved the democratic ideal. Nonetheless, he had a son fighting in the Japanese air force. Zeni was just one of many Japanese Americans emotionally torn by the war. So the news on October 26, 1943, did not help to put his mind at ease. The *Arizona Republic* reported that the Japanese suffered a big air loss, the largest count to date in the war effort. Was his son Kenji (Harry) part of the casualties? Zeni did not know and it would be months for him to learn the outcome. When word eventually reached Kenichi, he discovered that his son's plane did indeed crash in the Pacific Ocean, but not by enemy gunfire. Kenji Zenimura's plane ran out of gas and landed safely in the water. Kenji was fortunate enough to escape the wrecked plane, and near death.[176]

The post loyalty test seemed to elevate the level of patriotic expression at Gila River. For example, residents in both the Canal and Butte camps contributed $755 to the National War Fund and were on pace to exceed their goal of $2,000. Furthermore, community members continued to band together to build the Butte memorial to honor the names of 400 soldiers. The cornerstone was laid on Armistice Day, November 11.

December 1, 1943, marked the 15th birthday of Kenshi (Harvey) Zenimura, the youngest of the three Zenimura sons. Both his birthday celebration and the sense of patriotism generated from the previous weeks were overshadowed by the terrible news that twenty-two-year-old Butte resident Satoshi Kira was shot "attempting to gain freedom" from Gila River.[177] He was wounded in the left side after ignoring two warning shots by military police when he walked past a sentry point at the Chandler entrance despite orders to halt. The motive was reported:

> Relatives attributed Kira's failure to halt when ordered to an intense desire for freedom. They said that Kira, who is third generation American, had felt the evacuation keenly, and resented bitterly the fact of his detention in Rivers. Because in his resentment he had answered loyalty questions negatively, he had not been able to resettle despite many attempts to do so lately, they continued. For several days prior to the shooting, Kira had been extremely nervous, requiring considerable attention, they said. Hospital attendants stated that Kira's statements have been incoherent after hospitalization.[178]

Around the same time of the Kira shooting, reports from Tule Lake indicated that officials threatened the new arrivals, telling them to "join the crowd or die."[179] The news from Tule Lake and the shooting of Kira unsettled those living at Rivers. Officials could sense the tension, so the following memo was published in the *Courier* weeks later:

> "The comparison between internment camps in Japan and relocation centers cannot be adequately made," stated Hugo Wolter, community management lead. The relocation centers are in no sense internment camps nor are the people in the centers "prisoners of war." The articles of the Geneva Convention are not applicable to anyone except "prisoners of war," Wolters said. People may come and go from relocation centers depending on their compliance with the administrative procedure, he said. It is not the purpose of the WRA under orders of the President to detain anyone beyond such a time as is required for an adequate examination of his record and loyalties. Under present conditions those who have applied for repatriation or who have indicated their loyalties lie with Japan must go to Tule Lake. The Tule Lake center corresponds closely to civilian internment camps in Japan and therefore are governed more closely by the Geneva Convention, Wolter continued. It must always be remembered that the relocation centers are only stop-over situations between residence in evacuated areas and residence in other parts of the United States.[180]

On December 9, the Butte and Canal Community Councils also issued warnings that residents must not proceed beyond the project fence without consent from the proper authorities. Residents were further warned that they must stay within the fence around the immediate community areas from sunset to sunrise.[181]

Coach Zenimura announced that his Butte ballplayers would rest for two months after the winter baseball season came to close. He anticipated an interesting spring season, with Herbert "Moon" Kurima from the Denson Center in Arkansas making a trip, and with hopes he had for a return trip and possibly a tour with the cream of local young ball players. He intended to increase the class of ball by arranging games with Caucasian teams from nearby towns.[182]

The Intra-Camp Championship series kicked off on Saturday, December 18, with Zeni's Block 28 ball club defeating Block 65 by the score of 9 to 3. The next day Block 28 defeated G 66 by the score of 5 to 3 to take the Inter-Camp Horsehide League's First-Four Playoff Championship. This put Block 28 finishing first in the league's regular schedule.[183]

The *Courier* followed-up the victory by showcasing the 14 members of Championship Block 28 ballclub. "Piloted by Zenimura, the champs are: Sab and Goro Yamada, Kenso and Kenshi Zenimura, George Matsuda, Sam and Bob Yamasaki (assistant coach), Min and Masato Kinoshita, Key Kobayashi, George (Tojo) Sakumoto, and Scotty Mizukami."[184] The *Courier* added that "Field 28 Ground Managers Zenimura and Harry Komatsu hope to level and complete the field by the time spring ball rolls around."[185]

During the two-month hiatus from a formal baseball league, Zeni and assistant grounds manager Komatsu looked forward to putting the final touches on the Block 28 ballfield.[186] With a break from baseball, Gila residents found their outlet for physical activity in the form of golf, football and basketball. For entertainment they watched movies. And it was appropriate for Zeni's Block 28 team, as the movie running the week after their championship game was *The Pride of the Yankees*, starring Gary Cooper as the great Lou Gehrig.[187] In fact, *The Pride of the Yankees* received the top honors from the Gilans as the best received movie of the year. The combination of a heart-warming story, a baseball background, and Gary Cooper in the title role proved to be just what they needed in a motion picture. In contrast, it was reported that residents did not care for Orson Welles' *Citizen Kane*. Some Rivers resident's "walked out well nigh en masse" during Welles' award-winning film.[188]

December also saw considerable progress on the construction of the Rivers Honor Roll monument being built by the U.S. servicemen's parents and relatives associations. According to Kenji Arima, advisor for the monument, the project was almost halfway done by the end of 1943. "The hardest part of the job will be the construction of the name plate which will contain more than 400 names when completed," stated Arima. Relatives of servicemen were asked to help build the monument.[189]

Weeks before Christmas the Butte block managers issued a statement that residents were strongly discouraged from the exchange of holiday gifts in the center. Toshio Konoshito, Central Block Manager, declared that the block managers felt that exchange of gifts under the limited income state of the evacuees was an unnecessary luxury.[190]

Despite the ban on holiday "luxuries," the end of the year brought a welcome Christmas gift from generous Americans outside the barbed wire. Out of nowhere 26 books and 22 magazines arrived at the Gila library. According to the *Courier*, behind the donation is "a story of democracy at work." Mrs. George Reid of Chicago became interested in Rivers after meeting Mr. and Mrs. Jiro Oishi, ex–Gilans. But she became more than just an interested bystander. She told the young members of the Children's Society of Christian Service about Rivers. They too became interested in Rivers, so much so that at their next church bazaar they baked cookies and sold them, bought children's books and magazines with the proceeds, and sent them to Mrs. Fred Shimizu who in turn passed them on to the Toy and Loan Department.[191]

Among the new books in the library was *Lou Gehrig—A Quiet Hero*, by Frank Graham. The *Courier* announced its arrival: "Boys take special notice: It's the book you've been waiting for! It's the story of a fellow, who by the toughest kinds of work brought luxuries for his parents, who had sacrificed everything, including the necessities of life to give Lou an education. It also related how he became the 'Pride of the Yankees!' Smooth an' super!"[192]

By the close of 1943, the population of Rivers, Arizona, decreased by 3,619 residents, from a high of 13,325 to 9,706. Some Gilans relocated to the north for work, some joined the military, and some tragically took their own lives. The greatest single drain on the centers' population came through the loyalty segregation which sent 1,915 residents of Gila River to Tule Lake.[193]

Camp Director Bennett stated that he believed "the most serious and difficult times have passed" and that many new and positive opportunities were in store for the year. With their first full year at Gila River in the books, it appears that Bennett was right. Kenichi Zenimura had his *Yamato-Damashii* (meaning "way of the samurai") put to the test at Gila River, and he passed."[194] His entire life had led to this very moment, place and time. Zenimura leveraged his experience, skills and passion to build a spectacular baseball diamond in the middle of the desert. Doing so he helped create a sense of normalcy and hope for the internees, and improve relations with those living outside the barbed wire. As he had done in the past, Zenimura used the game of baseball to break down barriers and build bridges between people of different racial, cultural and geographic backgrounds. Best of all, Zenimura's accomplishments of the past year were just a hint of great things to come.

6

A Taste of Freedom (1944)

"Imagine our joy in breathing the fresh air of freedom after being incarcerated for two and a half years on an Indian reservation."[1]
— Tets Furukawa, pitcher, Gila River Jr. All-Stars, 1944

The 1944 Season—The Player and Coach

Attitudes towards Japanese Americans were mixed in the Unites States during 1944. In January headlines announced that the War Department would open up the draft to include Nisei men.[2] Yet a week later, Arizona officials were forced to tighten security at Gila River and Poston and evacuees were forbidden to leave Japanese relocation centers after it was announced that U.S. servicemen were killed while prisoners of war in Japan. Directors at the centers said they received no threats and anticipated no trouble but believed precautions should be taken to avoid any incident which might occur should the Japanese appear in neighboring white communities. In essence, for their own protection no one inside either Arizona camp was permitted to leave.[3]

Reports from the front lines revealed a new tactic used by Japanese soldiers to offend the opposition — they disrespected the American pastime by shouting "Screw Babe Ruth" and "To Hell with Ruth." According to Staff Sgt. Jeremiah A. O'Leary, a Marine Corps combat correspondent, more than 30 Japanese soldiers lost their lives shouting disparaging sentiments about the great Bambino. Word eventually got to Babe Ruth in New York, who replied: "I hope every Jap that mentions my name gets shot — and to hell with all Japs anyway."[4]

Positive news surrounding the war included the release of a new War Relocation Authority (WRA) film, *Go for Broke*, about the courageous Nisei soldiers serving in the 442nd. Also, just as former baseball great Sam Rice had done a year earlier, the future poet laureate of America, Carl Sandburg, welcomed evacuees from Poston, Arizona, and Jerome, Arkansas, to work on his farm in Michigan.[5]

The start of the spring 1944 baseball season marked the first time that Butte High School would not field a baseball team. Instead, all of the top teenage players chose to play in Zenimura's Butte League. This decision was viewed by some as a lack of school spirit.

There was no organized baseball for the Butte High Eagles in 1944, but there was a highly organized league for anyone in the camp who wanted to play. As the commissioner of the Butte League, Zenimura developed the following rules for a three-division league, a C-league, B-league, and A-league for the top players, regardless of age.

For Ayes, Bees & Cees Rules for Intercamp-Circuit, 1944 Season

The more important rules among those laid down for the three organized leagues are hereon printed:

1. The time limit for games will be two hours and will end by deadline, 8:15 o'clock. Any inning started before the deadline must be finished, however.
2. Players are transferable but must have the consent of the managers of both teams involved, and also of a baseball board in charge.
3. Transferred player must sit on the bench for two games before he enters for his new team. If a "B" player plays 18 innings of a "A"-league competition, he becomes automatically an "A" player.

ARGUMENTS

4. Any protesting of games must be written and turned in within 24 hours to the board.
5. In time of argument, only managers and captains of the teams may iron things out with umpire(s) on the field.
    a. Sportsmanship is to be enforced and no profane language is to be used by players or coaches.
    b. All disputes to be settled in a sportsmanlike manner and all violations of above rules to be punished with banishment of player(s) or team(s) from all the leagues.

GROUND RULES

6. All batters are to remain in the dugouts except the batter and the two following.
7. Should any opposing player interfere with a catcher or infielder trying to catch a foul ball, the batter automatically becomes out.
8. Players' dugouts are for players only and are not to be used as cheering section.
9. Any ball caught outside the bench by the support of backstop or dugout is not legal. The ball is dead.
10. Two bases are entitled to batter when the batted ball hits on fair territory and rolls beyond the marked playing field. Another runner, also on base will be allowed two bases.
11. The above rule will apply also when the batter is given three bases. Batters are entitled three bases when the ball rolls over the field's ditch.
12. A home run is when the ball clears the field's banks.

(The above rules were laid down and released by Ken Zenimura, director, as designated at a managers' meeting recently. It covers the field 16, 28 and 58.)

More rules remaining from previously, laid down for the three inter-camp aye, bee and cee leagues, numbered follows:

1. No player or coach is to smoke on the playing field.
2. During the course of game, if a runner is injured a substitute may run for him for just that time without the injured player losing his playing eligibility.
3. Pitchers are allowed to throw only five warm-up balls during the beginning of every inning on the mound. After the five warm-up balls are thrown, the chief umpire will call "play ball." This rule must and will be enforced strictly so as to save time.
4. In no time is the pitcher to be allowed to call "time out" and stay to warm up during the course of the game.
5. The ground must be cleared thirty minutes before the game and the home team is to take infield practice first.[6]

With the rules in place, Paul Sumii was selected to enforce them as the Major League's chief umpire for all Butte games at Zenimura field. The 1944 season opened up with less pomp and circumstance than the inaugural year. There was no ceremonial first pitch thrown by the camp director.[7]

Zeni's Block 28 opened the new season just as they had closed it, with a victory. On Sunday, March 26, Block 28 battled the Block 65 Peppers in the opening game of the Butte League season. Zeni's boys were down 10–4 up until the fifth inning when they exploded with an eight-run outburst to eventually win the free-scoring contest 12–10.[8]

Despite the on-field win, the first financial statement of the season for the Block 28 vs. Block 65 tussle reflected a bottom-line loss of $3.38.[9] Compared to the previous season, the gate receipts continued on a downward trend week after week. Zeni expressed his frustrations in the sports section of the *Courier*. "Fans who don't give their gate donations to Butte "A" games make it tough to keep up the expenses of the league," asserted Zenimura. He added that that the "donations" may have to be changed to required "admissions" if the trend continues. According to Zeni, the two opening games' donations for 1944 were $22.18, approximately a third of the $65.21 recorded in 1943.[10]

Good news arrived in Gila River in April 1944 in the form of an invitation to participate in the Arizona State Semipro baseball tournament. Zenimura as the Butte CAS baseball director received a verbal invitation for a local Butte-Canal all-star team to compete in an Arizona State Tournament to be held in Phoenix on July 16–23.[11] A few days later the good news was downgraded to an "unofficial invitation" to participate in the tournament.[12] In response to a letter written by Zenimura for a local request to be invited, John H. Morris, state semipro baseball commissioner, wrote to Ken Zenimura that it would be taken up with the board of directors prior to the tourney. "I am quite sure," wrote Morris, "it will receive favorable action."[13]

But the Butte-Canal all-star baseball team did not receive an invitation to compete in the 1944 Arizona State Semipro baseball Tournament in July. No official reason or report explaining why has surfaced. The most likely scenario is that camp officials determined that it was still unsafe for Japanese Americans to travel into Phoenix. So instead, more teams from the outside traveled into the camps for games.

While the Arizona State Semipro baseball tournament was underway in Phoenix, Zenimura received another invitation to participate in a series of games. This one, however, was more than 1,000 miles away. Russ Hinaga, manager of the San Jose Zebras (formerly Asahis) from Heart Mountain, Wyoming, extended an invitation for an all-star Butte team to reciprocate the visit from the previous year. Some of the expenses were guaranteed to help defray the costs of traveling.[14] Until official clearance was given by camp officials, Zeni and his team would have to settle for games against visiting teams from the outside.

The first to visit Gila River in July 1944 was the Tucson Post Jr. American Legion baseball team. At a Fourth of July luncheon, Arthur L. Griswol, CAS director, announced that Tucson would make a two-day appearance over the weekend. The schedule called for a game between the Cards in Canal on Saturday night and to play in Butte on Sunday. The Tucson team was led by Manager Joe Hanson, Director of the American Legion Junior baseball program.[15]

Tucson Jr. Legion split the two games, defeating Canal All-Stars 7 to 3, and then losing to the Butte All-Stars, 11 to 0, in pitcher Mas Kinoshita's 4-hit shutout. "The visiting team took the defeat well," reported the *Courier*. "It is hoped Gila will be able to meet more outsiders in the field of sports."[16]

The next team to visit Gila was the Yankees from Poston. Led by manager Jimmy Fujita, the club scheduled seven games against opponents at the Butte and Canal camps. The Yankees won 3 and lost 4 during their stay at Gila River. Among those from Poston who made the 211 mile journey to the southeast were administrator Wumino, Kay Hanada,

Jay Nishida, brothers Maya and Chokichi Miyamoto, Harry Sakamoto, and Frank Tanaka.[17] Tanaka hit an impressive .371 in 10 games while playing in the Poston "A" League, while Maya Miyamoto hit .333, and Chokichi Miyamoto hit .313 in nine games.[18] Of their seven games, one loss was handed them by the Canal All-Stars and Zeni's Block 28 team provided two more. At the end of their visit, the Poston Yankees' coach Fujita lauded the sportsmanship of the team and fans at Gila. On behalf of the entire Poston team, he also extended his sincere gratitude to Block 28 and especially to Kenichi Zenimura.[19]

On August 6, a rematch was held between the Gila River teams and the Tucson Jr. American Legion Post team. The doubleheader began with a Cardinal All-Star nine at Canal in the morning, followed by a Block 28 pickup team in the evening.[20] The Tucson Jr. American Legion baseball team's second two-game series ended with a split. The Tucson boys lost to the Canal Cardinal All-Star nine in the morning, 13–4, but bounced back in the evening to edge the Block 28 squad, 5–4, behind the pitching of young star Lowell Bailey. A double, a couple of fielder's choices and a pair of first-inning errors proved to be the deciding factors in the victory of Tucson against Block 28.[21]

The next team that Zeni arranged to pay a visit to Gila River was the Japanese American squad from the Granada Relocation Camp in Amache, Colorado. On August 8, the WRA newspaper, *The Amache Pioneer*, reported that 14 players were making the 632 mile trip to Gila.[22] The Amache All-Stars were composed of practically all army selectees which accounted for the administration approval to travel.

Shortly before the Amache visit, Zenimura received an airmail letter completing the arrangements — if plans were approved by Project Director Leroy Bennett — for a trip by a Butte-Canal All-Star team to compete at Heart Mountain, Wyoming. Zenimura and Harry Kono of Canal decided that the trip to the Wyoming Center would have to come after the Amache series. Kono and Zenimura would select their Butte-Canal All-Star team at that time.[23]

Zenimura and Kono scheduled a departure for August 29 to leave for Heart Mountain. Unfortunately the Amache squad was delayed a few days in their trip to Gila River due to a suicide attempt at the Relocation Camp in Colorado.[24] The Amache series opened on August 19, giving the teams only 10 days to play.[25]

The Amache players included Jack Hoshizu, Tad Ono, Hideo Noda, Yonami Ono, Joe Nakatogawa, Tom Shimazu, Bob Shiro, George Watanabe, Masao (Lefty) Nishijima, Bob Umekubo and Mits Omoto, all in the selective service. Advisor Taka Kimura accompanied the group.

The Canal All-stars swept three games from the Amache visitors. The guests then battled the Butte Block 28 all-stars in the first of three games. Tak Abo pitched a near shutout game with a final score of 8–1 with Butte prevailing.[26] In game two, "old-man" Zeni pitched a two-hitter against the boys from Colorado. According to the *Gila News Courier*, "Zenimura had Amache completely buffaloed with his sharp hooks and drops Sunday evening, giving up only two hits and taking the second game of the Butte series 5–1. Southpaw Hideo Noda and Bob Umekubo shared mound duties for Amache, giving up five hits. Amache's lone run came in the second on a walk and a hit.[27] The victory in the second game of the Butte-Amache series also featured "the shortest half-inning in Rivers baseball history.... Ken Zenimura retired the opposing batters with only four pitched balls." The *Courier* sports editors declared in amazement afterwards, "What we can't understand is how the extra pitch got in there."[28]

The results were the same for game three. Butte took its third and deciding game of the Amache series, 6–0. Abo scattered four hits and received excellent support out on the field from second-baseman Kenso Zenimura to secure a shutout. The Butte batters scattered seven hits against Amache pitcher Smokey Kimura. The highlights included two triples by Roy Nakamura, and a triple for both Key Kobayashi and Kenshi Zenimura.[29]

The Amache visit concluded with a two-game series against a combined Butte-Canal All-Stars contingency. The local all-stars swept its series with Amache 11–2 and 11–5. This particular series also marked the first time during their internment experience that all three Zenimura men contributed equally on the field of victory. As each inning passes at Gila River, we begin to see Kenso and Kenshi develop physically as ballplayers, while their father passes on the wisdom gained from playing, coaching and managing for decades.

With the Amache series in the books, Coach Zenimura made the final arrangements for the trip to Heart Mountain. In an effort to keep a low profile while on the road it was decided that the team of 14 players would split up and travel in two groups. The first group would leave on Monday, August 28, and the second on Tuesday, August 29. According to the *Courier:*

> Since many of the regular All-Stars selections could not make the trip, the group will be known as the Gila Junior All-Stars. The group is playing an abbreviated schedule of its proposed plans in order to enable its members to be back in time for the opening of school. Three adults are making the trip. Ken Zenimura is going as player-coach, Harry Kono as manager, and Tom Osada as treasurer-adviser. Arrangements have been made with Zenimura to wire scores of the games as soon as they are played so that Gilans may be able to know how the team is faring in the series. The Junior All-Stars are a youthful group, averaging 18 years not counting (coach) Zenimura. The oldest is Tom Murata who is 24, and the youngest is Harvey Zenimura who is 15. The following are the players who will make the Heart Mountain trip:[30]
>
> **1944 Gila Junior All-Stars**
> Kenichiro Zenimura — Pitcher/catcher-Coach
> Tom Murata — Catcher
> Key Kobayashi — LF
> Kay Ishimoto — 3B
> Toshio Nishino — 3B
> Howard Zenimura — 2B
> Harvey Zenimura — CF
> Ralph Osada — SS
> George Fujioka — Pitcher
> Takoshi Abo — Pitcher
> Tets Furukawa — 1B
> Tets Hasegawa — RF
> Kazuo Mizukami — Catcher

To ensure that the Jr. All-Stars were sharp upon arrival after the 20-plus hour and 1,200 mile trip to Wyoming, Zenimura scheduled a two-game series over the weekend with an all-star aggregation collected among the remaining ball players at Gila River. The games were also viewed as a farewell sendoff prior to the departure to Heart Mountain.[31]

According to pitcher Tets Furukawa, "boarding the Sante Fe Trailways bus at Phoenix and journeying forth was exciting to say the least. Imagine our joy in breathing the fresh air of freedom after being incarcerated for two and a half years on an Indian reservation."[32]

Years later Furukawa recalled, "We were divided into two group so as not to attract unnecessary attention. However, along the way we were accosted by whites who confronted us with derogatory remarks. We tactfully answered by explaining that we were just heading

Kenichi Zenimura and Russell Hinaga arranged to have a team from Gila River visit Heart Mountain, Wyoming, for an inter-camp series. With the older players unavailable for the tour, Zenimua recruited 14 young players, average age 18, to form the Gila Junior All-Stars. They made the 1,200 mile trip to Wyoming in September 1944. Pitcher Tets Furukawa (top row, fourth from right) said, "The Heart Mountain team ... got the impression that because we were young they would kick our ass. They got overconfident" (Nisei Baseball Research Project).

north to aid in the war effort by helping the potato and sugar beet harvest. This seemed to be a legitimate reason to defuse a potential crisis. I believe that coach Zenimura had our 'work permits' stashed away in his brief case."[33]

According to Japanese American baseball historian Kerry Yo Nakagawa, the travelers had another tactic to avoid trouble on the road. Gila Camp officials approved the trip to Heart Mountain under the condition that the young men wear their baseball uniforms while en route. As "so-called enemy aliens," the probability of trouble, and perhaps being arrested, would be increased if they wore civilian clothes.[34]

All covert efforts worked. The Gila players arrived safely on Wednesday and Thursday after their long journey. The boys were given time to practice on Friday, September 1, to work out their tired legs and regain their timing at the plate.

Takoshi (Tak) Abo of Fresno was in his early 20s and originally went to Jerome and then transferred to Gila River to be with friends and family. He was an all-round athlete who excelled in basketball on the Olympic Club team as well. Player Tets Furukawa recalls, "The Heart Mountain team was a lot older than Gila River and when we arrived on our first day ... they watched us practice and just by looking at us got the impression that because we were young they would kick our ass. They got overconfident."[35]

Between the reports in the *Heart Mountain Sentinel* and the summaries of telegrams sent back home by Harry Kono and printed in the *Gila News Courier*, the Gila River–Heart Mountain series is one of the best-documented contests in all of Japanese American internment camp baseball history. This depth of coverage offers a much deeper glimpse into life

Zenimura and his boys from Gila River won the Heart Mountain series, 9 games to 4. Unanimous choice as MVP for Heart Mountain was second-baseman Mori Shimada (back row, far left) who delivered two game-winning hits for the Zebras (Zenimura Family Archive).

and play during this period. For this reason, the space devoted to the series is far more substantial than for other games.

Best-of-Seven Series

The first series was a best of seven scheduled with the Gila boys taking on several individual teams from the Heart Mountain league. Daily the Gila squad battled the high altitude as much as the fresh legs of their new opponents, and that made the game results even more meaningful.

Saturday, Sept. 2, 1944—GAME 1: "Visitors Rout Ayes in Opener"

Coach Kenichi Zenimura's Gila all-stars displayed a powerful offensive as they subdued the Zebra Ayes, 7–3, before a capacity crowd of approximately 3,000 fans. The Gila batters pounced on the pitches of Billy Shundo for 12 hits. The Gila players drew first blood in the second inning when right-fielder George Fujioka smacked a sharp double over the shortstop's head to drive in Kay Ishimoto who was on base by virtue of a single. "The local champs took the lead in their half when George Shiraki pounded a round tripper to score Shundo ahead of him. The visitors came back in the third with three more runs on safe blows by second sacker Howard Zenimura, catcher Zenimura and Ishimoto and a Zebra error. Two more runs crossed the plate in the fourth on two errors and Howard Zenimura's second hit and a double by Ishimoto. Hits by Tak Sugiyama and Chi Akizuki accounted for the third Zebra tally."[36] The Heart Mountain batters were silenced the remaining four innings.

PLAYER PERSPECTIVE — KEY KOBAYASHI JOURNAL:

> Everyone arrived here safe and sound ... lady luck with us so far.... First game with Heart Mountain champions, the Zebra Ayes, Saturday, Sept. 2 ... quite a crowd to watch our first game.... Tak Abo started.... Zenimura behind the plate.... While Billy Shundo and Norman Yasui formed the battery for the Zebra Ayes. Abo allowed 6 hits and 3 runs with errorless defense.... Gila JAS's pounced on Shundo for 13 hits, 7 runs and stole 10 bases besides Zebra's 8 miscues. Zebra's leading by score of 2–1 ... top of 3rd inning the Gila JAS's bunched 4 hits and stole 4 bases to score 3 runs to acquire the lead to the final score of 7–3.[37]

Sunday, Sept. 3, 1944 — GAME 2: "Gilans Cop 10–7 Tilt in Eleventh"

A three-run barrage in the 11th inning gave the Gila all-stars a 10–7 victory over the Zebra Bees in the second game of the series. They held a comfortable 7–3 lead until the hectic seventh inning when Roy Suzuki, Rosie Matsui, Babe Namura and George Ishitani came through with base hits and three runs. In the eighth inning Frank Shiraki's double and a single by Russ Hinaga and Matsui brought in two more runs, tying the count at 7-all. After two scoreless innings, "the Gilans spiked the rubber three times in the 11th on a two bagger by Harvey Zenimura aided by a pair of Bee miscues. Shortstop Tosh Nishino sparked his mates at the plate with two doubles and two singles in four trips. Howard Zenimura, keystone sacker, followed with a triple, double and a single, while Kay Ishimoto hit three for five. In all, the Gilans garnered 19 blows."[38]

PLAYER PERSPECTIVE — KEY KOBAYASHI JOURNAL:

> The second game was against the Zebra Bees ... closest and most exciting game to date.... Lefty Fujioka and Ken Zenimura were the Gila JAS battery, while "old reliable" Russ Hinaga, and Frank Shiraki formed the Zebra Bee's battery ... composed mostly of old timers including players like Rosie Matsui, Babe Nomura and Russ Hinaga who made the trip to Gila last year ... managed to grab a early lead of 3 runs in the second ... started last half of 7th ... seemingly safe lead of 7–2 ... bats of Zebra's caught Lefty's slants for 4 hits and 3 runs ... Abo relieved Lefty ... 1st batter struck out, next batter tripled ... third batter issued a base on balls.... Russ laid down a perfect bunt that took the first baseman off base ... runner scores sending other to third.... Rosie Matsui came thru ... score tied with one away and runners on first and second.... Babe Nomura, hard-hitting left handed batter hit into a double play.... Ralph Osada stepped on second ... threw to first ... ninth and tenth inning both sides failed to score ... remained a tie.... Kenso Zenimura started the rally in the 11th by tripling.... Tets Furukawa grounded out.... Ken Zenimura hit by pitched ball.... Kay Ishimoto duck to avoid wild pitched ball ... hit measly grounder towards first ... the first baseman came in fast ... throw wide of the home plate.... Kenso scores. Kenshi pop up.... Tets Hasegawa hit a line drive on 2–2 count ... 2 more score.... Zebra Bees shocked and demoralized ... easily retired ... final score 10–7.... Gila JAS's have red letter day at the plate getting 20 hits.... Zebras got 13 hits."[39]

Heart Mountain Sentinel sports writer George Yoshinaga added,

> These two games proved to be as thrilling as could be expected. The Bee game was the longest ever played in Heart Mountain, the tilt going a full 11 frames before the Gilans edged out a 10–

7 win over the weary Bees. Russ Hinaga hurled the entire games for the oldsters, a remarkable feat considering his age. Another veteran performing in the series is Kenichi Zenimura, catcher of the Gilans. Zenny, who is more on in years than the great Hinaga, has caught all the games thus far. His regular backstopper is expected to arrive here for the All-Star series.

Tak Abo of the Gilans has so far proved to be the iron man as well as the wild man, turning back the Zebra Ayes with six hits last Saturday and returning in the relief role on Sunday to stop the Bees.[40]

Monday, Sept. 4, 1944 — GAME 3: "All-Stars Take Third Game, 5–3"

Although they outhit Gila River, 5–4, the Amateurs suffered a 5–3 defeat as the Gila all-stars garnered their third victory of the series. A base hit by Tets Furukawa and an error paved the way for the first Gila tally in the initial inning. The Amateurs made it one-all in their half when center-fielder Yuso Yasuhara singled to right field, scoring Chesty Okagaki, who landed on base via a free pass. "After five scoreless innings, the Gilans pushed across two runs in the seventh on a walk, a double by George Yamada and a line drive hit by short-stop Tosh Nishino. Two consecutive walks and an error accounted for two more runs in the eighth stanza to put the game on ice for the Gilans. Two errors and Fuzzy Shimada's two-bagger added two more runs to the Amateur scoring column, but their rally was two runs shy tieing the game."[41] The battery of pitcher Lefty Fujioka and "old-man" Zenimura went the entire distance in the Gila victory.

Player Perspective — Key Kobayashi Journal:

> The third game against the Amateurs Monday afternoon.... Lefty Fujioka on mound ... Zenimura catching.... Amateurs' George Isari toed the plate and Fuzzy Shimada donned the mask ... started even, for both sides scored ... 1–1 all the way to the 7th inning.... Goro Yamada tripled.... Tak Abo batting for Ralph earned a base on balls.... Tosh Nishino, pinch hitting for Tets H. connected with a 2 bagger ... inside third base by inches ... 2 runs scored ... in top of 8th, 2 walks and 2 errors enabled Gila JAS to score 2 more runs.... Amateur came back strong ... scored 2 runs on 2 hits and 1 error ... last half of ninth, with 2 outs Isori hit a double ... next batter hit by pitched ball.... "Ghosty" Okagaki, lead off man hit was grounder to Tosh Nishino ... throws wild ... runner advancing to 2nd went on to third with another man on base ... man on third, seeing runner, dashed for home ... meantime Tets threw to second.... Kenso threw home to put out final out. Again ... fortunate enough to eke out victorious by staving off a last inning rally ... don't see how we're going to keep having good luck. Tomorrow's game ... with Blk. 20 ... final game with individual teams ... then we face all-star teams ... keeping our fingers crossed in meantime and will try as hard as we can to win all the games we can.... Enjoying attitude (sic, altitude?) up here but miss the Arizona sunshine.[42]

The Heart Mountain Amateurs "were the surprise team of the week, coming the closest to dumping the Gilans," wrote *Heart Mountain Sentinel* sports writer George Yoshinaga. "A mixup on signals at third base robbed them of victory. On the particular play, the runner on second base advanced to third, but the man on third held his base and was caught at home after being forced off the bag." Yoshinaga was also impressed with the speed of the Gila River players. "The remarkable basestealing ability of the Zenimura men have bothered the local moundsmen a great deal. Kay Ishimoto pulled the best steal thus far in the series, when he sneaked home on the Zebra Bee game. So far the Gilans have stolen a total of 20 bases."[43]

Tuesday, Sept. 5, 1944 — GAME 4: "Abo Hurls Mates to 5–1 Triumph"

The Gila Junior All-Stars added its fourth consecutive victory as it routed the Block 20 team, 5–1. The Gilans grabbed an early lead, scoring a run in the second inning on a free pass, an error and a hit by left-fielder Harvey Zenimura. After a scoreless third frame, the Gila team came back in the fourth inning with another run on hits by Takeshi Abo and Zenimura, his second hit. An error and three consecutive hits paved the way for three tallies in the eighth inning. The Block 20 lone run came in the seventh inning "when Min Horino scored on Keso Osumi's two bagger which spoiled Abo's shut-out performance. Harvey Zenimura led the winners' offensive with three hits in four trips to the platter. Osami, first sacker, collected two of the six hits off Abo to spark the Block 20 attack."[44]

PLAYER PERSPECTIVE — KEY KOBAYASHI JOURNAL:

> September 6, 1944.... Sending results of fourth game against Blk. 20.... Abo went the route ... permitted 6 "measly" hits ... we got hold of curveball specialist, Texio Watambe for 8 hits ... aided by 9 errors ... our "Go For Broke" baserunning rattle their fielders.... Abo struck out 8 batters ... hit triple and single himself ... crazy base running ... nothing can beat Kay Ishimoto's running ... second game stole home on Russ Hinaga ... upset pitching.... Yesterday's game Kay started stealing second while pitcher had ball ... by luck managed to reach 1st safely after being trapped ... stole second ... wild peg to center field ... scored when center field bobbled ball all the way from first ... fans stunned by daring base running ... rattled pitcher to allow 2 succeeding hits ... 2 more runs made final score 5–1.[45]
>
> Enjoying day's rest before we take on combined teams.... Zebra Ayes combined with Amateurs.... Zebra Bees and Block 20.... Saturday, begin 3 out of 5 games series ... Heart Mountain All Stars. Idea of how we spend each day ... staying in 7 beam apartment ... 17 cots ... a coal stove ... profane language ... fine 10 cents ... set 11 o'clock curfew for players. Fellows pretty tired from 4 games ... high altitude makes it hard for breathing ... pant to catch our breath when we run to second ... all players fine just tired.... Key Kobayashi.[46]

After Zenimura's boys swept the individual squads in four straight victories, it was agreed that Heart Mountain would combine the best players from each team to assemble an all-star aggregation to take on the mighty boys from Gila River.

All-Star Series — Best-of-Seven Games

The series began with the Gila players competing against an all-star team with players from the Zebra Ayes and the Amateurs. The second game of the series combined players from the Zebra Bee and Block 20 teams. The remainder of the all-star games were composed of players pulled from all four teams. This is noteworthy because the Gila all-atars were still playing basically fresh teams until game four of the series.

Thursday, Sept. 7, 1944 — GAME 5: "Aye-Amateurs Trounced 11–2"

Handing the Zebra Aye-Amateur combination the worst shellacking since arriving in Heart Mountain, the Gila all-stars made it five games in a row with an 11–2 win. In the first inning Howard Zenimura walked and scored from third on an error. In the fifth inning the Gila players "pushed across two more runs after left fielder Key Kobayashi got life on a fielder's choice. A hit by Howard Zenimura scored Kobayashi and an error brought Zenimura across the plate. The sixth frame saw the Gilans bunch three hits with an error to add two more tallies. In their half the Aye Amateurs scored their two runs on two hits and a walk. The Gilans kept up their barrage, scoring three each in the seventh and final innings."

The *Gila News Courier* posted results back home. " Zeni (at catcher) started one of the neatest double plays ... bases loaded with 1 out ... signal for pitch ... whipped ball to second base ... Kenso chased runner to third to tag out ... trapped base-runner between third and home for 3rd out."[47]

Friday, Sept. 8, 1944 — GAME 6: "Gilans Capture Sixth Game, 5–4"

A three-run rally in the ninth inning gave Zeni's players a 5–4 victory over the combined Zebra Bee, Block 20 aggregation for the sixth consecutive triumph of their trip. The aggregate Heart Mountain team took the lead in the fourth inning by scoring two runs on hits by Min Horino and Tosh Asano. "After George Yamada came in on Tets Furukawa's single in the fifth, the Gilans tied the count in the eighth frame when Kay Ishimoto doubled scoring Howard Zenimura. The Hinagamen regained their half with a run on Babe Nomura's two bagger and Min Horino's second hit of the game. The Gilans clinched the game in the ninth with three runs denting the plate on three hits and an error, although Asano scored for the losers in their half after tripling to left field." Zeni started on the mound but was injured midway through the third inning when Heart Mountain's Snooks Kaato hit a line drive off Zeni's knee. Initially it was thought that Zeni suffered a broken patella (knee cap), but it was just a deep bruise. "George Fujioka was credited with the triumph. Russ Hinaga was charged with the defeat. Howard Zenimura and Kay Ishimoto shared batting honors with three hits apiece, while Asano connected for a triple and two singles for the locals."[48]

Saturday, Sept. 9, 1944 — GAME 7: "Shimada Sparks Locals to 5–4 Win"

In the first game with an aggregate of stars from four teams, Heart Mountain finally attained a victory. Mori Shimada was the hero of the day when he hammered out a triple to left field with two runners on the bases in the final inning. Shimada's timely shot gave the Heart Mountain all-stars their first victory in the series, 5–4. Heart Mountain pitcher Texie Watanabe had a shutout going into the seventh inning when Gila connected for three runs. George Iseri relieved Watanabe in the ninth inning, giving up one hit and one run. Tak Ikeda, Heart Mountain third baseman, swung the biggest bat of the day, going 3-for-6 at the plate. Shimada wrapped two triples in five at-bats. Gila pitcher Tak Abo suffered his first defeat of the series, while Iseri became the first Heart Mountain twirler to record a victory.[49]

Sunday, Sept. 10, 1944 — GAME 8: "Iseri Captures Second Tilt, 3–2"

The Heart Mountain all-stars made it two in a row when they defeated the Gila players, 3–2. It was pitcher George Iseri's second win of the series. The game was tied 1–1 going into the sixth inning when coach Russ Hinaga's ballclub staged a two-run rally on two Gila errors and Mori Shimada's second hit of the day. The Gilans were held scoreless until the eighth inning when slugger Tak Abo pounded a solo homer to center field. But the round-tripper was too little, too late. Pitcher Iseri aided his own effort with two hits. Kay Ishimoto collected two hits to lead the Gila bats in the loss.[50] Murata filled in as catcher while Coach Zenimura enjoyed another day off to rehab his injury suffered in the Friday afternoon game.

Monday, Sept. 11, 1944 — GAME 9: "Gila Nine Nabs 15–9 Slugfest"

"A comedy of errors paved way for the Gilans' first victory in the all-star series as they trounced the local horsehiders, 15–9."[51] After resting his injured knee, Coach Zenimura returned to the lineup to catch starter Tak Abo and reliever Lefty Fujioka. The two hurlers combined for eight innings, as the game was called due to darkness. John Santo started on the hill for Hinaga's club. Gila took a 5–0 lead in the first inning with three Heart Mountain errors and a hit by George Yamada. Zenimura's boys scored three more runs in the fourth inning behind the bats of Yamada, Ralph Osada, Howard Zenimura and Kay Ishimoto. Gila scored five more runs in the fifth inning, resulting from a combination of errors, walks and several hits by Tets Furukawa and Tak Abo off reliever Billy Shundo. Abo led the Gila hitting attack going 3-for-5 with a single and two doubles.[52]

Wednesday, Sept. 13, 1944 — GAME 10: "Hinaga Hurls 6–0 Shutout Win"

Following a day off on Tuesday, veteran Russell Hinaga hurled the first shutout game of the series as he blanked the Gilans, 6–0, for the Heart Mountain all-stars' third victory.

"The good people of Heart Mountain extended to the Gila team a warm welcome and home-run hospitality," said pitcher Tets Furukawa. Among those good people were Mr. and Mrs. Saburo Sugita, lifelong friends of Kenichi Zenimura's from Honolulu (Tets Furukawa).

Two Japanese American baseball pioneers, San Jose's Russ Hinaga and Fresno's Kenichi Zenimura, pose for a photograph at Heart Mountain in 1944. Hinaga's Asahi team toured Japan in 1925, and in 1935 he became a legend in Nisei baseball history when his late-inning single drove in the game winner against the visiting Tokyo Giants (Zenimura Family Archive).

"Chucker Hinaga yielded only four scattered hits as his mates pounded the deliveries of Tak Abo and Kenichi Zenimura for seven hits and six runs," reported the camp press. Zeni relieved Abo in the third inning, surrendering six hits and two runs for the remainder of the day. With Zeni on the mound, Hinaga singled and scored on Chi Akisuki's double. Heart Mountain's final run occurred when Fuzzy Shimada's tripled and scored on Tak Ikeda's two-bagger. Nicknamed the "war horse" by his Heart Mountain teammates, Hinaga's shutout was his first victory during the Gila series and Tak Abo's second defeat.[53]

Thursday, Sept. 14, 1944 — GAME 11: "Fujioka Tames Local Stars, 6–3"

Pounding the offering of Texio Watanabe for 9 hits and 6 runs, the Gila all-stars put the finishing touches on the series with a 6–3 triumph over Heart Mountain. "The Gilans went right to work on Watanabe in the first frame as Key Kobayashi walked, Howard Zenimura sacrificed and Tak Abo singled sharply to right field, scoring Kobayashi. The next few frames were listless as Lefty George Fujioka, Gila hurler, and Watanabe silenced the batsmen with their deliveries. In the sixth stanza Gila broke loose another barrage of blows, tallying three times on two hits and an error. The Gilans scored twice in the seventh on two hits. In the eighth and final innings Gila failed to score, but the Heart Mountain all-stars came to life." With bases loaded and two down for Heart Mountain, Babe Nomura doubled to center field, driving in their first two runs of the day. The final Heart Mountain run came in the ninth. With one down Fuzzy Shimada singled to left. Watanabe then drive in Shimada with a sharp line drive into left field.[54]

The results of the games during the best-of-seven series between Gila River and the Heart Mountain all-stars show that the contests were a better match of talent. Zenimura's ballclub ultimately won the series, four games to three, however the Heart Mountain boys demonstrated a lot of passion, ability and sportsmanship on the field.

There were fond memories off the field, too. Pitcher Tets Furukawa recalls how on their day off in Heart Mountain, he and a few other Gila River teammates were welcomed as special guests into the barracks of Frank Ito, a pharmacist from Guadalupe, California. Ito was assigned to Heart Mountain because he was a medical professional and each camp needed specialists in each area of medical expertise. A former ballplayer himself, a catcher for the Stockton Yamatos, Ito was kind enough to invite Furukawa, Tom Murata and Tets Hasegawa for a steak dinner with his family.[55]

Coaches Zenimura and Hinaga agreed to conclude the Gila River visit with a weekend series, a game Saturday against the combined squad of Heart Mountain's Zebra Aye and Block 20 teams, and a contest on Sunday against the San Jose Asahi veterans.

Saturday, Sept. 16, 1944 — GAME 12: "Local Nine Wins 5–4 in Eleventh"

A combined Zebra Aye-Block 20 team scored an 11-inning, 5–4 victory over the Gila players in the fourth triumph for Heart Mountain since the Gila River players had arrived. "Left fielder Texie Watanabe started the fireworks for the local nine in the opening inning with a smashing triple to deep right field, scoring Tak Ikeda and Norman Yasui. The Gilans opened their offensive in the second inning. Kenichi Zenimura was hit by a pitched ball and stole second base. Bespectacled George Yamada pounded the pellet to right field, driving in Zenimura for the first Gila score." Left-handed hitter Tets Furukawa belted a triple to right field to start the fifth inning. Furukawa scored on Kenso Zenimura's single giving Gila a 2–1 lead. Both sides went scoreless for seven innings until the ninth inning when George Shiraki scored on Chi Akizuki's triple. Like prize fighters going toe-to-toe, the Gilans battled back to take a 3–2 lead in the top of the tenth. Kay Ishimoto hit a triple to left center and then scored on an error. In the bottom of the tenth inning the Heart Mountain boys tied the game, 4–4, when Tak Ikeda singled to right and drive in Texie Watanabe. The final and decisive run came in the eleventh inning when Billy Shundo tripled to center and then scored on Mori Shimada's sacrifice fly to center. A second game against the combo squad was called in the third inning due to a dust storm.[56]

Sunday, Sept. 17, 1944—GAME 13: "Fujioka Blanks Locals, 8–0, in Finale"

In the final game at Heart Mountain, George "Lefty" Fujioka held the San Jose Asahi veterans to three hits in an 8–0 shutout victory. "Fujioka was in rare form as he allowed only four San Jose batters to reach base," reported the camp press. Zenimura's ballclub pounded pitcher Russ Hinaga for 14 hits, eight of which came in the first two innings. Hitting leadoff, Kenso Zenimura drive a triple to left field and then scored on Kenichi Zenimura's sacrifice fly to deep right field. Gila's southpaw Fujioka was credited with seven strikeouts, three of them in the final frame of the contest. Kenso Zenimura and Tak Abo led the Gila attack, both recording a 3-for-5 day at the plate.[57]

With the series complete and Gila River taking nine games to Heart Mountain's four, it was time for post-game analysis and awards. Ted Yano, a sports reporter for the *Heart Mountain Sentinel*, first honored Coach Zenimura with a career retrospective:

> Kenichi Zenimura, Gila's genial coach, who often sees service behind the plate or on the mound, is regarded as one of the all-time greats in Nisei athletic circles. To mention all of his achievements would be impossible in the little space we have, but we feel a few of his outstanding feats should be recorded. "Zeny" began his diamond career by cavorting at shortstop for the all–Nisei Fresno nine, which toured the Orient in 1924 and 1927. In one of the trips, the team scored nine consecutive victories over major universities. While performing for the Fresno outfit, Zenny played against such notable baseball headliners as Tony Lazzeri, famed Yankee veteran; Lefty O'Doul, SF Seal manager; Oscar Vitt (3b, Salt Lake City Bees, 1924, hit .238 in 10-year MLB career), Ray Fredricks (of, SLC Bees, 1924, hit .308 in six seasons) and Duffy Lewis. He was also chief mentor of Harry Kono's Alameda baseballers, who barnstormed the Orient in 1931 and 1937. Later he organized the Asahi semipro baseball team in Hawaii.[58]

Yano also paid tribute to their local hero, veteran Russell Noboru Hinaga. "(He) added another outstanding feat to his brilliant baseball career when he hurled a four-hit shutout victory against the Gilans last Tuesday." Yano featured other stars from the series: "Kay Ishimoto, who cavorts at third base or right field for the Gilans was selected on the 1943 Tule Lake all-star nine along with Tak Ikeda of the Block 20 outfit. Ishimoto performed with the Cal Aggie horsehiders in Davis before evacuation.... Al Fako (sp? Sako), newly appointed athletic director here (at Heart Mountain) has the distinction of being the first Nisei pitcher to defeat a Coast league team in 1923 when he played with Zenimura on the Fresno nine."[59]

Yano did not stop with the tributes and recaps. He also included what he called "dugout gossip." "According to the Gila players, their scorekeeper is lenient in recording of hits," wrote Yano. "On many occasions, hits that were awarded batters may well have been recorded as errors instead of too hot to handle."[60]

Box-score controversies aside, the Gilans outperformed the Heart Mountain ball club. According to a poll conducted by the *Sentinel* sports staff, Kenshi "Harvey" Zenimura and Tak "George" Abo emerged as the most outstanding Gila players of the 13-game series. The Gilans in turn selected Mori Shimada as the most outstanding player of the local teams. According to the *Sentinel*,

> (Kenshi) Zenimura's talent in cavorting at either left field or first base leaves no doubt as to his selection. During his performance on the local diamond, Harvey played errorless ball. His efforts with the hickory stick were also a big factor in Gila's nine victories. He batted .315 for the series. Incidentally, Harvey, 15, is the youngest member of the Gila team. Abo, chunky hurler and right fielder, finished in dead heat with Zenimura. Abo, who is often found in the clean-up spot of the batting order, captured the hitting honors for the Gilans with a .450 mark. His brilliant moundwork baffled many of the locals' heavy bat wielders. His leg injury hampered his performance in the last few games of the series.[61]
>
> Mori Shimada, Zebra second sacker, was the unanimous choice of the Gilans. He was the mainstay of the local all-star nine. On two occasions, Shimada came through in the pinches to win the games for the local twinks. He also turned in some fancy fielding at second base. Others who received mention were Howard and Kenichi Zenimura and Kay Ishimoto. Tak Ikeda was runner up for local honors, while Babe Nomura and Fuzzy Shimada followed close behind.[62]

One other Heart Mountain player not named by the *Sentinel* who received special praise from Coach Zenimura was George Iseri. The young pitcher was the only Heart Mountain hurler to win two games versus Gila River. After the tournament Zeni said, "I wish I had a pitcher like Iseri on our team."[63]

For safety purposes on the return trip, the team continued with its plan to travel in two groups, with the second group to arrive in Gila River on September 22.[64] Before their buses pulled away, Gila team members received one final gift—a souvenir towel with the words "Heart Mountain" embroidered on it. The gift was from some female friends of Key Kobayashi from the Alameda/Oakland, California, area who were relocated to Wyoming.[65]

In the September 21 issue of the *Heart Mountain Sentinel* a note of gratitude appeared from Manager Kono, Coach Zenimura, and Adviser Osada. It officially ended the chapter on one of the most uplifting baseball experiences for Zenimura and his Gila River ball club during their wartime incarceration.

Years later pitcher Tets Furukawa reflected on their visit to Wyoming. "All the good people of Heart Mountain extended to the Gila team a warm welcome and home-run hospitality. The royal treatment was accorded the visiting team with banquets, special parties and dance socials. Families invited players over for dinner at the barrack homes for an enjoyable evening topped with gifts. What priceless memories many of us who were a part of this experience have been left with to savor, so that when future generations ask, 'How was it done?' we have this baseball story to tell, as part of our historical legacy."[66]

For Furukawa, he was fortunate to have even made the trip. He was in the "minor leagues" in '43 to '44, playing for Lompoc in the Butte Camp. When the Lompoc ballclub folded in 1944, Coach Zenimura invited Furukawa and Tets Hasegawa to join the Butte all-stars. Furukawa, primarily an infielder, fondly recalls how Zenimura turned him into a solid pitcher. He especially remembers the countless hours of working with Zeni to perfect his pick-off move to first and hold runners on base.[67]

When Furukawa thinks of Zenimura, he recalls a good baseball mind and an even better human being. "On the field he was real stern and firm. He never cursed though.

There was no goofing off for the players. We ran laps around the field every day. Running was key. He showed us how to run bases, how to steal, round the bases (and by the way, he ran with us too). He would begin every game with the team huddled up in the outfield past first base.... He would get in the center, give a pep talk, go over the signs, get everyone fired up for the game."[68] According to Furukawa, there was more to Zenimura than just baseball. "Coach Zeni ... indeed possessed a tremendous knowledge of baseball savvy, but above all, he wanted every player to become a better human being by realizing his responsibility and compassion for his fellow man."[69]

The return from Heart Mountain marked the end of the 1944 baseball season at Gila River. Just like other towns across the U.S., Labor Day holiday meant that football season was about to kick off at Gila.

* * *

The Japanese American struggle for a place in the U.S. was a dominant theme at the end of 1944. In October, WRA director Dillon Myers was reported to have said on behalf of all Japanese Americans that he understood that "Americanism (was) a matter of mind and heart."[70] An editorial in the *Gila News Courier* observed that members of the 442nd were "fighting, not to kill, but for a place in this country."[71]

Persons of Japanese ancestry were not only dying on the front lines of the war, they were dying in the camps as well. According to an October 12 report in the *Gila News Courier*, "more than 1,000 Japanese internees in America, Canada, Australia and India" have died since January 1944.[72]

Virtually all politicians believed that the internment of Japanese Americans was a wartime necessity, except one. During his stump speeches for president of the United States in the 1944 election campaign, socialist candidate Norman Thomas said what an investigative committee and President Ronald Reagan would say in the 1980s: "It was 'greed and land' at the heart of the decision for Japanese American internment."

In a speech before the San Francisco Club on Sept 26, 1944, Thomas declared that Californians who oppose the return of the Japanese Americans to their homes in California—"Legally, if possible, illegally, if necessary"—do not believe in democracy. Thomas said the flareup of "racism" against the California-born Japanese is "a far greater danger to American liberty in general than to the Japanese Americans in particular." He stated that "[w]hat was done on the west coast was, as Justice Murphy admitted, painfully similar to the German treatment of the Jews." Thomas insisted that "greed for the land made fertile by Japanese skill and labor was partly at the bottom of the herding of these American citizens into concentration camps." He argued that if military necessity dictated the treatment accorded them, they should be paid damages for what was done to them, "just as we give property owners damage for things done to their property under military necessity."[73]

Thomas's position was supported by author Carey McWilliams, whose book, *Prejudice—Japanese Americans: Symbol of Racial Intolerance,* arrived in the Gila River library in October 1944.[74] According to a review by Leonard Bloom, McWilliams did an outstanding job in his book detailing all of the forces, agencies and persons responsible (especially General DeWitt) for the unnecessary evacuation of Japanese Americans.[75]

The dark veil of racism in organized baseball began to lift in 1944 when baseball commissioner Kenesaw Mountain Landis died on November 25. Landis perpetuated the color line and prolonged the segregation of organized baseball. His successor, Happy Chandler, said, "For twenty-four years Judge Landis wouldn't let a black man play. I had his records, and I read them, and for twenty-four years Landis consistently blocked any attempts to put blacks and whites together on a big league field."[76] Owner Bill Veeck claimed Landis stopped him from purchasing the Phillies when Landis learned of Veeck's plan to integrate the team. The signing of the first black ballplayer in the modern era, Jackie Robinson, came less than a year after Landis's death.[77]

The closing of 1944 provided an opportunity to reflect on the highlights from the previous season. Relocation teams from Poston, Arizona, and Amache, Colorado, as well as the Tucson Jr. American Legion, accepted invitations to play against teams at Gila River. Likewise, Zenimura and his players made the exciting journey to Heart Mountain, Wyoming, for a competitive series, and breath of fresh air and freedom. Despite the successes of the past year, there were still many unknowns for the future. Zenimura had no idea if he and his family had another 12 months or 12 years remaining at Gila River. With that, Zeni approached camp life one day at a time. He reminded himself that he had no control over the past, nor the future—"today" was the only day that mattered. Tomorrow was another day.

7

Rounding Third and Heading Home (1945)

"Coach Zeni ... indeed possessed a tremendous knowledge of baseball savvy, but above all, he wanted every player to become a better human being by realizing his responsibility and compassion for his fellow man."[1]
—Tets Furukawa, pitcher, Butte High Eagles, 1945

The 1945 Season—State Champ Upset

Japan and people of Japanese ancestry were the hot topic of the day in early 1945. On Tuesday, January 2, 1945, Fresno Insurance man Justin (Jud) Simons delivered a speech at the Hotel Fresno entitled "Japan as I Saw It" before the members of the Fresno Lions Club. Eighteen years earlier, Simons was the former semipro catcher who had toured Japan as a member of Kenichi Zenimura's Fresno Athletic Club baseball team.[2]

Californians were also meeting to discuss more nefarious topics related to Japanese Americans. Approximately 300 residents of Placer County, led by Sheriff Jack Hannon, commander of the Veterans of Foreign Wars Donner Post No. 1942, signed a petition agreeing to boycott returning Japanese Americans and "persons who do business with the Japanese." The action came as the climax of a meeting called to protest return of the Nisei to the fruit-growing and mining area of Central California. "We the undersigned agree not to purchase, do business or fraternize with any returning Japanese and that we also will boycott and refuse to do business with any other persons who do business with the Japanese," declared the Placer County residents. Several women said they would also withdraw their children from schools attended by Nisei.[3]

The West Coast attitudes were a stark contrast to those in the east. The *Gila News Courier* reported that the New York media had officially agreed to discontinue the use of the term "Japanese American" and instead use "Americans of Japanese Descent."[4] Caught in the middle of the hostile West Coast attitudes and liberal East Coast media were the Japanese Americans themselves, many of them still struggling with the realities of war-time internment.

At Tule Lake it was reported that more than 70 residents renounced their U.S. citizenship.[5] Even worse came the news on January 5 at Rivers, Arizona, that Joe Tsujimoto, a 29-year-old recently discharged World War II veteran, was found dead at his home, 65-6-A.

He was found with a self-inflicted knife wound through his heart. Tsujimoto was discharged from the Army in late December 1943, and had lived with parents at Gila River ever since. He was found dead by his father who, with other members of the family, had attended the Japanese movie at the camp amphitheater.[6]

A month later the second suicide of 1945 at Gila River occurred when resident Sanga Goto, 72, of 45-5-B, hanged himself. He was found dead February 1, suspended by rope from a beam of a canopy at the dump ground beyond the hills west of the camp. "Goto, formerly of Jerome, left no other identification and is apparently a bachelor," reported the *Courier*. "He is listed in the Japanese directory as a native of Kumamoto prefecture and formerly of Fresno. Chief John W. Nichol, who was called to the scene, stated that indications showed the man's first attempt to take his own life failed when the rope broke, and he had tried the second time."[7]

These were tragic reminders that not all residents at Gila River were able to find happiness in simple pleasures like baseball. Later in the spring, Canal resident Kazuo Kishimoto, 43, also committed suicide.[8] And officials announced that the body of 72-year-old Otomatsu Wada was discovered, solving a two-year-old mystery of his disappearance.[9]

Two weeks later another former Jerome resident made headlines at Gila River, this time on a more positive note. Herb "Moon" Kurima replaced Harry Kono as Canal baseball commissioner for the 1945 season.[10] Kurima got his nickname "Moon" because his father used to make moonshine during prohibition. Before the war "Moon" managed and pitched for the Florin Athletic Club. He became a legend in the annals of internment baseball when, on August 23, 1943, he shut out Arkansas A&M 6–0 at the Jerome, Arkansas, detention camp.[11]

With Kurima at the helm in the Canal camp, Zenimura was eager to begin laying the groundwork for the 1945 Butte Baseball Association.[12] Unfortunately for both men, the pool of players in Canal and Butte camps was depleting with each passing day.

WRA officials announced that by the end of 1945 it was projected that all of the relocation centers would be closed.[13] In early 1945 Gila River was viewed as the role model for relocation and led all relocation centers in terminal (indefinite) leaves. The majority of Gila residents were returning to California.[14]

Some Japanese Americans faced hostile attitudes and actions upon arrival. For example, shootings were reported in Lancaster, located 70 miles north of Los Angeles.[15] In San Jose a returnee from Gila, Joe Takeda, had his home set afire and was fired upon.[16] The WRA also had good news to report. By March 1945, more than 2,500 Nisei were enrolled in as many as 550 different colleges outside of the so-called restricted areas of the United States.[17]

In the spring of '45 the Butte High basketball team wrapped up their third and final season, led by star guard of the squad, Kenshi "Harvey" Zenimura.[18] A sure sign that spring was just around the corner, Zenimura held a meeting of enthusiasts on February 25. Plans were made to form an all-star team that would make a tour of other centers. Baseball equipment was getting harder to purchase.[19]

But there were hints that the dwindling population at Gila River would potentially threaten the quality of the '45 baseball season. In the Canal camp, Moon Kurima could only scrounge up enough men to fill three clubs.[20] After the meeting of the Butte Baseball Association, Zenimura and others realized that their league faced a shortage of players too. The solution was unprecedented. It is not known if he approached Butte High or vice-versa, however in late February Zenimura was named head coach of the Butte High School baseball team. The newest addition to the physical education department, Wilber Derr, was tapped by camp officials to serve as Zeni's assistant coach. With an initial turnout of only fourteen boys, on March 12 he debuted as the Butte High skipper.[21] Forever the salesman, Zenimura solicited the support of the editors of the *Desert Sentinel*— the Butte High newspaper — to recruit more players and fans.

Zenimura's first item of business as the new coach of Butte High was to plan games with outside teams, just as he had for the Butte All-Stars the previous two seasons. Arrangements were made with North Phoenix, Mesa, and Phoenix High School, and tentative plans were to book games with Glendale, Scottsdale, Litchfield Park and Peoria.[22] Determined to play, if they could not leave the camp, they would bring the games to them.

The 1945 season kicked off with an exciting contest between the Canal High Bears and the Block 55 nine from Butte. The Canal High Bears handed the visiting Block 55 players a 12–7 beating before about 1,500 fans.

On March 24, the Canal High Bears suffered a 4–1 defeat at the mercy of the Butte High Eagles bats on their own diamond. On the Bears' errors and their own timely hits, the Eagles drew in 2 runs each in the first two innings, while the Bears scored their lone run in the 4th.

Games of aggregated players appeared more frequently with the dwindling pool from which to pull. On Sunday, March 25, the Block 28 aggregation, aided by two home runs belted by Tets Furukawa and Tak Abo, triumphed 9–2 over the Canal Cardinals, at the latter's ballfield. The Block 28 squad scored in most of the innings while the Cards scored in the 7th inning. In Butte, the same afternoon, the Block 55 squad played hosts to the Old Timers of Canal and received an 8–5 beating on the Pasadena ball park.[23]

Shortly after being named to the Butte "Aye" Basketball All-Star team with Kenso and Kenshi Zenimura, star athlete Tak Abo was named one of 17 young men scheduled to leave for active duty in the U.S. Army.[24] Perhaps inspired by the new baseball season and the departure of young athletes like the mighty Tak, the *Gila News Courier* published a timely editorial on sportsmanship:

> Clean playing is just as important as clean living.... On the baseball diamonds, football fields, basketball courts, and many of "fields of friendly strife," you develop the strength and stamina, the speed, the coordination, sportsmanship, the fighting spirit, and the "will to win" that makes you not only a great athlete, but a better citizen. If you think that you are only playing the game for the fun of it, you are greatly mistaken. Do not forget for a minute that the habits you acquire, the traits you develop, the "seed" that you sow will show up in other fields in other years. It may be in the field of study; it may be in the field of work; or it may be in serving one's country. But somewhere in the field of life will be reflected the seed which you sow today.[25]

The call for sportsmanship came just in time for Butte High's first game against an outside team, Tolleson High School. Zenimura and school officials priced tickets for the contest at 25 cents for adults and 10 cents for students and children.[26] On Saturday, April 8, the Butte High Baseball nine were successful in downing the invading nine from Tolleson High by the score of 6 to 3 at Zenimura Field. Sharing hitting honors for Butte High were Kenso Zenimura and Tets Hasegawa slugging two hits apiece.[27]

There was no baseball played the week of April 12 at Gila River. In fact, there was no baseball played anywhere in the nation. Radio reports announced that President Roosevelt had died and that Harry Truman had been sworn in as the 33rd president of the United States. The next game on the horizon for the Butte High varsity baseball nine was Wednesday, April 18, when the Eagles were scheduled to play the Tucson High baseball team at 2:30 P.M. on the Zenimura Field. The visiting team had won the state championship title

In 1945 Mori Shimada visited the Zenimuras at Gila River. Shimada snuck his camera into the camp and from the dugout snapped this shot of Kenshi Zenimura batting, with pitcher Tets Furkawa on deck, during the Butte High vs. Tolleson High game. This rare photograph depicts the sunken dugouts, wooden bleachers, and hundreds of fans along the foul lines (Zenimura Family Archive).

14 times prior to the 1945 season, including six straight championships between 1939 and 1944.[28]

Coach Zenimura picked the following as his starters against the defending state champions:[29]

Kenso Zenimura — second base
Tets Hasegawa — left field
Tosh Nishino — short stop
Kenshi Zenimura — first base
Tets Furukawa — pitcher
Muscles Ushiro — center field
George Kataoka — third base
Masani Fukai — catcher
Shosan Shimasaki — right field

In preparation for the Tucson High contest, the Butte High Eagles took on the Canal High Cardinals and walloped the neighboring camp, 4–3. The Butte Eagles now turned their attention to the Tucson Badgers.

Thousands of Butte residents handed over their nickels and dimes to watch this contest. And for the first time in Gila River baseball history, Coach Zenimura authored the game summary himself:

Camp officials recruited Coach Zenimura to lead the Butte High School Eagles in 1945. The team's undefeated season included a thrilling extra-inning 11–10 victory over the defending state champions, the Tucson High Badgers (Nisei Baseball Research Project).

Butte High Edges Tucson Nine in 10th

Zenimura Comes Through to Upset State Champs

Playing an errorless defensive game, the undefeated Butte High Eagles, coached by Ken Zenimura, blasted a terrific rally in the last of the tenth frame to inflict upon the state champs from Tucson High their first defeat in three years in a ten inning thrill-packed baseball game on the 28 ball field by the narrow margin of 11–10 last Wednesday afternoon.

A Thrilling Finish

What the several thousand spectators witnessed in that decisive inning will be long remembered as one of the most thrilling chapters in the history of Butte baseball. It was in the last of the 10th frame, the score was at a 10–10 standstill, two outs, bases loaded, and the count three and two, Kenshi Zenimura singles sharply to left field, scoring Shosan Shimasaki for the deciding run.

In accomplishing the above feat, the Eagles came from behind three times in the second, sixth, and eighth innings before tying the score at 10–10 which continued throughout the ninth and tenth.

Close-up on the 10th

Then came the decisive inning. Lowell Bailey who hurled masterfully for Tucson was replaced by relief chucker Joe Tully. Lead off Shimasaki drew a base on balls and Osada followed, reaching first safely on a fielder's choice. As Hasegawa was grounding out, the runners advanced to second and third. All runners held base as Katakoka flied out to right. Nishino was given an intentional walk filling the bases. Then Zenimura came to bat and Tully delivered three consecutive balls followed by two consecutive strikes. With all runners advancing, Zenimura came through to annex another victory for Butte High.

Receiving excellent support, Tets Furukawa, though touched for 19 safeties on his mound debut, took his fifth straight victory.

Fukai and Ushiro hit 3 for 5 apiece for the Eagles while Lopez, Carey, and Weinstein did likewise for the visitors.[30]

According to pitcher Lowell Bailey, the Tucson ballclub initially did not know that they were playing Americans. "We thought we were going to play Japanese ball players ...

from Japan," he said. "We had no idea, until the game started and we heard them speak perfect English, that we were actually playing against U.S. citizens," recalled the Tucson hurler.[31] Bailey was amazed with the speed and hands of the Eagles. "I remember being impressed with how fast and quick they were on the bases. They were good fielders too.... I recall that the field was pretty rough ... a lot of rocks," said Bailey. "Then again, they were playing on the same field too," he confessed in a good-natured tone.[32]

At 5'9", 175 lbs., Lowell Bailey was often told he didn't have the physique to play baseball. A self-described junk-ball pitcher with a repertoire of a curve ball, fork ball, sliders and changeups, Bailey found himself in elite company in 1944 by becoming just one of four high school pitchers at the time to complete a season with a perfect 0.00 earned run average (ERA). Since Bailey accomplished the feat, 19 other pitchers have joined that elite group. Bailey never made it to the major leagues, but he played plenty of college and pro ball in the 1940s and 1950s.

At 6'1", 195 lbs., Joe Tully, relief chucker and disputed losing pitcher-of-record against the Butte Eagles, eventually played 13 years of pro ball all across North America, as far north as the New England League with the Lynn Red Sox in 1948, and as far south as the Mexican

Legendary coach Zenimura called the Butte Eagles victory over the Tucson Badgers "one of the most thrilling chapters in the history of Butte baseball." The 1945 Badgers were led by pitching sensation Lowell Bailey, who completed the previous season with a perfect 0.00 ERA, and third baseman Lee Carey, who became the highest paid recruit ever for the Cleveland Indians in 1945 (Lowell Bailey).

Pacific League with the Mexico City Red Devils. In 1959, Tully completed his professional baseball career with a respectable 89–74 record, 49 saves and 1,467 innings pitched in 297 games.[33]

Third-baseman Lee Carey, the man with the best view of Kenshi Zenimura's game-winning knock, was drafted by the Cleveland Indians in 1947. He was reported to have received the largest signing bonus of any draftee in Indians history at the time. In his six-year stint in the Indians minor league organization Carey hit .250, 2392 AB, 598 H, 102 2B, 21 3B, 46 HR.[34]

An injury to the Eagles' second baseman, Kenso Zenimura, led to a series of defensive changes that demonstrates the strategic mind of Coach Zenimura. Zeni's original Butte High Eagles lineup was:

Zenimura (Kenso), 2b
Hasegawa, lf
Nashino, ss
Kataoka, 3b
Zenimura (Kenshi), 1b
Ushiro, cf
Fukai, c
Furukawa, p
Shimasaki, rf

During the second inning the Eagles went for an out with the lead runner at second. Bernie Weinstein slid hard to break up the double play — as coached by Hank Slagle — and took out second baseman Kenso Zenimura. Kenso turned his ankle and was forced to leave the game. Coach Zenimura made the following changes: (1) Ushiro leaves centerfield to replace the injured Kenso Zenimura at second base; (2) Kenshi Zenimura leaves first base to replace Ushiro in centerfield; (3) Kataoka leaves third base to replace Kenshi Zenimura at first base; (4) Nashino leaves shortstop to replace Kataoka at third base; and (5) Osada enters the game to replace Nashino at shortstop.

Four players — Hasegawa, Fukai, Furukawa and Shimasaki — remained in their starting positions, which resulted in the new lineup:

Osada, ss
Hasegawa, lf
Nashino, 3b
Kataoka, 1b
Zenimura (Kenshi), cf
Ushiro, 2b
Fukai, c
Furukawa, p
Shimasaki, rf

All infielders and the centerfield were switched, the battery, and left and right field positions remained in place. All-star Pete Rose said, "It is the manager's responsibility to know his players strengths and weaknesses, and put them into positions to succeed."[35]With the five-player switch, Zenimura put his players in the best position to win, which they did, 11–10, in 10 innings.

Zenimura put his strategic mind to work off the field as well. "Coach Zenimura thought of everything," said Furukawa. "He ordered crates of watermelon to share with the Tucson team ... and then, we taught the Badgers how to sumo-wrestle."[36] Lowell Bailey recalls "dressing up" for sumo wrestling lessons and "being stuck"— as he put it — in the sumo ring drawn in the dirt with a stick.[37] Years later the game between the Tucson Badgers and Butte High Eagles is remembered as an impressive display of sportsmanship by all participants.

Before the Badgers returned home, Coach Zeni and Hank Slagle agreed to have a rematch, though this time at the Badgers home field in Tucson. On Saturday April 21, it was confirmed that the Butte High Eagles would play a rematch on the Badgers' home field.[38]

Sometime between the April 21 article and April 25 scheduled game, Zenimura received word that the Butte High boys were no longer welcome in Tucson. Despite the fact that teams from Gila River had previously traveled to Heart Mountain, Wyoming, to play ball, their request to travel to Tucson was denied. Local authorities cited the Japanese American team as a potential security threat. Many years later players on both sides remember the term "security threat" being used as an excuse, but the threat to whom was never really clear.

It seems apparent that hostility towards Japanese Americans in Tucson was the cause of the rematch cancellation. Zeni's letter to Coach Hank Slagle expressed his disappointment:

> Thursday, April 26, 1945
> To the members of Tucson B.B. Team:
>
> It was a great disappointment to myself and the members of the Butte baseball team when we learned of the cancellation of our return game.
>
> We know the circumstances which necessitated the cancellation and understand your position in the decision you had to take.
>
> This war has created many unpleasant incidents and I am sorry to have put you and yours in this spot in your district. I can only hope that in due time the difference in opinion can be overcome and that we may be able to resume our athletic rivalry.
>
> At this time I and the members of the team wish to thank you for your first game. It was a game we did not deserve to win and our return game would have been a humdinger I'm sure.
>
> If our return game can't be brought about, I sincerely hope that we may meet once again not as a team perhaps but as a single member of Uncle Sam and fight together for one principal.
>
> Sincerely yours,
> K. Zenimura
> Coach of the Butte High School (Gila River) Baseball Team

Coach Slagle's response echoed his own disappointment in the loss of the game and included disappointment in the citizens of Tucson. But, his letter also declared his admiration for the Gila River team:

> We shared your disappointment in not being to play you a return game on our field. We were not only anxious to avenge the defeat, but enjoyed the heads up smart competition you could give us. Your brand of ball was right down our alley, so to speak, and the boys could gain much from your heads up base running and infield play. As for the possibility of canceling our game — we had never given it a minute's thought — till we arrived home and started hearing from some of these so called 100% Americans. I sincerely hope it won't be too long till we are all thinking straight again and can live together in a true Democracy that we Americans of all races have created. I want to congratulate you all on your fine team — I only wish we had your base running and defensive ability — Not inferring that you can't hit — for 13 base knocks will win most games. I wish you all the best of luck, and continued success with your ball club.
>
> Sincerely yours,
> Hanley R. Slagle
> Baseball Coach[39]

The legendary Eagles-Badgers game was later described by Coach Zenimura as "one of the most thrilling chapters in the history of Butte baseball." The Eagles defeated the state champion Badgers 11–10 in ten innings. Hank Slagle won ten of Tucson High's national-record 29 state baseball championships, eight of them successive from 1939 through 1946. Tucson High's 52-game win streak spanning the 1942–46 seasons still stands as Arizona's longest.[40] Years later an 87-year-old Coach Slagle responded in a letter to Stacey Furukawa, the daughter of pitcher Tets Furukawa, "Our Tucson High team had won (12) state championships prior to playing your Dad's team so he should have felt good over this win."[41]

The game between the Tucson Badgers and Butte High Eagles is also remembered as an impressive display of sportsmanship by all participants. In the end, the Eagles-Badgers contest represented more than just a simple baseball game. It was a breaking of racial and cultural boundaries and a true example of sportsmanship and camaraderie. In the words of Butte High Eagle pitcher Tets Furukawa, "This is what baseball was meant to be."[42] "Played during a time when the nation was deeply divided by war, this single ballgame has become an important symbol of American brotherhood and goodwill," said Kerry Yo Nakagawa, founder of the Nisei Baseball Research Project, the non-profit organization established to preserve the history of Japanese American baseball.

Legendary Tucson coach Hank Slagle won 10 of Tucson High's national-record 29 state baseball championships. Tucson's 52-game win streak spanning the 1942–46 seasons under his reign still stands as Arizona's longest. After the Eagle-Badger rematch in Tucson was canceled by officials in 1945, Slagle wrote to Zenimura, "I sincerely hope it won't be too long till we are all thinking straight again and can live together in a true Democracy that we Americans of all races have created" (Nisei Baseball Research Project).

In his 2003 letter to Stacey Furukawa, Coach Slagle said that he enjoyed being a part of the Tucson-Badger game and then reflected on the lessons he and the nation learned from the war-time experience. "It was a sad and dark day in U.S.A. history when our government decided to set up relocation camps for our Japanese people," said Slagle. "It should never have happened, and in retrospect I believe all Americans regret that this action was taken."[43]

Just days after the cancelled contest in Tucson, Zenimura and his top players were back on the field playing in a weekend game as the Block 28 ballclub. "Allowing 7 scattered hits on their mound debut, right-handers Tak Abo and George Matsuda paced the strong 28 nine to another victory as they easily defeated the Block 65 aggregation by an impressive score of 11–3 on Zenimura's field Sunday afternoon. The main feature of this game was the terrific home runs hit consecutively by Tets Furukawa and Masani Fukai in the second frame after two outs."[44]

According to Tets Furukawa, after he hit a home run that cleared the castor bean fence line in right-centerfield, coach Zenimura stood in front of the dugout waiving a "green back." All of the players thought that Zeni was giving Tets a single dollar for his homer, but as they looked closer they saw that it was a $5.00 bill—big money back in 1945 (Note: Adjusted for inflation, $5.00 in 1945 is equivalent to approximately $60.00 in 2009). To Coach Zenimura's chagrin, the next batter, catcher Masani Fukai, hit a ball that cleared the fence almost exactly where Furukawa placed the ball. Coach Zeni had set a precedent and felt obliged to hand over another $5.00 bill to Fukai. Afterwards he yelled to his team, "no more home runs!"[45]

The Eagles played in Mesa as though they had a point to prove to those who doubted their skill level and loyalty towards the U.S. The Butte High Eagles blanked the Mesa High Jackrabbits 19–0. Zeni's boys started off with a five run rally in the first inning and continued to tally in every inning:

> The Butte nine appeared to be more like Jackrabbits as they ran wild stealing a total of 29 bases. Although the losers attempted to steal bases, the Butte battery composed of catcher Masani Fukai and Chucker Tets Furukawa was too secure, holding the Jackrabbits to no stolen bases. Allowing only 5 scattered hits on his mound debut for Butte High, southpaw Tets Furukawa took his sixth straight victory. Tets Hasegawa and Muscles Ushiro of the visitors were the potent batters of the tilt each garnering 2 hits.[46]

Weeks later the 1945 Arizona State Baseball Championship featured the Tucson Badgers and Mesa Jackrabbits. The Badgers defeated the Jackrabbits 10 to 2 to capture their seventh-consecutive crown. Despite the 16–5 season record and the well-documented loss to Butte High, the Badgers claimed to have kept their "consecutive game win streak" alive in 1945. Between 1939 and 1946 the Badgers claimed to have won 52 consecutive games. It appears that the streak must have included district games only.

On May 6 Germany surrendered to the United States, essentially ending the war in Europe. "After five years, eight months and six days of fighting after Hitler invaded Poland and struck the spark which set the world afire, the war in Europe was officially over."[47] However, the war for those at Gila River was not over.

With the high school baseball season coming to close, the Intra-Camp League, a combined league of Butte and Canal teams, began its play in May. In the final season of baseball at Gila River, there were enough players remaining in the camps to field 14 teams: four teams in the "Aye" League—the Cardinals, Block 65, Block 28 and the Old Timer Taiyos; and 10 teams in the "Bee" League—Block 49, Broncos, Block 55 4-A's, the News Courier, Canal High Golden Bears, Block 54, Block 47, the Fag Nine, and the Santa Anita Don Babes—which also offered an exciting brand of baseball for the camps.

The projected opening day batteries in the "Aye" League were:

Canal Cardinals: Herb "Moon" Kurima, catcher George Egusa
Block 65: Eddie Iwao, catcher (and brother) Mitch Iwao
Old Timers: Paul Ryono, catcher Kambo Minamide
Block 28: Tak Abo or George Matsuda, catcher Masani Fukai

Once again Zenimura set out to sell baseball and asked the Gila River baseball fans to donate generously for the new season.[48] In 1945 Zenimura no longer published the financial results of his contest, so it is unknown if fans answered his call.

In the initial opening A-league game at Zenimura Field, Block 28 defeated the visiting Old Timer Taiyos 20 to 4. The losers were having a tough time against right-hander Tak Abo. Every player on the Block 28 squad banged out a hit, with George Yamaguchi, Kenshi Zenimura and Tosh Nishino "taking the honors with 3 bingles."[49]

In the same issue of the *Gila River Courier* featuring Slagle's letter to Zenimura, it was announced that a letter from Washington stated that the land lease on the Gila River Relocation Center was to expire October 7 and that the land was to be returned to the Indian reservation. All the nurseries full of flowers, plants, and shrubs were to be closed down by that date. The WRA was already reducing livestock and replacing it with privately owned cattle. The camp harvest for the month of April was "394,414 pounds of vegetables, 70 tons of hay, 12,537 dozen eggs, 6,455 gallons of milk. The vegetable with the biggest harvest was strawberries with 6,301 pounds. Six carloads of vegetables have been sent to other relocation centers."[50] With the anticipated closing of the camp WRA officials announced that all of the schools at Gila River would close on June 8.[51] Things were changing at Gila River.

But the boys of summer played on. In the second week of play for the 1945 Intra-camp League the Block 28 nine overpowered the visiting Canal Cardinals by the overwhelming score of 15 to 6. At Canal, the Taiyo Old Timers enjoyed a surprising victory over the Block 65 nine by a score of 7 to 3.[52] Next on the hit list of Zenimura's Block 28 ballclub was the Block 65 aggregation. The undefeated Block 28 aggregation made a clean sweep in the first inning by defeating Block 65 by the score of 13 to 6.[53]

The relocation personnel of Gila River agreed to play a baseball game on May 27 against the internees:

> To give the fans an opportunity to display their skills and abilities in the field of baseball, the Caucasian personnel staff members and the Butte Old Timers will engage in a horsehiders tilt tomorrow afternoon at 12:45 at 28 field. Although both teams will field players who have had experience in the past, as well as the present, the game should prove an exceedingly interesting one, as the teams would be typical war time teams with many players in retirement called out to limber out their legs once more.[54]

The lineup for the Caucasian team included: Stringer, c; Couch, p; Jackson, 1b; Reynolds, 2b; MacAlpine, 3b; Martenson, ss; White, lf; Huso, cf; and Horitz, rf. The Butte Old Timers, managed by Sam Kawahata and captained by Fred Tsuda, included in its crew: Ken Zenimura, p; Harold Ouchida, lf; Hitoshi Ouchida, c; Kaz Suzukawa, 2b; Frank Kuwamoto; of; Sam Tamura, ss; Takeuchi, of; Hajime Miyagishima, ss; Joe Nakade, George Suenaga and Joe Osada as reserves. The final score was Caucasian personnel staff members 3 runs, Butte Old Timers 10.[55]

In late May, Block 28 defeated the Taiyos, 8 to 1. Tak Abo allowed 1 run and 4 hits over seven innings. George Matsuda pitched two innings of shutout ball in relief. The losing pitcher was Bobby Yamamoto. Hitting honors for the game were dominated by Tosh Nishino who cracked out 3 of the winner's 8 hits, with Kenso Zenimura collecting 2 more hits.

Weeks after the cancelled Badger-Eagle game, discussions were still stirring about the way the Japanese Americans were treated in Tucson. The editor of the *Arizona Daily Star* made a public call for Nikkei equality. "Nisei Deserve Equal Rights" said the *Star*, citing the record of Nisei soldiers and pointing out that they deserve the basic citizenship rights of American citizenship. After quoting photographer Joe Rosenthal's statement on the proven loyalty of Nisei soldiers, the editor of the *Star* stated: "These [Nisei soldiers] are the men whose families are being pushed around by some of our 'super-patriots' at home who have never heard a gun fired in anger. Their record should be guarantee enough of the basic rights to which they and their families are entitled as American citizens, regardless of ancestry."[56]

Conversations were being held inside and outside of the camp. The *Gila News Courier* discussed how the fight for the Nisei soldier was two-fold, one for democracy on the front line, and the other for respect back home. "No soldiers we have sent abroad have a more distinguished record than these Nisei [the men of the famous 100th Batallion] ... they have won every fight they have been in. But their hardest fight is still ahead and may outlast the war. It is the fight against prejudice roused by color of skin and slant of eye. It is easy to admire them while they are still in uniform. It would be kinder to remember and reward them when the battle is over."[57]

Additional battles for respect were being fought in towns all across the West as Japanese Americans began to return home. "A Fresno rancher plead guilty to firing two shots into the home of a returned Japanese American and drew a six month's suspended sentence in Justice Court at Parlier, Calif. The shooter, Levi Multanen, 33, was the first man arrested for shooting at Japanese Americans in Fresno county. He told the judge in court that he 'hadn't heard from his soldier nephew in the South Pacific for a long time, and that he was worried and 'very mad at the Japs.'"[58]

On July 9 the *Gila News Courier* gave the standings of the "Aye" League. After six games, Zenimura's men remained perfect:

A League Standings

	W	*L*	*T*	*Pct.*
Block 28	6	0	0	1.000
Taiyos	2	3	1	.400
Cards	2	3	1	.400
Block 65	1	5	0	.167

Top batters of the A League were also featured. Leading the league was "Freezer" Furuya of the Canal Cardinals, who was on a tear with a hefty .600 average and 10 stolen bases. The Zenimura brothers, Kenso and Kenshi, both hit over .350, to keep the Block 28 squad in first place.[59]

On Thursday, June 7, and Friday, June 8, 1945, approximately 230 seniors graduated from Canal and Butte High School. Among the graduates was Zenimura's son, Kenso.[60] Now that his high school studies were complete, Kenso started to make plans to leave Gila River. While he explored his college and career options, he continued to play ball.

On June 13 the *Gila News Courier* reported that Zenimura's Block 28 ball club extended their winning streak to seven games with 15 safeties and a 20–3 victory over the Canal Taiyos. "The first two innings were disastrous for the Taiyos as the Blk. 28 aggregation took advantage of every opportunity to score. In the first inning, lead-off batter Kenso Zenimura walked, Hasegawa and Nishino grounded out and Abo reached first on an error. Then three consecutive hits by Kenshi Zenimura, Furukawa, and Ushiro pushed across 4 runs. Kenso Zenimura led the winners at the plate with 2 singles and a double in the 4 trips to the plate while Furukawa, Nishino and Fukai each hit a triple. Kenshi Zenimura stole 5 bases. Tak Abo, who was relieved by Zenimura in the 6th frame, was the winning tosser.[61]

Following the Block 28-Taiyo game on Zenimura Field, the Butte Old Timers battled the Old Timers of Canal. The lineups for Butte included: Sam Kawahata, mgr.; Ken Zenimura, ss, coach; Fred Tsuda, 1st base, captain; Tomooka, P; Hitoshi Ouchida, c; K. Suzukawa, Ted Yamada, Masa Morinaga, 2nd base; Hajime Miyagishima, 3rd base; Harold Ouchida, LF; Ike Takeuchi, CF; Sam Tamura, RF. Sub—Masa Masada, outfield, and George Itogawa, infield. And for Canal they were: Fujii, C; Minemide, C; Kumano, P, mgr; Kaz Yamasaki, SS; Tanaka, OF; Tsuji, 3rd base; Fukuchi, 2nd base; Kahn Yamasaki, CF-P; Shiozaki, OF; Nakamura, 1st base. The Butte Oldtimers slapped out 13 safeties and easily defeated the Old Timers of Canal by the score of 11–6.[62]

Mid-June brought announcements that several services were being shut down or consolidated in anticipation of the camp closing in October. The discontinued services included a fish market and medical services in the Canal camp, and a mess hall for those with special diets in the Butte camp. In their place were new activities that prepared internees for jobs outside of the camps, including typing and stenography training, and training as a cook for students.[63]

Camp officials continued to discontinue services in preparation for the fall closings of the Canal and Butte Camps. The WRA announced that 1,007 internees returned home to southern California during the month of May. Trade schools opened on the camps and back home to help Japanese Americans return to the workforce. At both the Canal and Butte Camps, fewer supplies were ordered and internees were encouraged to return kitchen utensils, dishes and silver to the mess hall. In June the Canal watch repair shop closed. Relocation camp life was slowly and systematically being deconstructed.

Additional services continued to cease in preparation for the closing of the camps. In the Canal camp, summer school was discontinued, and a new course titled "How to Start a Grocery Store" was created. The Butte Camp faced a water shortage. Undoubtedly this impacted the frequency in which Zeni could water the grass on his baseball diamond. Officials described the water shortage as "grave" and asked for cooperation from all community members for help. "When the fire engine is heard, everyone is asked to turn off all water faucets so that the fire engine will get highest pressure possible. There are two pumps working 24 hours a day pumping 12,000 gallons per minute, but with the large consumption, there is no time for the tank to fill up, leaving it to dry up and crack."

The baseball games continued at Zenimura Field. In a twilight tilt on Wednesday, June 16, David beat Goliath when the unbeaten streak of Block 28 came to an end at the hands of the last place Block 65 club. "Behind the superb 2 hit chucking of George Kataoka and clouting 14 clean hits from the offerings of southpaw Tets Furukawa, the Blk. 65 nine came through with a stinging 12–2 victory over Blk. 28 to hand the league leading nine their first defeat of the season." The top hitters of the day for Block 65 were Tad Nakamura, who enjoyed a 3-for-5 day, and Nori Saki, Roy Nakamura, and Joe Osada, who each went 2 for 4 at the plate. Block 65's George Kataoka, the winning pitcher, hit two triples in three at-bats.[64]

The true sign of a champion is not how many games you win, but how well you handle loss and adversity. Zenimura instilled this mindset into his players, and they responded accordingly in their next game. Block 28 resumed their winning ways when they triumphed over the Canal Cardinals for their eighth win of the season by a score of 9 to 3. The game was tied three all in the third inning when Block 28 jumped out ahead scoring three runs on three hits, a walk and an error. Block 28 Pitcher Tak Abo held the Cards scoreless for the remainder of the game, allowing just two hits. The Block 28 batters touched Lefty Fujioka for three more runs in the fifth, sixth and seventh innings. Of the 12 hits recorded by Block 28, T. Hasegawa, T. Nishino, Y. Ushiro and M. Kikuchi collected 2 hits apiece.[65]

Back on Zenimura Field the final game of the "Aye" League season was played. "With Kenso Zenimura pacing the way with 4 of the team's 9 hits, the Block 28 nine, led by visiting chucker Lefty Fujioka, downed the Block 65 team by a score of 11 to 1 last Thursday evening...," the *Gila News Courier* reported on June 16. Block 65 scored their lone run in the third inning, after bunching three consecutive hits off Fujioka. The Block 28 lefty tightened up his game and kept the 65ers scoreless, allowing a total of 7 hits.[66]

On June 23, 1945, the *Gila News Courier* posted the final standings of the A, B and BB Leagues.[67] The 1945 Intra-Camp League was officially over.

SPORTS

June 23, 1945 Page 6

FINAL STANDINGS

Final A League Standings

	W	L	T	Pct.
Block 28	8	1	0	.889
Block 65	4	5	0	.444
Taiyos	2	5	2	.286
Cardinals	2	5	2	.286

Final B League Standings

	W	L	Pct.
Block 55	6	1	.857
Canal High	5	2	.714
News-Courier	4	3	.571
Broncos	3	4	.429
Don Juniors	3	4	.429

Final BB League Standings

	W	L	Pct.
Block 65	5	2	.714
Fag 9	5	2	.714
Block 54	3	4	.429
Block 49	1	6	.142
Block 47	0	7	.000

The final standings of the 1945 Gila River Baseball Season show that Zenimura's Block 28 ballclub finished in first place in the A League standings with an 8 and 1 record (*Gila News Courier*).[68]

Four days later the Intra-Camp officials announced the post-season honors for individual performances. George "Freezer" Furuya of the Cardinals topped all sluggers in the A league, hitting 19 safeties in 37 times at bat for an average of .513. He was awarded the YMCA batting trophy. Others who were awarded YMCA awards were Kenshi Zenimura for stealing the most number of bases, Tets Hasegaawa for the best outfielding, Kenso Zenimura for the best infielding and Tak Abo for the best pitching record.[69]

Perhaps sensing the end was near for Zenimura Field, teams continued to scrimmage one another in late June. "In a practice tilt at 28 field, the block 65 nine triumphed over the block 28 nine by a score of 12 to 6." Block 65 scored 9 runs off righty Tak Abo in the first two innings, 4 runs in the first inning and 5 in the second inning. Block 28 outslugged Block 65 with 11 to 8 hits, but they were unable to overcome the early run differential and lost the game. Pitchers George Kataoka and Hiro Shinmoto shared the hurling duties for Block 65, with Kataoka receiving the win. For Block 28, Kenso Zenimura slammed out 3 hits to pace the hitters.

On June 27, Zenimura called for a special meeting for all "Aye" and "Bee" league managers at his residence. They discussed plans for a farewell baseball tournament.[70] At the same time it was disclosed that Project Director Leroy H. Bennett would say farewell, too. Bennett's resignation was effective July 31. Bennett had entered WRA as project director of Rivers on Dec. 9, 1942, and would now return to San Francisco.[71]

With June coming to an end, plans began to unfold for the Fourth of July holiday. In the community of Rivers, Arizona, the Independence Day holiday this year would be recognized with little fanfare. From the baseball perspective, Coach Zenimura was working on securing one final game with an outside team. He also had more post-season honors to award. Zeni announced the 1945 Intra-Camp A-League All-Stars:

1945 A-League All-Stars

Catcher	*BA*	*SB*	*Shortstop*	*BA*	*SB*
M. Iwao (65)	.371	2	R. Osada (65)	.189	5
K. Minamido (T)	.458	0	*Infield utility*		
Pitcher			N.Saki (65)	.368	3
Abo (28)	.300	7	*Left field*		
P. Ryono (T)	.440	4			
G. Kataoka (65)	.241	0	F. Furaya (c)	.513	11
First Base			*Center field*		
T. Furukawa (28)	.324	5	Kenshi Zenimura (28)	.317	18
Second Base			*Right field*		
Kenso Zenimura (28)	.395	9	Tets Hasegawa (28)	.316	8
Third Base			*Outfield utility*		
T. Nishino (28)	.425	7	M. Ushiro (28)	.333	7

Perhaps speaking to the case of shortstop Ralph Osada who batted just .189 for the season, Zenimura stated that some players were selected for "their valuable defensive playing."

On Sunday evening, July 1, a scrimmage was played at 28 field. "The Olympic Club nine led by Lefty Fujioka and Mr. Ken Zenimura smothered the News-Courier nine convincingly by the score of 16–2." The game got out of control in the third inning when Zenimura's Olympic Club scored six runs on 3 hits, 2 errors and a passed ball. The News Courier club scored in the seventh inning with 3 hits off reliever Kenichi Zenimura. Pitcher Kiyo Nagai went the distance for the Courier nine, giving up 16 runs on 19 hits. The Olympic Club was led by Tak Abo with 4 hits, and Tets Furukawa who rapped out 3 hits.[72]

According to Kenso Zenimura, the team name "Olympic Club" had not been used since 1942 when Zenimura and others were temporarily housed at the Fresno Assembly Center. Most of the Olympic Club players were sent to Jerome, Arizona, in late 1942. A few arrived at Gila River after the Jerome camp closed. There is some speculation that the name "Olympic Club" was originally coined in '42 as a reference to Zeni's ballclub that never materialized for the cancelled 1940 Tokyo games. Perhaps Zenimura was feeling nostalgic and resurrected this team name to close the final chapter of his camp experience? We may never know.

On Wednesday evening, July 4, 1945, Block 65 celebrated Independence Day with a 7–3 victory over Block 28. The Block 65 club recorded 8 hits in an abbreviated 5-inning game. The game was called off because of a whirling dust storm. George Kataoka toed the mound for the winners, allowing 4 hits, while his mates were busy collecting runs in the first, third and fifth innings. Block 28 scored one in the fourth and two in the fifth after two way George Yamaguchi walked, Tosh Nishino hit safely and Tak Abo came up with a triple to left field. "Lefty" Fujioka was the losing tosser with Tosh Nishino on the receiving end. Belting two singles in three trips to the plate, Eddie Iwao took the batting crown for the game.[73]

The Fourth of July festivities were then followed by the final Bon Odori celebration to be held at Gila River. Bon Odori is a dance that accompanies the Japanese Buddhist custom of honoring the spirits of one's ancestors. Celebrated in Japan for more than 500 years, Bon-Odori is similar to the Mexican observance of el Día de los Muertos (Day of the Dead).

Internees continued to prepare to leave the camps. For some, it meant returning home to face a potentially hostile environment. In an effort to prevent conflict and violence, California attorney general Robert V. Kenney announced a reward of $1,000 for information leading to the arrest and conviction of any person attacking a person of Japanese ancestry.

Meanwhile, in Spokane, Washington, a member of the highly decorated 442nd faced some unexpected hostility when he returned home. News reports announced that the Spokane VFW denied the application of Pvt. Richard M. Noito, a wounded Japanese American soldier. His membership application was denied by the local VFW voting members. Clearly, the possibility of similar incidents was in store for Japanese Americans once the relocation camps were closed.

On Sunday, July 8, 1945, the final games in the history of the Block 28 diamond—Zenimura Field were played. Coach Zenimura invited the Mesa Junior American Legion baseball team to Rivers to play two games. The visiting Junior American Legion schoolboys from Mesa clashed with the Butte All Stars and fell short in both games by the score of 21 to 2 and 13 to 5.

In the first game Butte righties Tak Abo and George Kataoka battled pitchers Marvin Scott and Bob Morris of Mesa. The game was relatively close in the first two innings, but in the third and sixth innings Butte scored a combined 10 runs. Then the game got out of control in the seventh inning when the Japanese Americans pushed 10 more runners across home plate, fueled by a Kenso Zenimura home run. The boys from Mesa scored 2 runs on 5 hits, while Butte cracked out 12 hits.

In the second game, with visitor "Lefty" Masato Kinoshita taking the mound for Butte, Zenimura's ballclub defeated Mesa 13 to 5. Lefty was opposed by Milton Jackson. Butte scored 4 runs in the second inning, jumping to a lead, but Kinoshita had difficulty in the second, walking 5 batters and allowing 4 runs to score. Lefty was relieved by Kenichi Zenimura who stopped the Mesa rally.

Butte scored their 13 runs throughout the game, while Mesa was held scoreless after the sixth inning.[74]

Among the players included in the Mesa lineup were outfielder Wilford "Whizzer" White who would later play for the NFL Chicago Bears; an all-state wrestler—Bill Workman; future college baseball stars Delwyn Gardner, Bob Morris, Richard McCleve; and Marvin "The Marvel" Scott, a multi-sport athlete from California who would later pitch his team to a state championship in 1947 with a thrilling win over Hank Slagle's Tucson Badgers.[75]

Not included in the lineup was Mesa's only Japanese American ballplayer, Masumi Ikeda, a 15-year-old pitcher/infielder of the 1945 Mesa American Legion team. He was fortunate in that his family lived north of the dividing line in Arizona and they did not have to relocate in 1942. As a member of the Legion team he was invited to play in the game against the Butte All-Stars, but was unable to participate because it was played on a Sunday. The Ikeda family operated a vegetable farm in Mesa, and Sundays typically were the busiest days for picking because the farmers market was only open early in the week. Had the game been played on a Saturday, Ikeda would have been in a unique situation of being a "free" Japanese American visiting to play against an interned Japanese American team.[76]

According to second baseman Richard McCleve, the game between Mesa and the Japanese Americans interned at Gila River was witnessed by approximately 600 to 700 fans, and was arranged by Chuck Dayton of the Mesa American Legion.

After hitting a home run in what proved to be the final baseball game ever played on the Block 28 diamond, Kenso Zenimura packed his bags and hit the road for Chicago. He arrived shortly before July 15 and immediately began his summer job as a shipping clerk in the car battery factory where uncle Bob Yamasaki worked. When he was not at the factory he spent his free time enjoying big band leader Harry James and other musicians of the local jazz scene, taking in Cubs games at Wrigley Field, and even attended the 1945 Negro League All-Star game at Comiskey Park.

The last contest played at the relocation camp that involved a member of the Zenimura family occurred on Monday evening, July 16. According to the *Gila News Courier*, Kenshi Zenimura pitched for the Block 40 softball team in a 15 to 6 victory over the "Cold Storage" team at field 58. The top hitters of the day were "Moon" Kikuchi and K. Yoshinaga, each with 3 hits.[77]

Announcements continued in preparation for the closing of the relocation camps.

National WRA director Dillon S. Myer announced that Gila River would be closed on or before November 15, and that the lest of the seven centers would be closed on or before December 15. Butte High School was scheduled to close on August 4. Plans called for the hospital at Rivers to be closed prior to the relocations deadline.

Douglass M. Todd was named to succeed camp director Leroy Bennett. Todd, a native of Utah, came from the Heart Mountain Relocation Center. On July 21, 1945, the *Gila News Courier* reported the population of Rivers on its third anniversary:[78]

Population of Rivers, AZ

Year	*Population*
1942	520
1943	12,386
1944	10,024
1945	6,921

By August 1945, some 44,000 people remained in the internment camps across the United States. Thousands had nowhere to go after losing their homes and jobs and many were afraid of anti–Japanese hostility and simply refused to leave the camps. For Gila River internees returning to California, Fresno was the top destination.[79]

With the Butte school's closing on the fourth of August, it was time for the Zenimura family to leave Gila River. The *Gila News Courier* posted a letter on August 1 from "Baseball Czar" Kenichi Zenimura:

> May I take this opportunity to thank each and everyone for their fine co-operation shown to me during the past three years here at Gila. Also I appreciate the untiring efforts shown by all members of the various clubs and organizations in making the baseball league a successful one. I am about to leave the center soon and before I do, I wish to extend my deepest appreciation to all the players on the Gila "All-Star" team, who have an unblemished record for the last three seasons against outside competition. The fine men like conduct, great showmanship, and their every ready heads up baseball illustrated on the diamond makes me very proud [especially] their fine sportsmanship on and off the field. It was through your efforts that such a record can be boasted. Also many of the outside teams that have played us have praised the Gila boys. By playing a clean and fast game they wish that they had some of the boys on their team. For this I am very glad of the boys, who have played under my guidance and those who have been playing on the other teams in the league. I assure you that Gila had the strongest team in all the ten relocation centers.
>
> It was the willingness to learn and hard practice that such a team record was brought about. Through the help of all the players, Gila can also be proud of boasting to have the finest diamond in all the centers to play and practice on.

To you fans, I wish to express my thanks for your generous support and cooperation in making the league a success. Also in making it possible for the other centers, such as Poston, Heart Mountain, and Amache to visit our center to play a series of games with the team here at Gila. Also for letting us be able to make our visit to Heart Mountain in 1944, possible. The boys and I really appreciated what you have done for us.

Though I am on the outside I'll always remember the swell time I had playing baseball here in Gila. I will be thinking of you players and fans. My memories will always be here at Gila.

Sooner or later everyone will have to relocate and when you do, always remember that you are just as good as the other fellow, so don't be backward, show them what you can do. Those who have played under my guidance, on my team or on the "All-Star" teams, I have all the confidence in the world of your making the grade on any high school or college team, if given the chance, so don't make them come and ask you, but go out on your own accord and let yourself be seen. This is one of the easiest ways of making friends.

I will be returning to Fresno and while I am there, will try to make a team to play in the league in the city, try to speed up the mutual feeling between the Americans and the Japanese. It is much easier to make efforts of starting a better understanding between us in the field of sports then trying to talk your way through rough spots. So, if any of you fellows ever drop down Fresno way, drop in and see me, we can talk over old times. So 'til again may I wish all of you the best of luck and success.

Sincerely yours,
/a/ K. Zenimura[80]

The first of Zenimura's players to follow his advice was Mas Kinoshita of Block 28. The young Kinoshita was selected to pitch for the Fort Snelling nine in Minnesota after being transferred from Camp Wolters in Texas in August. Fort Snelling was the location for the Military Intelligence Service Language School where Nisei soldiers brushed up on their Japanese language skills to support the U.S. war effort.[81]

After months of bombing select cities throughout Japan, the United States issued an ultimatum. The Empire of Japan ignored the ultimatum, so on Monday, August 6, the U.S. dropped the atomic bomb known as "Little Boy" on the city of Hiroshima. Three days later the U.S. dropped a second bomb, "Fat Man," on Nagasaki. By the end of 1945, the bombs and its nuclear aftermath—flash burns, trauma, illness-related malnutrition, radiation sickness and cancer—would kill 220,000 people, approximately 140,000 in Hiroshima and 80,000 in Nagasaki. Japan surrendered on August 14, 1945.

At the time the bombings occurred, the Zenimura family, Kenichi, Kiyoko and Kenshi, had just returned to the San Joaquin Valley to live with the Yamasaki in-laws on their ranch in Bowles, California. The extended Zenimura family in Japan experienced the devastation in the Hiroshima bombing. Fortunately, his immediate family members were safe. Kenso Zenimura recalls where he was the day the A-bomb was dropped, "I was in Chicago when the Atomic bomb fell on Hiroshima and I know that they (my parents) were happy that my older brother was not in Hiroshima when the bomb was dropped. My father's mother had already passed away (in 1938) and my father's father was in Hawaii during the war."[82]

Back in Gila River, baseball was no longer played. In fact, there were so few athletic events that the *Gila News Courier* discontinued its sports coverage. Unlike Zenimura not everyone had left the camp. The population of Gila River was still approximately 7,000 people in August 1945. Men were now being hired to construct boxes to help with the packing of camp goods.[83] Among those who were returning to life back in California was Chiura Obata, the founder of the first Japanese American baseball team in San Francisco. He returned to the University of California at Berkeley to teach art.[84]

With the fall semester of college just around the corner, Kenso returned home and joined the family at the Bowles ranch. He enrolled at Fresno State College in September 1945 and moved in with the Nishioka family in Fresno to be closer to campus.

On September 27, the *New York Times* reported that a U.S. Army baseball team would soon tour Japan for a series of games with Nipponese teams. The plans called for gate receipts being turned over to "war sufferers in Japan." An editor with the *New York Times*, still passionate about the events of the war, took issue with the effort. "General Abner Doubleday, a military man himself, undoubtedly is spinning wildly in his grave at the thought of it," declared the editor. "He didn't invent the 'great American game' to help the Japanese."[85] Little did the *Times* editor know that baseball would do just that for Japan after the war, just as it did for Japanese Americans during the war.

Between 1943 and 1945, some of the best baseball in all the Japanese American relocation camps was played at Zenimura Field. The results from multiple games with outside semipro teams at Gila River show that Zenimura Field also hosted some of the best wartime baseball in the state of Arizona, period.

The field itself no longer exists. As of 2010, the historic site is occupied by a working olive orchard operated by the Gila River Indian Community. The only remnants of the ballpark are the box scores, articles, a few rare photographs, the memories of the ballplayers who played there, and a primitive home plate made of wood.

More important than the results of the games was the positive impact baseball had on the internees. In a 1998 interview with *Sports Illustrated*, Kenso Zenimura reflected on the importance of the national pastime to him. "Baseball was the only thing that kept us going. If we didn't play baseball, [camp life] would've been unbearable. Even when we didn't play, we were out there watching."[86]

The late Pat Morita, actor and former Gila River internee, echoed a similar sentiment. "Kenichi Zenimura showed that with effort and persistence, you can overcome the harshness of adversity.... Zenimura and others created a fraternal community in the desert — and baseball was the glue."[87]

8

Passing the Torch (1946–1968)

"It is much easier to make efforts of starting a better understanding between us in the field of sports than trying to talk your way through rough spots."[1]
— Kenichi Zenimura

The 1946 Season—Touching Home

When the Zenimuras left Gila River in August 1945 they could not afford to rent or buy their own home. So instead they moved in with Kiyoko's family, the Yamasakis, on their farm in Bowles, California, approximately 15 miles south of Fresno. Kenichi didn't return to his prewar job at the automobile dealership and instead found work on a ranch. He later became a crew boss at a vineyard.[2] Kenso returned to California from Chicago after spending the summer working with Uncle Bob Yamasaki in a battery factory. Upon arrival he and brother Kenshi received their first taste of grape picking. This period of hard labor convinced the young Zenimura boys of the importance of earning a college degree.

In the fall Kenso moved in with the Nishioka family in Fresno and enrolled at Fresno State College. Unfortunately, after one semester he was forced to leave school due to the draft. On March 26, he joined the U.S. Army and was shipped to Camp Beal located 214 miles north of Fresno in Yuba County (near Marysville). From there he embarked on a whirlwind of military assignments and relocations: Fort Lewis, Washington; Fort Monroe, Virginia; and Camp Stoneman, in Contra Costa County, 40 miles northeast of San Francisco. Along the way he took the Japanese language proficiency test and, to his surprise, passed. As a result, Kenso ceased his ball-playing stint with the Fort Monroe team and reported to the Military Intelligence Service (MIS) in Monterey, California.[3] While in Monterey, Kenso spent his weekends in San Jose with George Tak Abo playing ball as a member of Russell Hinaga's Zebras.[4]

In May 1946, Kenshi graduated from Fresno High School and followed his big brother's lead by enlisting in the Army. After serving in Italy for a year he was discharged. Upon his return in 1947 he signed up for the Army Reserves. This would later prove to be a risky decision because when the Korean conflict started in 1951 he was among the first to be called for service.[5]

Kenichi and Kiyoko eventually saved enough money to put a down payment on a house in Fresno, and in the spring of 1946 Coach Zeni resurrected the Fresno Athletic Club. With a new lineup powered by many relocation camp stars like pitchers Tak Abo and Nik

Nishi and catchers George "Hats" Omachi and Kaz Ikeda, the new FAC became one of eight teams in the American League division of the Fresno Twilight Baseball League.[6] Other teams included the Dairy Farmers, the Post Office, Camp Pinedale, the Rudolphs, the Warrior Boosters, Club Gaona and Kilburn's Prep. One of the few records available of the season featured a 6-to-2 Dairy Farmers victory over the FAC.[7] As the season unfolded, a young athlete in the neighboring town of Exeter caught the eye of Zenimura. He was a 5'4", 145 lb. star halfback and outfielder with great speed and cannon for an arm. His name was Satoshi "Fibber" Hirayama. Years later coach Zenimura would invite Fibber to join his Fresno nine.

The summer of '46 brought the first official Negro League to California. Led by sports entrepreneur Abe Saperstein, the West Coast Negro Baseball League (WCNBL) was founded in May with teams in Seattle, Portland, San Francisco, Oakland, Los Angeles, and Fresno. The Fresno franchise lasted only a short time before folding and relocating to San Diego. With Zenimura's long history of playing against the top Negro league talent in the West, the new Negro league included several opponents from his storied career.

In San Francisco, Harold "Yellowhorse" Morris was named president and general manager of the Sea Lions. Zeni and the FAC had defeated Morris as a hurler with Chet Bost's Oakland Pierce Giants back in 1923. Down south in Los Angeles, Wayne "Tank" Carr of Lonnie Goodwin's L.A. White Sox of the 1920s paid homage to his old team by resurrecting the moniker "White Sox." The new L.A. White Sox club included a left-handed outfielder from Phoenix named Leon "Sugar" Westbrooks. Just three years earlier Westbrooks was a member of the Phoenix Colored Nine who traveled into the Gila River internment camp to battle Zenimura's All-Stars.[8] Despite having big name backers like Olympic champion Jesse Owens, the WCNBL was not profitable enough to stay in business and folded in July 1946. One team, the San Francisco Sea Lions, survived as a barnstorming club and two years later added one of the greatest competitors of Zenimura's career, James Raleigh "Biz" Mackey.

The 1946 season saw the first African American to play for a minor league team since the color line was established in the 1880s. Jackie Robinson arrived in racially-charged Daytona Beach, Florida, for spring training with the Montreal Royals. He wasn't allowed to stay at the regular team hotel, so instead he stayed at the home of a local black politician. Jackie made his Royals debut at Daytona Beach's City Island Ballpark on March 17, 1946, in an exhibition game against the team's parent club, the Dodgers.

In July 1946, President Truman welcomed some special MVPs to the White House—the 442nd Regimental Combat Team composed of Japanese Americans. The 442nd was one of the most decorated combat teams of World War II, earning 7 Presidential Distinguished Unit Citations, 21 Medals of Honor, 53 Distinguished Service Crosses, and 9,846 Purple Hearts. Speaking from the White House lawn, President Truman declared, "You not only fought the enemy, but you fought prejudice ... and you won."

Truman's words of inspiration for the 442nd combat team also described the shared war faced by African Americans and Japanese Americans forced to play in their own leagues due to the bigotry and ignorance that held baseball's color line firmly in place. This war would see a new battle in the coming season.

The 1947 Season—Signs of Change

Baseball is not just about timing, it's also about opportunity. The inequity of playing opportunities available for Nisei ballplayers was underscored in February 1947 when third baseman and outfielder Lee Carey, 17, formerly of the Tucson Badgers, was signed by the Cleveland Indians. The Indians paid Carey the largest bonus ever given in the history of the organization in a player signing.[9] Just two seasons earlier Kenshi Zenimura roped a game-winning single past Carey to win the historic 10-inning Butte High Eagles victory over Tucson played at Gila River, Arizona.

Baseball commissioner Happy Chandler was a wise and brave man. He oversaw the initial steps toward integration of the major leagues, beginning with the debut of Jackie Robinson with the Brooklyn Dodgers in 1947. Chandler's position was controversial with team owners. It is reported that the owners voted 15–1 against integrating the sport in a secret January 1947 meeting.

Chandler didn't budge from his position. Some historians say that his controversial stance was the main reason why he was not selected for another term as commissioner after his term expired in 1951. It was a good thing for baseball that he cared more about his conscience than his career. Branch Rickey recounted Chandler's words in his autobiography:

> I've already done a lot of thinking about this whole racial situation in our country. As a member of the Senate Military Affairs Committee, I got to know a lot about our casualties during the war. Plenty of Negro boys were willing to go out and fight and die for this country. Is it right when they came back to tell them they can't play the national pastime? You know, Branch, I'm going to have to meet my Maker some day. And if He asks me why I didn't let this boy play, and I say it's because he's black, that might not be a satisfactory answer. If the Lord made some people black, and some white, and some red or yellow, he must have had a pretty good reason. It isn't my job to decide which colors can play big league baseball. It is my job to see that the game is fairly played and that everybody has an equal chance. I think if I do that, I can face my Maker with a clear conscience.

On April 15, 1947, Jackie Robinson became the first African American to play in the majors. For people of Japanese ancestry, the poignancy of the day might have been tainted with the presence of Babe Pinelli behind the plate as the umpire of this historic game. Pinelli was both vocal and unapologetic about his hatred towards Japanese Americans during World War II. Prejudice and racism would prevent any person of Japanese ancestry from playing in the big leagues for another 17 years.

At the age of 47, Zenimura continued to manage and coach. This season his squad was headquartered in Clovis, approximately 10 miles northeast of Fresno. As a member of the Central California Nisei League (CCNL), the Clovis Nisei Nine played against clubs in neighboring Bowles, Parlier, Reedly and Visalia. Newspaper coverage of the 1947 CCNL season was slim, however it was reported that under the leadership of "old man Zeni," Clovis won back-to-back championships (1947–48) of the CCNL. The toughest competition in the league came from the Visalia Nisei led by brothers Fibber and Truck Hirayama. Fibber received the American Legion Auxiliary award for athletic performance in 1947.

Ironically, while the *Fresno Bee* had only a few articles on the baseball exploits of local Japanese players, reporter Ed Orman detailed the pitching of Zenimura's colleague, Takizo Matsumoto (aka Frank Narushima), who pitched in a contest in Japan in October 1947. According to Orman, "Matsumoto pitched in a game in which the House of Representatives humbled the House of Councillors, 22 to 3, on Doolittle Field." Frank was highlighted as a close friend of Lefty O'Doul, San Francisco Seal manager; Connie Mack, manager of the Philadelphia Athletics; and the late Lou Gehrig. He also acted as interpreter for American baseball teams on tour of Japan in '31 and '34. Matsumoto was serving as a representative at the peace conference in Japan and had to retreat from the baseball game after a few innings on the mound to be present at the session.[10]

The 1948 & 1949 Seasons—Reestablishing Normalcy

Zenimura continued to play ball and manage the Clovis nine of the Central California Nisei League. His team won their second CCNL championship in 1948. That same spring, Kenso made the varsity squad at Fresno State College, now under the leadership of new coach Pete Beiden, a former competitor of Zeni's in the Twilight League.[11]

After his first collegiate season, Kenso and teammate Tak Abo landed jobs picking pears in Northern California, and spending their weekends playing ball with the San Jose Zebras. According to San Jose baseball historian Ralph Pearce, Kenso was in the San Jose lineup on August 15, 1948, in their game against the Richmond Athletic Club for the Coast Northern California Nisei Baseball League championship. San Jose won 20–5. For Kenso and Tak, playing with the Zebras reunited them with many of the players from the Heart Mountain, Wyoming series, including Chi Akizuki, George Hinaga and their former Gila All-Star teammate, Mas Kinoshita.[12]

Zeni's friend and former FAC teammate—Fred Yoshikawa—having officially retired from the diamond and fine-tuned his golf game behind barbed, was now a golf pro. Fred later won the Nisei Golf Championship in 1953. He also shot an 81 at Pebble Beach, California, the course Jack Nicklaus called the most beautiful golf course in the world. It is a par 72 course, and to put Yoshikawa's '53 performance in 21st-century perspective, pro golfers Hale Irwin and Sergio Garcia both shot an 81 at Pebble Beach as prize money winners in the 2000 U.S. Open.[13]

Just three years after the dropping of the bomb on Hiroshima and Nagasaki, America was doing its part to help rebuild the game in Japan. Both the Pacific Coast League and International Baseball League (IBL) donated twelve dozen big league baseballs and bats to high school and college teams in Japan in an effort to "further increase Japanese interest in America's national sport." The movement was started by Frank Shaughnessy, IBL president, whose son was a sergeant with the U.S. army occupation in Japan.[14] Zeni would soon lend his aid as well and again take up his matchmaking skills to rebuild teams and organizations. For now, he had a life to rebuild and baseball games to play and coach.

In late January 1949, the *Fresno Bee* covered the City League basketball team featuring the All-Nisei lineup of Zenimura, Kimura, Hirabayashi, Abo, Nishioka.[15] Many Nisei baseball players stayed active in other sports like basketball to keep their skills sharp in the off-season. The tactic must have helped. According to Kenso Zenimura, the Fresno Nisei baseball team won the state championship in '49 and '50. The league was comprised of teams from San Jose, Lodi, Florin, Walnut Grove and Placer. "We played ball every Sunday on the high school diamond or municipal stadium," said Kenso. "On occasion we'd even drive four to five hours one way by car to play San Jose," he added. Coach Zeni was primarily a catcher now, serving as an on-field mentor for his young pitching staff.

The 1949-50 championship Nisei Nine from Fresno was bolstered by the speed and powerful arm of Fibber Hirayama. He joined Zenimura's squad during the off-season when he wasn't playing for Fresno State. Second-year FSC coach Pete Beiden hoped to improve his 1948 record of 26 wins and 11 loses, so he also signed Hirayama and penciled the freshman football star in the lineup at center field.[16] Fibber joined Tak Abo and Kenso Zenimura, giving the FSC three Nisei players for the '49 season.[17]

Fibber, Tak and Kenso weren't the only Zeni protégés contributing at the major college level in 1949. Mas Kinoshita, the star southpaw of the Gila All Stars, joined the USC Trojans as a pitcher for co-coaches Sam Barry and Rod Dedeaux.

In the spring of 1949, in Tokyo, the Japanese professional baseball league named its first official commissioner in Matsutaro Shoriki. Called Japan's own "Happy Chandler," he took office intent on "rebuilding Japanese baseball on the American plan." Shoriki said he hoped to accomplish at least three things: to build up two major leagues like the American and the National in the United States; build more baseball stadiums; and get general MacArthur's approval to invite an American baseball team to Japan next fall. At the time, the league had eight teams, four in Osaka, three in Tokyo and one in Nogoya.[18]

MacArthur responded to Shoriki's request. In 1949, the general asked Lieutenant Cappy Harada, a former player from California once scouted by the St. Louis Cardinals organiza-

On May 18, 1949, Kenichi and Kiyoko Zenimura celebrated their 25th wedding anniversary. As a ballplayer, Zeni was "slowing down," primarily playing catcher to serve as an on-field mentor for his young pitching staff (Zenimura Family Archive).

tion, to help revive baseball in Japan. MacArthur asked Harada to look into bringing an American goodwill team to Japan. Cappy flew to San Francisco and invited Lefty O'Doul to bring the Seals. Lefty immediately agreed.[19]

The 1950 Season—

On January 25, 1950, Kenichi Zenimura celebrated his 50th birthday. Despite the sore joints, aching muscles and deteriorating vision, "old man Zeni" continued to compete with and against players half his age or younger. The Central California Nisei League roster of clubs remained the same as the previous season.

The series for the California Nisei Championship was played between Fresno and the San Jose Zebras. Fresno won the first game 3 to 1 in San Jose. The second game was played at Fresno State College Field in Fresno. John Horio and Mas Kinoshita pitched for San Jose, while George "Lefty" Fujioka, formerly of the Gila All Stars, pitched for Fresno. With coach Zenimura as the veteran backstop, Kenso at second, Kenshi in center field, and Fibber Hirayama in left field, Fresno defeated Russ Hinaga's boys 9 to 5 to win the 1950 California Nisei State Championship title.[20]

Looking for redemption, the San Jose Zebras challenged Fresno to another best of three series. On June 18, 1950, Fibber pitched game one for the Fresno Nisei against San Jose, winning 4 to 0. In game two, San Jose won 8 to 2 behind the stellar pitching of Jiro Nakamura. The third and final tie-breaking game between Fresno and San Jose never materialized.[21]

In 1950, Lefty O'Doul, the manager of the San Francisco Seals, signed Wally Yonamine (the first person of Japanese ancestry to play in the NFL when he was signed by the San Francisco 49ers in 1947) and assigned him to the team's Salt Lake City Bees farm club in the Pioneer League. Wally played outfield and first base and hit an impressive .355, fourth best in the league. O'Doul had originally planned on calling Yonamine up to the Seals in 1951 but Matsutaro Shoriki was looking to re-integrate Japanese baseball and Cappy Harada worked out a deal with O'Doul to send Yonamine to Japan. Wally was told he had little chance of playing in the majors because of post-war tensions toward Japanese American, so he agreed to sign with the Tokyo Giants. In 1951 Yonamine became the first American to play in Japan after World War II.

The 1951 Season—

Kenichi Zenimura and his Fresno Nisei nine continued their winning ways in 1951. According to the *Fresno Bee*, Zenimura's club won the national Nisei championship in a playoff with the Denver Nisei club in a game played in Fresno.[22] This Fresno Nisei squad was once again powered by Fibber Hirayama and Kenso Zenimua. Kenshi was a member of the Army Reserves in 1951. Zeni also brought in a few ringers from the California Nisei baseball scene—pitcher Mas Okuhura of Lodi, former hurler for Gila River Block 30 team; and Gordy Miyamoto of Monterey, former member of the Poston internment camp team. Gordy was also the brother of Ty Miyamoto, Zenimura's teammate on the 1937 Kono Alameda All-Stars. The veteran backstop, Coach Zenimura, called every pitch and kept the Denver batters guessing throughout the series.

The 1951 Denver Nisei club included George Akimoto, the club's leading hitter, and pitcher Dick Kitamura. After the loss to Zenimura's Fresno Nine, Kitamura joined the Colorado State A&M baseball team and starred at the shortstop position. Dick Kitamura, like Yonamine, was a Hawaiian who received a chance to play professional baseball in Japan. From 1952 to 1954, Kitamura was a member of the Mainichi Orions, led by fellow Hawaiian and future Japanese Baseball Hall of Famer Bozo Wakabayashi.

The military conflict in Korea was now several months old and Kenshi was among the first to be called up. He reported to Fort Lewis, Washington, and was immediately shipped overseas. While fighting in Korea, Kenshi contracted hepatitis from drinking unsanitary water in the jungle. He got sick and collapsed. The medics came in and took him to a hospital in Nara, Japan. In hindsight, the illness saved his life. Kenshi's platoon was ambushed shortly after he was taken to the hospital. Everyone in his platoon was killed. The illness proved serendipitous once more as his stay in the hospital in Nara, Japan, provided the opportunity for Kenshi to meet and reconnect with his big brother Kenji "Harry" Zenimura, the first time since they were infants in Hawaii.[23]

While a Zenimura family reunion was unfolding in Japan, middle son Kenso was doing his father proud by leading the Fresno State College Bulldogs on the diamond. The 1951 Fresno State ballclub played games against professional and military teams. The Bulldogs opened the season with a 7–1 victory over the Marines and defeated the San Francisco Seals "B" team. "They thought they were coming to Fresno to play a bunch of college guys, and they found out a little different," Bulldogs catcher Don Bricker said. "They couldn't believe what they saw."[24]

In May, Fresno State chalked up a double win over the California Polytechnic College Mustangs to finish with a season record of 36–4 for one of the best collegiate records in the nation and the distinction of being only one of five teams in NCAA Division 1 history to post a .900 winning percentage.[25] The Bulldogs had a chance to represent the West in the College World Series and were invited to play against USC for the honor. However, Fresno State had a scheduling conflict and the matchup never materialized. The '51 Fresno State team is considered one of the best in the program's history, and fifty-two years later in 2003 it was inducted into the Fresno Sports Hall of Fame.[26] It had to make a father proud.

With their nation-leading winning record, the Bulldogs dominated the post-season award selections. Six Fresno players were named to the California Collegiate Athletic Association (CCAA) all-conference team. They were: Don Barnett, p; Don Bricker, c; Fred Bartell, 1B; Frano Oneto, 2B; Bob Donkersly, ss; Fibber Hirayama, of.[27] One name missing from the list was the team's leading batter, Kenso Zenimura. His absence from the all-conference team list remains a mystery to this day.

Another post-season honor awarded to the Fresno State team was the opportunity to play in Hawaii. Through the networking efforts of Kenichi Zenimura, several members of the FSC team went to Hawaii and competed against Hawaiian League teams in the summer of 1951.[28] Playing in their Fresno State uniforms, the team included the outfield of Kenso Zenimura, Fibber Hirayama and Zip Brown. The pitching aces of the club included Truman Clevenger and Don Barnett. When freshman catcher Bob Bennett struggled with keeping the Hawaiian players from stealing bases, Coach Pete Beiden donned the catcher's gear. Among the star players faced during the tour on the Islands was pitcher Bill Nishida, a future Tokyo Giant, who defeated Fresno in a 10-inning thriller. Even though Zeni was struggling to rebuild his finances in the early 1950s, he was still quietly working his diplomatic magic.

The 1952 Season—Finally, an American Citizen

The Fresno State Bulldogs were ready to defend their CCAA championship title in 1952. Coach Beiden had lost stars like Barnett, Jake Abbott, Tom Yost, Bricker and Howard Zenimura to graduation, but he still had the services of team captain Fibber Hirayama in center field. Replacing Kenso "Howard" Zenimura in the outfield was Kenshi "Harvey" Zenimura.[29] Even though Howard hit left-handed and Harvey hit right-handed, the younger brother's presence on the team often created some confusion for the media, fans, coaches and players. Harvey not only resembled Howard physically, both played outfield and both wore uniform number 16. By the end of the season, the right-handed Harvey Zenimura was even among the team's leading hitters with a hefty .344 average.

Like Beiden, Coach Ken Zenimura was eager to defend his championship title. Zeni kicked off the new season with an early Sunday morning practice in mid–April 1952. The Fresno Nisei played their home games on the Fresno High school diamond in 1952. As Zeni's sons were preparing to take on the San Pedro Skippers ballclub that won the '52 southern Nisei championship, his own ballclub was boosted by the presence of his son Harvey after the end of the FSC season.[30]

The Fresno Nisei starting lineup in the summer of '52 included:

> Ken Zenimura, catcher/manager
> Ben Yano, first base/pitcher
> Howard Zenimura, second base;
> Jimmy Morioka, third base;
> George Toyama, shortstop;
> Jim Takemoto, left field,
> Harvey Zenimura, center field;
> Ken Obata, right field.[31]

On June 27, the U.S. Senate and House defeated President Truman's veto and voted the Walter-McCarren Act into law. The new bill gave a small number of Japanese the opportunity to immigrate to the U.S. and allowed Issei like Kenichi Zenimura to become naturalized U.S. citizens. According to Howard, his father prepared diligently for the U.S. citizenship and passed with flying colors. "I remember my dad going to citizenship class after the law was passed," said Howard. "He didn't have any problem in passing because he could speak and write English very well. When he got his citizenship, we didn't have a big party ... we were still struggling [financially] to get ahead."[32]

That summer Lefty O'Doul attempted to import an established Japanese Professional Baseball League player into the United States. O'Doul told the *Los Angeles Times* that "the next great innovation in organized baseball—following the advent of night games and Negroes—will be the introduction of Japanese ball players." Lefty spearheaded an effort to invite Japanese baseball's home run king Kaoru Betto to try out for the San Diego Padres in the PCL. Unaware of the past attempts of Japanese players to cross "the yellow color line," like Sorakichi with the Cleveland Spiders in 1897, and Sugimoto with the New York Giants in 1905, the press called Betto's efforts the "the first Japanese born athlete ever to try out for organized baseball" in the U.S.[33] "They're fast afoot and quick with their hands, and on the base paths should drive pitchers crazy. You can't beat them for speed. Defensively, the Japanese are every bit as good as our top stars," Lefty declared.[34] No reasons were reported as to why Betto did not join the San Diego Padres.

In May 1952 an announcement was made that a team of baseball players selected from California colleges would make a barnstorming tour of Japan in the summer. The team, piloted by Coach John Scolinos of Pepperdine, was composed of players from the California Intercollegiate Baseball Association, the California Collegiate Athletic Association (CCAA) and other state baseball loops.[35] The team of California college stars was scheduled to meet the Japanese all-stars in the first game on August 9 in Tokyo.

According to *Stars and Stripes*, the games against the American College Coast Stars would be the "hypothetical collegiate world series contests" with the Japanese All-Stars in Osaka and Nagoya.[36] Players selected as the barnstorming "Pacific Coast All-Stars" were:

Harvey Zenimura, Fresno State
Dick Camill, Santa Clara
Ed Thile, San Diego State
Al Matthews, California
Warren Goodrich, Stanford
Joe Segura, UCLA
Ron Gerst, UCLA
Pete Moody, UCLA
Darryl Nelson, Oregon (player manager)
Jim Drews, Pepperdine
Willie Davis, Santa Barbara
Carl Thomas, Santa Ana Junior College
Frank Romero, Cal Poly
John Garten, USC

Their seven-game series in 14 days was extended to 17 games in 30 days. When it was all said and done, they won 10 games, lost 5 and tied 2 against Japanese college nines.[37]

Standouts for the Americans were outfielder Kenshi Zenimura of Fresno State and pitcher Dick Camill of Santa Clara.[38] Throughout the course of the tour the U.S. faced several future Japanese professional baseball players, including outfielder Takashi Iwomoto of the Tokyo Giants and catcher Katsuhiko Hara of the Kintetsu Buffaloes. Coach Scolinos was not only impressed with Kenshi's play on the diamond, he took notice of his leadership ability as well. As Zeni's son, he had the benefit of a lifetime role model. When Scolinos received a call from the U.S. with news that his father was critically ill, he selected Harvey to serve as acting manager of the team prior to returning home.[39]

In late 1952, Harvey was back in Fresno and again playing ball for his father's ballclub. Kenichi Zenimura called his Twilight Winter Baseball League addition the "Nichi Bei Baseball Club" and on November 3 the *Fresno Bee* stated that they had "moved into undisputed first place." The Nichi Bei showcased some sharp hitting and "sparkling base running." Coach Zenimura's team was an integrated mix of Japanese American, Caucasian, African American and Hispanic ballplayers. The Nichi Bei lineup:[40]

Fibber Hirayama, cf
Norman Tanner, 2b
Kenso Zenimura, 2b
John Morse, 3b
Len Bourdett, ss
Kenshi Zenimura, lf

Rudy Garcia, p (Fresno State pitcher, transfer from the University of San Francisco)
Frank Hayes, 1b-rf
Larry Burgess, p-rf
George Toyama, rf
Glen Lewis, c
Truman Clevenger, p
Kenny Stacks, p
Bernard Martinez
Don Asplund, p
George Omachi, ph

By Thanksgiving, Zenimura's Nichi Bei team held first place in the standings with a 4–1 record.[41] The Nichi Bei lost one game to the second place Cardinals, 9–2, in early November when their defense imploded with seven errors and allowed 9 unearned runs. The Fresno Winter League played twin bills on Saturdays, free to the public, at the Fresno State College Park. The Nichi Bei offensive was fueled by the hot bats of Hirayama, Toyama, Bourdet, Kenso Zenimura and Lewis.[42] On November 30, pitchers Clevenger and Garcia combined for a two-hit shutout against the Mid Valley Sports nine, securing a 7–0 victory, a 5–1 season record, and first place for Coach Zenimura.[43]

The 1953 Season—The Master Negotiator Is Back

After in less than one year of enjoying life as a U.S. citizen, Ken Zenimura and other Issei now had to cope with those trying to turn back the clock to the good ole' days. One vocal opponent to Issei citizenship was Eugene Nixon, former Pomona football coach who mentored Zenimura's high school coach "Banty" Given. "I think we should repeal the McCarren-Walter Immigration and Naturalization Act," said Nixon. "I favor repealing the present immigration law, and substituting for it an act forbidding any further immigration whatever into this country for the next five to 10 years," he added.[44] Fortunately, the law remained.

Neither Coach Ken Zenimura nor Coach Pete Beiden would have the services of outfielder Fibber Hirayama in 1953. In January he was drafted into the army and sent to Fort Ord, California.[45] Fortunately for Fibber, he was invited to roam the outfield for the Fort Ord Warriors. For the opening series of the '53 season, the Warriors battled Fibber's old club, the Fresno State College Bulldogs.[46]

In a three-game series, Fort Ord defeated Fresno State in the first two games, 10 to 0 and 8 to 4. Fibber was the star of the game, playing classic small ball. He generated a run with a base on balls and a stolen base. On March 15, Fresno State took the third game 4–3. This series was the last time for Harvey Zenimura and Fibber Hirayama to battle against each other as opponents.

Later that spring the *Fresno Bee* reported that Fibber was "deliberating two professional offers—one from the Fresno Cardinals and the other from the Stockton Ports ... [however] some of Fibber's advisors are urging him to negotiate a contract to play ball in one of the professional leagues in Japan."[47] Looking back Fibber said that his advisor at the time was Coach Ken Zenimura, who was quietly negotiating contracts behind the scenes for him and other players in the Fresno area to play in Japan.

The Tokyo Giants, with the help of special advisor Cappy Harada, were due to arrive in San Francisco on February 16. The touring group numbered around 60 people, with 33 ballplayers making the trip. The Giants were scheduled to play several games with major and Pacific Coast League teams during spring training in California and Arizona.

In late February the *Fresno Bee* announced that the touring Tokyo Giants were to play against a squad of local all-stars. "Ken Zenimura, the manager of the Fresno Nisei All Stars made the arrangements to bring the Giants to Fresno and he and Fresno State College coach Pete Beiden are organizing the team. It will be a combination of local Nisei and professional ball players who will compose the Fresno team to play the powerful visitors."[48] Coach Zenimura had assembled "a potent lineup of local players" and would open with the following starters and batting orders: Harvey Zenimura, lf; Fred Sommers, ss; John Morse, 1b; Bob Moniz, cf; Jake Helmuth, rf; John Walker, 2b; Len Bourdet, 3b; and Don Bricker c.

Truman Clevenger was slated to start the first game. Coach Zenimura armed his team with lots of pitching options with nine other hurlers: Ted Wills, Jack Hannah, brothers Bob and Dick Drilling, Jerry Meyer, Jim Perkins, Charley Beene, Bill Vanderlaan and Al Garcia. Other reserve players selected for the Valley All-Star team were Howard Zenimura, Isiah Jackson, Howard Phillips, Glen Lewis and Bob Bennet.[49]

The barnstorming Tokyo Giants schedule called for a series of exhibition games starting with game one on Saturday in Fresno, game two on Sunday in Visalia, and game three in Fresno on Monday — all against Zenimura's Valley All-Stars. The Nipponese would then go on to play the San Francisco Seals, Hollywood, San Diego, Oakland, Portland and Sacramento of the Pacific Coast League, and the St. Louis Browns, New York Giants and Chicago White Sox in California before returning home March on 27. The cost for the Giants tour was an estimated $100,000.[50]

The *Fresno Bee* profiled four Tokyo Giant star players: outfielder Wally Yonamine, first baseman Tetsuharu Kawakami, and pitchers Takehiko Bessho and Hideo Fujimoto:

> It was six years ago last fall when Wally Yonamine, a versatile halfback, sparkled for the Honolulu All Stars in a football game in Fresno's Ratcliffe Stadium.... The Hawaiian born Yonamine will return to Fresno in the role of the leading hitter for the Tokio Giants, who will help inaugurate the local baseball season in a game against the Valley All Stars in the Fresno State College Park. Twenty-seven-year-old Yonamine batted .344 for the Giants last season, appearing in 116 games. He hit 10 home runs, the second best for the Giants.[51]
>
> The outstanding pitcher among the Giants is Tekahike [*sic*] Bessho, a 29-year-old flinger who won 33 games while losing 13. He emerged with the imposing earned average of 1.94. Bessho struck out 192 opponents. Hideo Fujimoto, another ace pitcher, chucked two no hitters and ran up a string of 68 consecutive scoreless innings while winning 16 and losing six games. First baseman Tetsuju [*sic*] Kawakami, twice voted the most valuable player among the Giants, ranked second to Yonamine in hitting with a .320 mark. Japanese players are supposed to be light hitters, but last year Kawakami hit a 400 foot home run.[52]

GAME 1: Tokyo Giants 3, Valley All Stars 2

"The Tokyo Giants from Japan opened their exhibition baseball tour ... by scoring a 3 to 2 victory over the Valley All-Stars in the first of a three game series before about 1,500 fans in the Fresno State College Park," reported *the Bee*.[53]

Tokyo started former University of California star Bill Nishida who gave up three hits and one unearned run in the first three innings. Nishida was relieved by Masayoshi Miura and Minoru Suzuki, in the final three innings. For the local All-Stars, Truman Clevenger took the mound for the first six innings, giving up one earned run and five hits. Southpaw

In 1953, Kenichi Zenimura and Shigeru Mizuhara (far right) face one another in Fresno 18 years after their first encounter when Fresno played the 1935 Tokyo Giants. Tokyo's consultant, Cappy Harada (center), watches as managers Zenimura and Mizuhara exchange line-up cards (Nisei Baseball Research Project).

Ted Wills relieved in the seventh and was tagged with the loss. The Giants scored in the third inning as Wally Yonamine reached first on catcher's interference, advanced to third, and then tagged up and scored on Yuko Minamimura's deep fly to left.

For the locals, Kenshi Zenimura matched efforts with an RBI single to right in the third inning. In the eighth, brother Kenso Zenimura poked a looper just over third to tie the game 2–2. Yonamine drove home pitcher Suzuki for the game winner with one out in the ninth. The hitting stars of the day were Yonamine, Chiba, Kenshi Zenimura and Moniz, who each had two hits. Defensively, Kenshi Zenimura made the top fielding play of the game with a running glove hand stab of Kawakami's 360 foot shot to right center in the eighth inning.

The crowd was entertained by the antics of home plate umpire Emmett Ashford, who would later become the first African American umpire in Major League Baseball in 1966.[54]

GAME 2: Tokyo 5, Valley All-Stars 3

The Tokyo Giants won the second game against Kenichi Zenimura's Valley All-Stars, 5 to 3. The guests from Japan used six different pitchers in the contest, with Takumi Otomo starting and earning the victory. The big bats of the day were carried by Tokyo shortstop Saburo Hirai, 1-for-3 with a home run, and second baseman Shigeru Chiba, 2-for-3 at the plate. For the Valley All-Stars, Beene was the losing pitcher of record, striking out one and walking two Tokyo batters. Catcher Bricker hit a double, while Kenshi Zenimura had a 2-for-5 day at the plate. The coach's son would have had another hit if it were not for the defensive play of the game, when Wally Yonamine robbed him of an extra-base hit in the ninth with a diving shoestring catch after a long run. After the contest in Visalia, Tokyo left for its spring training base in Santa Maria, holding a two-game edge on the Valley All Stars. The third game between the Tokyo Giants and Zenimura's All-Star squad was rained out.[55] The winning pitcher of the day, Otomo, would later go on to have a stellar season in 1953: a 27–6 win-loss record, 173 strikeouts, and a 1.85 ERA in 281.1 innings. For his on-field accomplishments, Otomo was named the winner of the 1953 Sawamura Award, the Cy Young Award equivalent in Japan.[56]

According to *Fresno Bee* reporter Bruce Ferris, before the Tokyo Giants left the Valley they were invited to Zenimura's home for food and festivities. When the first member of the Tokyo Giants bowed to greet Zenimura, Zeni stuck out his right hand and said, "Why don't we just shake? We're in America now."[57] This greeting, in contrast with the traditional Japanese meal served to the Tokyo guests, highlights Zeni's sense of humor and the cultural complexities he faced as a Japanese American.

After the Tokyo Giants left Central California for the remaining games of their tour, Coach Zenimura announced that he was heading to Hawaii. The *Fresno Bee* detailed his plans:

> Kenny Zenimura, the veteran Fresno baseball figure, will fly over the Pacific Ocean Friday for Honolulu where he will spend a month with his mother and father, extensive property owners in Honolulu, and at the same time do some scouting for Fresno State College and attempt-to cook up some baseball deals. Kenny revealed he has received many letters from athletes in Honolulu wishing to learn about the possibility of getting in FSC and playing football and baseball. "The trip of Pete Beiden and his baseball Bulldogs to Honolulu two seasons ago [1951] really paid off," Zenimura said. "They made many friends there and many athletes are interested in FSC.
>
> Zenimura will be in Honolulu when the Tokyo Giants, currently barnstorming California and Arizona, stop there en route home from the west coast. He will confer with Cappy Harada relative to taking a Fresno baseball club on a tour of Japan next year. Zenimura will also attempt to book a Hawaiian team for a series of games in Fresno and other California cities this year [1953]. Zenimura will return to Fresno late in March to organize his Nisei All Stars for their annual diamond campaign.[58]

The Fresno press reported Zeni's visit:

> Kenny Zenimura, the veteran Fresno baseball man is doing some wonderful work in behalf of Fresno and the Fresno State College on his current trip to Honolulu. The goodwill athletic ambassador from the Raisin City already has made arrangements to bring an all star club from the islands to Fresno in 1954; he may import one or two all star teams this year and is trying to arrange another trip to the islands by the Fresno State College baseball team and its coach, Pete Beiden, plus a trip to Japan, too.
>
> ...We've known Zenimura for many years, but not until we picked up a copy of the column of Red McQueen, the veteran Honolulu sports editor, in the Honolulu Advertiser, did we learn that Zenimura is one of the all time prep and Hawaii League stars. He was a stellar shortstop for the Midpacific Institute and later for the Asahis of the Hawaii League.

The *Fresno Bee* printed his letter to long-time friend and sports writer Ed Orman:

Dear Ed:

Ever since I came here I have been busy visiting my old teammates, coaches of various high schools, meeting boys interested in attending Fresno State and watching inter island high school league and other league games.

I have met all the league officials and I hope to induce the AJA League to send an all star team to the states in 1954. After several meetings I came to terms and the visit of the All Star Japanese American team will be a reality. Most of the Hawaiian All Stars are now playing in Japan so the deal for 1953 is off. But in all probability when the Red Sox champions of the Honolulu League go to Brooklyn to play in the world semipro tournament, the chances are I might have an opportunity to schedule a few games in California, mostly around Fresno. The Kanebo champions of Japan are invited to the same tournament and also may bring that team to the San Joaquin Valley.

And thanks to the Fresno State College team and Pete Beiden. Beiden is known throughout the island as one of the greatest coaches Hawaii ever has seen. The trip really is paying off because the coaches are recommending their star players to attend FSC.

I am figuring on a deal for the baseball coaches to extend an invitation to Beiden for a clinic here.

I have been talking to friends of mine in Honolulu about underwriting a trip to the islands by the Fresno State team and with proper handling I am sure the team also could go to Japan.

I am hoping to bring fine news back to Fresno and FSC about many high school seniors coming to FSC to play baseball and basketball.

Regards,
Kenny Zenimura[59]

Zenimura's return from Hawaii in April 1953 also marked the resurrection of the long-revered Twilight League. "Prospects are bright for the best twilight league baseball which has existed in Fresno for many years, said Fresno City Playground Supervisor R. L. (Ray) Quigley, who pioneered the Twilight League before World War II." Eight teams were lined up for a season of high class evening ball.[60]

Team	*Manager*
Fresno State College	Pete Beiden
Fresno Junior College	Ray McCarthy
American Legion #4	Oliver Bidwell
Fresno Indians	Melvin Combs
Police Department	Joe Osterberg
Fresno High School	Toby Lawless
Nisei All Stars	Ken Zenimura
Telephone Company	Ed King

Each team would play two games a week with five games on the Holmes playground and one at Romain, Cosmos and Fink-Smith.[61]

Coach Zenimura held the first practice of the season for the Fresno Nisei All Stars baseball club on Sunday, April 16, on the Frank H. Ball playground diamond. The *Fresno Bee* also announced that Zenimura would inform his Nisei players about the prospects of playing professional baseball in Japan.[62]

During the summer of 1953 Zenimura's Nisei club resumed play in the California Nisei Baseball League. Nisei teams competing in the loop included Coalinga, Fresno, Madera, San Jose and San Pedro.

In late May the Fresno Nisei Nine defeated the San Jose Zebras 6–5 at the Fresno State College ballpark. "Howard [Zenimura] did a fine job of relief pitching to halt a three run ninth inning rally by the Zebra's which just missed tying the score. Fresno had its big inning in the third when they tallied five runs on six hits. John Horio held the Fresno nine scoreless for the remaining distance. Howard Zenimura had three hits and Harvey two for the winners. Tom Okagaki, former San Jose State shortstop, had two hits for the losers."[63]

This particular game was significant because it had just been announced that three members of the Fresno team would join the professional Hiroshima Carps in the Japanese Central League. Kenso and Kenshi Zenimura were to make the Japan trip along with pitcher Ben Mitsuyoshi.[64] The following week the Fresno Nisei traveled north to battle the San Jose Zebras. The *Fresno Bee* traveled to San Jose to see Ben Mitsuyoshi pitch the Fresno Nisei All Stars to a 2-to-0 shutout over the San Jose Zebras. In what was called his "most impressive performance of the baseball season," Mitsuyoshi struck out five, allowed four hits and one base on balls. In the victory Kenso Zenimura had a 2-for-4 day at the plate, while brother Kenshi made "a fine catch and then a long throw to first for a double play." After the game, it was announced that the three stars of the day, Ben, Kenso and Kenshi, would leave the following week to play pro ball in Hiroshima, Japan.[65]

The Zenimura brothers and Mitsuyoshi left for the U.S. to play in the Japanese Professional Baseball League in mid–June 1953. Kenichi Zenimura's sons wrote home and sent press clippings about the incredible reception the three Fresno baseball players received in Japan. Facing a crowd of about 15,000 at the railroad station in Hiroshima, they were paraded through the streets for an hour and a half while thousands of fans cheered and besieged them for autographs. A crowd of 36,000 attended the first game in which they played.[66]

Kenso recalled just how proud his father was of him and his brother for signing with the Hiroshima Carp. "He always said, practice hard. Learn what you can. Be confident in what you are capable of doing, and do it," said Kenso. "He had a lot of confidence in me at that time. Just out of college, in good shape. So when we went over to Japan to play he was pretty happy," added Kenshi.[67]

After a month in Japan it became clear to the Zenimura brothers that their careers were heading down different paths. Harvey quickly became a star for the Hiroshima Carps. Early in the '53 season he hit safely three times, walked once and scored four times against the second place Nagoya Dragons, thus helping Hiroshima split a doubleheader before 10,000 fans. As a result of his stellar play on the field, Harvey became a fan favorite in the circuit. After experiencing a zero-for-eight drought at the plate, Howard was designated a utility player for the Carps. Unhappy with the prospect of riding the pine in Japan, Howard made the difficult choice of returning to Fresno for a teaching job in the neighboring town of Madera.[68]

Despite his struggles on the field, Howard's month-long stint in Japan did have its positive highlights. The experience gave him the opportunity to reunite with his older brother Kenji (Harry). Actually, both Harvey and Howard lived with Harry while playing with the Hiroshima Carp. "I did not meet my brother [Harry] until Harvey and I went to play for the Hiroshima Carp in the summer of 1953," said Howard. "He had a house and was married so we both stayed with him and commuted back and forth to the ball park."[69] Howard also recalls that grandfather Masakicihi Zenimua played an important role while the Zenimura brothers were in Japan. They were paid in yen, and they relied on grandfather Zenimura to convert the yen into dollars and then deposit the funds into their accounts in Hawaii.[70]

Years later pitcher Ben Mitsuyoshi reflected on the influence Coach Zeni had on him as a player and as a human being. "You'd have to say that he [Zenimura] was a coach similar to the Atlanta coach [Bobby Cox]. He really had full control of the game when we played. He more or less coached every play, every opportunity for a bunt, hit and run. He was a

After World War II, a wave of Japanese Americans signed to play baseball in Japan partially due to racial tensions in organized baseball in the U.S. In 1953, Kenichi Zenimura was instrumental in negotiating the contracts for (left to right) Kenso Zenimura, Ben Mitsuyoshi, a pitcher from Hanford, California, and Kenshi Zenimura, to play with the Hiroshima Carp (Zenimura Family Archive).

Signing with the Hiroshima Carp in 1953 gave Kenshi (left) and Kenso (right) the opportunity to reunite with their older brother Kenji (center) in Japan. "He (Kenji) had a house and was married so we stayed with him and commuted back and forth to the ball park," recalled Kenso (Zenimura Family Archive).

real student of the game. That is the way I will always remember him." And once the game was over, Ben learned the lessons of generosity from his coach. "He and his wife, Mrs. Zenimura, treated me just like one of their sons ... before and after the games. So I really felt like one of the family."[71]

According to Japanese American baseball historian Kerry Yo Nakagawa, Nisei ballplayers like Yonamine, the Zenimuras and Mitsuyoshi played an important role in helping to build a diplomatic "bridge across the Pacific." The Nisei with their aggressive American style brought the level of baseball in Japan to a higher standard of play," said Nakagawa. "They laid the foundation for many future players to achieve success. Many players honed their skills and spirit and returned to the U.S."

In the fall of 1953, Zenimura continued his efforts as a U.S. Japanese baseball ambassador. His good friend Nobuo Fujita, director of the Six Universities Baseball League in Japan, was in the U.S. making a tour of Pacific coast colleges and universities in an effort to improve the physical education system in the Japanese schools. During his visit to California, Fujita told the *Bee* that he had known Zenimura for some 20 years (since the 1924 tour) and could remember the Fresnan when he toured Japan as a player and a manager. After spending time with the Zenimura family, Fujita made a complete tour of both Fresno State and Stanford University campuses and took many pictures and notes on the athletic plants in both schools.[72]

The 1954 Season — Exporting to Japan

In February, Kenshi Zenimura's prowess in the batting box in Japan received high praise from former "Yankee Clipper" Joe DiMaggio as he coached the Hiroshima Carp professional baseball team. "Zenimura was acclaimed the outstanding rookie in the Japanese professional league during the past 71 game season."[73]

DiMaggio's scouting prediction about Harvey Zenimura came true that July when the Hiroshima Carp outfielder was selected to the all star team of the Central League. Kenshi was penciled in the lineup to play left field in the series against the Pacific League All Stars. Proud papa Zenimura told the *Fresno Bee* that "between 65,000 to 80,000 fans will see each of the games and seats have been sold for months in advance." At the time of the '54 all-star game, Mrs. Zenimura was in Japan visiting her Kenshi and other relatives.[74]

Back in California the Fresno Nisei baseball team began practice for the 1954 season in early May at the Frank H. Ball diamond. Coach Zenimura issued a call for all Nisei players who were interested in playing to be on hand for the workouts. He lined up a full summer schedule of games highlighted by a series against an all star university squad from Japan. The Japanese all star team was scheduled to arrive in Fresno in July.[75]

Zenimura also began play in the Fresno Twilight baseball league in June 1954. The new season was also an attempt on the part of the local recreation department to reestablish the American Baseball Congress in Fresno. Coach Pete Beiden of FSC was elected president of the local ABC setup. Twilight League games were played Monday through Thursday evenings from 6 o'clock until 8 o'clock or seven innings, whichever came first. The participating teams of the Fresno ABC included the Red Sox, led by Pete Beiden; the Japanese Association team, led by Ken Zenimura; the Fresno Indians with skipper James Brown; and the Telephone nine headed by Ed King and (Deal E.) Reynolds. Sacramento, Stockton, San Jose and Bakersfield also expressed interest in reviving the ABC in California.[76]

The standings of the new Twilight League spring season were published in July. The Zenimura Japanese and the Telephone were tied for first place in the American League division race. Zenimura's ballclub held the edge percentage wise, with one less loss, but each had six wins.[77]

1954 Twilight League, American League Division Standings

	W	*L*	*T*	*PCT*
Zenimura Japanese	6	2	0	.750
Telephone	6	3	0	.667
Beiden's Red Sox	4	4	0	.500
Fresno Indians	1	8	0	.111

Up north approximately 190 miles away, a crowd of 5,187 turned out to see an old-timers game in which the San Francisco Old Timers Association team defeated a team of ex–Seal greats 2 to 1. The game highlights included a 350-foot double off the wall by Joltin' Joe DiMaggio.[78]

The 1954 Nisei baseball season brought new additions to the Fresno club — mascots and ball girls. Two young women from the Fresno Buddhist Church, Ricky Yagura, 17, and Alice Clover, 20, joined to team up for publicity purposes.

Coach Zenimura reported that his Fresno Nisei team would be the strongest in several seasons. He had hard hitting former Fresno State star Fibber Hirayama in center field and batting cleanup for the Nisei team. Despite still being official property of the St. Louis

Browns and the Fort Ord Warriors military teams, Fibber made time to play with the Fresno Nisei.

Zenimura's infield was solidified with Hawaiian imports Robert Rii at first base and Tom Takamoto at catcher. Both players arrived in mid–July and would attend FSC in the fall. At second base was Kenso Zenimura; Mac Sanwo was at shortstop; and FSC freshman slugger Keiji Tsuhako was on third. The starting Nisei pitcher was lefthander Willie Yashiro, a native Hawaiian who pitched for the FSC freshman during the '53 season and for the Wasco town team. Rieko Yagura was another new outfielder for the Nisei team.[79]

Keiji Tsuhako was one of many players imported from Hawaii whose lives were changed by Coach Zenimura. Tsuhako recalls how when he arrived in Fresno Zeni hired him and a few other ballplayers to help pick grapes at a local farm. Zenimura worked as a labor crew chief and each morning he would arrive in a military-type transport truck, large enough to seat several men in the back. "He got us all jobs and brought food for us while we worked. He was a generous man who did everything possible to make sure we had what we needed to be successful," said Tsuhako. "He was a good man, a kind man, and I will forever be grateful for his generosity," Keiji added.[80]

In July the Fresno Nisei and Beiden Red Sox were neck and neck in the battle for first place in the Twilight loop.[81] But by August momentum had shifted in favor of Zenimura's Japanese Association and they held on to win the American League division of the Twilight League.[82]

In the California Nisei circuit, Zenimura's boys continued to dominate their competition. On August 29, the Fresno Nisei All Stars pounded out an 18 to 5 win over the San Jose Zebras in an exhibition baseball game played in San Jose. George Toyama led the hitting attack with two triples and a single in six trips to the plate. Kenso Zenimura also had three hits. After securing a victory over long-time rival San Jose, Fresno looked ahead to the Nisei tournament in Lodi. Fresno defeated the Placer ballclub in the first game, and battled the winner of the Lodi vs. San Pedro game in its second contest. Press coverage of the state Nisei tournament was not located, however those who participated in the tourney reported that Zenimura's Fresno Nisei ballclub won the 1954 State Championship.

The closing of the 1954 season also saw the end of Fibber Hirayama's service in the military at Fort Ord. When his commitment ended, Zenimura contacted the center fielder, this time not as a coach, but as a scout. Zeni asked Fibber if he would be interested in joining Harvey Zenimura as a member of the Hiroshima Carp. Despite still belonging to the now Baltimore Orioles organization contractually, Fibber decided to play pro ball in Japan.[83]

Years later Fibber said, "[Coach] Zenimura was a constant student of the game. He always looked for the little details. He would beat you with speed, bunt, double steal. It was a very fast and aggressive style of baseball. He was the best at teaching those principles. His sons were already stars with the Hiroshima Carp, so I went to join them soon after. The reason I was able to go to Japan and have a great career was because of Mr. Zenimura's faith in me."[84]

The 1955 Season—Handing Over the Reins

The Nisei ballclub of Placer, a town approximately 60 miles northeast of Sacramento, won the California Nisei Baseball state championship in 1955. At age 55, Kenichi Zenimura could feel the end of his playing and managing career approaching. Legend has it that Zeni played his final game as a catcher during the 1955 season, although a supporting game summary or box score has yet to surface. What is known is that after the end of the California Nisei baseball season, Zenimura hung up his cleats and clipboard and handed over the managerial reins to his long-time right fielder and protégé George Omachi.

In September Takizo "Frank" Matsumoto, Zenimura's lifelong colleague and now a member of the Japanese Diet representing the prefecture of Hiroshima, visited Fresno. The Japanese dignitary, visiting his many Japanese and American friends in the San Joaquin Valley for the first time since 1951, was primarily concerned with Japan in the 1956 Olympics. In this later capacity he was responsible for the overall policy and conduct of the 1956 Olympic Games preparations and particularly the task of seeking financial support to assure that the Japanese athletes had enough cash to buy their round trip tickets and food while in Australia the next summer.[85]

When asked about the presence of Fresno baseball players in Japan, Matsumoto replied, "Sure, I know Harvey Zenimura and Fibber Hirayama. Who doesn't?" He added, "They're almost national heroes in Hiroshima. Each has his fan clubs. So do most of the baseball stars of Japan these days."[86]

It was an annual tradition of *Fresno Bee* sports editor Ed Orman to wish his friends and fans a Merry Christmas and Happy and Prosperous New year in a special, year-end column. "We acknowledge the thoughtfulness of the following ... Kenny Zenimura, the *former baseball club manager*, who still takes an interest in the national pastime, and whose son Harvey is playing for the Hiroshima Carps in Japan."[87] For the first time since 1912, Kenichi Zenimura was no longer an active participant in the game of baseball.

The 1956–1967 Seasons

In May 1956 the Fresno Nisei baseball nine began its first season without Coach Kenichi Zenimura at the helm. The team got off to a winning start in its season opener with a 10-to-3 victory over the Walnut Grove Deltans (Nisei team) of Sacramento County with Kenso as captain. George Omachi was now managing the team. The *Fresno Bee* gave little attention to the 1956 Fresno Nisei ball club. The few game summaries and line-ups featured in the press included the names of players Kenichi Zenimura recruited from the Islands of Hawaii, such as star pitcher Tom Higa.

* * *

After losing the NCNBL championship to the San Jose Zebras in 1956, the Fresno Nisei All-Stars regrouped and won the crown in 1957. The team was strong and made even stronger with the presence of Kenshi Zenimura, who returned home after a three-year career in Japan with the Hiroshima Carp. The '57 Nisei championship marked the first of five-consecutive championships achieved under new manager George "Hats" Omachi.

The 1957 Fresno Nisei Roster included:

George Omachi
Harvey Shiraga, pitcher, (stocky right-hander and former Roosevelt HS star)
Mac Sanwo, veteran catcher
Fred Watari, p (formerly of FSC)
Mike Tonai, p (formerly of FSC)
Harvey Zenimura

Howard Zenimura
Tom Higa, 3b
George Toyoma, of

The 1957 season also marked the first time in decades that a National Nisei Baseball Championship was not played. "We do not have a national tournament anymore," said Omachi. "The winner of this tournament [in California] will be declared the national champion because the teams in Salt Lake City and Denver are not strong enough now to compete with the California teams."[88]

* * *

In 1958, Zeni experienced a number of losses. On June 25, he received the sad news of the passing of sporting goods store owner, civic leader and close friend, Frank Homan. From the beginning of Zenimura's playing days in Fresno during the early 1920s until the closing of Homan's sporting goods store in the 1950s, Frank was always there to help Zenimura with his baseball equipment needs. Homan's willingness to help Zenimura even while interned behind barbed wire in Arizona was a remarkable gesture of kindness.[89]

Then on November 1, he learned that his friend Takizo "Frank" Matsumoto had died. The former Fresnan and Japanese vice minister was remembered in the press as "a popular figure in Japan through his activities as teacher, politician and sportsman."[90]

* * *

Zenimura said farewell to yet another friend in early 1959. He lost his speedy outfielder from the 1920s Fresno Athletic Club, Harvey Iwata. Iwata was 55 years of age and was stricken while working in the Geographic Names Branch Army Map Service in Washington, D.C.[91]

In the summer of '59 it was announced that a team of all-star high school baseball players from Japan would visit Fresno on August 31 for an exhibition game against a group of San Joaquin College and high school players assembled by Fresno State College coach Pete Beiden.

The Fresno contest was billed as one of five appearances in California by the visiting Japanese team. Zenimura said that T. P. (Cappy) Harada, head scout of the Tokyo Giants, had arranged the tour with the support of the *Asahi Shimbun,* one of the leading Japanese newspapers. The members of the Japanese team were selected from the top performers in a series of tournament games played in Osaka, Japan. "Several of the players chosen for this team will go directly into Japanese professional ball," said Zenimura. "It should be a high class team. It will play games in Lodi, San Jose, Santa Maria and Los Angeles before coming to Fresno to conclude the trip."[92] Zeni was looked to as a source of player and team information.

* * *

Press coverage of Nisei baseball activity in Fresno, California, was scarce in 1960. For Kenichi Zenimura, his time was occupied as an active and involved grandfather. Between his sons Harry, Howard and Harvey, papa Zenimura now split his time and attention between 14 grandchildren

In late October 1960, reporters with the *Fresno Bee* reflected on the all-time baseball greats who contributed to the game in the San Joaquin Valley area. Among the all-time greats listed were Zeni and Fred Yoshikawa.

* * *

The 1961 season was a year for both records to be broken and traditions coming to an end. At the major league level, Roger Maris belted 61 home runs to surpass Babe Ruth for the single-season record. Zenimura's coaching peer from Arizona, Hank Slagle, was erased from the record books as well. Joe Skaisgir of the 1961 University of Arizona baseball team broke Slagle's record of .405 single-season batting average when he hit an impressive .425 for the '61 season.[93] In California, the Northern California Nisei Baseball League disbanded at the end of the season. San Jose player Roy Matsuzaki lamented, "I guess we were too old and nobody wanted to play anymore. When we disbanded, the interest had dropped and a lot of the younger kids had decided that their interest in baseball wasn't there anymore."[94]

* * *

On May 20, 1962, the 25th anniversary of Kenichi Zenimura's last tour to Japan (in 1937) was celebrated by the Fresno community. Reporter Tom Meehan featured Zenimura in a full-page spread in the Sunday *Fresno Bee*. "The history of Nisei baseball in the United States would not be complete without the name of Zenimura somewhere in its timeworn pages. He is the dean of Nisei baseball in America."[95] His influence was noted. "Zenimura still receives mail from the Japanese Hall of Fame, club owners and scouts seeking his advice on Japanese baseball players in America.... Several of Zenimura's first students are managing in the Japanese pro leagues and his influence still is felt throughout the Japanese empire."[96] Zeni was quoted in the article on his reflections of organizing the first California first tour to Japan. "'Our Fresno team hardly ever lost and I wanted to take it to play in Japan,' said Zenimura. 'The Seattle Asahis supposedly was the best Japanese team in the United States. So I challenged them to play is for the right to tour Japan. Ken Nushida pitched us to a 5 to 0 win.'"[97]

Zenimura's favorite team, the San Francisco Giants, made it to the 1962 World Series behind the star power of Willie Mays, Willie McCovey, Juan Marichal, Orlando Cepeda and the Alou brothers, Matty and Felipe. Despite the Giants' powerful lineup, the mighty New York Yankees led by Yogi Berra, Whitey Ford and Mickey Mantle won the series 4 games to 3.

* * *

On May 3, 1964, the *Fresno Bee* sports section featured a photograph of four former star players on the Fresno Japanese baseball team of the 1920s with the minor league Fresno Giants' import from Japan—pitcher Masanori Murakami. The Fresno Japanese legends were Ken Zenimura, Sam Yamasaki, John Nakagawa and Fred Yoshikawa.[98] Murakami was brought over from Japan by the Giants to learn the American style of baseball. But Fresno Giants Manager Bill Werle was so pleased with his performance that he gave him his first pro starting assignment.[99] He went on to become the first Japanese national to play major league ball in the United States.

* * *

The Fresno Athletic Hall of Fame had enshrined a total of forty people since its founding in 1959. Of those honored with a statuette of Apollo, the Greek God of the Sun, the symbol of the FAHF, seven were baseball players: Frank Chance (1959), Dutch Leonard (1960), Frenchy Bordagaray, Orval Overall (1962), Dick Ellsworth, Jim Maloney (1963), and Pete Beiden (1964). The nominees for the baseball category in 1966 were: Wade Blasingame, Pat Corrales, Fibber Hirayama, Lloyd Meriman, Alex Metzler, Monte Pearson, Ted Wills Jr., Don Barnett and Ken Zenimura. Sportswriter Ed Orman was nominated in the general category.[100] When the votes were tallied, Metzler and Orman made the cut. Zenimura and the other stars of the San Joaquin Valley were not selected for the Fresno Sports Hall of Fame in 1966.[101] Zeni would have to wait another year for his career to be celebrated.

* * *

On March 5, 1967, Zenimura joined his peers Jackie Heizenrader, Foy Frazier and Jack Savory as the latest inductees into the Fresno Twilight League Hall of Fame. The 1967 class represented the top 25 all-time players in Fresno's Twilight League history.

The 1968 Season—Zeni's Final Season

Political and social unrest were in the air in 1968. Martin Luther King Jr. was assassinated on April 8 in Memphis, Tennessee; and Robert F. Kennedy, the top presidential candidate for the Democratic Party, was assassinated on June 26 in Los Angeles. During the Summer Olympic Games in Mexico City, sprinters Tommie Smith and John Carlos were banned from the games after raising their fists wearing black gloves to protest the treatment of African Americans in the U.S.

Earlier that spring, the final renunciation case was settled. Some 23 years after people of Japanese ancestry were forced to renounce their U.S. citizenship during World War II,

Kenichi Zenimura was inducted into the Fresno Twilight League Baseball Hall of Fame in 1967, but it was his role as grandfather that brought him the most joy in his later years (Zenimura Family Archive).

they now had the opportunity to have it restored. Of the 5,589 persons whose applications for renunciation were accepted during World War II, 5,409 (approximately 97 percent) asked to have their citizenship returned.

In May 1968 Kiyoko Zenimura reported a burglary in their home. A thief stole wedding and engagement rings, other jewelry and watches worth $1,215 from their home at 708 Collins Ave. A door was forced open to gain entry.[102] According to the Zenimura family, 68-year-old Kenichi was fast asleep on the couch when the burglary occurred.

Zeni loved watching ballgames on TV while enjoying a cold beer after a long day of work as a labor crew chief. In early October Zeni watched the Detroit Tigers surprise the baseball world by defeating the mighty Bob Gibson and the St. Louis Cardinals in Game 7 of the World Series. Immediately after their loss to the Tigers, the Cardinals embarked on a goodwill tour to Japan.

Tuesday, November 5, 1968, marked the fourth time Zenimura received the opportunity to vote in a presidential election since becoming a U.S. citizen 16 years earlier. Running on a campaign promise to restore "law and order," the Republican nominee, former Vice President Richard Nixon won the presidential election over the Democratic nominee, Vice President Hubert Humphrey.

Five days later, Sunday, November 10, Zeni was returning from work to make it home in time for a birthday party for one of his granddaughters. After stopping for a right-hand turn at the corner of A and Inyo street, less than a mile from his house, he was blindsided by a drunk driver who ran a stop sign. Zeni was driving a large military-type transport truck, one big enough to haul workers for his job as a day labor crew chief. Apparently the truck was not equipped with seat belts, and when the oncoming car hit the driver's side of the vehicle, the truck turned over on its right side. The tilting truck, combined with the impact of the crash, sent Zeni towards the ground where he hit his head on the curb. With the blunt-force trauma to the head, he lost consciousness immediately.

It is said that statistically most car accidents occur close to home. This was doubly true for Zenimura. The exact location of the collision was approximately .2 miles (1,052 ft.) from the front door of his house, and 660 ft. from the home plate on the diamond of Frank H. Ball playground, the field on which he had often practiced and played since his arrival in the U.S. in the early 1920s.

On Wednesday, November 13, 1968, sports reporter Bruce Ferris of the *Fresno Bee* expressed his sorrow and sent prayers to the Zenimura family in his "Sport Thinks" article. Just as sports fans were reading Bruce Ferris's words, Zenimura said farewell to the world. The *Fresno Bee* memorialized his life the following day:

> **Dean of Nisei Baseball Dies**
> Kenichi "Ken" Zenimura, 68, one of the oldest amateur baseball players in his time and considered the dean of Nisei baseball in America, died Wednesday in a Fresno hospital of injuries suffered Sunday in an automobile accident.... A wake service will be held Friday at the Calaveras Chapel of the Lisle Funeral Home. Final rites will be heard Saturday morning in the Fresno Buddhist Chapel Annex.[103]

It was standing room only at the Fresno Buddhist Church Annex on Kern Street. Hundreds of friends and family gathered to pay their final respect to Kenichi Zenimura. The nine men selected for Zeni's "final lineup" were Satoshi "Fibber" Hirayama, who delivered the eulogy; and eight honorary pallbearers: Hidechi "Ed" Tsukimura, Johnny Nakagawa, Kazuo "Pug" Mimura, Fred Yoshikawa, Shig Tokumoto, Shiro Kawakami, Fred Tsuda and Fresno State's legendary coach Pete Beiden. All those in attendance were also reminded by the Buddhist Priests about the impermanent nature of existence with a reading of the "Letter on White Ashes" (or hakkotsu no gobunsho), a letter written by Rennyo of the Jodo Shinshu Buddhist sect to his followers. The term "white ashes" refers to the Buddhist funerary tradition of cremation.

> Letter on White Ashes
>
> Now, if we look realistically at the nature of human life, we see that it is fleeting and unpredictable, illusive almost. Birth, life and death pass by in the twinkling of an eye. Thus we never hear of the human body lasting for ten thousand years.
>
> And who today can keep the body young and healthy for even one hundred years? Yes, how quickly our lives slip away. Whether I am the first or someone else, whether today or tomorrow, our lives on earth do indeed one day come to an end. Life seems to vanish unseen like ground water, or to evaporate like the morning dew on the summer lawn.
>
> Thus our bodies may be radiant with health in the morning, but by evening they may be white ashes. If the right causes and conditions prevail, our two eyes are closed forever, our breathing ceases and our bodies lose the glow of life. Our relatives in great numbers and with great wealth can assemble, but they are powerless to change our situation. Even the rites and rituals of grief and mourning change nothing. All we can do is prepare the body for cremation; all that is left is white ashes.
>
> In view of these facts, does it not make sense to focus on the things we can change? We cannot control the passing away of both young and old alike, but each of us can take refuge in the Buddha of Infinite Life who promises to embrace, without exception, all beings who but recite his Holy Name — Namo Amida Buddha. This you can do here and now, freeing yourself of any worries concerning your future life.
>
> With friendly reverence, I remain,
>
> Rennyo (1414–1499)[104]

Zenimura's funeral services concluded at one of the oldest cemeteries in Fresno, the Chapel of the Light, located on Belmont Avenue, just a few miles north of the old Japanese Ball Park. In an ironic twist of fate, years later Highway 99 just next to the cemetery was renamed "Pearl Harbor Survivors Memorial Highway." Perhaps this was fitting, given that Zenimura's life had always seemed to be intertwined with the events of World War II. A modest headstone marks the location of his grave. On the marker are etched four lines to remind visitors of the little man who made a big impact on the world as a hall of fame player, manager, international ambassador — and most important of all — human being:

Father
Kenichiro Zenimura
1900–1968
Dean of the Diamond

Appendix A: Select Box Scores

To date, hundreds of articles, line scores and box scores have been uncovered detailing the exciting career of Kenichi Zenimura. During the 1920s–30s he competed against the top talent in the Pacific Coast League, the Negro Leagues, the Nisei Leagues, barnstorming major leaguers and the newly formed Nippon Professional Baseball League of Japan. In the box scores below, Zenimura compiled an impressive .303 batting average (10 hits/33 at-bats) and .378 on-base percentage (reached base 14 times/37 plate appearances) as a player. These box scores closely mirror his career .312 batting average and .396 on-base percentage in approximately 130 identified games. An additional box score from 1945 reflects what is considered by Zenimura, as a manager, to be the most exciting game ever played at the Gila River Relocation Camp in Arizona during World War II.

Fresno Athletic Club 6, Salt Lake City 4 (Pacific Coast League)
Firemen and Policemen's Baseball Park, Fresno
March 9, 1924

FRESNO A.C.	*AB*	*R*	*H*	*PO*	*A*
Iwata, lf	3	2	0	4	0
Zenimura, 2b	3	1	0	2	4
Yoshikawa, c	4	0	1	6	1
Sako, p	4	0	1	0	1
Nakagawa, cf	4	1	1	4	0
Sakata, 1b	4	0	0	9	0
Nakamura, ss	4	0	1	2	0
Santos, 3b	4	1	2	0	4
Tsukimura, lf	3	1	0	0	0
Totals	33	6	6	27	10

SALT LAKE	*AB*	*R*	*H*	*PO*	*A*
Gillespie, rf	3	0	1	2	0
Horton, 2b	2	1	1	1	2
Hepting, 3b	2	1	1	0	1
Hulvey, lf	4	0	1	2	0
Govenor, cf	4	0	0	1	0
Graff, ss	3	0	0	1	1
Hester, 1b	1	0	2	8	1
Wachenfeld, c	3	1	1	7	1
Mulcahy, p	4	0	0	0	2
Merrit, 2b	2	0	0	2	1
Lazzeri, ss	1	0	0	1	1
Cleary, 3b	1	0	1	0	0
Blunt, c	3	0	1	2	1
*Leslie	1	1	1	0	0
**Lewis	1	0	0	0	0
Totals	35	4	10	27	11

*Leslie batted for Hester in ninth[1]
**Lewis batted for Mulcahy in ninth

Score by inning:

Fresno	1	0	0	0	1	1	3	0	0	= 6
Salt Lake	2	1	0	0	0	0	0	0	1	= 4

Fresno Athletic Club 5, Los Angeles White Sox 4 (Negro League semipro)
White Sox Park, Los Angeles
September 6, 1925

FRESNO ATHLETIC CLUB	*AB*	*R*	*H*	*O*	*A*
Zenimura, ss	5	1	2	3	2
Tsukimura, cf	5	1	2	2	1
Yoshikawa, c	5	0	0	5	2
Tsuda, 1b	4	1	1	9	0
Furabayashi, rf	4	1	2	0	1
Tamiyama, lf	4	0	1	3	1
Hirokawa, 2b	4	1	1	3	2
Muira, 3b	3	0	0	2	2
Nushida, p	4	0	0	0	1
Totals	38	5	9	27	12

L.A. WHITE SOX	*AB*	*R*	*H*	*O*	*A*
Foote, rf	5	0	0	1	0
Savage, lf	4	1	2	4	1
Pullen, c	4	1	1	6	2
Wilson, cf	3	1	1	3	1
Adams, 1b	4	0	2	9	2
Riddle, 3b	4	0	1	1	2
Salisbury, ss	4	0	2	1	4
Johnson, p	4	0	0	0	1
Fagan, 2b	4	1	3	2	2
Totals	36	4	12	27	15

Score by inning:

Fresno	0	0	0	2	0	0	2	1	0	= 5
Los Angeles	4	0	0	0	0	0	0	0	0	= 4

L.A. White Sox 4, Fresno All-Stars 9
Firemen and Policemen's Baseball Park,[2] Fresno
July 4, 1926

L.A. White Sox	*AB*	*R*	*H*	*PO*	*A*	*E*
Riddle, ss	5	1	3	3	3	1
Fagan, 2b	5	1	3	2	2	1
Savage, lf	5	0	2	1	0	1
Pullen, c	4	0	1	6	0	0
Adams, 1b	4	0	2	7	0	0
Evans, rf	4	0	0	1	0	1
Green, cf	4	1	2	1	1	1a
Walker, 3b	4	1	1	2	1	1
Johnson, p	4	0	1	0	2	0
Totals	39	4	15	23	9	6

Fresno All-Stars	*AB*	*R*	*H*	*PO*	*A*	*E*
Zenimura, ss	4	3	3	4	3	0
Tsukamura, cf	4	2	1	1	0	0
Ritchie, 2b	4	1	2	2	5	0
Hill, rf	3	0	1	2	0	0
Iwata, lf	2	1	1	0	0	0
Nakamura, 1b	5	1	0	10	2	0
Kunitomo, 3b	4	0	2	1	0	0
Yoshikawa, c	3	0	0	5	1	0
Lawson, p	4	1	1	1	1	0
Nitta, p	0	0	0	5	0	0
Totals	33	9	11	26	12	0

Score by inning:

Los Angeles	1	0	1	0	0	0	1	0	1	= 4
Fresno	0	0	1	2	2	0	0	2	2	= 9

Philadelphia Royal Giants 9, Fresno Athletic Club, 1
Hiroshima, Japan
April 14, 1927

Philadelphia Royal Giants	*AB*	*R*	*H*	*PO*	*A*	*E*
Duncan, 1b	5	2	1	9	1	0
Fagan, 2b	5	1	3	5	3	2
Mackey, ss	4	2	3	3	4	1
Dixon, cf	5	0	3	1	1	0
Pullen, c	5	0	2	4	1	0
Cady, lf	5	1	1	0	0	0
Green, rf	3	1	0	3	0	0
Walker, 3b	4	1	2	2	2	1
Cooper, p	3	1	2	0	2	0
Totals	39	9	17	27	14	4

Fresno Athletic Club	*AB*	*R*	*H*	*PO*	*A*	*E*
Zenimura, ss	3	0	0	1	8	0
Yoshikawa, c	4	0	0	4	0	0
Nakano, 1b	2	0	1	13	0	0
Simons, ph	1	1	1	0	0	0
Nakagawa, cf	3	0	0	1	1	0
Kawasaki, ph	1	0	0	0	0	0
Iwata, lf	2	0	0	1	1	0
Yamasaki, ph	1	0	1	0	0	0
Furubayashi, cf	4	0	1	4	0	0
Kunitomo, 2b	4	0	0	1	3	0
Miyahara, 3b	3	0	0	0	2	0
Mamiya, p	3	0	0	2	2	0
Hendsch, ph	0	0	1	0	0	0
Totals	31	1	5	27	17	0

Score by inning:

Philadelphia	1	0	0	0	0	1	4	3	0	= 9
Fresno	0	0	0	0	0	0	0	0	1	= 1

Bustin' Babes 3, Larrupin' Lou's 13
Firemen's Baseball Park,* Fresno
October 29, 1927

Bustin' Babes	AB	R	H	PO	A	E
Adams, 3b	3	1	0	0	0	0
Kohl, 2b	2	0	0	3	4	0
Bier, 2b	1	0	0	0	0	1
Ruth, 1b-p	5	1	2	5	1	0
Lary, ss	4	0	0	1	0	1
Shepherd, rf-p	2	0	0	3	0	0
Baker, lf	0	0	0	0	0	0
Miller, lf	2	1	2	2	0	0
Mitchell, c	3	0	2	6	1	0
Curry, 2b	2	0	1	0	1	0
Brunderson, 3b	3	0	0	1	0	1
Bidwell, rf	3	0	0	0	0	0
Hollerson, p	1	0	0	0	0	0
Crawford, p	0	0	0	0	0	0
Hansen, p	1	0	0	0	0	0
Totals	32	3	7	24	8	3

Larrupin' Lou's	AB	R	H	PO	A	E
Metzler, cf	3	3	3	0	0	0
Nakagawa, cf	2	0	1	1	0	0
Frazier, rf	3	2	2	1	0	0
I. Jacobsen, rf	1	0	0	0	0	0
Gehrig, 1b	4	2	2	7	1	0
Cartwright, 2b	3	2	2	1	0	0
Santos, 2b	2	1	1	3	1	0
Parret, lf	3	1	1	0	0	0
Coffman, lf	1	0	0	1	0	1
Ostenberg, 3b	2	1	1	1	0	0
Fries, 3b	3	0	0	0	0	1
Zenimura, ss	0	0	0	1	1	0
D. Jacobsen, ss	2	0	1	0	1	0
Simonds, c	2	0	0	8	0	0
Yoshikawa, c	1	1	1	2	1	0
Craghead, p	1	0	0	0	3	0
McHenry, p	1	0	0	1	1	0
Cano, p	1	0	0	0	1	0
†Jewett	1	0	0	0	0	0
Totals	35	13	15	26	9	2

†Batted for Craghead in third

Philadelphia Hilldale Colored Giants 12, Fresno Athletic Club 7
Firemen's Baseball Park, Fresno
March 19, 1928

Colored Giants	AB	R	H	PO	A	E
Warfield, ss	6	2	2	2	2	0
Fagan, 2b	4	2	2	2	3	0
Dixon, 3b	4	1	2	2	1	0
Hubbard, rf	5	1	3	1	0	0
Carr, 1b	4	1	1	8	0	2
Cade, cf-lf	5	1	1	1	0	0
Holland, p-cf	5	1	1	1	0	0
Butcher, c	5	1	2	10	0	0
Flournoy, lf-p	4	2	1	0	0	0
Totals	42	12	15	27	6	2

FAC All-Stars	AB	R	H	PO	A	E
Zenimura, ss	6	0	1	1	2	1
Kohl, 2b	4	1	1	1	2	1
Cartwright, 1b	4	4	3	9	0	0
Nakagawa, rf	5	1	2	2	0	0
Iwata, lf	5	0	1	5	0	0
Sako, p	4	0	0	1	2	0
Tsukimura, cf	3	1	1	3	0	0
Yoshikawa, c	4	0	2	5	0	0
Hensen, p	1	0	0	0	0	0
Totals	40	7	11	27	8	3

**From 1922 to 1926 the park was known as the Firemen and Policemen's Baseball Park; in 1927 the name changed to Firemen's Baseball Park.*

FAC Old Timers 6, Fresno Japanese 12
Fresno Japanese Ballpark, Fresno
October 14, 1934

FAC OLD TIMERS

	AB	R	H	O	A
Zenumura, ss	5	0	2	2	5
Yoshikawa, c	5	1	3	8	0
Tsukimura, cf	5	1	1	1	0
Iwata, lf	5	2	2	2	0
Nakagawa, rf	5	0	1	2	0
S. Yamasaki, 3b	5	2	1	0	0
Tokumoto, p	4	0	0	0	1
Nakamura, 1b	5	0	1	5	0
Tachino, 2b	5	0	1	4	1
Totals	44	6	12	24	7

FRESNO JAPANESE

	AB	R	H	O	A
W. Ishida, cf	4	2	1	3	0
B. Yamasaki, 1b	5	1	1	8	0
Fujita, c	5	2	4	5	0
Saiki, p	4	2	2	0	1
Yano, 3b	5	1	1	3	0
Y. Kawakami, ss	4	2	3	0	5
Wada, lf	0	1	0	0	0
B. Ishida, lf	4	1	2	3	0
Yamato, 2b	5	0	1	3	2
Kumano, rf	2	0	0	0	0
S. Kawakami, rf	2	0	0	2	0
Totals	40	12	15	27	8

Score by inning:

FAC Old Timers	0	0	0	1	0	1	0	1	3	= 6
Fresno	0	0	1	2	2	0	1	6	x	= 12

Tokyo All-Stars 6, Fresno Japanese 4
Fresno Japanese Ballpark, Fresno
April 30, 1935

TOKYO ALL-STARS

	AB	R	H	O	A
Yajima, rf	6	0	0	1	0
Tabe, 2b	6	1	2	3	1
Kerita, ss	6	0	0	1	3
Shintmi, lf	5	1	0	0	0
Horio, cf	5	1	1	2	0
Ngsawa, 1b	5	1	3	10	2
Mzhara, 3b	5	0	0	0	3
Nchibori, c	4	1	0	10	1
Aoshiba, p	4	1	0	0	1
Totals	46	6	6	27	11

FRESNO JAPANESE

	AB	R	H	O	A
Iwata, lf	5	1	1	0	0
Zenimura, c	5	0	0	4	2
Tsukimura, cf	4	1	2	2	0
Kawakami, 1b	4	0	2	2	3
Yano, 3b	4	0	1	2	3
S. Ymsaki	4	1	1	14	1
Takagai, ss	4	1	0	0	1
Ishida, rf	4	0	0	2	0
Moryama, p	4	0	0	0	3
Saiki, p	1	0	0	0	1
B. Ymsaki, 3b	0	0	0	0	0
Fujita, c	0	0	0	1	0
Tokumoto, 2b	0	0	0	0	0
Totals	39	4	7	27	14

Umpires: Jones and Yoshikawa

Score by inning:

Tokyo All-Stars	0	1	0	0	3	0	2	0	0	= 6
Fresno	0	1	2	1	0	0	0	0	0	= 4

Tucson High School Badgers 10, Butte High School Eagles 11
Block 28 Baseball Field (aka Zenimura Field), Rivers, Arizona
April 18, 1945

Badgers	*AB*	*R*	*H*	*PO*	*A*	*E*
Weinstein, lf	6	1	3	2	0	0
Hassey, cf	6	2	2	3	0	1
Bailey, p, rf	4	1	1	1	6	1
Carey, 2b	6	0	3	2	1	1
Lopez, rf	5	1	3	2	0	2
Tully, p	0	0	0	0	0	0
Dodson, c	3	1	1	3	0	0
Robinson, 1b	5	1	1	12	1	1
Vasey, 3b	5	2	3	1	2	0
Smith, ss	4	1	2	1	6	1
Totals	44	10	19	27	16	7

Eagles	*AB*	*R*	*H*	*PO*	*A*	*E*
Zenimura (Kenso), 2b	2	0	0	2	0	1
Osada, ss	4	1	1	2	2	0
Hasegawa, lf	6	1	1	0	0	0
Nashino, ss, 3b	5	0	1	3	2	0
Kataoka, 3b, 1b	6	0	2	6	1	0
Zen'mra (Kenshi), 1b, cf	6	1	1	3	0	0
Ushiro, cf, 2b	5	2	2	2	0	0
Fukai, c	5	2	3	5	0	0
Furukawa, p	5	0	0	2	3	0
Shimasaki, rf	5	4	4	2	0	0
Totals	49	11	15	27	8	1

Score by inning:

Tucson	2	2	0	1	4	0	0	1	0	0	= 10
Butte	0	4	0	0	0	5	0	1	0	1	= 11

Appendix B: Who's Who in Zenimura's Career

Statistics are based on hundreds of articles and box scores which reflect the performance of players in games featuring Kenichi Zenimura between 1920 and 1936.

Players from the Nisei Leagues — Batting Statistics

	G	PA	SAC	BB	AB	H	2B	3B	HR	SB	AVG	OBP
Fujita, Tom	3	9	0	3	6	5	1	0	0	0	0.833	0.889

Tom Fujita (b. 1915) was a hard-hitting catcher from Hanford, CA, who played briefly with Zenimura's Japanese ballclub during the early 1930s.

	G	PA	SAC	BB	AB	H	2B	3B	HR	SB	AVG	OBP
Furubayashi, Kenichi	68	270	19	18	234	58	6	6	0	6	0.248	0.303

Ken Furubayashi (b. 1900) was a multi-position player from Honolulu who joined Zenimura for both the 1924 and 1927 tours of Japan. Once in the mainland U.S., he worked as a farm laborer in Dinuba, CA. Furubayashi made his first trip to Japan in 1924. He pitched on his high school team, Orosi High. On the '24 trip to Japan he was a pitcher but was moved to the outfield during the '27 tour because of his heavy hitting.

	G	PA	SAC	BB	AB	H	2B	3B	HR	SB	AVG	OBP
Hendsch, Charles	9	28	0	5	23	9	3	1	0	0	0.391	0.500

Charlie Hendsch (b. 1903) was a two-sport athlete who lettered in football and baseball at Fresno State College between 1922–1925. During the FAC 1927 tour to Japan, Hendsch pitched in six games, winning five.

	G	PA	SAC	BB	AB	H	2B	3B	HR	SB	AVG	OBP
Hinaga, George	2	10	0	1	9	4	0	0	0	0	0.444	0.500

Brother of Russ Hinaga, member of the San Jose Asahi during the late 1930s–40s

	G	PA	SAC	BB	AB	H	2B	3B	HR	SB	AVG	OBP
Hinaga, Russ	2	9	0	0	9	2	0	1	0	2	0.222	0.222

Russell Noboru Hinaga (b. 1903) was a Hawaiian native who moved to the mainland in 1906. He co-founded the San Jose Asahi's Nisei team in 1918 at age 15, playing and managing the team through its last game in 1942. Between 1925 and 1941, the Asahi won 6 championships. Russell led his team on a tour of Japan in 1925, and in 1935 he was the winning pitcher and recorded the game winning hit against the visiting Tokyo Giants. He was a star pitcher who won more than 200 games. Known as "Mr. Baseball" in

San Jose, Russell was a humorous and soft-spoken man who is recognized as one of the great pioneers in Japanese American baseball history.

	G	PA	SAC	BB	AB	H	2B	3B	HR	SB	AVG	OBP
Hirano, John	3	4	0	0	4	3	0	0	0	0	0.750	0.750

Jenichi "John" Hirano (b. 1904) was a solid middle infielder from Honolulu.

	G	PA	SAC	BB	AB	H	2B	3B	HR	SB	AVG	OBP
Hirano, Tom	5	23	0	5	18	2	0	0	0	4	0.111	0.304

Takeo "Tom" Hirano (b. 1902) was a solid middle infielder from Honolulu.

	G	PA	SAC	BB	AB	H	2B	3B	HR	SB	AVG	OBP
Hirokawa, James	23	84	6	2	76	14	1	0	0	2	0.184	0.205

Katsue "James" Hirokawa (b. 1904) of Honolulu, HI, a cousin of Kenichi Zenimura's, was a light-hitting second baseman who played for Fresno State during the early 1920s.

	G	PA	SAC	BB	AB	H	2B	3B	HR	SB	AVG	OBP
Hunt, Eldridge	10	28	2	2	24	3	0	0	0	0	0.125	0.192

Eldridge Josse "Al" Hunt (b. 1904) was member of the 1927 FAC squad that toured Japan.

	G	PA	SAC	BB	AB	H	2B	3B	HR	SB	AVG	OBP
Ishida, Wilson	19	82	1	3	78	26	5	1	0	2	0.333	0.358

Wilson Tsumoru Ishida (b. 1917–d. 2006), namesake of President Woodrow Wilson, was born in Fresno. He died in Marion, Ohio.

	G	PA	SAC	BB	AB	H	2B	3B	HR	SB	AVG	OBP
Iwata, Harvey	91	419	19	38	362	134	14	8	1	19	0.370	0.430

Satoru "Harvey" Iwata (b. 1904, Fresno, CA–d. 1959, Washington, DC), left fielder, was a graduate of Fresno High and attended college for agricultural science. He was captain of the Fresno High team that won the Pacific Coast Championship in 1920. Iwata participated in both the '24 and '27 tours to Japan.

	G	PA	SAC	BB	AB	H	2B	3B	HR	SB	AVG	OBP
Kawakami, Shiro	14	51	2	4	45	13	1	1	0	0	0.289	0.347

Shiro Kawakami (b. 1915, Fresno, CA), at 6 feet tall, he was the tallest member of the 1937 Kono Alameda Tour of Japan. He signed a contract to play pro ball in China during the '37 tour. He returned in 1938 when war escalated between China and Japan.

	G	PA	SAC	BB	AB	H	2B	3B	HR	SB	AVG	OBP
Kawakami, Yukio	19	75	5	1	69	23	8	2	1	4	0.333	0.343

Yukio Kawakami (b. 1913, Fresno, CA), was the older brother of Shiro.

	G	PA	SAC	BB	AB	H	2B	3B	HR	SB	AVG	OBP
Kawasaki, Satoshi	40	137	6	3	128	41	1	0	1	2	0.320	0.336

Richard Kawasaki (b. 1904, Hawaii) pitched for both Los Angeles High School and the L.A. Nippons. He joined the FAC in 1926 as a member of the pitching staff and participated in the 1927 tour to Japan.

	G	PA	SAC	BB	AB	H	2B	3B	HR	SB	AVG	OBP
Kunitomo, Anthony	50	200	7	17	176	47	0	0	0	2	0.267	0.332

b. 1904, NY, attended school in Colorado. Was a member of the FAC 1927 tour to Japan. Played second base, joined the Fresno Club in 1926. He attended Regis College in Denver.

	G	PA	SAC	BB	AB	H	2B	3B	HR	SB	AVG	OBP
Mamiya, Thomas	37	123	1	5	117	29	2	0	0	1	0.248	0.279

Thomas Mamiya was a graduate of McKinley High School in Honolulu. He joined Fresno to pursue higher education in the states. He pitched for his high school and for the Asahi team and had the reputation of being the best Japanese pitcher in Hawaii.

	G	*PA*	*SAC*	*BB*	*AB*	*H*	*2B*	*3B*	*HR*	*SB*	*AVG*	*OBP*
MIYAHARA, TY	60	240	12	5	223	71	13	5	0	4	0.318	0.333

Taijiro Miyajara (b. 1897, Hawaii), third baseman, proud of the fact that he was received at the White House by President Coolidge in 1926. He made his first trip to Japan with the Honolulu Asahi team in 1920. He also made a trip with the Fresno team in 1924. He studied at Center College, in Danville, Kentucky. He attended graduate school at Columbia University.

	G	*PA*	*SAC*	*BB*	*AB*	*H*	*2B*	*3B*	*HR*	*SB*	*AVG*	*OBP*
MORIYAMA, G	18	44	1	5	38	9	2	0	0	2	0.237	0.326

Left-handed pitcher for the Fresno Japanese during the 1930s. Originally a star player with Fowler High School (CA).

	G	*PA*	*SAC*	*BB*	*AB*	*H*	*2B*	*3B*	*HR*	*SB*	*AVG*	*OBP*
NAKAGAWA, JOHNNY	76	326	8	2	316	119	10	24	8	8	0.377	0.381

Junichi John Nakagawa (b. 1905–d. 1972), centerfielder, is known as the Japanese "Babe Ruth." He pitched and played outfield for Fresno High, finishing there in 1926. He participated in both the '24 and '27 Tours to Japan.

	G	*PA*	*SAC*	*BB*	*AB*	*H*	*2B*	*3B*	*HR*	*SB*	*AVG*	*OBP*
NAKAMURA, WILLIAM 1923–1934	22	87	6	9	72	18	1	2	0	2	0.250	0.333

William Nakamura, (b. 1901, Hawaii). Pitcher and shortstop from Hawaii was often called the Christy Mathewson of Japan.

	G	*PA*	*SAC*	*BB*	*AB*	*H*	*2B*	*3B*	*HR*	*SB*	*AVG*	*OBP*
NAKANO, MIKE 1927–1929	59	273	12	36	225	82	12	17	1	3	0.364	0.452

Makito "Michael" Nakano (b. 1908, Alameda, CA), was a first baseman who attended college in Alameda, California. He was considered the best first baseman in the Japanese baseball league in 1926 on the west coast. Nakano was a member of the '27 FAC tour to Japan.

	G	*PA*	*SAC*	*BB*	*AB*	*H*	*2B*	*3B*	*HR*	*SB*	*AVG*	*OBP*
NARUSHIMA, FRANK	3	4	0	0	4	1	0	0	0	0	0.250	0.250

Takizo "Frank" Narushima Matsumoto, b. 1901, Hiroshima, Japan.

	G	*PA*	*SAC*	*BB*	*AB*	*H*	*2B*	*3B*	*HR*	*SB*	*AVG*	*OBP*
NITTA, SHOICHI	4	9	0	1	8	5	1	0	0	0	0.625	0.667

Shoichi Nitta (b. 1899, Hiroshima, Japan), was a pitcher and third baseman who played for the professional Daimai ballclub in 1925, later joining the Fresno Japanese in 1926.

	G	*PA*	*SAC*	*BB*	*AB*	*H*	*2B*	*3B*	*HR*	*SB*	*AVG*	*OBP*
NUSHIDA, KENSO	8	29	1	1	27	8	3	1	0	1	0.296	0.321

Kenso "The Boy Wonder" Nushida (b. 1900–d. 1983) was a star pitcher and teammate of Zenimura's in Hawaii at Mills High. He pitched for the Honolulu Asahi prior to joining the Hawaiian All-Stars who toured the West Coast in 1922. He stayed in California and joined teams in Fresno and Stockton. In 1932 he became the first Japanese American to play in the PCL when he was signed by the Sacramento Solons, who at the time boasted an All-Nations lineup (minus African American representation). In 1935 he led a Japanese All-Star team to the National Baseball Congress tournament in Wichita, KS, and served as a coach during the 1937 Kono Alameda Tour of Japan.

	G	*PA*	*SAC*	*BB*	*AB*	*H*	*2B*	*3B*	*HR*	*SB*	*AVG*	*OBP*
OANA, HANK	1	4	0	0	4	2	1	0	0	0	0.500	0.500

Handsome Henry Oana, the Hawaiian Prince, spent the first thirteen seasons of his twenty-three year professional career as an outfielder/first-baseman, and proved himself a solid batter in the Pacific Coast League. As related in the PCL history by Bill O'Neal, his timber lines for the 1931 San Francisco Seals and 1933 Portland Beavers ran .345 (23 HR & 161 RBI) and .332 (29 HR & 163 RBI). During the decade Oana also took turns on the mound, however, two of his best showings occurred in the Texas League.

	G	*PA*	*SAC*	*BB*	*AB*	*H*	*2B*	*3B*	*HR*	*SB*	*AVG*	*OBP*
SADAMUNE, SATORU	2	9	0	0	9	4	1	0	0	0	0.444	0.444

Alfred Saturo Sadamune (b. 1915, Hawaii–d. 1988, Santa Clara, CA), resident of Oakland who played for the Alameda Japanese during the 1930s, served in the U.S. Army, 442nd regiment, 2nd battalion, Company F during World War II

	G	*PA*	*SAC*	*BB*	*AB*	*H*	*2B*	*3B*	*HR*	*SB*	*AVG*	*OBP*
SAIKI, TY	22	88	2	6	80	30	5	0	4	3	0.375	0.419

Taro T. Saiki (b. 1912–d. 2002) was a power hitter and pitcher with the Fresno Japanese during the late 1930s. It was reported that he received and declined an offer to sign with the Tokyo Giants in 1935 after Fresno lost to the visiting club 11–7. Off the field he gained notoriety in the poultry industry as an expert in "chick sexing," a specialty in identifying the gender of roosters and chickens. Before World War II Saiki serendipitously moved to Mankato, Minnesota, and avoided the relocation of Japanese Americans on the West Coast.

	G	*PA*	*SAC*	*BB*	*AB*	*H*	*2B*	*3B*	*HR*	*SB*	*AVG*	*OBP*
SAKO, AL	17	53	2	1	50	9	1	1	0	0	0.180	0.196

Alfred Hideo Sako (b. 1902, Hawaii–d. 1998), member of the Fresno Japanese ballclub that toured Japan in 1924, member of the Hollywood Japanese All-Stars during the 1930s. Relocated to Jerome, AR, during World War II.

	G	*PA*	*SAC*	*BB*	*AB*	*H*	*2B*	*3B*	*HR*	*SB*	*AVG*	*OBP*
SHIBATA, MITSURA	8	23	0	2	21	8	0	0	0	1	0.381	0.435

(b. 1918, Fresno, CA–d. ??), brother of Kazo Shibata

	G	*PA*	*SAC*	*BB*	*AB*	*H*	*2B*	*3B*	*HR*	*SB*	*AVG*	*OBP*
SIMONS, JUD	16	53	4	1	48	12	0	0	0	0	0.250	0.265

Justin F. Simons (b. 1904–d. 1979) was a member of the 1927 tour to Japan. He was a prep star at Fresno Tech and later caught for the Association Oil and Sun Maid teams in the TWL before signing to play professional baseball. He played in the PCL and Texas League. It is widely believed that Simons caught more games than any other TWL catcher.

	G	*PA*	*SAC*	*BB*	*AB*	*H*	*2B*	*3B*	*HR*	*SB*	*AVG*	*OBP*
TACHINO, YOSHIO	7	28	0	3	25	3	0	0	0	0	0.120	0.214

Yosh (b. 1908–d. 1986) was a light-hitting second baseman who joined the Fresno Japanese club in 1928. He was relocated to Jerome, AR, during World War II.

	G	*PA*	*SAC*	*BB*	*AB*	*H*	*2B*	*3B*	*HR*	*SB*	*AVG*	*OBP*
TOKUMOTO, SHIG	16	55	1	6	48	14	3	1	0	0	0.292	0.370

Shigeo Tokumoto (b. 1915, Hanford, CA–d. 2001), dominate righty with a deceptive submarine delivery. Faced Joe DiMaggio in 1933 and forced the future hall of famer to pop-up. He was relocated to Jerome, AR, during World War II.

	G	*PA*	*SAC*	*BB*	*AB*	*H*	*2B*	*3B*	*HR*	*SB*	*AVG*	*OBP*
TOMIYAMA, ISAMU	4	8	1	0	7	2	1	1	0	0	0.286	0.286

Isamu "Tom" Tomiyama, (b. 1905–d. 1998) pitcher from Los Angeles who was a member of the FAC during the 1924 tour. Later played for the Nippons and Hollywood All-Stars. Relocated to Manzanar during World War II.

	G	*PA*	*SAC*	*BB*	*AB*	*H*	*2B*	*3B*	*HR*	*SB*	*AVG*	*OBP*
Tsuda, Fred	10	40	0	2	38	10	1	1	0	1	0.263	0.300

Fred Kozuo Tsuda (b. 1899, Hawaii–d. 1979, Los Angeles, CA), made two tours to Japan, first in 1924 as a member of the FAC, second in 1928 with the Guadalupe Aratani club. Relocated to Rowher, AR, and then Gila River, AZ, during World War II.

	G	*PA*	*SAC*	*BB*	*AB*	*H*	*2B*	*3B*	*HR*	*SB*	*AVG*	*OBP*
Tsukimura, Ed	39	152	5	10	137	43	7	4	1	6	0.314	0.361

Hideichi Edward Tsukimura (b. 1905, Hiroshima, Japan–d. 1992, Danville, CA), was a speedy 5'2" outfielder who participated in both the 1924 and 1927 tours to Japan. Relocated to Jerome, AR, during World War II.

	G	*PA*	*SAC*	*BB*	*AB*	*H*	*2B*	*3B*	*HR*	*SB*	*AVG*	*OBP*
Wakabayashi, Bozo	1	3	0	0	3	0	0	0	0	0	0.000	0.000

Tadashi "Bozo" Wakabayashi (b. 1905, Hawaii–d. 1965), member of the 1927 Honolulu Asahis who lost to FAC during the 1927 tour. Later became an all-star pitcher for the Hanshin Tigers and changed Japanese baseball with his aggressive style. Became the first American inducted into the Japan Hall of Fame in 1964.

	G	*PA*	*SAC*	*BB*	*AB*	*H*	*2B*	*3B*	*HR*	*SB*	*AVG*	*OBP*
Yamamoto, Ken	12	43	0	5	38	15	1	0	0	2	0.395	0.465

Kenichi Russell Yamamoto, (b. 1901, Hawaii–d. 1986, Los Angeles, CA), Relocated to Gila River, AZ, during World War II.

	G	*PA*	*SAC*	*BB*	*AB*	*H*	*2B*	*3B*	*HR*	*SB*	*AVG*	*OBP*
Yamasaki, Bob	10	28	2	1	25	6	1	0	0	0	0.240	0.269

Sataoshi Robert Yamasaki (b. 1910–d. 1989) Zenimura's youngest brother in-law, he was a pitcher and infielder with the Fresno Japanese during the 1930s. Relocated to Poston, AZ, during World War II.

	G	*PA*	*SAC*	*BB*	*AB*	*H*	*2B*	*3B*	*HR*	*SB*	*AVG*	*OBP*
Yamasaki, Sam	38	104	6	5	93	32	3	2	0	4	0.344	0.378

Isami Yamasaki (b. 1909), Zenimura's brother in-law, was youngest member of the 1927 FAC team that toured Japan

	G	*PA*	*SAC*	*BB*	*AB*	*H*	*2B*	*3B*	*HR*	*SB*	*AVG*	*OBP*
Yamashiro, Andy	1	3	0	0	3	2	0	0	0	0	0.667	0.667

Masayoshi Andrew Yamashiro (b. 1896, Honolulu, HI). Considered first player of Japanese ancestry to play organized ball, with Gettysburg Ponies, in 1917. Long-time member of the Honolulu Asahi. Toured Japan in 1926 with members of the Guadalupe Aratani ballclub.

	G	*PA*	*SAC*	*BB*	*AB*	*H*	*2B*	*3B*	*HR*	*SB*	*AVG*	*OBP*
Yano, Masao	15	68	0	2	66	19	2	4	0	1	0.288	0.309

b. 1913 in Oso Flaco, CA, resident of Delano, CA, member of the 1937 tour to Japan

	G	*PA*	*SAC*	*BB*	*AB*	*H*	*2B*	*3B*	*HR*	*SB*	*AVG*	*OBP*
Yoshikawa, Fred	99	417	30	24	363	103	20	10	7	25	0.284	0.328

Captain Fred Yoshikawa, catcher, played for four years on the McKinley High School team in Honolulu. He captained the team through a series of games with Mills High which was headed by Kenichi Zenimura. He is a graduate of the Technical College of Kansas. He was a member of the 1924 & '27 FAC tours to Japan.

	G	PA	SAC	BB	AB	H	2B	3B	HR	SB	AVG	OBP
Yoshioka, G	2	10	0	0	10	5	2	1	0	0	0.500	0.500

Member of the 1934 San Jose Asahi

	G	PA	SAC	BB	AB	H	2B	3B	HR	SB	AVG	OBP
Zenimura, Kenichi	130	583	21	68	494	154	15	5	1	50	0.312	0.395

Ken Zenimura, manager and shortstop, was the mainstay of the Fresno Japanese teams from 1920 to 1941. He steered the team to several championship seasons. Upon leaving Mills High School in Honolulu in 1920, where he was captain, he went to the U.S. mainland to join the Fresno Club and continue his higher education. While in Honolulu he was captain of the Asahi ball club. He made three tours to Japan, in 1924, 1927 and 1937.

Players from the Pacific Coast League (AAA Level)—Batting Statistics

	G	PA	SAC	BB	AB	H	2B	3B	HR	SB	AVG	OBP
Craghead, Howard	2	4	0	0	4	1	0	0	0	0	0.250	0.250

Howard Craghead (b. 1908–d. 1962), appeared in 15 games over two seasons with the MLB Cleveland Indians, 1931 and '33. Recorded a 16-year career in West Coast leagues between 1926–40, including teams such as Oakland, Ogden, Toledo, Seattle and San Diego of the PCL, UTID and AA leagues. Achieved a lifetime 221–208 record (.515). Was teammate of Bobby Doerr, Dom DiMaggio and Ted Williams in '36 with San Diego, and Rod Dedeaux in '39.

	G	PA	SAC	BB	AB	H	2B	3B	HR	SB	AVG	OBP
DiMaggio, Joe	1	3	0	0	3	2	1	0	1	0	0.667	0.667

Joe DiMaggio (b. 1914–d. 1999) joined SF in the PCL at age 17 in 1932. In four seasons with the Seals he hit .361 in 463 games (1825 AB, 659 H, 74 HR). In 13 seasons with the NY Yankees Dimaggio hit a lifetime .325, including .381 in 1939. In 10 world series appearance with the Yankees, he hit .271 in 51 games to help the team win nine championship titles. He was named the League MVP three times ('39, 41' and '47).

	G	PA	SAC	BB	AB	H	2B	3B	HR	SB	AVG	OBP
Hulvey, Hank	2	5	0	0	5	2	1	0	0	0	0.400	0.400

Hank Hulvey (b. 1897–d. 1982) had a cup of coffee in the majors with the Philadelphia Athletics in 1925. He spent 18 years in professional baseball with Martinsburg, Portsmouth, SLC, FW, Hollywood, Chattanooga, Knoxville, Little Rock, Birmingham, Tacoma, Bartlesville, and Harrisonburg.

	G	PA	SAC	BB	AB	H	2B	3B	HR	SB	AVG	OBP
Lazzeri, Tony	4	13	0	0	13	5	1	0	1	0	0.385	0.385

Tony Lazzeri (b. 1903–d. 1946) played seven seasons in minors, including 5 with PCL teams, recording a .290 average in 896 games (2883 AB, 835 H, 135 HR). His performance was similar in 14 years in the majors, hitting .292 in 1,740 games (6,297 AB, 1,840 H, 178 HR). His best season was 1929 when he hit .354 with 18 HRs and was in the top 10 for almost all offensive hitting categories. In seven world series appearances with the NY Yankees and Chicago Cubs, he hit .262 in 32 games to help his teams win five championship titles.

	G	PA	SAC	BB	AB	H	2B	3B	HR	SB	AVG	OBP
Leslie, Roy	3	9	0	0	9	4	0	2	0	0	0.444	0.444

Roy Leslie (b. 1894–d. 1972) began his 26 year career in baseball in 1913 with Bonham of the Texas Oklahoma League. In 15 seasons with teams in the Texas League and PCL he hit .296 (5,983 AB, 1,772 H, 107 HR). His major league experience includes three seasons with the Cubs ('17), Cardinals ('19) and Phillies ('22). As the starting 1b with Philadelphia, he hit .271 in 141 games (573 AB, 139 H, 6 HR).

	G	PA	SAC	BB	AB	H	2B	3B	HR	SB	AVG	OBP
Lewis, Duffy	2	5	0	0	5	1	0	0	0	0	0.200	0.200

George Edward "Duffy" Lewis (b. 1888–d. 1979) played 11 seasons in the majors with the Red Sox, Yankees and Senators, and 10 seasons in the minors, primarily with PCL teams. His minor league lifetime batting average was .330, including .403 with the 1921 SLC Bees, compared to a lifetime .284 in the majors.

	G	PA	SAC	BB	AB	H	2B	3B	HR	SB	AVG	OBP
Metzler, Alex	2	7	0	0	7	3	2	1	0	0	0.429	0.429

Alex Metzler (b. 1903–d. 1973) hit a lifetime .328 during eight seasons in the TX, WA, AA and PCL leagues. In six seasons in the majors with the Cubs, Athletics, White Sox, and Browns he hit .285 (1968 AB, 561 H, 9 HR).

	G	PA	SAC	BB	AB	H	2B	3B	HR	SB	AVG	OBP
O'Doul, Lefty	1	5	0	0	5	1	0	0	0	0	0.200	0.200

Francis Joseph "Lefty" O'Doul (b. 1897–d. 1969) enjoyed a 39-year career in professional baseball, including 16 seasons in the minors primarily with PCL teams, and 11 seasons in the majors (Yankees, Red Sox, Giants, Phillies, Dodgers). He hit a lifetime .352 in the minors, including a .392 clip during the 1924 season with the SLC Bees; and .349 lifetime in the majors, including a .398 season with the Phillies in 1929.

Other PCL Players (Significant players who competed against Zenimura, but no box scores or line scores were located).

Coumbe, Fritz The slender junkballer won a career-high 13 wins with Cleveland in 1918. He played centerfield for the Reds in the major leagues' last triple-header in 1920. He finished his eight year MLB career with a 38–38 record and 212 strikeouts in 193 games. During his 10 year minor league career, Coumbe appeared in 334 games and finished with a 91–75 (.548) record.

Duchalsky, Jimmy James Duchalsky (b. 1900–d. 1924) was a half Russian and half Hawaiian pitcher who played for SLC in 1923, where was the top hitting pitcher in the PCL with a .400 avg. He was traded to Decatur, IL in the Three-I League, in 1924, and tragically was shot to death while visiting Hawaii in the winter. A local taxicab driver confessed to shooting Duchalsky in a jealous argument over a woman. He finished his career with a 12–12 record while appearing in 51 games.

Mails, Walter Lefty John Walter Mails ("Duster" or "The Great") (b. 1915–d. 1974) played seven years in MLB compiling a 32–23 record and 4.10 ERA with Brooklyn, Cleveland and the St. Louis Cardinals. In 1920 he joined the Indians and he won seven straight, including a pennant-clinching shutout over Chicago, then did not allow a run in his two World Series starts. Mails also pitched 18 seasons in the minors, including 14 seasons in the Pacific Coast League (1917–36) where he won over 20 games 3 times. During his minor league career he appeared in 602 games and finished with a 226–210 (.518) record.

McCabe, Dick Richard James McCabe (b. 1896–d. 1950) was a right-handed pitcher for the Boston Red Sox (1918) and Chicago White Sox (1922). In his two MLB seasons he posted a 1–1 record with a 3.46 ERA in six appearances. McCabe spent a total of 19 years in the minors where he compiled a 259–212 (.550) record in 661 games. He was a career journeyman who played in all corners of the United States, including Bridgeport, Lewiston, Lynn, Buffalo, Jersey City, Binghamton, Newark, Salt Lake City, Hollywood, Fort Worth, Dallas, Montreal and Birmingham.

Mulcahy, Phil John Phillip Mulcahy (b. 1906–d. 1946) was signed to a pro contract off the sandlots of Oakland, CA. He played for the SLC Bees in 1924–25 seasons and was traded to the Hollywood Stars in 1926. In 1928 the Stars sold the "bad boy" pitcher to the Little Rock club of the Southern Association. Management declared Mulcahy a great prospect who never developed past the prospect stage. During his six-year minor league career Mulcahy appeared in 245 games, with a 39–60 record (.394 winning percentage).

NEWKIRK, FLOYD Floyd Newkirk (b. 1908–d. 1976) enjoyed a nine-year career in pro ball between 1930 and 1938. He experienced a cup of coffee in the bigs when he pitched one inning for the NYY in 1934. During the off-season of '34 he and three other players were traded to the S.F. Seals of the PCL for Joe DiMaggio. During his eight years in the minors, Newkirk appeared in 182 games and compiled a 64–49 (.566) record.

MYERS, ELMER Elmer Glenn Myers (b. 1894–d. 1976) pitched 8 years in the majors with Philadelphia, Cleveland and Boston where he compiled a 55–72 (.433) record in 185 games. Myers saw better success during his 11-year career in the minors where he won 165 games, lost 143 (.536) in 381 appearances.

NUSHIDA, KENSO Kenso "The Boy Wonder" Nushida (b. 1900–d, 1983) was a star pitcher and teammate of Zenimura's in Hawaii at Mills High. He pitched for the Honolulu Asahi prior to joining the Hawaiian All-Stars who toured the west coast in 1922. He stayed in California and joined teams in Fresno and Stockton. In 1932, he became the first Japanese American to play in the PCL when he was signed by the Sacramento Solons, who at the time boasted an All-Nations lineup (minus African American representation). In 1935 he led a Japanese All-Star team to the National Baseball Congress tournament in Wichita, KS, and served as a coach during the 1937 Kono Alameda Tour of Japan.

PEARSON, MONTE Montgomery Marcellus Pearson (b. 1908–d. 1978) was a starting pitcher in Major League Baseball who played for the Cleveland Indians (1932–1935), New York Yankees (1936–1940) and Cincinnati Reds (1941). In a ten-season career, he posted a 100–61 (.621) record with 703 strikeouts and a 4.00 ERA. In four World Series appearances with the Yankees, he posted a 4–0 record with 28 strikeouts, 1.01 ERA, pitching three complete games and one shutout. He also spent 6 seasons in the minors with Bakersfield, Phoenix, Oakland, Toledo and Hollywood, posting a 42–39 (.519) record.

PHEBUS, BILL Raymond William Phebus (b. 1909–d. 1989) spent 15 years in professional baseball, 13 as a player and two as a manager in the minor leagues. Between 1936 and 1936 he appeared in a relief role in 13 games with the Washington Senators, finishing his brief career in the majors with a 3–2 (.600) record. During his 12 years in the minors he moved around from Bakersfield, Oakland, Mission, Davenport, Albany, Chattanooga, Hollywood, Indianapolis, Wenatchee and Fresno, appearing in 189 games with a 57–73 (.438) record.

PONDER, ELMER Ponder (b. 1893–d. 1974) began his ML career with Pittsburg in 1917. After serving in the military during World War I, he returned home to earn a spot in Pittsburgh's starting rotation. In 1920 he was 11–15 with a 2.62 ERA. In 1921 he was traded to the Chicago Cubs, and then to Los Angeles of the PCL in 1922. Ponder appeared in 350 games during his 11-year minor league career and finished with a 124–113 (.523) record.

STUTZ, EDDIE Edward Francis Stutz (b. 1912–d. 1959) spent his entire 12-year career with the San Francisco Seals of the PCL. He began his career in 1932 and missed three seasons due to military service between 1942–45. After pitching one final season in 1946, Stutz retired with a 124–129 (.490) record in 418 career games.

THURSTON, SLOPPY Hollis John Thurston (b. 1899–d. 1973) enjoyed an 18-year career between 1920 and 1938. He spent nine seasons in the majors with the Browns, White Sox and Dodgers, where he compiled a 89–86 (.509) record in 288 games. He had similar success in the minors with a 106–97 (.522) record in 291 games. Against Negro League and Major League talent in the California Winter League, Thurston appeared in 27 games, with a 9–16 (.360) record.

Players from the Fresno Twilight League (A Level)—Batting Statistics

The symbol ‡ indicates a Twilight League Hall of Fame member

ADAMS, LEFTY Maurice "Lefty" Adams (b. 1909–d. ?) was a pitcher and outfielder who competed against Zenimura in the Fresno Twilight League (TWL), playing for Billings & Meyering ('23) and Pipe Line ('26). In four games against Zeni's Japanese ballclub, Adams hit .444, recording 4 hits in 9 official at-bats. Also a professional billiards player, Adams was enshrined into the TWL Baseball Hall of Fame in 1973.

ALLISON, PAUL Allison (b. 1915–d. ?) was a pitcher, 3b, lf, with the Rialto Recreation club and Fresno Tigers. In partial stats from the 1935–36 seasons, Allison recorded 2 hits in 10 at-bats against Nisei pitching.

	G	*PA*	*SAC*	*BB*	*AB*	*H*	*2B*	*3B*	*HR*	*SB*	*AVG*	*OBP*
BIDWELL, HASTY	16	43	3	0	40	9	0	0	0	1	0.225	0.225

Hastings Albert Bidwell (b. 1895–d. 1978), a pitcher and outfielder, broke into professional baseball with Bisbee, AZ, in 1917 and played with Vernon of the PCL in 1917–18. He made his debut in the Twilight Leagues in 1919. Bidwell hit .225 against Zeni's ballclubs in 16 games, including 9 hits in 40 at-bats.

	G	*PA*	*SAC*	*BB*	*AB*	*H*	*2B*	*3B*	*HR*	*SB*	*AVG*	*OBP*
CANO, MOOSE	4	11	0	0	11	3	0	0	0	0	0.273	0.273

John R. "Moose" Cano (b. 1903–d. ?) pitched five seasons in professional baseball (1928–30; 1934–35), primarily in the PCL clubs in Hollywood and Sacramento. He recorded a 12–17 record (.414) appearing in 56 games. Partial stats against Japanese American teams show him batting .273 (3 hits, 11 at-bats). Cano was elected to the Twilight League HOF in 1972.

	G	*PA*	*SAC*	*BB*	*AB*	*H*	*2B*	*3B*	*HR*	*SB*	*AVG*	*OBP*
CARTWRIGHT, JOE‡	7	29	0	0	29	10	2	2	0	0	0.345	0.345

Joseph L. Cartwright (b. 1899–d. ?) was one of four brothers who were standouts in the TWL and later in the Valley and PCL. He played semipro ball in Del Rey and Selma in the old Raisin Belt League.

	G	*PA*	*SAC*	*BB*	*AB*	*H*	*2B*	*3B*	*HR*	*SB*	*AVG*	*OBP*
COFFMAN, JOHNNY‡	4	12	1	0	11	3	0	0	0	1	0.273	0.273

John Issac Coffman (b. 1901–d. ?), a pitcher and infielder, started his TWL career with Standard Oil in 1919. In 1921 he had a tryout with Sacramento of the PCL. He was an excellent long ball hitter and fielder. He played with Dinuba in the Central Valley League and performed in 10 "little world series" (TWL championships).

	G	*PA*	*SAC*	*BB*	*AB*	*H*	*2B*	*3B*	*HR*	*SB*	*AVG*	*OBP*
FORD, SCOTT‡	11	24	0	0	24	7	0	1	0	1	0.292	0.292

Ford moved to Fresno from Atcheson, KS, in 1904 and played in the first TWL in 1907. He later organized and managed teams in Fresno, Dinuba and Lemoore.

	G	*PA*	*SAC*	*BB*	*AB*	*H*	*2B*	*3B*	*HR*	*SB*	*AVG*	*OBP*
FRAZIER, FOY‡	3	13	2	0	11	6	2	0	0	0	0.545	0.545

Foy Francis Frazier (b. 1908–d. 1989) was a portly, power-hitting lefthander who popped many balls over the right field fence at Holmes Playground in the glory days of the TWL. Big Foy was a classy fielder and played several season for Oakland and San Francisco in the PCL. During his seven years in the minors he hit .316 (2,224 AB / 703 H) in 610 games.

	G	*PA*	*SAC*	*BB*	*AB*	*H*	*2B*	*3B*	*HR*	*SB*	*AVG*	*OBP*
FRIES, AUGIE‡ (1923–1930)	7	18	1	0	17	2	0	1	1	1	0.118	0.118

Auto service station owner who played infield and pitcher for several teams, including: Bingham-Wenks ('23), Post Office club ('26), Larrupin Lous ('27), Fresno Sciots ('29) and Jaynes & Sons ('30) with Zenimura and Yoshikawa. He was enshrined into the TWL Hall of Fame in 1972.

	G	*PA*	*SAC*	*BB*	*AB*	*H*	*2B*	*3B*	*HR*	*SB*	*AVG*	*OBP*
FUNKNER, PHIL‡ (1929–1930)	3	5	0	1	4	3	1	1	0	0	0.750	0.800

Funkner (b. 1904–d. 1980) was a pitcher and 1b, teammate of Zenimura's on the 1930 Jaynes & Sons TWL club. Also joined the FAC in games against Meiji University ('29) and Aratani's Guadalupe Japanese ('30). Funkner was enshrined into the TWL Hall of Fame in 1970.

	G	PA	SAC	BB	AB	H	2B	3B	HR	SB	AVG	OBP
HANSEN, JIMMY‡ (1924–1929)	6	18	1	1	16	2	1	0	0	0	0.125	0.176

Hansen (b. 1917–d. 1993) was a pitcher and outfielder for several teams including the Fresno Tigers ('24), Fresno Eagles ('26), Bustin Babes ('27) and Fresno Sciots ('29). Incomplete stats show that Hansen pitched twice for Zenimura in 1928, first against the Negro League Hilldale Colored Giants of the California Winter League and then the Fresno Tigers. Hansen was enshrined into the TWL Hall of Fame in 1976.

	G	PA	SAC	BB	AB	H	2B	3B	HR	SB	AVG	OBP
HEIZENRADER, JACK‡	3	16	0	0	16	9	2	2	2	0	0.563	0.563

Heizenrader (b. 1912–d. 2001) was one of the most versatile and finest hitters to ever perform in the TWL. He played every position and was several-time batting champion of the TWL, hitting .426 in 1940 and .444 in 1942. He broke into the TWL with the 1928 Cosmos Yanigans, which won 29 straight games.

	G	PA	SAC	BB	AB	H	2B	3B	HR	SB	AVG	OBP
JACOBSEN, DOC‡	4	13	1	0	12	4	0	0	0	0	0.333	0.333

Irvin "Doc" Jacobsen (b. 1904–d. 1968) started his TWL career in 1921 and later played with the Fresno Tigers, SLC Bees, SF Seals and Ogden, UT. He competed for 20 years in the TWL. A 3b with a powerful arm, Doc also wielded a healthy bat.

	G	PA	SAC	BB	AB	H	2B	3B	HR	SB	AVG	OBP
JACOBSEN, EARL‡	4	16	0	0	16	5	2	0	0	1	0.313	0.313

Earl Martin Jacobsen (b. 1911–d. 1952) was known as "Little Jake." He was a 2B and basketball star who later played for the Fresno Oaks, Fresno Sciots and Fresno Tigers. Besides the TWL he also played throughout the San Joaquin Valley. His career was cut short by an automobile accident in the late 1930s. He died of a heart attack at age 41 in 1952. He was enshrined into the TWL HOF in 1968.

	G	PA	SAC	BB	AB	H	2B	3B	HR	SB	AVG	OBP
JACOBSEN, JAKE‡	11	33	1	0	32	10	1	1	5	0	0.313	0.313

Big Jake (b. 1900–d. ?) began his career with the Fresno Reds in 1919 and played pro ball with Emporia, KS, in the Southwestern Association in 1924–25. He spent 20 years in the Twilight Leagues. He was an outstanding pitcher and outfielder with a lifetime average of .345. Often referred to as "Mr. Twilight League," he was one of the most colorful performers with a "blooper" pitch and hidden ball plays.

	G	PA	SAC	BB	AB	H	2B	3B	HR	SB	AVG	OBP
KOHL, JACKIE‡	8	29	0	0	29	8	1	0	1	1	0.276	0.276

Kohl (b. 1901–d. 1976), began his TWL career with the Fresno Reds in 1919. A stellar 2B, Kohl played 23 years in the TWL circuit. He also played semipro ball with Selma and Fowler in the old Raisin Belt League and with the Fresno Tigers. Kohl had a trial with Oakland of the PCL.

	G	PA	SAC	BB	AB	H	2B	3B	HR	SB	AVG	OBP
LAWSON, TY‡	4	11	0	0	11	3	0	0	0	0	0.273	0.273

Tyre P. Lawson (b. 1893–d. 1968) was a Kentucky native and police officer. Pitcher with the Fresno Tigers who often joined Zenimura's ballclubs when tough competition came to town. He was posthumously enshrined into the TWL Hall of Fame in 1974.

	G	PA	SAC	BB	AB	H	2B	3B	HR	SB	AVG	OBP
LEYVA (1924–1926)	6	20	0	1	19	5	0	0	2	0	0.263	0.300

Pitcher and infielder with the Bee All-Stars, Fresno Tigers and TWL Post Office club that invited Zeni and Yoshikawa to join them in 1926.

	G	PA	SAC	BB	AB	H	2B	3B	HR	SB	AVG	OBP
OSTENBERG, LEO‡	3	11	0	0	11	3	0	1	2	1	0.273	0.273

Leo Ostenberg (b. 1908–d. ?) spent 13 years in professional baseball between 1926–1940. Playing primarily in the West, he spent time in the PCL, TX, AZ and ID leagues. He hit a career .309 in 1,106 games (3,723 AB / 1,151 H). In 1933 as a teammate of Joe DiMaggio of the SF Seals, he hit 23 HRs and hit .328.

	G	PA	SAC	BB	AB	H	2B	3B	HR	SB	AVG	OBP
RAMAGE, ART‡	3	14	0	1	13	4	2	0	0	0	0.308	0.357

James Arthur Ramage (b. 1894–d. ?) 1b, played college baseball at Santa Clara in 1912–14. Was a member of the New York Americans in the spring of 1916. Appeared briefly with the Sacramento Senators of the PCL in 1918. Manager of the Fresno Tigers. Enshrined into the TWL Hall of Fame in 1972.

	G	PA	SAC	BB	AB	H	2B	3B	HR	SB	AVG	OBP
SANTOS, MIKE (1924–1927)	12	41	1	3	37	6	1	0	0	2	0.162	0.225

Infielder who played 3B primarily was one of the few Latinos to substitute on Zenimura's FAC Japanese ballclub between 1924–27. As manager of the Santos Pirates in 1919 he often featured the battery of pitcher Ben Shintaku and catcher Frank Narushima, founders of the FAC. Santos also played for the Fresno Tigers and Sugar Pine nine in the TWL. Santos played 2B and hit 1–2 for the Larrupin Lous when Ruth and Gehrig barnstormed Fresno in 1927.

	G	PA	SAC	BB	AB	H	2B	3B	HR	SB	AVG	OBP
SAVORY, JACK‡	5	22	0	1	21	7	2	0	2	0	0.333	0.364

Long and lean Savory (b. 1903–d. 1988) was a fastball pitcher who also played several season of semipro ball. He was the ace for the strong Sciots team that won the 1928 city title. He coached for 15 years at Roosevelt HS in Fresno.

	G	PA	SAC	BB	AB	H	2B	3B	HR	SB	AVG	OBP
SHEPHERD, PETE,‡ (1924–1927)	3	6	0	0	6	1	0	0	0	0	0.167	0.167

James I. "Pete" Shepherd (b. 1891–d. 1968), a native of TN, started his baseball career as a $5 a game pitcher for Carterville, MO, in the Trolley League of 1908. He pitched for Kansas City in the American Association and the St. Louis Browns in 1914. He was stationed with the marines at Mare island during World War I and came to Fresno in 1921. Pete played for several TWL clubs for 14 seasons and later with the Fresno Tigers in the Valley League and Sanger in the Raisin Belt league. Shepherd also played OF and was a long ball hitter. He was enshrined in the TWL Hall of Fame in 1965.

	G	PA	SAC	BB	AB	H	2B	3B	HR	SB	AVG	OBP
TOCHER, JOY,‡ (1924–1926)	8	26	0	1	25	7	0	0	0	0	0.280	0.308

Dr. Lloyd Tocher (b. 1899–d. 1978), a dentist, was an all round athlete and star from Fresno High who started playing in the TWL in 1915. Tocher, an outfielder with numerous teams from Del Rey, Porterville, Dinuba and Hanford, reportedly turned down offers to join PCL clubs throughout his career.

	G	PA	SAC	BB	AB	H	2B	3B	HR	SB	AVG	OBP
WACKENFELD, DUTCH	5	17	0	0	17	9	0	1	0	0	0.529	0.529

Walter Grover Wackenfeld (b. 1900–d. 1964) catcher, played three seasons in professional baseball with the Sacramento Senators of the PCL (1922, 1925) and Ogden of the Utah League (1926). In three seasons he hit .306 (96 H, 316 AB) in 101 games. During the 1924 season he played for the spring squad of the SLC Bees and was cut before the regular season. He landed a position with the Fresno Tigers in 1924.

Players from the Major Leagues—Batting Statistics

	G	PA	SAC	BB	AB	H	2B	3B	HR	SB	AVG	OBP
GEHRIG, LOU, 1927	1	5	0	1	4	2	2	1	0	0	0.500	0.600
RUTH, BABE, 1927	1	5	0	0	5	2	0	0	1	1	0.400	0.400

Players from the Negro Leagues (Major-AAA-AA Levels)

CADE, JOE Cade (b. July 16, 1901, or April 5, 1900) was a Missouri native and member of the LA White Sox selected by Lon Goodwin to join the Philadelphia Royal Giants on the 1927 tour to Japan. Also participated in barnstorming tours to Hawaii in 1928 and 1929 with O'Neal Pullen and Robert Fagan. In two games versus Zenimura's ballclubs, Cade recorded 2 hits, both doubles, in 10 at-bats.

BUTCHER, SPENCER Butcher (b. 1896–d. 1967) was a Galveston, Texas, native who moved to the West Coast sometime between 1910 and 1920. He was a member of the semipro Los Angeles White Sox who was picked up by the Alexander Giants and Philadelphia Royal Giants in the CWL between 1920 and 1928. He hit .248 (491 AB, 122 H) in 128 CWL games.

COOPER, ANDY Cooper (b. 1898–d. 1941) pitched in the Negro Leagues from 1920 to 1941, compiling a record of 121–54 (.691). He recorded a 22–6 (.786) record in the California Winter League between 1922–31, and participated in tours to Japan in 1925 and 1932 that helped contribute to the start of professional baseball in Japan in 1936. He was elected to the National Baseball Hall of Fame in 2006. In one game versus Zenimura's FAC, Cooper recorded 2 hits in 3 at-bats.

COOPER, SAM (b. 1897, New York), Negro League pitcher with nine years experience with the Richmond Giants, Baltimore Black Sox, Harrisburg Giants, Bacharach Giants and Homestead Grays. Cooper was one of several West Coast Negro League players to barnstorm Hawaii in 1928 with Zenimura.

DAY, WILSON C. "CONNIE" Day was a sensational defensive second baseman in the Negro Leagues for 13 years. He hit .261 (532 AB, 139 H) in six seasons in the California Winter League. He barnstormed Hawaii in the spring of 1928 and 1929.

DIXON, RAP Dixon was an outstanding all-round player in the Negro Leagues from 1922 to 1937. He hit .326 in five seasons in the California Winter League, including a .380 clip with the 1927–28 Royal Giants. In two games versus Zenimura's ballclubs, Dixon recorded 5 hits (2 doubles, 1 triple) in 9 at-bats for a .556 average.

DUNCAN, FRANK Frank Duncan Jr. was one of the top catchers in the Negro Leagues between 1920 and 1948, playing mostly with the KC Monarchs. He was an average hitter with a .268 clip in the Negro Leagues and .304 in two seasons in the California Winter League. As a member of the Philadelphia Royal Giants touring Japan in 1927, Duncan hit 1–5 against Zenimura's FAC.

EVANS, ALEXANDER Evans (b. Oct. 17, 1897, South Carolina–d. ?) was a member of the LA White Sox selected by Lon Goodwin to join the Philadelphia Royal Giants on the 1927 tour to Japan. He also participated in barnstorming tours to Hawaii in 1928 and 1929 with O'Neal Pullen and Robert Fagan. In two games versus Zenimura's ballclubs, Evans recorded 3 hits in 8 at-bats.

FAGAN, ROBERT Fagan (b. March 27, 1900, Indiana–d. ?) had a short four-year career in the Negro Leagues. He was a member of the 25th Infantry team in Hawaii and Arizona who joined the KC Monarchs in 1920. He participated in tours to Japan in 1927 and 1932, and barnstormed Hawaii several times between 1928 and 1932. Fagan played against Zenimura in Hawaii during the later 1910s. In five games against Zenimura's ballclubs, he hit an impressive .522, going 12 for 23 against Nisei pitchers.

FLOURNOY, JESSE Jesse Willis "Pud" Flournoy was an outstanding pitcher in the Negro Leagues from 1919 to 1933. He was a chubby southpaw with good control, an excellent fastball and a variety of curveballs. As a member of the 1927–28 Philadelphia Royal Giants, he led the league in innings pitched (92).

GREEN, JULIUS Julius "John" Green (b. June 25, 1900, Texas–d. ?) was a member of the LA White Sox selected by Lon Goodwin to join the Philadelphia Royal Giants on the 1927 tour to Japan. Green also participated in barnstorming tours to Hawaii in 1928 and 1929 with O'Neal Pullen and Robert Fagan. Green was a light-hitting infielder who recorded 2 hits in 10 at-bats in 3 games against Zenimura.

HOLLAND, BILL Elvis "Bill" Holland (b. 1901–d. 1973) pitched in the Negro Leagues from 1920 to 1941. According to McNeil, incomplete statistics credit him with a 127–99 record (.562). In the 1927-28 CWL season, he led the league in complete games pitched (10), wins (7) and shutouts (4). In 1930 he became the first black pitcher to pitch in Yankee Stadium. In one game against Zenimura's Nisei ballclub, Holland hit 1–5 (.200).

HUBBARD, JESS Jess "Mountain" Hubbard (b. 1895–d. 1992) was a big, rugged right-handed pitcher who spent 18 seasons in the Negro Leagues. In addition to being an outstanding pitcher, he was a solid hitter with a lifetime .316 batting average. In one game versus Zenimura's Fresno ballclub, Hubbard went 3 for 5 (.600), including a triple.

JOHNSON, AJAY Ajay Deforest Johnson (b. 1901–d. 1996) began his career in 1924 with the L.A. White Sox, one of the top teams in Joe Pironne's Greater Southern California Baseball Association (GSCBA) integrated semipro league. Manager Lon Goodwin signed the native Texan to pitch and play outfield with his team comprised of several former Negro league players, including Alexander Evans, Robert Fagan and O'Neal Pullen. Johnson joined the Philadelphia Royal Giants at the end of the 1926-27 California Winter League season when Bullet Joe Rogan declined Goodwin's offer to accompany the club on their upcoming tour of Asia and Hawaii. Johnson became the number-two ace behind lefty Andy Cooper and helped lead the Royal Giants to a phenomenal 25–0–1 record against competition in Japan and Korea. He won seven (28 percent) of the teams' 25 victories. Once out of baseball, Johnson became a police officer in L.A, and in 1943 earned the distinction of becoming one of the first black uniformed patrol lieutenants and sergeants in LAPD history.

MACKEY, BIZ Mackey (b. 1897–d. 1965) is considered by many to be the greatest all-round catcher in Negro Leagues history. A lifetime .322 hitter in the Negro Leagues, he recorded a .366 average (957 AB / 350 H) in the California Winter League. He participated in tours to Japan in 1927 and 1931–32 that helped contribute to the start of professional baseball in Japan in 1936. In the historic match-up between the Zenimura's Fresno Athletic Club and the Philadelphia Royal Giants, Mackey was a single shy of hitting for the cycle. His home run was the first ever at Meiji Shrine field in Japan. Mackey was elected to the National Baseball Hall of Fame in 2006.

MORRIS, HAROLD Harold "Yellow-horse" Morris, was a great pitcher with the Kansas City Monarchs, Detroit Stars and Chicago American Giants in the '20s and '30s. As a member of the 1924 KC Monarchs, Morris appeared in 18 games and helped the team to the first Colored World Series with a 6–4 record and 4.02 ERA. In 1946, Morris became the owner and manager of the San Francisco Sea Lions of the West Coast Negro League.

PULLEN, O'NEAL, 1925–1927 Pullen (b. 1895–d. 1944) played in the Negro Leagues eight years. He started his career in the Texas Negro Leagues with Beaumont in 1915 and missed two years of play due to service in World War I. He was a good defensive catcher who had a career .314 average (437 AB, 137 H) in 127 games against PCL and ML talent in the California Winter League. He toured Japan with Philadelphia Royal Giants in 1927, and barnstormed in Hawaii several times between 1928 and 1932. During 4 games versus Zeni's Japanese American ballclubs, O'Neil hit .235, recording 4 hits in 17 at-bats.

REID, CHARLIE Charles Rodgers Reid (b. 1898–d. 1979) learned the game of baseball as a child from his Berkeley, CA neighbors, the Hafey family, who produced several major leaguers in Bud, Tom and cousin Chick Hafey. During his three-year career with the Shasta Limited and Oakland Pierce Giants, once considered the strongest Negro team on the west coast, Reid received an offer to play with the Detroit Stars in the Negro National League. He declined the $150-a-month offer because he could earn more playing ball and working in California. Reid was the losing pitcher in the 1923 Fresno Athletic Club victory over the Oakland Pierce Giants. In 1947 he became the head of the parks and recreation department in Richmond,

CA, and was actively involved in increasing sports participation in the black community. His legacy is honored today with the Shields-Reid Community Center in Richmond, CA.

RIDDLE, JOHN John Thomas Riddle (b. 1900–d. ?), a native of Ohio was a two-sport athlete at the University of Southern California. He starred at Pasadena High School as a halfback prior to joining the Trojans in 1922. Nicknamed "Up-the-middle Riddle," he played three seasons (1922–24) with USC and gained notoriety as the first African American for the Trojans to play in the Rose Bowl when USC defeated Penn State 14–3 in 1923. After touring Japan with the Philadelphia Royal Giants in 1927, he accepted a position as an architect in Hawaii. Riddle hit .462 in three games versus Zenimura's Nisei ballclubs, with 6 hits in 13 at-bats.

SAVAGE, AZEL Savage (b. April 16, 1897, Macon, GA–d.?) was an outfielder with the Los Angeles White Sox during the 1920s. He appeared in the 1924–25 California Winter League, and in 1928 barnstormed Hawaii with Zenimura, O'Neal Pullen and Robert Fagan. In three games against Zenimua's ballclubs, Savage recorded 5 hits in 14 at-bats (.357).

WALKER, JESSE Jesse "Hoss" Walker (b. 1904–d.?) was a 3b, ss, who spent more than 20 years in the Negro Leagues and managed the Indianapolis Clowns and Baltimore Elite Giants at the end of his career. He was described by Riley as "a pull hitter with a little power, an average gloveman with good arm strength and accuracy." In three games versus Zeni's teams, he squeaked out 3 hits in 12 at-bats.

WARFIELD, FRANK Warffield (b. 1888–d. 1967) was a star pitcher for various Negro Leagues teams between 1910 and 1925, including nine seasons with Rube Foster's Chicago American Giants. According to Riley, in 1913 and 1914 he gained his most notoriety when he outdueled Walter Johnson in 2 of 3 games. In the 1928 matchup against Zenimura's Japanese American nine, Warfield stroked 2 hits in 6 at-bats, including a double.

Appendix C: F.A.C. 1924 Tour of Japan

During their 22-game tour of Japan in late 1924, Zenimura's Fresno Athletic Club finished with a 14–8 record (.636 winning percentage). Results of individual games are as follows:

Date	*Opponent*	*Score*	*Winner*	*Location*
October 11	Daimai	5–0	Fresno	Hanshin Koshien Stadium
October 12	Star Club	7–0	Fresno	Hanshin Koshien Stadium
October 14	Daimai	4–3	Daimai	Hanshin Koshien Stadium
October 15	Kyoto U Alum	4–0	Kyoto U Alum	Keihan Neyagawa Stadium
October 17	Diamond Club	11–2	Fresno	Hanshin Koshien Stadium
October 18	Diamond Club	6–2	Fresno	Hanshin Koshien Stadium
October 21	Takarazuka C	2–1	Fresno	Takarazuka Stadium
October 2*	Kure Kenchiku	14–1	Kure Kenchiku	Hiroshima
October 2*	Kure Zenrin	8–2	Fresno	Hiroshima
October 2*	Hiroshima Star	8–7	Hiroshima Star	Hiroshima
October 30	Takarazuka C	1–0	Fresno	Kasugabaru Ground*
November 1	All Fukuoka	17–3	Fresno	Kasugabaru Ground
November 7	Hohyuh Club	4–2	Hohyuh Club	Nakano Ground (Tokyo)
November 9	Meiji U	8–3	Meiji U	Komaba Ground
November 11	Rikkyo U	11–8	Fresno	Ikebukuro Ground
November 15	Keio U	8–4	Fresno	Meguro Ground
November 16	Waseda U	3–2	Waseda U	Tokyo Totsuka Ground
November 19	Takarazuka Club	6–0	Fresno	Tokyo Totsuka Ground
November 21	Yokohama Shoyu Club (Yokohama Commercial High Alumni)	9–0	Fresno	Yokohama Yamashita-cho Park
November 23	Sundai Club	16–3	Sundai Club	Tokyo Totsuka Ground
November 25	Toyu Club (Waseda Alum)	13–2	Fresno	Yokohama Shin-Yamashita-cho Park
November 26	All Yokohama	5–1	Fresno	Yokohama Shin-Yamashita-cho Park

**Exact date unknown*

Source: Asahi Sports, *No. 32–34, 1924,*[1] *Japan (Shared by Kyoko Yoshida).*

Appendix D: Nisei League vs. Negro League

According to hundreds of articles and box scores, between 1920 and 1935, Zenimura faced Negro Leagues competition 11 times, with 10 of the scores reported. Zenimura and his teammates won seven of those games (a .700 winning percentage).

With the addition of another game from 1943 inside the Japanese American Internment Camp at Gila, River, Arizona, his Nisei teams were successful in eight of 11 games against Negro Leagues competition (a .727 winning percentage).

All games in Fresno, CA, unless otherwise noted.

Date	*Opponent*	*Captain/Mgr.*	*Score*	*Winner*
10/17/1920	Fresno Colored Giants	Chet Bost	8–2	Colored Giants
7/2/1923	Oakland Pierce Giants	Chet Bost	11–7	F.A.C.
9/6/1925	Los Angeles White Sox (@ LA, CA)	Lon Goodwin	5–4	F.A.C.
7/4/1926	Los Angeles White Sox, game 1	Lon Goodwin	9–4	Fresno All-Stars
7/5/1926	Los Angeles White Sox, game 2	Lon Goodwin	4–3	Fresno All-Stars
4/15/1927	Philadelphia Royal Giants (@ Tokyo)	Lon Goodwin	9–1	Royal Giants
4/27/1928	Philadelphia Hilldale Royal Giants	Frank Warfield	12–7	Royal Giants
7/24/1933	Fresno Colored Athletic Club	Gene Hinds	unknown	unknown
5/27/1934	Fresno Colored Athletic Club	Gene Hinds	14–1	F.A.C.
7/17/1934	Detroit Colored Giants	Albert Moorehead	17–16	Fresno All-Stars
5/5/1935	Fresno Colored Cubs	Gene Hinds	20–2	F.A.C.
10/17/1943	Arizona Compress, Phoenix Negro Nine (@ Rivers, AZ)	James Searcy	11–2	Butte All-Stars

Appendix E: Butte Baseball League Statistics, 1943–1945

1943 Butte Baseball League

Club Batting

Team	*G*	*AB*	*H*	*AVG.*
YMBA	20	735	217	.288
Firemen	19	705	146	.266
Lompoc	19	633	164	.258
Pasadena	19	635	163	.256
Giants	14	485	124	.255
Hinode	19	627	156	.248
Block 30	15	555	137	.246
Block 28	19	692	141	.203

Individual Batting

Player	*G*	*AB*	*H*	*AVG.*
B.Tsutsumi (G&Y)	12	49	16	.469
Nob Oki (L)	19	83	33	.397
Sei.Ikeda (G&P)	12	42	16	.380
K. Nishino (Y)	20	82	30	.365
J. Tomooka (Y)	14	59	20	.350
K. Ikeda (G&Y)	12	44	15	.340
K. Okuhara (30)	14	59	20	.338
Ken Z'imura (28)	19	69	23	.333
H. Yamanaka (P)	19	69	23	.333
M. Tomooka (Y)	17	76	25	.328
G. Kanagaki (66)	18	52	17	.326
H. Inouye (P)	19	74	24	.324
M. Mitani (Y)	20	76	24	.315
J. Nishino	13	49	16	.306
K. Nagai (28)	10	40	12	.300
Others				
Kso. Z'mura (28)	19	77	22	.285

Legend: Y, YMBA; G. Giants: P. Pasadena; L. Lompoc; F. Firemen; 30, Block 30; 66, Block 66; and 28, Block 28.[1]

Pitching Averages

(All pitchers who won or lost at least two games.)

Players	*W*	*L*	*T*	*AVG.*
T. Morishita (Y)	8	0	1	.944
J. Sakuma (F)	4	1	0	.750
T. Tomooka (G-Y)	2	1	1	.666
Bob Toyoda (P)	2	1	1	.666
Mas Mitani (Y)	6	4	0	.590
L. Nishimura (P)	10	7	0	.578
G. Kanagaki (H)	4	3	1	.562
Mas Okuhara (R)	6	5	2	.538
Mas Kinoshita (*)	8	7	2	.529
S. Shimasaki (F)	6	6	2	.500
Y. Shimada (H)	1	1	0	.500

Legend: *Block 28, R-Block 30 Rods, H-Hinodo's, Y-YMBA, P-Passadena, G-Giants, F-Firemen and L-Lompoc (Compiled by the *News-Courier*)

Butte High School Eagles, 1943 Season Record

Opponent	*W-L*	*Score*
Casa Grande (semi-pro team)	loss	10–3
@ Mesa High School	win	3–2
Canal High	loss	10–4
@ Peoria High	loss	3–1
Glendale JA All-Stars	win	10–0

1944 Butte Baseball Season Stats

Club Batting

Team	*G*	*AB*	*H*	*Avg.*
Block 28	11	393	124	.318
Block 65	11	298	79	.265
Cards	10	296	79	.244

Team	*G*	*AB*	*H*	*Avg.*
White Sox	7	232	53	.244
Lamp. Guad.	11	390	91	.233

INDIVIDUAL BATTING[2]

(All regular players of three or more games including the first game of the 28–65 play-off. Number in parenthesis is games played.)

Player	*AB*	*H*	*Avg.*
H. Shimoto-W(4)	11	3	.455
Ko. Zenimura*(11)	47	21	.446
T. Hasegawa-L(3)	9	4	.444
H. Inouyo — W(4)	18	7	.388
T. Sakamoto*(9)	31	12	.386
Kn. Zenimura*(7)	22	6	.353
F. Furuya-C(5)	17	6	.353
R. Nakamura-B(11)	41	14	.341
Ki. Zenimura*(7)	44	15	.340
D. Kanon-L(8)	24	8	.333
Y. Hirano-B(8)	27	9	.333
S. Yamada*(3)	12	4	.333
G. Egusa-C(10)	37	12	.324
K. Toya-L (11)	44	14	.318
B. Yoshimoto*(11)	44	14	.318
N. Iwahashi-C(4)	13	4	.308
M. Okuhara*(6)	26	8	.307
T. Egusa-C(10)	30	9	.300
T. Nakamura-B(11)	40	12	.300

TOP HURLERS[3]

(Including the first game of Block 26–65 play-off.)

Player	*W*	*L*	*Pct.*
M. Okuhara (28)	2	0	1000
T. Abo (G-L)	1	0	1000
M. Mitani (G-L)	4	1	.800
K. Kinoshita (28)	5	2	.714
D. Kanon (G-L)	2	1	.666
Y. Hirota (65)	7	4	.540
J. Muranishi (C)	2	2	.500
G. Matsuda (28)	1	1	.500
T. Egusa (C)	1	4	.200

(G-L) — Guad-Lompoc, (W) — White Sox, (C) — Cards

1945 Post-Season Honors, Top Players, Batting, Fielding, Pitching

Player (team)	*AB*	*H*	*Avg.*
F. Furuya (C)	37	19	.513
M. Minamido (T)	33	15	.458
Player (team)	*AB*	*H*	*Avg.*
P. Ryono (T)	25	11	.440
T. Nishino (28)	40	17	.425
Ke. Zenimura (28)	38	15	.395
M. Iwao (65)	35	13	.371
M. Saki (65)	38	14	.368

STOLEN BASES

Kenshi Zenimura	(28)	18
George Furuya	(C)	11
Tom Ehara	(C)	8
Tets Hasegawa	(28)	8
Kenso Zenimura	(28)	8

OUTFIELD FIELDING	*P.O.*	*E.*
Tets Hasegawa	13	1

INFIELD FIELDING	*E.*	*Ass.*	*P.O.*
Kenso Zenimura	1	18	9

PITCHER'S RECORD	*W*	*L*
Tak Abo	7	0
George Kataoka	2	0

Appendix F: Zenimura Legacy Timeline

"The reason I was able to go to Japan and have a great career was because of Mr. Zenimura's faith in me."
— Satoshi "Fibber" Hirayama, Hiroshima Carp All-Star Outfielder and Japanese Professional Baseball League Scout

The legacy of Kenichi Zenimura as the Father of Japanese American baseball is alive and well in the game today. During his four decades in baseball he touched the lives of hundreds, if not thousands, across the globe. From players, protégés, modern art and hall of fame museums, the following is a timeline of significant events since Zenimura's passing on November 13, 1968, that shine the light on his legacy.

1968 — Newspapers across the globe announce the passing of Zenimura, calling him the "Dean of Nisei Baseball in America."

1968 — Sotaro Suzuki, Zenimura's opponent during the 1927 Japan tour, is elected to the Japanese Baseball Hall of Fame.

1969 — Former Japanese American internees start making pilgrimages back to relocation camps. The first occurred at Manzanar when 200 people paid tribute to those who died in that camp, and were buried at the foot of the Sierra Nevada foothills.

1969 — Saburo Miyatake, Jiro Morioka and Takeo Tabe, opponents from Zenimura's career, are elected to the Japanese Baseball Hall of Fame.

1970s — Zenimura's protégé and MLB scout George Hatsuo "Hats" Omachi, forms the Omachi All-Stars, comprised of the best players in the San Joaquin Valley area. His players include future MLB stars Bobby Cox, Tom Seaver, Will Clark, Rex Hudler and Geoff Jenkins.

1970— Shunichi Amachi and Nobuaki Nidegawa, opponents from Zenimura's 1924 tour, are elected to the Japanese Baseball Hall of Fame.

1975 — St. Louis Cardinals pitcher Ryan Kurosaki becomes the first Japanese American ballplayer break into the majors.

1976 — President Gerald Ford officially terminates Executive Order 9066.

1977 — Shigeru Mizuhara, Zenimura's opponent during the 1935 Tokyo Giants U.S. tour, is elected to the Japanese Baseball Hall of Fame.

1978 — Shinji Hamazaki, Genzaburo Okada, Kenjiro Matsuki and Yasuhiro Itami, opponents from Zenimura's career, are elected to the Japanese Baseball Hall of Fame:

1979 — Zenimura is enshrined in the Fresno Athletic Hall of Fame, joining the ranks of San Joaquin Valley sports legends Frank Chance, "Dutch" Leonard, Pete Beiden, "Len" Bourdet and Victor Lombardi.

1979 — Goro Taniguchi, Zenimura's opponent during the 1927 Japan tour, is elected to the Japanese Baseball Hall of Fame.

1980— Congress establishes the Commission on Wartime Relocation and Internment of Civilians (CWRIC) to investigate whether a wrong had been committed with the forced relocation of 120,000 Japanese Americans.

1981—Tatsuo Saeki, Zenimura's opponent during the 1927 Japan tour, is elected to the Japanese Baseball Hall of Fame.

1982—Kenso "Howard" Zenimura is named the manager of Fresno-Alameda youth team to compete in the International Boys League (IBL). He accompanies his team of 14–15 year olds from California to play a series of friendship games in Osaka, Japan. Zenimura selects a young Don Wakamatsu to serve as one of the coaches for the IBL team.

1986—Miyoshi Nakagawa, Zenimura's opponent during the 1935 Tokyo Giants U.S. tour, is elected to the Japanese Baseball Hall of Fame.

1987—Minoru Yamashita, Zenimura's opponent during the 1927 Japan tour, is elected to the Japanese Baseball Hall of Fame.

1987—Nobuo Fujita, Zenimura's life-long friend and international baseball colleague, is elected to the Japanese Baseball Hall of Fame.

1988—President Ronald Reagan signs HR 442 into law acknowledging that Japanese American internment was unjust. In doing so he offered an apology and announced reparation payments to each person incarcerated under Executive Order 9066.

1988—Saburo Yokozawa, Zenimura's opponent during the 1924 Japan tour, is elected to the Japanese Baseball Hall of Fame.

1989—Maseo Date, Zenimura's opponent during the 1931 Hosei University tour of the U.S., is elected to the Japanese Baseball Hall of Fame.

1990s—Satoshi "Fibber" Hirayama, Zenimura protégé and former NPB all-star outfielder becomes a scout for the Hiroshima Carp organization in Japan and in the Dominican Republic and signs future major leaguers Timon Perez and Alfonso Soriano.[1,2]

1991—The importance of Japanese American Internment Camp baseball and Zenimura's role begins to gain national attention in the early 1990s. The '91 winter edition of *Whole Earth Review* featured an article titled "Baseball Behind Barbed Wire."

1991—Tony Lazzeri, Zenimura's opponent during the early 1920s with the Salt Lake City Bees, is elected to the National Baseball Hall of Fame.

Kenso Zenimura (third from left) and Don Wakamatsu (third from right) applaud the national anthems of the U.S. and Japan prior to an International Boys League tournament game in Osaka, Japan, in 1982 (Zenimura Family Archive).

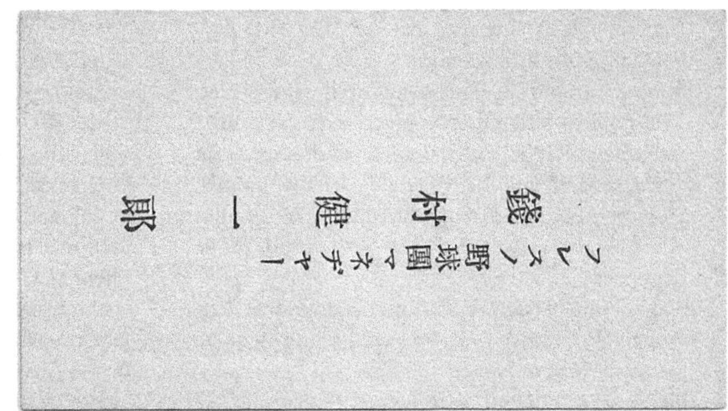

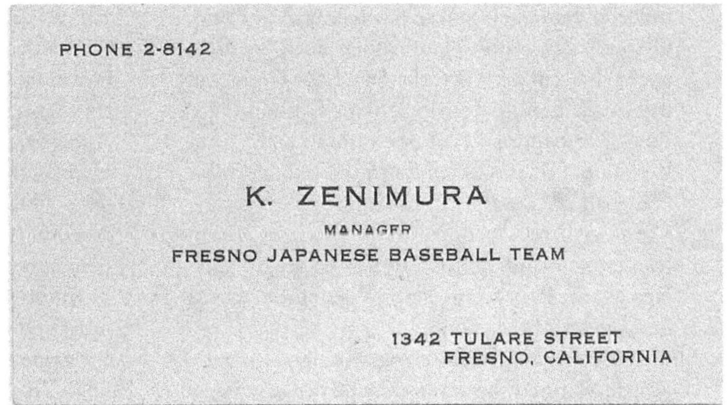

The business card of Kenichi Zenimura, circa 1937, was printed in English on one side and Japanese/Kanji on the other (Nisei Baseball Research Project).

1992 — Baseball becomes a recognized medal sport in the 1992 Barcelona Olympic Summer games. In five Olympic games (1992 to 2008), the Cuban national wins five medals, including three gold and two silver. Japan wins three medals: two silver and one bronze; the U.S. wins three: one gold and two bronze.

1994 — Hideo Nomo, pitcher with the Kintetsu Buffaloes from 1990 to 1994, signs with the Los Angeles Dodgers to become the second player from Japan in MLB.

1996 — Mac Suzuki, the first Japanese player to enter the majors without having first played in the NPB, makes his major league debut with the Seattle Mariners. He becomes the third Japanese player to play in the major leagues, after Masanori Murakami and Nomo.

1995 —*Baseball Saved Us* by Ken Mochizuki is published by Lee & Low Books. Mochizuki was inspired by both the Zenimura family legacy and his own parents who were sent to the Minadoka internment camp in Idaho during World War II.

1996 — Kerry Yo Nakagawa, historian, filmmaker and author, founds the Nisei Baseball Research Project (NBRP; www.niseibaseball.com), a nonprofit 501(c)3 organization established to preserve the history of Japanese American Baseball.

1996 — Kenichi Zenimura's widow, 90-year-old Kiyoko, cuts the ribbon at the opening of the exhibit *Nisei Baseball: Diamonds in the Rough.*

1996 — Nisei baseball pioneers are honored in a *Tribute to the Legends of the Nisei Baseball League* with 50,000 fans at 3Com Park before a San Francisco Giants home game.

1998 — The exhibit *Nisei Baseball: Diamonds in the Rough* travels to Sacramento, Phoenix, Portland, Los Angeles, San Diego, ultimately reaching the Japan Baseball Hall of Fame and Museum in Tokyo, and the National Baseball Hall of Fame and Museum in Cooperstown, NY.

1998 — Several of Zenimura's former players make a pilgrimage back to the Butte camp location at Gila River, AZ. During the same trip, the Arizona Diamondbacks honor Nisei baseball legends at a game, which included the national anthem sung by former Gila River internee Pat Morita.

1998 — Chiba Lotte Marines pitcher Hideki Irabu signs with the New York Yankees.

1998 — Shinjiro Iguchi, Zenimura's opponent during the 1927 Japan tour, is elected to the Japanese Baseball Hall of Fame.

1999 — Yokohama BayStars pitcher Tomokazu Ohka signs with the Boston Red Sox.

2000— Yokohama BayStars relief pitcher Kazuhiro Sasaki signs with the Seattle Mariners and is named American League Rookie of the Year. His 37 saves in a rookie season remains an MLB record.

2000— The documentary *Diamonds in the Rough: Legacy of Japanese American Baseball* is released. The film focuses of Zenimura, his Nisei baseball peers, and tells the story of Japanese Internment and the role of baseball as a means of survival during an unjust incarceration.

2001—Ichiro Suzuki signs a landmark, three-year, $13 million-$15 million contract with the Seattle Mariners in 2001. He is later named the American League MVP and the Rookie of the Year awards, joining Boston Red Sox outfielder Fred Lynn as the only two players to receive both awards in the same season.

2002—Fujio Nakazawa, Zenimura's opponent during the 1927 Japan tour, is elected to the Japanese Baseball Hall of Fame.

2002—Lefty O'Doul, who helped resurrect U.S.-Japanese baseball relations after World War II, is inducted into the Japanese Baseball Hall of Fame. O'Doul's first exposure to ballplayers of Japanese ancestry occurred when the Salt Lake City Bees battled Zenimura's Fresno Athletic Club in 1923.

2002—The handmade wooden home plate from Zenimura field is selected for the traveling exhibit "Baseball as America." Zeni's home plate was one of 500 artifacts scheduled to travel across American cities including Los Angeles, Chicago, Cincinnati, St. Petersburg, Fla., Washington, D.C., St. Louis, and Houston.

2003—Pitcher Shigetoshi Hasegawa signs with the Seattle Mariners, becoming the team's closer and named to the American League All-Star team.

2003—Hideki Matsui signs a three-year contract with the New York Yankees. He was a three-time MVP in the Japanese Central League (1996, 2000, and 2002) with the Yomiuri Giants. He led his team into four Japan Series and winning three titles (1994, 2000 and 2002).

The handmade wooden home plate from Zenimura field was one of the most popular artifacts in the National Baseball Hall of Fame traveling exhibit "Baseball as America" (Nisei Baseball Research Project).

2004—Takizo Matsumoto (aka Frank Narushima), one of the original founders of the Fresno Athletic Club and Zenimura's life-long friend and international baseball colleague, is elected to the Japanese U.S. Football Hall of Fame. Matsumoto is recognized as a pioneer for introducing the American sport to Japan in 1936.

2004—Artist Ben Sakoguchi begins *The Unauthorized History of Baseball.* Among his 225 paintings are two pieces celebrating Zenimura and other Japanese American baseball pioneers.

2005—Arizona Governor Janet Napolitano declares November 10th Kenichiro Zenimura Day throughout the state. The day marked the 60th Anniversary of the closing of Butte Camp, and in essence, the end of an era at Zenimura Field.

2005—The City of Chandler, AZ, votes to create Nozomi Park to honor the 13,000 people wrongly incarcerated at Gila River. The word *nozomi* is Japanese for "hope" and was inspired by Zenimura's efforts to make camp life bearable through the game of baseball.

2006—The World Baseball Classic is established as the global stage to determine the best in international baseball competition. Led by manager Sadaharu Oh, the Japanese national team defeats the powerhouse of Cuba, 10–6, to win first WBC championship in 2006.[3]

2006—Members of the 1945 Butte High Eagles and state champion Tucson High Badgers baseball teams reunite 61 years after their historic game in Rivers, Arizona.

2006—The Fresno Grizzlies, Triple-A affiliate of the San Francisco Giants and member of the Pacific Coast League, name one of the luxury suites at Chukchansi Park after Zenimura.

2007—The major motion picture *American Pastime* is released. Inspired by the story of Kenichi Zenimura, the film's story centers around one family in Utah's Topaz camp where the interned community uses baseball as a way to rise above their daily hardships and adversity.

2006—Along with Josh Gibson and Fernando Valenzuela, Zenimura is inducted into the "Shrine of the Eternals" by the Baseball Reliquary, a non-profit organization in Southern California dedicated to fostering an appreciation of American art and culture through the context of baseball history.

Kenichi Zenimura and other Nisei baseball pioneers have been immortalized in artist Ben Sakoguchi's award-winning Orange Crate Label Series: "The Unauthorized History of Baseball in 100–Odd Paintings" (Ben Sakoguchi, www.bensakoguchi.com).

2006—Andy Cooper and Biz Mackey, members of the Negro Leagues all-star Philadelphia Royal Giants and Zenimura's opponent during the 1927 Japan tour, are elected to the National Baseball Hall of Fame.

2006—At the 18th annual Cooperstown Symposium on Baseball and American Culture, the case is made for Japanese American baseball pioneers to be honored with plaques and player induction, just as their Negro League peers received. The case was made for Zenimura, as the recognized Father of Japanese American Baseball, to be the first.

2007—Seibu Lions pitcher Daisuke Matsuzaka signs a contract with the Boston Red Sox in 2007.

2007—The Negro Leagues Baseball Museum in Kansas City, MO, unveils plans to develop an exhibit featuring the historic tours of Japan by the 1927 Philadelphia Royal Giants, Zenimura's role, and their collective influence on the game in Japan.

2007—MLB.com recognizes the 80th anniversary of the 1927 Goodwill Tour to Japan with features on the Philadelphia Royal Giants and Zenimura.

2008—Marking 65 years since the start of internment baseball, MLB.com

Top: **In April 1945, Zenimura wrote to Tucson High School Coach Hank Slagle: "I sincerely hope that we may meet once again not as a team perhaps but as a single member of Uncle Sam." In October 2006, the surviving members of the Butte High School Eagles and Tucson High School Badgers fulfilled Zenimura's hope with a reunion (Nisei Baseball Research Project).** ***Bottom:*** **The 2007 major motion picture *American Pastime* featured the character of Kaz Namura (played by Japanese actor Masatoshi Manamura) inspired by Kenichi Zenimura (Nisei Baseball Research Project).**

spotlights how Zenimura kept the game alive in Japanese internment camps in the article "Baseball cast light in shadow of war."

2008 — Don Wakamatsu is named the manager of the Seattle Mariners, making him the first Japanese American and Asian-American manager in MLB history.

2009 — The Japanese team repeats as WBC champions, defeating rival Korea, 5–3, in 10 innings on Ichiro Suzuki's two-run single off right-handed reliever Chang Yong Lim.

2009 — Rare home movies from the late 1920s are discovered in Fresno, CA. Included on the reel are 21 seconds of Zenimura and his Nisei teammates interacting with Babe Ruth and Lou Gehrig leading up to the famous photograph captured in 1927.

2010 — The Nisei Baseball Research Project launches a campaign to nominate Kenichi Zenimura for the Buck O'Neil Lifetime Achievement Award. The National Baseball Hall of Fame receives thousands of letters from all over the globe supporting Zenimura's nomination.

2011 — The Fresno Grizzlies, Triple-A affiliate of the San Francisco Giants and member of the Pacific Coast League, honor Zenimura and Nisei Baseball pioneers by wearing throw-back 1927 Fresno Athletic Club jerseys on May 7.

2011 — Filmmakers in Japan begin work on a documentary about Kenichi Zenimura for Japanese audiences.

2011 — On May 20, 2011, Neal Katyal, Acting Solicitor General of the United States, issues an official Confession of Error, admitting that the office was wrong in defending the country's war-time internment policy.

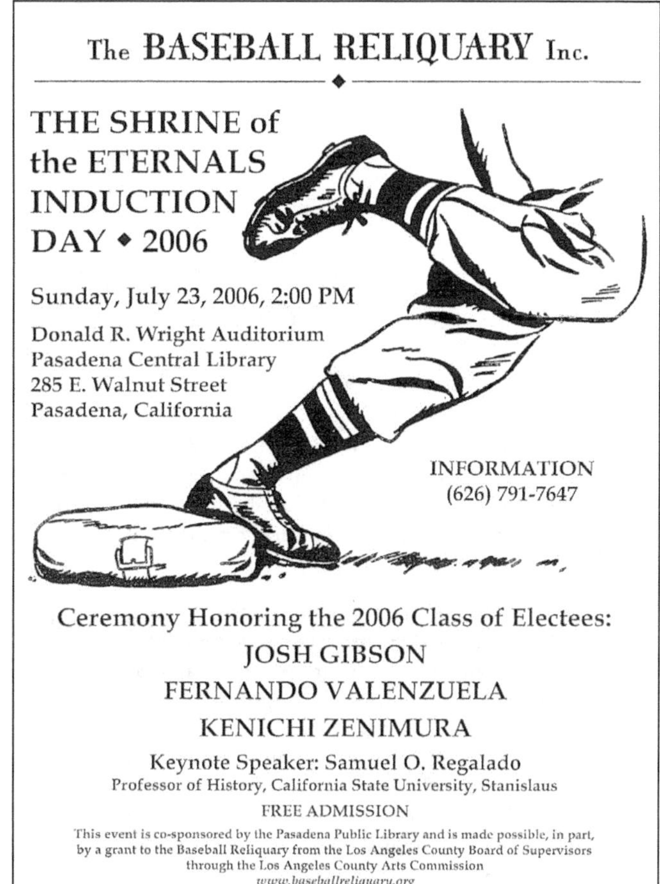

Kenichi Zenimura joined Negro League slugger Josh Gibson and pitching phenom Fernando Valenzuela in the Class of 2006 inductees into the Baseball Reliquary Shrine of the Eternals (Baseball Reliquary).

Appendix G: Japanese American Glossary of Terms

Alien land acts laws enacted by various Western states that prevented Japanese (and other Asian) immigrants from purchasing land. First enacted in the 1910s, the laws generally remained in effect until well after World War II.

"Aliens ineligible to citizenship" a phrase used in the wording of alien land law legislation. This phrase was a way to make sure the legislation applied to people of Asian ancestry without specifically mentioning them as the targeted group. Until 1952, existing federal naturalization laws discriminated on the basis of ancestry. The right to become a naturalized U.S. citizen was given only to "free white persons and to aliens of African nativity and to persons of African descent."

American Civil Liberties Union (ACLU) a private organization dedicated to fighting civil liberties violations. The ACLU has often defended the civil rights of unpopular groups or individuals — those who need the protection of the Bill of Rights the most. Given its purpose of defending civil liberties, it is not surprising that the ACLU was one of the only organizations to come to the defense of the Japanese Americans who were forcibly removed and detained during World War II.

American Friends Service Committee (AFSC) a Quaker organization committed to social justice, peace and humanitarian service. One of the few organizations that provided help to the Japanese American community during World War II, especially through the student relocation program.

Assembly centers temporary incarceration camps that imprisoned Japanese Americans who had been forcibly removed from the West Coast in the early months of World War II. By mid–1942, Japanese Americans were transferred to more permanent "relocation centers," also known as concentration camps. The terms "temporary incarceration camps" or "temporary prison camps" better convey the nature of these facilities. Denshō's policy, however, is to still use the term "assembly center" as part of a proper noun, e.g. "Puyallup Assembly Center," and in quotation marks: "assembly center" when referring to the facilities. The reason for this is to avoid confusion, since many people would not associate "temporary incarceration camps" with "assembly centers."

Buddha-head a term for Japanese Americans from Hawaii.

Civil rights the freedoms and rights that a person has as a member of a given state or country.

Commission on Wartime Relocation and Internment of Civilians (CWRIC) a Congressional commission charged with studying the mass removal and incarceration of Japanese Americans during World War II and recommending an appropriate remedy.

Concentration camps euphemistically called "relocation centers" by the War Relocation Authority (WRA), the concentration camps were hastily constructed facilities that housed Japanese Americans who had been forcibly removed from their homes and businesses on the West Coast during World War II. This term was also used to refer to the Justice Department internment camps where enemy aliens were detained. See internment camps for definition.

Evacuation forced removal of Japanese Americans in early 1942 from the West Coast. They were forbidden to return. The government called this an "evacuation," a euphemism that implies it was done as a precaution for Japanese Americans' own safety, when in fact, it was motivated by economic greed and racial prejudice. "Mass removal" and "exclusion" are better terms for the event, because Japanese Americans were expelled from the West Coast and forbidden to return.

Executive Order 9066 this order, signed by President Franklin D. Roosevelt on February 19, 1942, authorized the War Department to prescribe military areas from which "any and all persons may be excluded." This provided the basis for the exclusion and mass incarceration (or "internment") of all Japanese Americans from the West Coast.

522nd Field Artillery Battalion part of the 442nd Regimental Combat Team — an all–Nisei U.S. Army regiment that served in Europe during World War II. The 522nd had the distinction of liberating survivors of the Dachau concentration camp from the Nazis on April 29, 1945.

442nd Regimental Combat Team a segregated U.S. Army regiment made up of Nisei that saw heavy action during World War II. The 442nd fought in Italy, France and Germany. The 442nd rescued the "Lost Battalion," liberated survivors of the Dachau concentration camp, and was the most decorated unit for its size and length of service in U.S. military history.

Gaman a term of Zen Buddhist origin which means "enduring the seemingly unbearable with patience and dignity." Gaman is generally translated as "perserverance" or "patience."

Gentlemen's Agreement the 1908 agreement between Japan and the United States that halted Japanese labor migration to the United States.

Gosei a Japanese term meaning American-born great-great grandchildren of Japanese immigrants; fifth generation Japanese Americans.

Gothic Line the last important defense of the German army in Italy during World War II.

Hakujin "white person" in Japanese. This term is used to refer to a person of European descent.

Hoshidan informal name for pro-Japanese group in Tule Lake incarceration camp. Short for Sokuji Kikoku Hoshi Dan ("Organization to Return Immediately to the Homeland to Serve").

Immigration Act of 1924 legislation that restricted overall immigration to the United States and banned further Japanese immigration.

Incarceration the state of being in prison, or being confined.

Incarceration camps camps administered by the U.S. War Relocation Authority to detain Japanese Americans during World War II. These were prisons surrounded by barbed wire fences and patrolled by armed guards, which inmates could not leave without permission. The U.S. War Relocation Authority called these camps "relocation centers." Because "relocation center" inadequately describes the harsh conditions and forced confinement of the camps, terms such as "incarceration camp" or "prison camp" are more accurate. As prison camps outside the normal criminal justice system, designed to confine civilians for military or political purposes on the basis of race and ethnicity, they fit the definition of "concentration camps."

Internment camps camps administered by the Justice Department for the detention of enemy aliens (not U.S. citizens) deemed dangerous during World War II. Most of the several thousand people in these camps were Issei and Kibei who had been rounded up after the attack on Pearl Harbor because they were perceived as "dangerous." Japanese Latin Americans were also placed in these camps. "Internment camp" is used by some to describe the "incarceration camps." The term "internment" is problematic when applied to U.S. citizens. Technically, internment refers to the detention of enemy aliens during time of war, and two-thirds of the Japanese Americans incarcerated were U.S. citizens. Although it is a recognized and generally used term even today, we prefer "incarceration" as more accurate, except in the specific case of aliens.

Inu "dog" in Japanese. This term was used in the incarceration camps to refer to Japanese Americans who were suspected of informing authorities about "suspicious" incarcerees.

Issei the first generation of immigrant Japanese Americans, most of whom came to the United States between 1885 and 1924. The Issei were ineligible for U.S. citizenship and considered "enemy aliens" during World War II.

Jap a derogatory, hostile term used to refer to Japanese and Japanese Americans.

Japanese American two-thirds of those imprisoned during World War II were Nisei born in the United States and thus U.S. citizens. The proper term for them is "Japanese American," rather than "Japanese." Their parents, the Issei, were immigrants who were legally forbidden from becoming naturalized citizens. While they were technically aliens, the Issei had lived in the U.S. for decades by the time of World War II and raised their children in this country. Many of them considered themselves to be culturally Japanese, but were committed to the United States as their home. Calling the Issei "Japanese American" as opposed to "Japanese" is a way to recognize that fact.

Japanese American Citizens League (JACL) a Japanese American civil rights organization that has emphasized assimilation and Americanization. The JACL is the largest and most influential Japanese American political organization, and has been controversial, particularly during World War II.

Kanji a Japanese term for the Chinese characters used in Japanese writing.

Kibei American-born person of Japanese ancestry sent to Japan for formal education and socialization when young and later returned to the United States.

Lost Battalion the Texas battalion of 211 men surrounded by German troops in eastern France and rescued by the all–Nisei 442nd Regimental Combat Team during World War II.

"Loyalty questions" two questions on questionnaires distributed to Japanese Americans in incarceration camps. Despite serious problems with the wording and meaning of the questions, government officials and others generally considered those who answered "no" to the two questions to be "disloyal" to the United States. "Yes" answers to these questions made internees eligible for service in the U.S. Army, and some became eligible for release and resettlement in areas outside of the West Coast exclusion zones.

McCarran-Walter the immigration statute passed in 1952 that gave the Issei the right to become naturalized U.S. citizens. Also known as the Immigration and Nationality Act of 1952.

Military Intelligence Service (MIS) a U.S. Army branch in which many Japanese Americans served during World War II, utilizing their language skills in the Pacific War. Japanese American soldiers in the MIS translated enemy documents, interrogated Japanese prisoners of war, intercepted enemy communication, and persuaded enemy units to surrender.

NCJAR National Council for Japanese American Redress.

NCR National Committee for Redress.

NCRR National Coalition for Redress/Reparations.

Nihonmachi Japan Town.

Nikkei a person of Japanese ancestry.

Nisei American-born children of Japanese immigrants; second generation Japanese Americans. Most mainland Nisei were born between 1915 and 1935; in Hawaii, large numbers were born about a decade earlier. Many Nisei share a common background. Many grew up in a rural setting; were part of a large family; attended both a regular public school and private Japanese language schools; and had their lives dramatically changed by events stemming from World War II (which nearly all see as a key turning point in their lives).

Non-alien the government sometimes referred to Nisei as "non-aliens," a way of evading the fact that they were U.S. citizens.

"No-no boy" a term that refers to Japanese Americans (both male and female) who refused to answer the "loyalty questions" or answered in the negative. Many were unfairly stigmatized as being "disloyal" to the United States and were segregated to the Tule Lake camp.

100th Infantry Battalion a U.S. Army battalion made up of Nisei from Hawaii that saw heavy action during World War II. The 100th carved out an exemplary military record during their service in the European Theater, paving the way for the 442nd Regimental Combat Team, which arrived later.

Picture bride Issei women who participated in marriages that included the exchange of photographs between them or their families in Japan and their prospective husbands in the U.S. This was an affordable way for Issei men to marry and begin families without the cost of returning to Japan.

Power of attorney a legal instrument authorizing one to act as the attorney or agent of the grantor.

Redress and reparations two terms used to refer to Japanese American efforts to get compensation from the U.S. government for being wrongfully detained in incarceration camps during World War II. While often used as synonyms, "redress" can imply an apology; "reparations" specifically refers to monetary compensation.

"Relocation centers" a term used by the U.S. War Relocation Authority to refer to the camps in which most Japanese Americans were detained during World War II. These were prisons surrounded by barbed wire fences and patrolled by armed guards, which inmates could not leave without permission. Because "relocation center" inadequately describes the harsh conditions and forced confinement of the camps, terms such as "incarceration camp" or "prison camp" are more accurate. As prison camps outside the normal criminal justice system, designed to confine civilians for military or political purposes on the basis of race and ethnicity, they fit the definition of "concentration camps."

Resettlement a term used by the War Relocation Authority to refer to the migration of Japanese Americans from the incarceration camps in which they were imprisoned during World War II. Those who were allowed to leave the camps for resettlement could not return to the West Coast; they were told to move to the eastern and northern areas of the United States.

Sansei American-born grandchildren of Japanese immigrants; third generation Japanese Americans.

Shin-Issei new Issei; newcomers to the United States after World War II.

War Relocation Authority (WRA) the U.S. government agency charged with administering the incarceration camps in which Japanese Americans from the West Coast were imprisoned during World War II.

Writ of error coram nobis a legal term meaning "error before us." Legal petitions were filed on behalf of Fred Korematsu, Gordon Hirabayashi, and Minoru Yasui in 1983 to reopen their cases, claiming that the courts had made major errors when their cases were decided during World War II.

Yellow peril a term used by anti–Japanese agitators in the early 1900s to describe the "threat" of Japanese immigration as a precursor to a Japanese invasion.

Yonsei American-born great-grandchildren of Japanese immigrants; fourth generation Japanese American.

Source: Densho (http://www.densho.org/resources/default.asp). Many definitions were adapted from Brian Niiya, ed., Japanese American History *(New York: Facts on File, 1993).*

Notes

Foreword

1. "Mariners Manager Eager to Help Others — Few Asian-Americans Among Sports Stars," *San Jose Mercury News*, February 3, 2009, 1D.

Preface

1. Nisei is the Japanese word for "second-generation Japanese American."

2. "Fresno's Ken Zenimura, Dean of Nisei Baseball in US, Recalls Colorful Past," *Fresno Bee*, May 20, 1962, 3S.

3. Nikkei is the Japanese word for "Japanese Americans of all generations."

4. George "Horse's Mouth" Yoshinaga, columnist for the *Rafu Shimpo*, is reported to have said this about Zenimura circa 2000.

5. David Marasco, "The Diamond at Manzanar — Controversy in the Desert," http://www.thediamondangle.com/archive/july04/manzanardiamond.html.

6. Kerry Yo Nakagawa, *Through a Diamond: 100 Years of Japanese American Baseball* (San Francisco: Rudi Publishing, 2001).

7. Issei is the Japanese word for "first-generation Japanese American."

8. Robert Peterson, *Only the Ball Was White* (New York: Oxford University Press, 1992).

9. Joe Morgan, *Baseball My Way* (New York: Atheneum, 1976), 4.

Introduction

1. "New Ball Park at Livingston Opened, Japanese Defeated," *The Fresno Bee*, May 1, 1923, 12.

2. "Editorial: Huge Signs Disappeared," *Gila News Courier*, September 25, 1943, 6.

3. *Ibid.*

4. Tetsuo Furokawa, "When Gila Fought Heart Mountain," National Japanese American Historical Society, *Nikkei Heritage, Sports 2006*, 11.

Chapter 1

1. "Around the World with the Giants by John J. McGraw, Manager of the New York Giants," *New York Times*, January 4, 1914, S3.

2. Nakagawa, *Through a Diamond*, 10.

3. United States Federal Census, M. Zemimura (*sic*), Year: 1930; Census Place: Honolulu, Honolulu, Hawaii Territory; Roll 2633; Page: 7B; Enumeration District: 29; Image: 902.0.

4. Honolulu, Hawaii, Passenger Lists, 1900–1953, Kenichi Zenimura, December 12, 1907.

5. Denshō, Sites of Shame, Historic Timeline, http://www.densho.org/sitesofshame/timeline.xml.

6. *Ibid.*

7. Meiji Period (1868–1912), http://www.japan-guide.com/e/e2130.html.

8. United States Federal Census, Masakichi Zenimura, Year: 1920; Census Place: Honolulu, Honolulu, Hawaii Territory; Roll T625_2036; Page: 9A; Enumeration District: 35; Image: 312.

9. Nakagawa, *Through a Diamond*, 10.

10. "A Japanese Baseball Player," *Auburn Bulletin*, June 8, 1891.

11. "May Beat the Orioles," *Washington Post*, June 7, 1897, 8.

12. "News and Comments," *Sporting Life Magazine*, July 3, 1897, 5; "Line Hits from the Bat," *Evening Herald* (Syracuse, NY), July 14, 1897, 2.

13. "Japanese for McGraw's Team," *New York Times*, Feb 10, 1905, 8.

14. "M'Graw Signs a Jap," *Hartford Courant*, Feb 11, 1905, 14.

15. "New York Nuggets," *Sporting Life Magazine*, February 25, 1905, 8.

16. *All About Hawaii: The Recognized Book of Authentic Information on Hawaii, Combined with Thrum's Hawaiian Annual and Standard Guide* (Honolulu, HI: Honolulu Star-Bulletin, 1917), 17. Original from the University of Michigan, digitized Mar 2, 2007, http://books.google.com.

17. Jim Becker, The Father of Baseball, Hawaiian Historical Society, http://www.hawaiianhistory.org/moments/baseball.html.

18. Japanese American Baseball: A Goodwill Ambassador, Japanese American National Museum, http://www.janmstore.com/jabaseball.html.

19. *Diamonds in the Rough: The Legacy of Japanese-American Baseball*, DVD (Derry, NH: Chip Taylor Communications, 1998).

20. Nakagawa, *Through a Diamond*, 6.

21. "Legislators See Chance for New Working Period; Sunday Baseball Bill," *Hawaiian Gazette*, April 25, 1903, 3.

22. "Baseball for the Orient," *New York Times*, July 19, 1908, S2.

23. "Diamond Dust," *Fresno Republican*, December 16, 1908, 9.

24. *Ibid.*

25. "Ball Stars to Invade Far East Next Winter," *Chicago Heights Star*, July 30, 1908, 6.

26. Bill Weiss and Marshall Wright, "Top 100 Teams: 1970 Hawaii Islanders," MinorLeagueBaseball.com, http://web.minorleaguebaseball.com/milb/history/top100.jsp?idx=38.

27. *Ibid.*

28. "Around the World with the Giants by John J. McGraw, Manager of the New York Giants," *New York Times*, January 4, 1914, S3.

29. "South Americans to See Baseball," *New Castle News* (New Castle, PA), November 22, 1916, 14.

30. John Henry Nankivell, *Buffalo Soldier Regiment: History of the Twenty-Fifth United States Infantry, 1869–1926, Blacks in the American West* (Lincoln: University of Nebraska Press, 2001), 172.

31. *Ibid.*

32. "Visitor from Hawaii Tells of Life There," *Galveston Daily News*, October 3, 1917, 5.

33. United States Federal Census, Nell L. Moore, Year: 1920; Census Place: Honolulu, Honolulu, Hawaii Territory; Roll T625_2036; Page: 9A; Enumeration District: 35; Image: 316.

34. Hawaii Medical Library, 1996–2003, William L. Moore, August 29, 2005, http://hml.org

35. *Ibid.*

36. "Gila Parade of Baseball Stars," *Gila News Courier*, October 7, 1943, 6.

37. "Form League in Honolulu," *Elyria Chronicle* (Ohio), January 20, 1915, 8.

38. "Gila Parade of Baseball Stars," *Gila News Courier*, October 7, 1943, 6.

39. *Ibid.*

40. Hawai'I Timeline: 1892, Hawaii History.org, http://hawaiihistory.com/index.cfm?fuseaction=ig.page&year=1892.

41. "Around the World with the Giants by John J. McGraw, Manager of the New York Giants," *New York Times*, January 4, 1914, S3.

42. "'Banty' Out for Good," *Los Angeles Times*, November 9, 1916, III2.

43. "Old Grads Remember the Day That Tiny Pomona College Toppled SC, 10–6," *Los Angeles Times*, November 6, 1955, H4.

44. "Coach Nixon at Pomona," *Los Angeles Times*, September 7, 1916, III1.

45. "Mills Wins 1918 School Pennant," *Pacific Commercial Advertiser*, June 12, 1918.

46. *Ibid.*

47. *Ibid.*

48. Charlotte Davis and Edith Stickney, eds., *The Emerging Minorities in America: A Resource Guide for Teachers* (Santa Barbara: ABC-Clio Press, 1972), 105.

49. Kenichi Zenimura Mills High Enrollment form, 1919, Mid-Pac High Administration Office.

50. World War I Draft Registrations Cards, 1917–1918, Jacob Kenichiro Zenimura, Registration Location: Hawaii County, Hawaii; Roll 1452097; Draft Board: 1.

51. Email correspondence with Kenso Zenimura, February 28, 2006.

52. "Micks and Mills Trim Collegians and Pun Outfit," *Honolulu Star-Bulletin*, May 3, 1919.

53. "Mills School Slash Thirteen Bingles in Game with Saint Looey Aggregation," *Honolulu Star-Bulletin*, May 10, 1919.

54. "Mills School Team, Champions of 1919 Interscholastic Baseball League," *Honolulu Star-Bulletin*, May 28, 1919.

55. "Mills Swamps Fort Kamites," *Honolulu Star-Bulletin*, June 27, 1919.

56. "Asahi Win Out in a Tight Game," *Honolulu Star-Bulletin*, June 16, 1919.

57. "Big Shakeup in Ranks of Oahu-Service League," *Honolulu Star-Bulletin*, June 21, 1919.

58. *Ibid.*

59. United States Federal Census, Sinchi Kozicki, Year: 1910; Census Place: Hilo, Hawaii, Hawaii; Roll T624_1752; Page: 31B; Enumeration District: 115; Image: 366.

60. Correspondence with the Mid-Pac High Administration Records department, 2006.

61. California Passenger and Crew Lists, 1893–1957, Knichiro Znimura (*sic*), April 4, 1920.

62. Interview with Kenso Zenimura, Fresno, CA, February 2008.

63. "American League's Birthday Is Today," *Atlanta Constitution*, January 2, 1918, 14.

64. "Sport Shrapnel by Harry A. Williams," *Los Angeles Times*, January 21, 1923, 19.

65. United States Federal Census, Blayney F Matthews, Year: 1920; Census Place: Dubuque Ward 4, Dubuque, Iowa; Roll T625_488; Page: 2A; Enumeration District: 135; Image: 373.

Chapter 2

1. "Race Upholds Japs on Coast Declares DuBois," *Chicago Defender*, May 24, 1913, 1.

2. Race for the United States, Regions, Divisions, and States: 1920; Historical Census Statistics on Population Totals by Race, 1790 to 1990, and by Hispanic Origin, 1970 to 1990, for the United States, Regions, Divisions, and States, by Campbell Gibson and Kay Jung; Population Division, U.S. Census Bureau, Washington, D.C. 20233, September 2002; http://www.census.gov/population/www/documentation/twps0056/twps0056.html.

3. "Senior League Starts Tomorrow," *Fresno Morning Republican*, November 20, 1919, 23.

4. "HS Pups-FAC Juniors at Fink Smith Playground," *Fresno Morning Republican*, December 9, 1919.

5. *Ibid.*

6. "Winter League Starts Sunday," *Fresno Morning Republican*, December 27, 1919, 14.

7. "Winter League Starts Today," *Fresno Morning Republican*, December 28, 1919, 19.

8. "Plans to Discuss Japanese Question," *Fresno Morning Republican*, December 22, 1919.

9. United States Federal Census, Hichiza Narushima, Year: 1920; Census Place: Fresno, Fresno, California; Roll T625_96; Page: 20A; Enumeration District: 20; Image: 842.

10. Honolulu, Hawaii, Passenger Lists, 1900–1953, Hisa Hirokawa, December 11, 1907.

11. William McNeil, *The California Winter League* (Jefferson, NC: McFarland, 2002), 67.

12. "White Sox Have Sweet Ball Club," *Los Angeles Times*, June 17, 1920, III1.

13. "Get Japanese Ballplayer," *The News* (Des Moines, IA), August 31, 1920.

14. "Japanese as Baseball Players," *Oakland Tribune*, February 24, 1905, 9.

15. "Labor Day Ball Game for City," *Fresno Morning Republican*, September 5, 1920, 12.

16. "Giants Meet FAC," *Fresno Bee*, October 16, 1920, 20.

17. "Colored Giants Defeat F.A.C. 8–2," *Fresno Bee*, October 18, 1920, 6.

18. "Fresno League Is Drawing Big Crowds," *Fresno Bee*, September 30, 1917.

19. "Our Letter Box," *Baseball Magazine* 12 (December 1913): 91–96.

20. "Oak Leafs Begin Today," *Oakland Tribune*, February 20, 1916, 36.

21. *Ibid.*

22. "Protect West from Japan," *Fresno Bee*, September 15, 1920.

23. Denshō, Sites of Shame, Historic Timeline, http: Source: http://www.densho.org/resources/default.asp//www.densho.org/sitesofshame/timeline.xm.

24. McNeil, *The California Winter League*, 66.

25. "All-Star Baseball Club May Go to Japan," *Chicago Defender*, February 21, 1921, 6.

26. "Baseball Fans in Honolulu Have Tough Time Trying to Pronounce Players Names," *Olean Evening News*, May 9, 1921, 10.

27. "Japan Invaded by American Ball Teams," *Los Angeles Times*, September 22, 1921, III3.

28. "Pitches No-Hitter," *Los Angeles Times*, September 27, 1921, III3.
29. "Brindza and Sommerville Now in Camp," *Evening Independent* (Massillon, OH), April 16, 1927, 14.
30. *Ibid.*
31. "Athletic Club Nine Plays at San Jose Today," *Fresno Bee*, October 29, 1921, 16.
32. Kerry Yo Nakagawa, *Through a Diamond: 100 Years of Japanese American Baseball* (San Francisco: Rudi Publishing, 2001), 65.
33. "Semi-Pros Mix Today, by Joe Bush," *Los Angeles Times*, July 30, 1922, 18.
34. "Twenty Years Ago (1922)," *Fresno Bee*, June 30, 1942, 4-B.
35. "Gila Parade of Baseball Stars," *Gila News Courier*, October 7, 1943, 6.
36. Email correspondence with Kyoko Yoshida, March 18, 2008.
37. "Orientals to Clash Tomorrow," *Los Angeles Times*, September 16, 1922, III2.
38. Honolulu, Hawaii, Passenger Lists, 1900–1953, Keichiro Zinamura, October 22, 1922.
39. "Majors' Club Picked to Tour Japan," *Ogden Standard-Examiner*, June 22, 1922, 8.
40. "Baseball Tourists Start Trip Today," *New York Times*, October 14, 1922, 16.
41. SABR Asian Baseball Committee, Japanese Baseball, http://asianbb.sabr.org/japanesebaseball.html.
42. "Big Leaguers Boot One in Japan, Herbert Hunter Takes Major League All-Stars to Japan," *Fresno Bee*, December 14, 1922, 9.
43. "Hoyt Arrives Here After Long Jaunt," *New York Times*, February 8, 1923, 22.
44. Denshō, Timeline, Causes of the Incarceration, http://www.densho.org/assets/sharedpages/timeline.asp.
45. "All Set for Opening Nov. 19," *Fresno Bee*, November 8, 1922, 15.
46. "Two Games on Winter League Baseball Card," *Fresno Bee*, December 2, 1922, 7c.
47. "Real Battles on League Schedule," *Fresno Bee*, December 16, 1922, 7c.
48. "Gila Parade of Baseball Stars," *Gila News Courier*, October 7, 1943, 6.
49. "Nipponese Tossers to Play Ball Here," *Oakland Tribune*, January 6, 1923, 8.
50. "Hard Contest for League Leaders," *Fresno Bee*, January 13, 1923, 7c.
51. "Brotherhood Forfeits Game to Bee Club," *Fresno Bee*, January 29, 1923, 7c.
52. "Tail-Enders Trim Fast Bee Club," *Fresno Bee*, February 19, 1923, 10.
53. California Passenger and Crew Lists, 1893–1957, Knichiro Znimura, February 11, 1923.
54. "Valley Tossers Drop Two Games to Island Stars," *Fresno Bee*, February 23, 1923, 14.
55. "First Practice Game," *Fresno Bee*, February 24, 1923, 6c.
56. "Sport Shrapnel by Harry A. Williams," *Los Angeles Times*, January 21, 1923, 19.
57. *Ibid.*
58. "Fresno Semi-Pros to Meet Salt Lake Club in Spring Game," *Fresno Bee*, March 9, 1923, 16.
59. "Rally in Seventh Gives Biola Victory Over Japanese Team," *Fresno Bee*, March 12, 1923, 12.
60. "Fresno Semi-Pros to Meet Salt Lake Club in Spring Game," *Fresno Bee*, March 9, 1923, 16.
61. "Bees-Tigers to Tangle Saturday," *Fresno Bee*, March 14, 1923, 12.
62. "Lewis Trades Siglin to Solons," *Fresno Bee*, March 13, 1923, 13.
63. "Bees Have Three Games on Week-End Schedule," *Fresno Bee*, March 16, 1923, 18.
64. "Bees Trim Japanese," *Fresno Bee*, March 19, 1923, 10.
65. "Twilight League to Have Great Season, Quigley Predicts," *Fresno Bee*, March 14, 1923, 12.
66. "Japanese to Hold Track Meet Here," *Fresno Bee*, March 29, 1923, 12.
67. "Three Games on Card for Bees, Lewis Adds Setto with Japanese," *Fresno Bee*, March 30, 1923, 16.
68. "Rain Halts Final Game of Salt Lake Training Season, Bees All Set," *Fresno Bee*, April 2, 1923, 10.
69. "Japanese Club Will Be First Saturday Opponent for Tigers," *Fresno Bee*, March 27, 1923, 16.
70. "Ten Years Ago," *Fresno Bee-Republican*, April 21, 1933.
71. "Japanese League Will Be Organized," *Oakland Tribune*, April 14, 1923, 11.
72. "New Ball Park at Livingston Opened, Japanese Defeated," *Fresno Bee*, May 1, 1923, 12.
73. "Huge Signs Disappeared," Editorial, *Gila News Courier*, September 25, 1943, 6.
74. "Blewett's Hopefuls Win from Madera," *Fresno Bee*, May 9, 1923, 12.
75. "Fresnans Plan Entertainment for Colored Players," *Fresno Bee*, June 28, 1923.
76. "Local Japanese Win from Fast Oakland Colored Club, 11–7," *Fresno Bee*, July 2, 1923, 10.
77. "Japanese Clubs to Play Series Here for Title," *Fresno Bee*, July 3, 1923, 4.
78. "Win Championship from Seattle Club," *Fresno Bee*, July 5, 1923, 12.
79. "Bingham-Wenks Hope to Defeat Japanese to Get Chance at Aristo Cubs," *Fresno Bee*, December 8, 1923, 4c.
80. "Fresno Athletic Club Wins from Bingham-Wenks," *Fresno Bee*, December 10, 1923, 8.
81. "Coast League Stars Will Play Athletic Club on Christmas," *Fresno Bee*, December 20, 1923, 12.
82. "Jap Gets Contract," *Lowell Sun*, August 22, 1932, 7.
83. "Bee All Stars Defeat FAC Team 7–6," *Fresno Bee*, February 4, 1924, 4.
84. "Bee Stars Beat FAC 7 to 5," *Fresno Bee*, February 11, 1924, 4.
85. "Valley League Organized with Six Ball Clubs," *Oakland Tribune*, February 12, 1924, 27.
86. *Ibid.*
87. "Porterville Would Bar Japanese," *Fresno Bee*, February 26, 1924, 10.
88. "Four Clubs Ready to Start," *Fresno Bee*, March 5, 1924, 22.
89. "Salt Lake Schedules Three Practice Games," *Fresno Bee*, March 4, 1924, 4.
90. "Japanese Win from Bees 6 to 4," *Fresno Bee*, March 10, 1924, 4.
91. *Ibid.*
92. "Strong Club Will Battle Japanese," *Fresno Bee*, March 13, 1924, 12.
93. "Bees Wallop Japanese 13–0," *Fresno Bee*, March 17, 1924, 10.
94. "Salt Lakers Trample Over Fresno Outfit," *Los Angeles Times*, March 17, 1924, B3.
95. "Bees Wallop Japanese 15–2," *Fresno Bee*, March 31, 1924, 4.
96. "Fresno A.C. Wins from Stockton by Score of 5 to 4," *Fresno Bee*, April 14, 1924, 14.
97. "Local Florists to Play Japanese 'U,'" *Oakland Tribune*, April 17, 1924, 18.
98. Pearce, *From Asahi to Zebras*, 17.
99. Denshō, Timeline, Causes of the Incarceration, http://www.densho.org/assets/sharedpages/timeline.asp.
100. "Fresno Japs Will Invade the Orient," *Los Angeles Times*, July 18, 1924, 11.
101. "Fast Japanese Club Will Oppose Fresno Tigers Tomorrow," *Fresno Bee*, August 2, 1924, 4A.
102. "The Tigers Beat Japanese 9 to 8," *Fresno Bee*, August 4, 1924, 10.
103. "FAC Loses to Tigers 7 to 5," *Fresno Bee*, August 11, 1924, 10.
104. "Japanese Team Ready for Trip," *Fresno Bee*, August 23, 1924, CL4.
105. "Fresno Nipponese Are Given Baseball Bat Autographed by Cobb," *Fresno Bee*, August 23, 1924, CL4.
106. "Fresno Trims Army Nine 9 to 3," *Fresno Bee*, August 25, 1924, 13.

107. "Fresno Japanese Challenge Tigers," *Los Angeles Times*, August 17, 1924, 13.
108. Honolulu, Hawaii, Passenger Lists, 1900–1953, Lilian Zenimura, September 8, 1924.
109. Interview with Kenso Zenimura, 2010.
110. Nakagawa, *Through a Diamond*, 66.
111. "Fresno's Ken Zenimura, Dean of Nisei Baseball in US, Recalls Colorful Past," *Fresno Bee*, May 20, 1962, B9.
112. Nakagawa, *Through a Diamond*, 18–19.
113. "Fresno Tigers Take Game from Japanese Club," *Fresno Bee*, December 29, 1924, 4.
114. California Passenger and Crew Lists, 1893–1957, Knichiro Znimura, January 27, 1925.

Chapter 3

1. Kansas City Monarchs display, Negro Leagues Baseball Museum, Kansas City, MO.
2. Email correspondence with Kenso Zenimura, February 28, 2006; California Passenger and Crew Lists, 1893–1957, Knichiro Znimura, January 27, 1925.
3. "Fresno State Hopes to Win Championship in Baseball and Track," *Fresno Bee*, February 1, 1925, C1.
4. William McNeil, *The California Winter League* (Jefferson, NC: McFarland, 2002), 102.
5. "Tigers Trimmed by St. Louis Club by 7 to 2 Score," *Fresno Bee*, March 22, 1925, C1.
6. "Colored Giants Win Final Game from Tigers 3–2," *Fresno Bee*, March 23, 1925, 9.
7. "Harry Morton Is Fresno Cubs Boss," *Fresno Bee*, May 26, 1925, 15.
8. Interview with Kenso Zenimura, February 2008.
9. "Fresno Cubs Win from Japanese in Ten Innings, 5–4," *Fresno Bee*, May 31, 1925, 17.
10. "30,000 Yen Offered to Ruth for Baseball Tour of Japan," *New York Times*, June 17, 1925, 17.
11. "Osaka Nine to Leave Japan on March 28 for Tour of the U.S.," *New York Times*, March 21, 1925, 10.
12. "N.Y.U. Nine to Play Japanese Two Games," *New York Times*, May 31, 1925, S7.
13. "Japanese Club Downs Visitors," *Fresno Bee*, July 5, 1925, C1.
14. "Fresno Team to Play Fast Team from Japan To-Day," *Fresno Bee*, July 7, 1925, 3b.
15. "Fresno Ball Club Beats Japanese 6–2," *Fresno Bee*, July 8, 1925, 3B.
16. "Fresno A.C. Wins from Fowler 7–6," *Fresno Bee*, July 20, 1925, 15.
17. "Around the Bases in the Twilight Leagues," *Fresno Bee*, August 10, 1925, 15.
18. "Salt Lake Sells Lazerre (*sic*) to NY Yankees," *Fresno Bee*, August 3, 1925, 17.
19. "Star Jap Nine to Play Series Here," *Los Angeles Times*, September 6, 1925, A1.
20. "Fresno, 5; White Sox, 4," *Los Angeles Times*, September 7, 1925, 13.
21. Former Manzanar internee Rose Ochi recalls reading the headline "Japs Beat the Niggers." Email correspondence with Kerry Yo Nakagawa, May 30, 2006. Newspapers containing this headline have yet to surface.
22. Email correspondence with Glynn Martin, Executive Director, Los Angeles Police Historical Society, March 28, 2008.
23. McNeil, *The California Winter League*, 120.
24. "Sports of the Times," *New York Times*, Jun 3, 1956, 206.
25. *Lincoln Sunday Star*, January 31, 1926, A6.
26. "Shan Kilburn's Team to Tangle with FAC Team," *Fresno Bee*, February 7, 1926, 23.
27. "Hazelwood Defeat FAC in Fast Contest," *Fresno Bee*, February 8, 1926, 7.
28. "Japanese Baseball League Organized," *Modesto News-Herald*, March 6, 1926, II-1.
29. "Fresno Japanese Baseball Outfit Blanks Stockton," *Fresno Bee*, March 8, 1926, 7.
30. *New Castle News* (New Castle, PA), April 15, 1926, 19.
31. "Stockton Beats Fresno A.C. Team in Game Here, 8–6," *Fresno Bee*, May 3, 1926, 7.
32. "Fresno Athletic Club Beats Stockton Team in Japanese League, 5–2," *Fresno Bee*, May 10, 1926, 7.
33. "Sciots Win Game from F.A.C. by Score of 11 to 0," *Fresno Bee*, May 24, 1926, 8.
34. "FAC Defeats Sciot Ball Team by 8 to 3 Score, *Fresno Bee*, June 28, 1926, 11.
35. "Fresno All-Stars Beat Los Angeles Crack Team, 9 to 4," *Fresno Bee*, July 5, 1926, 10.
36. *Ibid.*
37. Interview with Kenso Zenimura, February 2008.
38. "Fresno All-Stars Win Again from L.A. Team, 4 to 3," *Fresno Bee*, July 6, 1926, 10.
39. *Ibid.*
40. "Postoffice Wins City League Flag," *Fresno Bee*, July 27, 1926, 13.
41. "Sako Holds the Printers to Two Hits," *Fresno Bee*, July 30, 1926, 13.
42. "Yoshikawa Hits Hard Enough to Beat Little Lake," *Fresno Bee*, August 3, 1926, 10.
43. "FAC Defeats Firemen's Team in Slugfest 14–11," *Fresno Bee*, July 26, 1926, 8.
44. "Around the Bases in the Twilight Leagues," *Fresno Bee*, August 25, 1926, 11.
45. "Fresno Athletic Club Loses to Alameda Pastimers by 5–4 Count," *Fresno Bee*, October 4, 1926, 10.
46. "FAC Falls Before Pastimers from Capital City," *Fresno Bee*, October 11, 1926, 10.
47. "Fresno Fans to See Oakland's Best Here Today," *Fresno Bee*, October 31, 1926, 3D.
48. *Ibid.*
49. "Oakland Outfit Beats Locals in Fast Game, 5 to 4," *Fresno Bee*, November 1, 1926, 10.
50. "Stockton Pastimers Defeat FAC in Series Opener, 12 to 5," *Fresno Bee*, November 22, 1926, 10.
51. "Japanese Ball Club to Invade Orient Again," *Fresno Bee*, January 4, 1927, 10.
52. "Philadelphia Royal Giants Going to Japan," *Rafu Shimpo*, February 13, 1927.
53. Kazuo Sayama, *Black Baseball Heroes: The Rise and Fall of the "Nigro League"* (Tokyo, Japan: Chuo Shinsho, 1994), 11–12.
54. Email correspondence with Kyoko Yoshida, 2007.
55. Comment 144, Hall of Merit Discussion: Biz Mackey, BaseballThink Factory Blog, comment posted April 15, 2005, http://www.baseballthinkfactory.org/files/hall_of_merit/discussion/biz_mackey/P100.
56. "Smallpox Scare Threatens Club," *Fresno Bee*, March 31, 1927, 10.
57. "Fresno Japanese Nine to Play Meiji in 1st Game," *Japan Times*, April 4, 1927.
58. "Fresno Combine Arrives to Play Local Tossers," unknown Honolulu paper, August 2, 1927, from the Harvey Iwata 1927 Tour Scrapbook, National Baseball Hall of Fame.
59. "Firemen Ready to Meet Calpets This Afternoon," *Fresno Bee*, June 12, 1927, D1.
60. Harvey Iwata 1927 Tour Scrapbook, National Baseball Hall of Fame.
61. *Ibid.*
62. "Rikkyo Baseball Team to Visit Southern, Central, Northern Calif.," January 12, 2010 news release, http://www.hokubei.com/en/news/2010/01/Rikkyo-Baseball-Team-Visit-Southern-Central-Norther-Calif.
63. "Fresno Japanese Plays Basketball 1st Game April 20," *Japan Times*,

April 14, 1927, from the Harvey Iwata 1927 Tour Scrapbook, National Baseball Hall of Fame.

64. Email correspondence with Kyoko Yoshida, 2007.

65. "Royal Giants Swamp Fresno Japanese 9–1," *Japan Times*, April 21, 1927, from the Harvey Iwata 1927 Tour Scrapbook, National Baseball Hall of Fame.

66. *Ibid.*

67. *Ibid.*

68. *Ibid.*

69. *Ibid.*

70. *Ibid.*

71. Stephen Ellsesser, "Black Giants Were Treated Like Royalty," MLB.com, February 23, 2007, http://mlb.com/news/article.jsp?ymd=20070223&content_id=1812798&vkey=news+mlb&fext=.jsp&cid=mlb.

72. "Royal Giants Won 26, Tied One on Their Japanese Tour," *Chicago Defender*, June 25, 1927, 9.

73. David King, "Finally Getting His Due," *San Antonio Express-News*, July 30, 2006, 1C.

74. Kazuo Sayama, *Black Baseball Heroes: The Rise and Fall of the "Nigro League"* (Tokyo, Japan: Chuo Shinsho, 1994), 11–12.

75. Stephen Ellsesser, "Black Giants Were Treated Like Royalty," MLB.com, February 23, 2007, http://mlb.com/news/article.jsp?ymd=20070223&content_id=1812798&vkey=news+mlb&fext=.jsp&cid=mlb.

76. From the Harvey Iwata 1927 Tour Scrapbook, National Baseball Hall of Fame.

77. *Ibid.*

78. *Ibid.*

79. "Firemen Ready to Meet Calpets This Afternoon," *Fresno Bee*, June 12, 1927, D1.

80. "Fresno Baseball Club Back from Orient," *Fresno Bee*, September 8, 1927, 12.

81. "Ruth to Make Tour with Gehrig to Coast," *New York Times*, September 27, 1927, 20.

82. "Plans Progress for Ruth-Gehrig Game in Fresno," *Fresno Bee*, October 18, 1927, 15.

83. "Veterans Defeat F.A.C. Nine in 11-Inning Game," *Fresno Bee*, October 24, 1927, 7.

84. "Babe Ruth and Gehrig to Play Here Tomorrow," *Fresno Bee*, October 28, 1927, 17–18.

85. "Fans Pack Park to Watch Ruth Gehrig Perform," *Fresno Bee*, October 29, 1927, 7.

86. *Ibid.*

87. *Ibid.*

88. *Ibid.*

89. "A Man Who Met the Babe and Treasured a Baseball," *Fresno Bee*, July 23, 1989, G3.

90. "A Slice of Japanese Americana; Second Generation Japanese-Americans Learned to Play Baseball Behind the Barbed Wires of Internment Camps," *Fresno Bee*, May 3, 1996.

91. "All-Stars Lose to FAC Team," *Fresno Bee*, October 30, 1927, 10.

92. "Speedy Waseda Quintet to Play Here Saturday," *Fresno Bee*, January 11, 1928, 11.

93. "State Nine May Play Keio Team in Early April," *Fresno Bee*, February 21, 1928.

94. McNeil, *The California Winter League*, 127.

95. BaseballThinkFactory.org blog.

96. "Colored Giants Defeat FAC Outfit," 12 to 7, *Fresno Bee*, March 19, 1928, 6.

97. "Rain Halts Iron Boys FAC Ball Game," *Fresno Bee*, April 2, 1928, 4.

98. "Eleven Teams Are Entered in Japanese Meet," *Fresno Bee*, April 6, 1928, 18.

99. "Fresno YMBA Leads Field in Japanese Meet, *Fresno Bee*, April 9, 1928, 6.

100. "FAC Nine Will Battle Tollhouse," *Fresno Bee*, April 15, 1928, 3D.

101. "FAC Pastimers Upset Tollhouse," *Fresno Bee*, April 16, 1928, 12.

102. "Japanese Nines to Stage Series Here Next Week," *Fresno Bee*, April 17, 1928, 11.

103. "Tigers Schedule Three Ball Games," *Fresno Bee*, April 20, 1928, 18.

104. "Tigers Will Play L.A. Nine Sunday," *Fresno Bee*, May 1, 1928, 6.

105. "Tigers Smother LA Club Under 18 to 4," *Fresno Bee*, May 7, 1928, 6.

106. "Open Season April 28, Japanese Nine Is Booked," *Afro-American* (Baltimore), April 21, 1928, 13.

107. "Hilldale Tops Keio," *Afro-American* (Baltimore), May 19, 1928, 12.

108. "FAC Tossers Trounce Merced," *Fresno Bee*, April 23, 1928, 6.

109. "Merced Club in Double Victory Over Weekend," *Fresno Bee*, May 7, 1928, 6.

110. "FAC Nine Wins District Title," *Fresno Bee*, June 4, 1928, 9.

111. "FAC Tossers Bump All-Stars," *Fresno Bee*, June 11, 1928, 4.

112. "Keio University Squad to Arrive Here Tomorrow," *Fresno Bee*, June 14, 1928, 15.

113. "Keio Slab Star Smothers FAC Under 10–6 Count," *Fresno Bee*, June 17, 1928, D1.

114. "Keio University Drubs FAC Pastimers 28–8," *Fresno Bee*, June 18, 1928, 6.

115. "FAC Pastimers Stop Tigers 6–4," *Fresno Bee*, June 25, 1928, 9.

116. "Second Game of Series on Books at Firemen's Lot," *Fresno Bee*, July 1, 1928, 3D.

117. "Tiger Chucker Wins Own Game," *Fresno Bee*, July 2, 1928, 6.

118. Honolulu, Hawaii, Passenger Lists, 1900–1953, Kenso Zenimura, July 14, 1928.

119. *Ibid.*

120. McNeil, *The California Winter League*, 127.

121. "Negro and Jap to Umpire Ball Game," *Woodland Daily Democrat*, August 30, 1928, 8.

122. "FAC Pastimers Lose to All-Stars 7–4," *Fresno Bee*, October 8, 1928, 10.

123. "Zenimura to Play with FAC Nine Sunday," *Fresno Bee*, March 12, 1929, 3B.

124. "Cobb to Sail Oct. 20 for Tour of Japan," *New York Times*, October 10, 1928, 24.

125. "FAC Nine Jumps on Firemen for 20–3 Win," *Fresno Bee*, March 4, 1929, 8A.

126. "Zenimura to Play with FAC Nine Sunday," *Fresno Bee*, March 12, 1929, 3B.

127. "Meiji Baseball Team from Japan Will Play Here," *Fresno Bee*, March 27, 1929, 3C.

128. "Sciots Land on FAC Pitchers for 8–3 Victory," *Fresno Bee*, April 1, 1929, 2B.

129. "Meiji Nine Wins," *Fresno Bee*, April 8, 1929, 4B.

130. "Sciots Take Beating at Hands of All-Star Japanese Club 10–3," *Fresno Bee*, April 15, 1929, 4B.

131. "Chinese Association Sponsors Program of Sports and Dancing," *Fresno Bee*, April 26, 1929, 3B.

132. "FAC Pastimers Down LA Outfit," *Fresno Bee*, April 29, 1929, 3B.

133. "Fresno Sciots to Play Ball on Hawaii Trip," *Oakland Tribune*, May 3, 1929, B49.

134. "Objects to Paying $1 to See Sunday Ball Game," *Fresno Bee*, May 4, 1929, Editorial Page.

135. Inflation calculator, http://www.westegg.com/inflation/infl.cgi.

136. "Sciot Baseball Team Entertains Pyramid Members," *Fresno Bee*, July 22, 1929, 6A.

137. California Passenger and Crew Lists, 1893–1957, Kenichiro Zenimura, October 30, 1929.

138. United States Federal Census, Masakichi Zenimura, Year: 1930; Census Place: Honolulu, Hawaii.

139. Interview with Kenso Zenimura, February 2008.

Chapter 4

1. "At Dawn, There was Twilight Circa 1920s—Weeknight Baseball League was Fresno's First Passion," *Fresno Bee*, October 9, 1997, D1.

2. "Fresno High to Play Chowchilla Nine on Friday," *Fresno Bee*, March 11, 1930, 2B.
3. "Japanese Ball Sked Announced," *Fresno Bee*, February 26, 1930, 3C.
4. "Valley Japanese Will Stage Meet Here Next Sunday," *Fresno Bee*, April 1, 1930, 2B.
5. "Fresno Japanese to Play Stockton Here April 26–27, *Fresno Bee*, April 16, 1930, 10B.
6. "Fresno Japanese Win League Title for Fourth Time," *Fresno Bee*, May 13, 1930, 3B.
7. "Around the Bases in the Twilight Leagues," *Fresno Bee*, April 19, 1930, 2B.
8. "Jaynes Shade Lumbermen as Darkness Halts Game," *Fresno Bee*, April 19, 1930, 2B.
9. "Jaynes Loses to Hanford All Stars," *Fresno Bee*, July 14, 1930, 6A.
10. *Diamonds in the Rough: The Legacy of Japanese-American Baseball*, DVD (Chip Taylor Communications, 1998).
11. "Japanese Meet All-Star Team Tomorrow Night," *Fresno Bee*, September 5, 1930, 14A.
12. "Fresno Outfit Shades Aratani Pastimers 6–5," *Fresno Bee*, September 8, 1930, 2B.
13. "Stars of Big Leagues Will Play Tonight," *Fresno Bee*, October 27, 1930, 2B.
14. "Grove, Shires and Big League Comedians Steal Show at Baseball Game," *Fresno Bee*, October 28, 1930, 6B.
15. Stewart Tolnay and E.M. Beck, *A Festival of Violence: An Analysis of Southern Lynchings, 1882–1930* (Champaign: University of Illinois Press, 1995).
16. "Japanese Nine to Invade US," *Vidette-Messenger* (Valparaiso, IN), March 12, 1931, 12.
17. Interview with Kenso Zenimura, February 2008.
18. "Alamedan Will Take Baseball to Japan," *Oakland Tribune*, January 29, 1931, B21.
19. "Sport Tidbits, by Red Tano," *Heart Mountain Sentinel*, September 16, 1944, 6.
20. "Japanese to Observe Birthday of Buddha," *Fresno Bee*, March 5, 1931, 12A.
21. Interview with Kenso Zenimura, February 2008.
22. "FAC Playing in Diamond Tourney," *Fresno Bee*, May 30, 1931, 4A.
23. "FAC Nine to Tussle All-Stars," *Fresno Bee*, June 12, 1931, 2B.
24. "FAC Club Will Not Play Hosei Nine Here," *Fresno Bee*, July 3, 1931, 7A.
25. "FAC Nine to Play Stockton," *Fresno Bee*, July 10, 1931, Sports Section, 1.
26. "FAC Trounces Stockton 14–5," *Fresno Bee*, July 13, 1931, 2B.
27. "Japanese Stars Will Play Here," *Fresno Bee*, August 6, 1931, 3B.
28. "Japanese Prep Wins from Fresnans," *Fresno Bee*, August 9, 1931, 3D.
29. "Fresno Japanese Lose Title Game," *Fresno Bee*, October 1, 1931, Sports Section, 1.
30. "Heflin Engages Japanese Park, *Los Angeles Times*, September 20, 1931, 6.
31. "National Affairs: Again, Heflin," *Time Magazine*, Monday, Feb. 17, 1930.
32. "Heflin Hits City County Boards for Speech Bans, " *Fresno Bee*, September 23, 1931, 1C.
33. *Ibid.*
34. "Old Timers Twilight Benefit Rosters Named," *Fresno Bee*, October 2, 1931, 2C.
35. "Babe Slated to Play First and Pitch for Sciots at Local Park, Second Trip Here," *Fresno Bee*, October 21, 1931, Sports Section, 1.
36. "Ruth Hits Home Run, Makes Two Errors at First," *Fresno Bee*, October 22, 1931, Sports Section, 1.
37. "Sport Thinks by Ed W. Orman," *Fresno Bee*, October 22, 1931, Sports Section, 1.
38. "Touring Big Leaguers Win Another in Japan," *Fresno Bee*, December 16, 1931, Sports Section, 1.
39. "About Matsumoto," *Fresno Bee*, October 29, 1947, 16.
40. "Tuning in with Our Children," *Oakland Tribune*, October 27, 1931.
41. "Fresno's Ken Zenimura, Dean Of Nisei Baseball In US, Recalls Colorful Past," *Fresno Bee*, May 20, 1962, B9.
42. "Fresno Colored Ball Club Beats Bakersfield," *Fresno Bee-Republican*, May 16, 1932, Sports Section, 1.
43. "Around the Bases in the Twilight Leagues," *Fresno Bee-Republican*, June 21, 1932, 3B.
44. "Japanese Down DePrima Club," *Fresno Bee-Republican*, June 27, 1932, Sports Section, 1.
45. "Fresno Coming Here for Tilt with Nippons," *Rafu Shimpo*, June 1932, Daily English Section.
46. "Fresno Coming with Large Squad for Nippon Series," *Rafu Shimpo*, June 27, 1932, Daily English Section.
47. "Nippons Easily Win Both Fresno All-Star Games," *Rafu Shimpo*, July 5, 1932, Daily English Section.
48. "Guadalupe Nine Bats to Victory," *Rafu Shimpo*, July 6, 1932, Daily English Section.
49. "Japanese to Play Aviators Tonight in Series Opener," *Fresno Bee-Republican*, July 16, 1932, Sports Section, 1.
50. "Aviators Will Play Japanese," *Fresno Bee-Republican*, July 26, 1932.
51. "Aviators Trim Japanese, 19–11," *Fresno Bee-Republican*, August 1, 1932, Sports Section, 1.
52. "Boy Confesses Setting Fires," *Fresno Bee*, May 23, 1935, 1.
53. "Auto Dives Off of 300-Ft Bank and Catches on Fire," *Hayward Review*, September 26, 1932, 1.
54. "Hanford Nine Beats Dinuba," *Fresno Bee-Republican*, April 5, 1933.
55. "Japanese Nine Trims All-Stars," *Fresno Bee-Republican*, July 17, 1933, Sports Section, 1.
56. *Diamonds in the Rough: The Legacy of Japanese-American Baseball*, DVD (Chip Taylor Communications, 1998).
57. "Have Twilight Pennant Sewed Up," *Fresno Bee-Republican*, July 30, 1933, 2C.
58. "Colored Clubs to Clash," *Fresno Bee*, August 31, 1933, Sports Section, 1.
59. "Challenge Fresno Clubs," *Fresno Bee*, September 17, 1933, 3C.
60. "Fete Queen to Receive Crown," *Fresno Bee-Republican*, September 15, 1933, 2A.
61. "Colored Athletics to Play Bakersfield Cubs," *Fresno Bee*, October 15, 1933, 3C.
62. "All-Stars Win from Sciots Exhibition Here," *Fresno Bee*, October 15, 1933, 3C.
63. "Japanese Clubs to Play Here," *Fresno Bee*, May 6, 1934, 3C.
64. "Japanese Ball Clubs Tussle Here Today," *Fresno Bee*, May 20, 1934, 3C.
65. "Fresno A.C. Beats Alameda," *Fresno Bee*, May 21, 1934, Sports Section, 1.
66. "Japanese Trim CAC, 14 to 1," *Fresno Bee*, May 28, 1934, 3B.
67. Email correspondence with Kenso Zenimura, July 11, 2007.
68. "Double Plays Aid San Jose Victory," *Fresno Bee*, June 4, 1934, Sports Section, 1.
69. "Fresno Japanese Defeat Stockton," *Fresno Bee*, June 11, 1934, Sports Section, 1.
70. "Major League Clubs Seeking College Talent," *Fresno Bee*, June 11, 1934, Sports Section, 1.
71. "Athletic Club Wins from Salinas Outfit," *Fresno Bee*, June 19, 1934, Sports Section, 1.
72. "Fresno Japanese Ball Club Captures Game," *Fresno Bee*, July 2, 1934, 5B.
73. "Elks Club Defeats Japanese Nine," *Fresno Bee*, July 9, 1934, Sports Section, 1.
74. "Ruth to Make Tour Abroad

Next Fall," *New York Times*, July 6, 1934, 22.

75. "Fresno Stars Beat Detroit Team, 17-to-16," *Fresno Bee*, July 18, 1934, 1B.

76. "New Mexico," *Chicago Defender*, July 14, 1934, 20.

77. "Fresno Stars Beat Detroit Team, 17-to-16," *Fresno Bee*, July 18, 1934, 1B.

78. "Japanese Trim All-Stars, 15–5," *Fresno Bee*, July 16, 1934, Sports Section, 1.

79. "Fresno Japanese Ball Club Wins at Hanford," *Fresno Bee*, July 30, 1934, 3B.

80. "Dwelling Burned; Baseball Park Is Damaged by Fire," *Fresno Bee*, July 30, 1934, 3B.

81. "Ball Clubs Go Run-Crazy and Play 22–22 Tie," *Fresno Bee*, August 6, 1934, 3B.

82. Interview with Kenso Zenimura, February 2008.

83. "Japanese Ball Clubs to Meet," *Fresno Bee*, August 18, 1934, Sports Section, 1.

84. "Fresno Japanese Beat San Jose," *Fresno Bee*, August 20, 1934, Sports Section, 1.

85. "Japanese Ball Club Wins Game," *Fresno Bee*, September 4, 1934, 10.

86. "Seattle Japanese to Play Here," *Fresno Bee*, September 12, 1934, 3C.

87. "San Jose Club Beats Japanese," *Fresno Bee*, September 17, 1934, Sports Section, 1.

88. "Hollywood All-Stars to Meet Fresno Club Today," *Fresno Bee*, October 7, 1934, 2C.

89. "Japanese Ball Club is Winner," *Fresno Bee*, October 7, 1934, 3D.

90. "Fresno Japanese Will Play FAC Club To-day," *Fresno Bee*, October 14 1934, 2C.

91. "Japanese Beat Old-Timers, 12–6," *Fresno Bee*, October 15, 1934, 2C.

92. "Stars Leave Chicago," *New York Times*, October 16, 1934, 33.

93. "Mack Hails Ruth as Peace Promoter," *New York Times*, January 6, 1935, 57.

94. "Some Crank," *New York Times*, February 24, 1935, E1.

95. "Bye, George! Ichiro Passes Sisler's Mark," mlb.com, http://mlb.mlb.com/mlb/events/ichiro_hits_tory/index.jsp.

96. *Directory of City and County of Honolulu*, vol. 1933–1934.

97. "Coast League Puts Okeh on Valley Circuit," *Fresno Bee*, January 8, 1935, 3B.

98. "Japanese Pro Baseballers May Play Here," *Fresno Bee*, February 28, 1935, Sports Section, 1.

99. "Seals Hope to Even Series with Japanese," *Fresno Bee*, March 26, 1935, Sports Section, 1.

100. "Cavney Will Use Young Bob Cole on Mound," *Fresno Bee*, March 24, 1935, 2C.

101. "Tokio Giants Will Play in Two Games Here," *Fresno Bee*, April 24, 1935, Sports Section, 1.

102. Pearce, *From Asahi to Zebras*, 54.

103. "Three Baseball Games Slated at Chance Field," *Fresno Bee*, April 28, 1935, 2C.

104. "Tokio Giants Defeat Fresno Japanese," 6–4, *Fresno Bee*, April 30, 1935, Sports Section, 1.

105. "Fresno Japanese Beat Colored Cubs," *Fresno Bee*, May 6, 1935, 3B.

106. "Fresno Japanese Ball Club defeats Le Grand," *Fresno Bee*, July 15, 1935, Sports Section, 1.

107. "Japanese A.C. Scores Another League Victory," *Fresno Bee*, July 25, 1935, Sports Section, 1.

108. "Japanese Club Rallies in Ninth But Drops Game," *Fresno Bee*, July 29, 1935, Sports Section, 1.

109. "Brewers Beat Japanese, 5–4, at Chance Field," *Fresno Bee*, August 1, 1935, 3B.

110. "Japanese Stars Listed for Game with S.F. Seals," *Fresno Bee*, August 1, 1935, 3B.

111. "Seals Trounce Fresno Club in Drab Contest," *Fresno Bee*, August 6, 1935, Sports Section, 1.

112. "Japanese Club Whips Sera in League Contest," *Fresno Bee*, August 5, 1935, Sports Section, 1.

113. "Japanese Ball Club Beats Sun Maids, 6–2," *Fresno Bee*, August 10, 1935, Sports Section, 1.

114. "Brewers Lose League Lead to Japanese Club," *Fresno Bee*, August 12, 1935, Sports Section, 1.

115. "Japanese A.C. Is Beaten, 17 to 11, by Mt. Whitney," *Fresno Bee*, August 28, 1935, Sports Section, 1.

116. "Japanese Play Here To-day in Title Contest," *Fresno Bee*, September 1, 1935, Sports Section, 1.

117. "Japanese A.C. Divide Games with LA Nine," *Fresno Bee*, September 2, 1935, Sports Section, 1.

118. "Fresnans Down L.A. Japanese," *Fresno Bee*, September 3, 1935, 3B.

119. "McMurtry Brothers Lead Sun-Maids to Bat Title," *Fresno Bee*, September 15, 1935, 3B.

120. "Japanese Play Watsonville Nine," *Fresno Bee*, September 27, 1935, 3B.

121. "Fresno Japanese Play San Jose," *Fresno Bee*, October 16, 1935, 3B.

122. "Japanese Will Meet All-Stars," *Fresno Bee*, October 12, 1935, 5A.

123. "Tokio Giants Beat Rookies," *Fresno Bee*, March 13, 1936, 3B.

124. "Tokio Giants Defeat Fresno Japanese, 10–3," *Fresno Bee*, March 14, 1936, 1B.

125. Hall of Famers List: Takeo Tabe, Japanese Baseball Hall of Fame and Museum, http://english.baseball-museum.or.jp/baseball_hallo/detail/detail_031.html.

126. "Policemen to Meet Japanese Tossers To-Day," *Fresno Bee*, April 12, 1936, 3C.

127. "Police Lose to Japanese," *Fresno Bee*, April 13, 1936, 11.

128. "Hawaiian Ball Club Will Play," *Fresno Bee*, April 12, 1936, 3B.

129. "Japanese Will Play Chinese Ball Club Sunday," *Fresno Bee*, May 16, 1936, Sports Section, 1.

130. "Fresno Nines Beats Wa Sung," *Fresno Bee*, May 18, 1936, 3B.

131. "Zenimura Will Lead New Twilight Club," *Fresno Bee*, May 15, 1936, 11B.

132. "Japanese Play in State Series," *Fresno Bee*, May 27, 1936, Sports Section, 1.

133. "Fresnans Head Japanese Teams," *Fresno Bee*, June 1, 1936, 11A.

134. "Fresnans Win at Sacramento," *Fresno Bee*, June 8, 1936, 3B.

135. "Brewers Beat Barbano Club by 4–2 Score," *Fresno Bee*, June 12, 1936, 5B.

136. "Merced Club Beats Fresnans," *Fresno Bee*, June 15, 1936, Sports Section, 1.

137. "Merced Merchant Play Fresno Japanese Club," *Fresno Bee*, June 13, 1936, 3B.

138. "Merced Trims Japanese, 6 to 1," *Fresno Bee*, June 23, 1936, 5B.

139. "Waseda U. Will Play Fresno Club," *Fresno Bee*, June 24, 1936, Sports Section, 1.

140. "Waseda U. Club Plays Fresnans this Afternoon," *Fresno Bee*, June 28, 1936, 3C.

141. "Fresno Japanese Play Champions of Nippon Nines," *Fresno Bee*, June 27, 1936, Sports Section, 1.

142. "Fourth of July Fete Is Planned," *Fresno Bee*, June 23, 1936, 5B.

143. "Corbett Club Smashes Out Shutout Hit," *Fresno Bee*, July 16, 1936, Sports Section, 1.

144. "Fresno Japanese Play Stockton Here To-Morrow," *Fresno Bee*, July 11, 1936, Sports Section, 1.

145. "Fresno Tigers Tame Japanese Ball Club, 11–10," *Fresno Bee*, July 31, 1936, 3B.

146. "Japan Wins Award for 1940 Games," *Fresno Bee*, July 31, 1936, Sports Section, 1.

147. "Japanese Team Beaten, 6–3 in Deciding Game," *Fresno Bee*, August 21, 1936, 3B.

148. "Fresno Twilight League Banter," *Fresno Bee*, August 21, 1936, 3B.
149. "Zenimura Will Lead New Twilight Club," *Fresno Bee*, May 15, 1936, 11B.
150. "Doc Jacobsen Wins Twilight Bat Battle," *Fresno Bee*, August 23, 1936, 2C.
151. "Fresno Japanese Beat Monterey," *Fresno Bee*, September 8, 1936, Sports Section, 1.
152. "Fresno Japanese Club Will Play Alameda Team," *Fresno Bee*, September 17, 1936, Sports Section, 1.
153. "Fresno Japanese Defeat Alameda," *Fresno Bee*, September 21, 1936, Sports Section, 1.
154. "Brewers, Nippons to Meet Today," *Fresno Bee*, October 4, 1936, 3C.
155. "West Coast Is Seething Over League Snubs," *Chicago Defender*, June 6, 1936, 13.
156. "Local Pitcher to Make Japan Tour," *Hayward Daily Review*, February 12, 1937, 3.
157. "Fresno Players Will Sail for Japan Tonight," *Fresno Bee*, March 2, 1937, 3B.
158. "Zenimura Writes About Trip of Baseball Club," *Fresno Bee*, April 6, 1937, 3B.
159. "Japanese Club Picks Officers," *Fresno Bee*, July 12, 1937, 3B.
160. "Bucky Harris Has Namesake Playing Pro Ball in Japan," *Fresno Bee*, December 1, 1937, 10.
161. John Findling et al., *Encyclopedia of the Modern Olympic Movement* (Santa Barbara, CA: Greenwood Publishing Group, 2004), 120.
162. "'Old Timers' Play in Benefit Contest Today," *Fresno Bee*, October 9, 1938, 2C.
163. "Slim Crowd Sees Benefit Baseball Game," *Fresno Bee*, October 10, 1938, 3B.
164. "Brewers Bow to Giants by 4–3 Decision," *Fresno Bee*, March 20, 1939, 2B.
165. "Laton Oaks Trip Central, 6–3," *Fresno Bee*, July 24, 1939, 2B.
166. "Fresno Japanese Are Defeated at Central," *Fresno Bee*, August 14, 1939, 3B.
167. "Japanese Nines Clash Today," *Fresno Bee*, September 3, 1939, 2C.
168. "Grudge Diamond Tilt Is Set for Sunday," *Fresno Bee*, September 7, 1939, 6B.
169. "Bakersfield Negro Nine Seeks Contest in Fresno," *Fresno Bee*, March 24, 1940.
170. "Bowles Japanese Nine Trims Hanford Club," *Fresno Bee*, April 1, 1940, 2B.
171. "City Will Share in Cost of New Armory Site Here," Fresno Bee, July 5, 1940, 4A.
172. Interview with Fumio Ikeda, September 26, 2009.
173. *Diamonds in the Rough: The Legacy of Japanese-American Baseball*, DVD (Chip Taylor Communications, 1998).
174. *Ibid.*
175. Interview with Fumio Ikeda, September 26, 2009.
176. "Negro Ball Club Claims Discrimination, Files Suit for Injunction," *Fresno Bee*, July 3, 1941, 5A.
177. McNeil, *The California Winter League*, 207.
178. "Edison Tech School News," *Fresno Bee*, October 18, 1941, 3A.
179. "Roosevelt Team Is Topped in Playoff Series," *Fresno Bee*, February 21, 1942, 3B.
180. James E. Turner, "Moment in History: Japanese Flag Flies Over Old Main?" University of Arizona News, December 5, 2003, http://uanews.org/node/4061.
181. Stephen Vaughn, *Ronald Reagan in Hollywood: Movies and Politics* (New York: Cambridge University Press, 1994), 75.

Chapter 5

1. Nakagawa, *Through a Diamond*, 78.
2. President Franklin Roosevelt Green Light Letter — Baseball Can Be Played During the War, Baseball Almanac, http://www.baseball-almanac.com/prz_lfr.shtml.
3. "Japs Believe Baseball Players Are Supermen," *Kingsport Times*, March 25, 1943, 2.
4. "Edison Tech School News," *Fresno Bee*, February 7, 1942, 3B.
5. "Japanese Give $142 to Cause," *Oakland Tribune*, January 5, 1942, 12B.
6. "Old Residents Among Enemy Aliens Ordered to Leave Alameda Restricted Zone," *Oakland Tribune*, February 14, 1942, 1.
7. "Enemy Alien Curfew Is Effective Today," *Fresno Bee*, March 27, 1942, 5B.
8. "FBI Arrest of Valley Japanese Climb to 139," *Fresno Bee*, March 27, 1942, 5B.
9. "Fresno Prep Baseball League Opens Tonight," *Fresno Bee*, March 31, 1942, 2B.
10. "Preps Forsake Ball for Army Housing Work," *Fresno Bee*, March 31, 1942, 2B.
11. "Sale Is Scheduled," *Fresno Bee*, April 28, 1942, 8A.
12. "Warrior Nine Plays to Tie with P-Z Club," *Fresno Bee*, April 29, 1942, 2A.
13. Nakagawa, *Through a Diamond*, 78.
14. Interview with Kenso Zenimura, August 19, 2008.
15. Nakagawa, *Through a Diamond*, 78.
16. Poston Relocation Center, Becoming Arizona, http://www.becomingarizona.org/entries/poston.html.
17. A.D. Hopkins, Del E. Webb Rich (1899–1974): Man of the Years, *Las Vegas Review Journal*, http://www.1st100.com/part2/webb.html.
18. "Fresno's Yesterdays: Twenty Years Ago," *Fresno Bee*, June 30, 1942, 4B.
19. "Latest Arrivals Swell Population of Colony," *Gila News-Courier*, September 12, 1942, 1.
20. "Butte Buddhist Initiate Program," *Gila News-Courier*, September 19, 1942, 4.
21. Eric Enders, Timeline of International Baseball, 1847–present, http://www.wricenders.com/internationalbb.htm.
22. Nakagawa, *Through a Diamond*, 79.
23. Fresno Goes to Arkansas, *Gila News-Courier*, October 10, 1942.
24. Interview with Kenso Zenimura, 2008.
25. "University Extension Courses Denied Japs," *Arizona Republic*, October 14, 1942.
26. UCLA Daily Bruin, http://www.dailybruin.com/db/issues/99/12.09/news.internment.html.
27. Caleb Foote, *Outcasts! The Story of America's Treatment of Her Japanese-American Minority* (New York: Fellowship of Reconciliation, 1943), 1 (available online, http://content.cdlib.org.).
28. "In Retrospect," *Gila News-Courier*, January 1, 1943, 4.
29. "Stockton, Fresno, Arrive Today," *Gila News-Courier*, October 17, 1942, 1.
30. *Diamonds in the Rough: The Legacy of Japanese-American Baseball*, DVD (Chip Taylor Communications, 1998).
31. Interview with Kenso Zenimura, February 2008.
32. David Davis, "A Field in the Desert That Felt Like Home: An Unlikely Hero Sustained Hope for Japanese-Americans Interned in World War II," *Sports Illustrated*, November 16, 1998, 48.
33. *Diamonds in the Rough: The Legacy of Japanese-American Baseball*, DVD.
34. *Ibid.*
35. Davis, "A Field in the Desert That Felt Like Home," 48.
36. *Ibid.*
37. "Military Plans Call for Fence

Enclosure — Cozzens," *Gila News-Courier*, December 12, 1942, 2.

38. *Diamonds in the Rough: The Legacy of Japanese-American Baseball.*

39. "Sport Sightings," *Gila News-Courier*, November 14, 1942, 6.

40. "Not Prisoners Says De Amat," *Gila News-Courier*, December 17, 1942, 3.

41. "Bennett Calls Mass Meetings," *Gila News-Courier*, December 19, 1942, 1.

42. "It Was a Challenge," *Gila News-Courier*, December 28, 1942, 2.

43. "New Eligibility Rules," *Desert Sentinel*, December 5, 1942, 5.

44. "Eligibility Rules Lifted!" *Gila News-Courier*, December 19, 6.

45. "Doubleday's Game Attracts Seven Teams," *Gila News-Courier*, December 22, 1942, 5.

46. Frank Graham Jr., "When Baseball Went to War," *Sports Illustrated*, April 17, 1967, 82.

47. *Ibid.* 82–83.

48. "Semi-Pro Baseball to Start May 5 in Tucson," *Tucson Daily Star*, April 1943.

49. "1937 All American NBC Team," National Baseball Congress, http://www.nbcbaseball.com/images/content/files/allamericanteams/37_allamerican_team.pdf.

50. "Press Box," *Tucson Daily Citizen*, September 1, 1942, 8.

51. "Red Sox Sign Arizonans," *Fresno Bee*, May 16, 1938, 2B.

52. "1939 All-American NBC Team," National Baseball Congress, http://www.nbcbaseball.com/images/content/files/allamericanteams/39_all american_team.pdf.

53. "New Year's Edition," *Gila News-Courier*, January 1, 1943.

54. *Ibid.*

55. "Butte High Defeats Chandler in Basketball Game, 33–15," *Gila News-Courier*, January 1, 1943, 6.

56. "Phoenix Journal Free to Public," *Gila News-Courier*, January 14, 1943, 3.

57. "Student Misdemeanors," *Gila News-Courier*, February 9, 1943, 2.

58. "Baseball Supplies Now Available," *Gila News-Courier*, February 9, 1943, 3.

59. "Guadalupe, Stockton in Season's Baseball Opener," *Gila News-Courier*, February 25, 1943, 5.

60. "Okuhara Bros. Lead Block 30 to Win Over YMBA 7–6," *Gila News-Courier*, March 2, 1943, 5.

61. "Bleachers to Be Constructed," *Gila News-Courier*, March 6, 1943, 5.

62. "Field Inaugural at Block 28," *Desert Sentinel*, March 6, 1943, 5.

63. "The Rambler," *Desert Sentinel*, March 6, 1943, 2.

64. "Parlier Cards Face YMBA; Block 28 Meets Vikings," *Desert Sentinel*, March 6, 1943, 5.

65. *Ibid.*

66. "Mas Kinoshita to Pitch," *Gila News-Courier*, March 6, 1943, 5.

67. Davis, "A Field in the Desert That Felt Like Home," 50.

68. *Ibid.*

69. *Ibid.*

70. "Parlier Cards Face YMBA; Block 28 Meets Vikings," *Desert Sentinel*, March 6, 1943, 5.

71. *Diamonds in the Rough: The Legacy of Japanese-American Baseball.*

72. *Ibid.*

73. "To Overcome Prejudice Barriers," *Gila News-Courier*, March 9, 1943, 2.

74. "Canal Hi School Travels," *Gila News-Courier*, March 20, 1943, 6.

75. "Block 28 Dumps Pasadena," *Gila News-Courier*, March 23, 1943, 7.

76. "12 Teams Sign Up for Class 'A,'" *Gila News-Courier*, March 23, 1943, 7.

77. "Stored Lumber to Be Collected," *Desert Sentinel*, March 27, 1943, 1.

78. "Zenie Has Pamphlets," *Desert Sentinel*, March 27, 1943, 4.

79. "Hinodes Lose 14–14, Blk. 28 Drops Blk. 30," *Gila News-Courier*, March 30, 1943, 5.

80. "Horsehiders Plan Outside Games," *Desert Sentinel*, April 1, 1943, 4.

81. "Despondency Blamed in Suicide Case," *Gila News-Courier*, April 3, 1943, 4.

82. "Lookout Usefulness Ended," *Gila News-Courier*, April 15, 1943, 2.

83. "Baseball Notes," *Gila News-Courier*, April 15, 1943, 6.

84. "Ballplayers Say People Friendly," *Desert Sentinel*, April 16, 1943, 4.

85. "Sports Spot, Sports Editor, George Toyoda," *Desert Sentinel*, April 16, 1943, 2.

86. "Sports Shorts," *Gila News-Courier*, April 29, 1943, 4.

87. "Baseball Notes," *Gila News-Courier*, April 15, 1943, 6.

88. Interview with Kenso Zenimura, February 2008.

89. Tim W. Schorzman, "Caught in a Rundown: Baseball and the Japanese American Struggle for Acceptance" (Master's thesis, Northern Arizona University, 2009).

90. *Gila News-Courier*, April 24, 1943.

91. Davis, "A Field in the Desert That Felt Like Home," 50.

92. "First Lady Roosevelt Visits Camp," *Gila News-Courier*, April 24, 1943, 1.

93. Gila River Relocation Center, Arizona Japanese American Veterans, http://www.javadc.org/gila_river_relocation_center.htm

94. "Ickes Hires Japanese to Work on His Farm," *Los Angeles Times*, April 16, 1943, 7.

95. "YMBA Batting .336 in 4 Tilts," *Gila News-Courier*, April 29, 1943, 4.

96. "Seats for Those Who Pay Only," *Gila News-Courier*, April 24, 1943, 4.

97. "Baseball Butte Financial Standings Shown," *Gila News-Courier*, May 6, 1943, 6.

98. Inflation calculator, http://www.westegg.com/inflation/infl.cgi.

99. "Ball Purchase Urged Soon," *Gila News-Courier*, May 6, 1943, 6.

100. Interview with Kenso Zenimura, February 2008.

101. "Wildcats Sweep Mexican Series," *Tucson Daily Citizen*, April 30, 1943, 8.

102. "Cats to Meet Jap Relocation Team," *Tucson Daily Citizen*, May 5, 1943, 8.

103. "Canal to Play University of Arizona," *Gila News-Courier*, May 4, 1943, 6.

104. "Blk. 28-vs-YMBA Thursday!!" *Gila News-Courier*, May 11, 1943, 5.

105. "Butte Class 'C' Circuit May Form," *Gila News-Courier*, May 8, 1943, 6.

106. "Butte Major League," *Gila News-Courier*, May 11, 1943, 5.

107. "All-Star Series Hope Waning, Representative Poston Bound," *Gila News-Courier*, June 3, 1943, 6.

108. *Ibid.*

109. "Keadle Refutes 'Best-Fed Civilians' Charge by Dies," *Gila News-Courier*, June 3, 1943, 1.

110. "Pampered So They Leave," *Gila News-Courier*, June 3, 1943, 2.

111. "2CAC Managers Reported Agrees Tournament," *Gila News-Courier*, June 17, 1943, 6.

112. "All-Stars Series Hope Waning, Representative Poston Bound," *Gila News-Courier*, June 3, 1943, 6.

113. "Tickets May Be Used as Passes," *Gila News-Courier*, June 3, 1943, 6.

114. "Despondent Girl Commits Suicide," *Gila News-Courier*, June 8, 1943, 5.

115. "Phoenix Passes Reduced to Bare Minimum," *Gila News-Courier*, June 10, 1943, 1.

116. "Tempe Coach in U.S.–Jap Group," *Tucson Daily Star*, May 26, 1943, 10.

117. "Sam Yamasaki Now Manager '28 Club," *Gila News-Courier*, June 19, 1943, 6.

118. "Masato Kinoshita's 3 Hitter Gives '28 4–2 Win Over Reds," *Gila New Courier*, July 1, 1943, 2.

119. "Arizona Statute Illegal," *Gila News-Courier*, July 8, 1943, 1.

120. "'28-'30 Takes Tourney Title," *Gila News-Courier*, July 8, 1943, 6.

121. "'Patrolmen' New Warden Title," *Gila News-Courier*, July 10, 1943, 4.

122. "Parker Dam Threatened by Japs," *Tucson Daily Citizen*, July 17, 1943, 6.

123. "Gen. Peterson Making Survey of Jap Camps," *Tucson Daily Citizen*, July 22, 1943, 2.

124. "Segregation to Commence September 1, Rivers Is Not Affected by First Moves," *Gila News-Courier*, July 20, 1943, 1.

125. "Russell Hinaga, Zebras Mgr. in Heart Mountain, Seeks Series Here," *Gila News-Courier*, July 24, 1943, 6.

126. "Still Play Baseball," *Fresno Bee*, July 29, 1943, 2b.

127. "No Aye, Bee Players to Change Teams or Clubs from August 5," *Gila News-Courier*, July 31, 1943, 6.

128. Davis, "A Field in the Desert That Felt Like Home," 50.

129. "Block of 28 Ties Firemen," *Gila News-Courier*, August 5, 1943, 6.

130. "Zenimura to Plant Grass on Field," *Gila River Courier*, August 7, 1943, 6.

131. Davis, "A Field in the Desert That Felt Like Home," 48, 50.

132. *Ibid.*, 50.

133. "Expenses Too High for Series," *Gila News-Courier*, August 14, 1943, 6.

134. "Hinaga's Team Enters Second Game of Canal Series Tonight," *Gila River Courier*, August 26, 1943, 6.

135. "Hinaga: Rusty Ain't Rusty Yet," *Gila News-Courier*, September 2, 1943, 6.

136. "Asahi's Guadalupe Open Series In Butte Tomorrow," *Gila News-Courier*, August 28, 1943, 6.

137. "Horsehiders Ball Monday," *Gila News-Courier*, September 4, 1943, 5.

138. *Ibid.*

139. Davis, "A Field in the Desert That Felt Like Home," 51.

140. "From Asahis," *Gila News-Courier*, September 9, 1943, 6.

141. "Nisei Players Attend Try-Outs," *Gila News-Courier*, September 9, 1943, 6.

142. "Hunt Compete in Semi-Pro Tourney," *Gila News-Courier*, September 4, 1943, 6.

143. "Batting Averages for the Season Listed," *Gila News-Courier*, September 11, 1943, 4.

144. *Ibid.*

145. "Farm Prepares for Record Year," *Gila News-Courier*, September 16, 1943, 1.

146. "Workers Needed to Replace 700 Tule Lake Goers," *Gila News-Courier*, September 21, 1943, 1.

147. "Horsehiders Ball Monday," *Gila News-Courier*, September 4, 1943, 5.

148. "Censors Reject Only Two Letter," *Gila News-Courier*, October 2, 1943, 3.

149. "'Yes Yes' Against 'No No' Nine Battle Set for Saturday Nite," *Gila News-Courier*, September 16, 1943, 6.

150. "Yes Yes, No No Nine Split Series Even 1 All," *Gila News-Courier*, September 21, 1943, 6.

151. "'Outside' Clubs from Nearby Cities May Make Appearance Here Soon," *Gila News-Courier*, September 21, 1943, 6.

152. "Phoenix Nine 'Thunderbirds' Make Appearance Against Local Butte, Canal All-Stars Sunday, 2 & 5 P.M.," *Gila News-Courier*, September 23, 1943, 6.

153. "Thunderbirds Face All-Star Nines Tomorrow Afternoon, Night," *Gila News-Courier*, September 25, 1943, 6.

154. "Huge Signs Disappeared," *Gila News-Courier*, September 25, 1943, 6 (editorial).

155. "Caucasians' in Rohwer Games," *Gila News-Courier*, October 2, 1943, 6.

156. "Birds Score Easy Victory," *Arizona Republic*, October 5, 1943, II-4.

157. "Thunderbirds Face All-Star Nines Tomorrow," *Gila News-Courier*, October 9, 1943, 6.

158. "Thunderbirds Series Sunday," *Gila News-Courier*, October 7, 1943, 6.

159. "Birds Lose Two Games," *Arizona Republic*, October 12, 1943, II-4.

160. Interview with Lowell Bailey, October 29, 2007.

161. "Butte Pick-Ups Edge Visitors from Phoenix by 3–2 Margin," *Gila News-Courier*, October 12, 1943, 6.

162. "Butte Pick-Ups Edge Visitors from Phoenix by 3–2 Margin," *Gila News-Courier*, October 12, 1943, Japanese Section, 8.

163. "Sunday's Visiting Club Gets Haul of Ball Games Receipts," *Gila News-Courier*, October 12, 1943, 6.

164. "President Asks for Racial Unity," *Gila News-Courier*, September 30, 1943, 5.

165. "Use of Japs to Teach Navajos is Protested," *Tucson Daily Citizen*, October 2, 1943, 1.

166. "Phoenix Colored Horsehiders to Appear Sunday," *Gila News-Courier*, October 14, 1943, 6.

167. "Phoenix Colored Nine, Butte Pick-Ups Cross Bats Tomorrow," *Gila News-Courier*, October 16, 1943, 6.

168. "Phoenix Colored Nine Smashed by Butte, 11–3," *Gila News-Courier*, October 19, 1943, 6.

169. Interview with Cornell Fisher Jr., September 2008.

170. "Livestock Class Offers Experience," *Gila News-Courier*, October 12, 1943, 3.

171. "Three Hundred Hogs Arrive," *Gila News-Courier*, December 23, 1943, 5.

172. Interview with Kenso Zenimura, February 2008.

173. Interview with Kaz Ikeda, September 2008.

174. "Caucasians' in Rohwer Games," *Gila News-Courier*, October 2, 1943, 6.

175. "Tule Lake Athletes Hold New Gym as Promising," *Gila News-Courier*, October 23, 1943, 6.

176. Interview with Kerry Yo Nakagawa.

177. "Tragedy Follows Gilan's Attempt to Gain Freedom," *Gila News-Courier*, December 2, 1943, 1.

178. *Ibid.*

179. "Join Crowd or Die — Nisei Told," *Gila News-Courier*, December 2, 1943, 4.

180. "WRA, Internment Camps Not to Be Compared, " *Gila News-Courier*, December 21, 1943, 1.

181. "Gilans Asked to Stay Within the Fence," *Gila News-Courier*, December 9, 1943.

182. "Inter-Camp Ball," *Gila News-Courier*, December 2, 1943, 6.

183. "1st Place Winners Block 28 Takes," *Gila News-Courier*, December 21, 1943, 6.

184. "Horsehide Champs Number 14," *Gila News-Courier*, December 23, 1943, 6.

185. *Ibid.*

186. *Ibid.*

187. "Motion Picture Parade: No Banknight Here, but Residents Throng to Movies," *Second Yeara at Gila, Rivers, Arizona*, July 20, 1944, 32.

188. *Ibid.*

189. "Monument Half Finished," *Gila News-Courier*, December 28, 1943, 4.

190. "Gift Exchange Discouraged," *Gila News-Courier*, December 9, 1943, 1.

191. "Story Behind Book Donation," *Gila News-Courier*, December 31, 1943, 4.

192. "New Book in Library," *Desert Sentinel*, January 14, 1944, 3.

193. "Rivers Loses 3,619 Residents," *Gila News-Courier*, December 30, 1943, 1.

194. *Diamonds in the Rough: The Legacy of Japanese-American Baseball.*

Chapter 6

1. Tetsuo Furokawa, "When Gila Fought Heart Mountain," *Nikkei Heritage*, Winter 2006, 11.
2. "Year in Review," *Second Year at Gila, Rivers, Arizona*, July 20, 1944, 38.
3. "Guard Doubled on Jap Camps for Evacuees," *Tucson Daily Citizen*, January 28, 1944, 3.
4. "Japs Shout, 'To Hell with Ruth;' Marines Fan 30," *Chicago Daily Tribune*, March 3, 1944, 25.
5. "Two Evacuees Work for Carl Sandberg in Michigan," *Gila News Courier*, March 9, 1944, 4.
6. "National League Schedule," *Gila News Courier*, April 29, 1944, 6.
7. "News Brief," *Gila River Courier*, April 27, 1944, 6.
8. "28 Grabs 2nd Practice Win," *Gila River Courier*, March 28, 1944, 4.
9. "1st Report of Gate Intakes," *Gila River Courier*, March 28, 1944, 4.
10. "Groundskeeper on Gate Intakes," *Gila River Courier*, April 25, 1944, 6.
11. "News Brief," *Gila River Courier*, April 27, 1944, 6.
12. "State Tourney," *Gila News Courier*, April 29, 1944, 6.
13. "State Tourney," *Gila River Courier*, May 23, 1944, 6.
14. "Locals Receive Unofficial Bid," *Gila News Courier*, July 18, 1944, 4.
15. "Tucson Nine: Tentatively Set 2 Games," *Gila News Courier*, July 6, 1944, 6.
16. "Tucson Nine Wins and Loses," *Gila News Courier*, July 11, 1944, 6.
17. "Ball Team Visits Gila," *Poston Chronicle*, July 4, 1944, 5.
18. "Himaka Wins Batting Title," *Poston Chronicle*, July 6, 4.
19. "Dust and Desert," *Poston Chronicle*, July 15, 1944, 3.
20. "Tucson Nine's 2nd Invasion," *Gila News Courier*, August 5, 1944, 6.
21. "Tucson Nine Splits Series Here," *Gila News Courier*, August 8, 1944, 6.
22. "Amache 'Pioneer' Says They've Left," *Gila News Courier*, August 8, 1944, 6.
23. "Amache All-Star Series Here Confirmed," *Gila News Courier*, August 10, 1944, 6.
24. "Amache Delayed," *Gila News Courier*, August 12, 1944, 6.
25. "Amache Opens Butte Series Tonight," *Gila News Courier*, August 19, 1944, 6.
26. "Zeni Pitches a Two Hitter," *Gila News Courier*, August 22, 1944, 6.
27. *Ibid.*
28. "From the Bench," *Gila News Courier*, August 24, 1944, 6.
29. "Abo Shuts Out Amacheans 5–0," *Gila News Courier*, August 24, 1944, 6.
30. "Ht. Mountain Series Set; Fourteen Players to Go," *Gila News Courier*, August 26, 1944, 6.
31. "Sendoff Series for Jr. All-Stars," *Gila News Courier*, August 26, 1944, 6.
32. Furokawa, "When Gila Fought Heart Mountain," 11.
33. *Ibid.*
34. Nakagawa, *Through a Diamond*, 90.
35. Interview with Tets Furukawa, February 5, 2009.
36. "Visitors Rout Ayes in Opener," *Heart Mountain Sentinel*, September 9, 1944, 7.
37. "Players Description of the Heart Mountain Series," *Gila News Courier*, September 9, 1944, 6.
38. "Gilans Cop 10–7 Tilt in Eleventh," *Heart Mountain Sentinel*, September 9, 1944, 7.
39. "Players Description of the Heart Mountain Series," *Gila News Courier*, September 9, 1944, 6.
40. "Sport Tidbits, by George Yoshinaga," *Heart Mountain Sentinel*, September 9, 1944, 7.
41. "All-Stars Take Third Game, 5–3," *Heart Mountain Sentinel*, September 9, 1944, 7.
42. "Luck of Gila Junior All Stars Hold as They Win," *Gila News Courier*, September 12, 1944, 6.
43. "Sport Tidbits, by George Yoshinaga," *Heart Mountain Sentinel*, September 9, 1944, 7.
44. "Abo Hurls Mates to 5–1 Triumph," *Heart Mountain Sentinel*, September 9, 1944, 7.
45. "Luck of Gila Junior All Stars Hold as They Win," *Gila News Courier*, September 12, 1944, 6.
46. *Ibid.*
47. "Jr. All Stars Edge Combines," *Gila News Courier*, September 14, 1944, 6.
48. "Gilans Capture Sixth Game, 5–4," *Heart Mountain Sentinel*, September 16, 1944, 7.
49. "Shimada Sparks Locals to 5–4 Win," *Heart Mountain Sentinel*, September 16, 1944, 7.
50. "Iseri Captures Second Tilt, 3–2," *Heart Mountain Sentinel*, September 16, 1944, 7.
51. "Gila Nine Nabs 15–9 Slugfest," *Heart Mountain Sentinel*, September 16, 1944, 7.
52. *Ibid.*
53. "Hinaga Hurls 6–0 Shutout Win," *Heart Mountain Sentinel*, September 16, 1944, 7.
54. "Fujioka Tames Local Stars, 6–3," *Heart Mountain Sentinel*, September 16, 1944, 7.
55. Interview with Tets Furukawa, February 5, 2009.
56. "Local Nine Wins 5–4 in Eleventh," *Heart Mountain Sentinel*, September 23, 1944, 7.
57. "Fujioka Blanks Locals, 8–0, in Finale," *Heart Mountain Sentinel*, September 23, 1944, 7.
58. "Sport Tidbits, by Ted Yano," *Heart Mountain Sentinel*, September 16, 1944, 6.
59. *Ibid.*
60. *Ibid.*
61. *Ibid.*
62. *Ibid.*
63. Interview with Tets Furukawa, February 5, 2009.
64. "Gila Takes Fifth Game 6–3; Loses 5–4 to Zebra-Block 20," *Gila News Courier*, September 21, 1944, 6.
65. Interview with Tets Furukawa, February 5, 2009.
66. Furokawa, "When Gila Fought Heart Mountain," 11.
67. Interview with Tets Furukawa, February 5, 2009.
68. *Ibid.*
69. Furokawa, "When Gila Fought Heart Mountain," 11.
70. "Myer Speaks on Behalf of Japanese Americans," *Gila News Courier*, October 7, 1944, 5.
71. "Pfc. Higa, Relates War Experience," *Gila News Courier*, October 10, 1944, 1.
72. "99% Die from Natural Causes," *Gila News Courier*, October 12, 1944, 1.
73. "Thomas: Expresses Views on Evacuation," *Gila News Courier*, October 14, 1944, 2.
74. "Libe. Gets Book by McWilliams," *Gila News Courier*, October 28, 1944, 6.
75. Leonard Bloom, review of *Prejudice—Japanese Americans: Symbol of Racial Intolerance*, by Carey McWilliams, *American Sociological Review* 10 (1945): 313–314.
76. Peter Golenbock, "Breaking Baseball's Color Barrier," excerpt from *Bums: An Oral History of the Brooklyn Dodgers* (New York: G.P. Putnam's Sons, 1984), http://thatsbaseball1.tripod.com/id147.htm.
77. *Bill Veeck, Veeck—As in Wreck: The Autobiography of Bill Veeck* (Chicago: University of Chicago Press, 2001), 171.

Chapter 7

1. Tetsuo Furokawa, "When Gila Fought Heart Mountain," *Nikkei Heritage*, Winter 2006, 11.

2. "Japan Is Topic," *Fresno Bee*, December 31, 1944, 4A.
3. "Jap Boycott Group Forms in Pacer Co.," *Oakland Tribune*, January 17, 1945, 1.
4. "New Term for 'Nisei American,'" *Gila News-Courier*, January 17, 1945, 5.
5. "Seventy Tuleans Cast Citizenship," *Gila News-Courier*, January 3, 1945, 4.
6. "Resident Found Dead Last Night," *Gila News-Courier*, January 6, 1945, 1.
7. "Aged Resident Hangs Himself," *Gila News-Courier*, February 3, 1945, 1.
8. "Resident Found Dead Yesterday," *Gila News-Courier*, March 24, 1945, 1.
9. "Finding of Body Solves Two-Year-Old Mystery," *Gila News-Courier*, March 24, 1945, 1.
10. "Canal Maps Out 1945 Program," *Gila News-Courier*, February 17, 1945, 6.
11. "Japanese American Baseball: A Goodwill Ambassador," Japanese American National Museum, http://janmstore.com/jabaseball.html.
12. "Zenimura Calls Meeting Sunday for Butte Baseball Association," *Gila News-Courier*, February 24, 1945, 6.
13. "Relocation Centers to Close by December 31," *Gila News-Courier*, February 10, 1945, 1.
14. "Rivers Leads Leave Parade," *Gila News-Courier*, March 3, 1945, 1.
15. "More Shootings in California," *Gila News-Courier*, March 3, 1945, 1.
16. "San Jose Returnee Home Set Afire, Fired Upon," *Gila News-Courier*, March 10, 1945, 3.
17. "2500 Nisei in 550 Colleges," *Gila News-Courier*, March 7, 1945, 5.
18. "Prepsters Whip Chandler Five," *Gila News-Courier*, February 14, 1945, 6.
19. "Zenimura Calls Meeting Sunday for Butte Baseball Association," *Gila News-Courier*, February 24, 1945, 6.
20. "Canal to Have 3 Clubs," *Gila News-Courier*, February 24, 1945, 6.
21. "Zenimura to Coach Team," *Desert Sentinel*, March 13, 1945, 4.
22. "Horsehiders Plan Outside Games," *Desert Sentinel*, March 13, 1945, 4.
23. "Baseball Games Results Given," *Gila News-Courier*, March 28, 1945, 6.
24. "Seventeen Men Leave Rivers for Active Duty," *Gila News-Courier*, April 4, 1945, 1.
25. "Sportsmanship Award," *Gila News-Courier*, April 4, 1945, 2.
26. "Butte to Player Tollerson (*sic*)," *Gila News-Courier*, April 4, 1945, 6.
27. "Butte Hi Downs Tollerson (*sic*) Nine," *Gila News-Courier*, April 11, 1945, 6.
28. Arizona Interscholastic Association, State Champion Archives, http://www.aiaonline.org/athletics/archives.php [link to Baseball Team Champs].
29. "Baseball: Butte Preps to Play Tucson Hi," *Gila News-Courier*, April 14, 1945, 6.
30. "Butte High Edges Tucson Nine in 10th," *Desert Sentinel*, April 23, 1945, 3.
31. Interview with Lowell C. Bailey Jr., December 2005.
32. *Ibid.*
33. Minor league records, Joe Tully, BaseballReference.com, http://www.baseball-reference.com/minors/player.cgi?id=tully-001jos.
34. Minor league records, Lee Carey, Baseball-Reference.com, http://www.baseball-reference.com/minors/player.cgi?id=carey-001lee.
35. Interview with Pete Rose, April 2002.
36. Interview with Tets Furukawa, September 2009.
37. Interview with Lowell C. Bailey Jr., December 2005.
38. "Butte High to Play at Tucson," *Gila News-Courier*, April 21, 1945, 6.
39. "Tucson Coach Writes to Butte," *Gila News-Courier*, May 16, 1945, 6.
40. "Southern Arizona's All-Time High School Athletes," *Tucson Citizen*, May 16, 2009.
41. Letter from Hank Slagle to Stacy Furukawa, August 25, 2003, Tets Furukawa Archive.
42. Damien Alameda, "Baseball Behind Barbed Wire," February 20, 2009, Tucson KOLD News 13, http://www.kold.com/global/story.asp?s=5605750.
43. Letter from Hank Slagle to Stacy Furukawa, August 25, 2003, Tets Furukawa Archive.
44. "Blk. 65 Taken by Blk. 28, 11–3," *Gila News-Courier*, May 2, 1945, 6.
45. Interview with Tets Furukawa, September 2009.
46. "Butte Blanks Mesa High 19–0," *Gila News-Courier*, May 5, 1945, 6.
47. "Germany Surrenders, Ending the War in Europe," *Gila News-Courier*, May 7, 1945.
48. "Baseball Fans Asked to Donate," *Gila News-Courier*, May 5, 1945, 6.
49. "Block 65, Block 28 Take Cardinals, Oldtimers," *Gila News-Courier*, May 9, 1945, 6.
50. "Gila Land Lease Expires Oct 7," *Gila River Courier*, May 16, 1945, 2.
519. "Closing Dates Listed," *Gila News-Courier*, May 23, 1945, 1.
52. "Blk. 28, Taiyos Beat Cards, 65," *Gila News-Courier*, May 16, 1945, 6.
53. "Block 28 Cops First Round," *Gila News-Courier*, May 23, 1945, 6.
54. "Personnel to Play Evacuees," *Gila News-Courier*, May 26, 1945, 6.
55. "Evacuees Defeat Caucasian Nine 10–3," *Gila News-Courier*, May 30, 1945, 6.
56. "Editor Says: Nisei Deserve Equal Rights," *Gila News-Courier*, May 26, 1945, 3.
57. "Fight Is Two-Fold," *Gila News-Courier*, June 6, 1945, 2.
58. "Parlier Gunman Gets Probation," *Gila News-Courier*, June 6, 1945, 2.
59. "65, Cards Beaten by 28, Taiyos," *Gila News-Courier*, June 6, 1945, 6.
60. "Rivers High Schools Graduate 230 Seniors," *Gila News-Courier*, June 9, 1945, 1.
61. "28 Continues Winning Streak," *Gila News-Courier*, June 13, 1945, 6.
62. "Butte Old Timers Win 11–6, Butte Easily Defeats Canal," *Gila News-Courier*, June 13, 1945, 6.
63. "Canal Adult Ed Training Starts Monday," *Gila News-Courier*, June 16, 1945, 1.
64. "Block 28 Loses First Game, 7–1 Record," *Gila News-Courier*, June 16, 1945, 6.
65. "Block 28, Block 65 Take Cards, Taiyos 9–3, 9–2," *Gila News-Courier*, June 20, 1945, 6.
66. "Block 28 Defeats Blk. 65, 11 to 1," *Gila News-Courier*, June 23, 1945, 6.
67. "Final Standings," *Gila News-Courier*, June 23, 1945, 6.
68. *Ibid.*
69. "Furuya with .513 Leading Batsmen," *Gila News-Courier*, June 27, 1945, 6.
70. "Mgrs. Meeting Tonight at 7:30," *Gila News-Courier*, June 27, 1945, 6.
71. *Ibid.*
72. "Olympic Club Wins, 16–2, Blk 55 Beats Blk 65, 9–2," *Gila News-Courier*, July 4, 1945, 6.
73. "Blk 65 Takes Win Over Blk 28 in Abbreviated Game," *Gila News-Courier*, July 7, 1945, 6.
74. "Butte Takes 2 Tilts from Mesa," *Gila News-Courier*, July 11, 1945, 6.
75. Arizona High School Hall of Fame, Whizzer White, http://www.azcentral.com/flash/sports/halloffame/halloffame.html?player=wwhite.

76. Interview with Kaz Ikeda, July 2009.
77. "Blk 55, Blk 40 Win 7–0, 15–6," *Gila News-Courier*, July 18, 1945, 6.
78. "Third Anniversary," *Gila News-Courier*, July 21, 1945, 1.
79. "To Homes, Old and New," *Gila News-Courier*, August 11, 1945, 6.
80. "Baseball Czar K. Zenimura Gives Thanks and Regards," *Gila News-Courier*, August 1, 1945, 6.
81. "Kinoshita Wins Hardball Tilt," *Gila News-Courier*, August 4, 1945, 6.
82. Email correspondence with Kenso Zenimura, December 17, 2005.
83. "Men Detailed to Make Boxes," *Gila News-Courier*, August 18, 1945, 3.
84. "Obata Returns to University," *Gila News-Courier*, August 22, 1945, 2.
85. "Sport of the Times, Short Shots in Sundry Directions," *New York Times*, September 27, 1945, 27.
86. David Davis, "A Field in the Desert That Felt Like Home: An Unlikely Hero Sustained Hope for Japanese-Americans Interned in World War II," *Sports Illustrated*, November 16, 1998, 48, 51.
87. *Ibid.*

Chapter 8

1. "Baseball Czar K. Zenimura Gives Thanks and Regards," *Gila News-Courier*, August 1, 1945, 6.
2. David Davis, "A Field in the Desert That Felt Like Home: An Unlikely Hero Sustained Hope for Japanese-Americans Interned in World War II," *Sports Illustrated*, November 16, 1998, Pgs. 48–51.
3. Email correspondence with Kenso Zenimura, August 29, 2009.
4. *Ibid.*
5. Email correspondence with Kenso Zenimura, March 11, 2009.
6. "Two More Teams Join City Play," *Fresno Bee*, May 14, 1946, 10.
7. "Farmers Nip Fresno Athletic Club, 6–2," *Fresno Bee*, May 20, 1946, 4.
8. "Larks Play L.A. White Sox Here Tomorrow," *Oakland Tribune*, July 3, 1946, Section C, 7.
9. "Charley Trippi All Set; Signs Baseball Pact," *Chicago Daily Tribune*, February 13, 1947, 28.
10. "Sport Thinks by Ed Orman," *Fresno Bee*, October 29, 1947, 15.
11. "Zenimura Named to FSC Varisty Team," *Fresno Bee Republican*, April 11, 1948.
12. Pearce, *From Asahi to Zebras*, 93.
13. 2000 U.S. Open, Recap and Scores for the 2000 U.S. Open Golf Tournament, http://golf.about.com/library/weekly/bl2000usopen.htm.
14. "PCL to Give Jap Kids Baseball Bats," *San Mateo Times*, July 3, 1948, 5.
15. Top Teams Win in Muny Leagues, *Fresno Bee*, January 21, 1949, 19.
16. "FSC Baseballers Begin Workouts; Prospects Good," *Fresno Bee*, January 16, 1949, 24.
17. *Ibid.*
18. "Japanese Baseball Czar Outlines Expansion Plan," *New York Times*, April 17, 1949, S3.
19. John B. Holway, "Lefty and the Geisha," BaseballGuru.com, http://baseballguru.com/jholway/analysisjholway32.html.
20. Pearce, *From Asahi to Zebras*, 95.
21. *Ibid.*
22. "Hirayama Will Play for Nisei in Benefit Tilt," *Fresno Bee*, July 22, 1954, 14A.
23. Email correspondence with Kenso Zenimura, March 11, 2006.
24. "2003 Fresno Athletic Hall of Fame Inductees," *Fresno Bee*, November 4, 2003.
25. "Rainout Pushes Back Reunion of '51 Bulldogs," *Fresno Bee*, April 21, 2001.
26. *Ibid.*
27. "Fresno Dominates All-Star Selections," *Reno Evening Gazette*, June 2, 1951, 7.
28. Interview with Kenso Zenimura, February 2008.
29. "FSC Baseballers Will Start Work for Big Schedule," *Fresno Bee*, February 3, 1952, 4S.
30. "San Pedro and Fresno Nisei Teams Will Play," *Fresno Bee*, June 28, 1952, 8A.
31. "Nisei All Stars Will Play Lodi Team Tomorrow," *Fresno Bee*, July 3, 1952, 8A.
32. Email correspondence with Kenso Zenimura, March 11, 2006.
33. "Lefty O'Doul Importing Home-Run King of Japan for Tryout Here," *Los Angeles Times*, June 18, 1952, C3.
34. *Ibid.*
35. "College Nine to Tour Japan," *Long Beach Press*, May 13, 1952, 14.
36. West Coast All-Stars Clip Waseda U, *Stars and Stripes*, August 25, 1952, 13.
37. "Coast College Baseball Team Leaves for Home," *Los Angeles Times*, September 8, 1952, C2.
38. "Zenimura Hits But All-Stars Lose," *Fresno Bee*, August 16, 1952, 8A.
39. "Sport Thinks by Ed Orman," *Fresno Bee*, September 4, 1952, 14B.
40. Fresno line-ups from *Fresno Bee*, November 3, 1952, 8B, and November 10, 1952, 8A.
41. "Nichi-Bei Nine, Mid Valley Win Baseball Games," *Fresno Bee Republican*, November 28, 1952, 5B.
42. Fresno line-ups from *Fresno Bee*, November 3, 1952, 8B, and November 10, 1952, 8A.
43. "Nichi-Bei Tops Goodfellow, 7–0, Boosts Loop Lead," *Fresno Bee Republican*, December 1, 1952, 6B.
44. "Immigration Repeal by Eugene Nixon," *Los Angeles Times*, February 3, 1953, A5.
45. "Fibber Headed to Army," *Fresno Bee*, January 29, 1953.
46. "FSC Bulldog Nine Will Open with Fort Ord Warriors," *Fresno Bee Republican*, February 27, 1953, 13.
47. "Sport Thinks," *Fresno Bee Republican*, February 14, 1953, 28.
48. "Tokio Giants in Fresno," *Fresno Bee*, February 8, 1953, 6B.
49. "Tokio Nine Will Open US Tour in Fresno Contest," *Fresno Bee*, February 18, 1953, 4B.
50. "Sport Thinks by Ed Orman," *Fresno Bee*, February 20, 1953, 10A.
51. *Ibid.*
52. *Ibid.*
53. "Tokio Giants Win from Valley All Stars, 3–2; Play in Visalia Today," *Fresno Bee*, February 22, 1953, 12A.
54. *Ibid.*
55. "Heavy Showers Cancel Giants, All Star Game," *Fresno Bee*, February 23, 1953, 4B.
56. 1953 in Japanese Baseball, Baseball-Reference.com, http://www.baseball-reference.com/bullpen/1953_in_japanese_baseball.
57. Interview with Bruce Ferris, 2008.
58. "Zenimura Travels to Honolulu," *Fresno Bee*, February 25, 1953, 12A.
59. "Sport Thinks by Ed Orman," *Fresno Bee*, March 22, 1953, 3B.
60. "Plan Strong Twilight League," *Fresno Bee*, April 14, 1953, 8B.
61. "Eight Team Fresno Twilight League Will Open Monday," *Fresno Bee*, May 13, 1953, 13B.
62. "Nisei Nine will Practice Sunday," *Fresno Bee*, April 16, 1953, 23A.
63. "Nisei Nine Wins Over Zebras, 6–5," *Fresno Bee*, June 1, 1953, 8B.
64. *Ibid.*
65. "Nisei All Stars Blank San Jose," *Fresno Bee*, June 8, 1953, 4B.
66. "Sport Thinks by Ed Orman, Zenimuras Are Greeted, but Good," *Fresno Bee*, July 1, 1953, 18A.
67. Email correspondence with Kenso Zenimura, March 11, 2006.
68. "Zenimura Stars in Japan," *Fresno Bee*, August 4, 1953, 6B.
69. Email correspondence with Kenso Zenimura, March 11, 2006.

70. Interview with Kenso Zenimura, February 2008.
71. *Diamonds in the Rough: The Legacy of Japanese-American Baseball*, DVD (Chip Taylor Communications, 1998).
72. "Sport Thinks, by Bruce Farris," *Fresno Bee*, September 2, 1953, 8B.
73. "Makes All Star Team," *Fresno Bee*, July 9, 1954, 12A.
74. *Ibid.*
75. "Nisei Will Open Baseball Practice," *Fresno Bee*, May 1, 1954, 6B.
76. "Twilight League Baseball Play Will Begin This Week," *Fresno Bee*, June 6, 1954, 2S.
77. "Zenimura Team, Telephone Lead American League," *Fresno Bee*, July 11, 1954, 2S.
78. "Seals Win; 5,187 See DiMag Hit 350 Double," *Fresno Bee*, July 11, 1954, 2S.
79. "Hirayama Will Play for Nisei in Benefit Tilt," *Fresno Bee*, July 22, 1954, 14A.
80. Interview with Keiji Tsuhako, 2009.
81. "Beiden's Red Sox Are Threatening Zenimura's Lead," *Fresno Bee*, July 25, 1954, 2S.
82. "Zenimura Nine Holds AL Lead in Twilight Loop," *Fresno Bee*, August 1, 1954, 3S.
83. "Jack Shepard, Fresno Catcher with Pittsburgh, Say Bucs Will Move Up," *Fresno Bee*, January 25, 1955, 3B.
84. *Diamonds in the Rough: The Legacy of Japanese-American Baseball.*
85. "Former Fresno Japanese Says 800,000 Fans See Prep Baseball Playoffs," *Fresno Bee*, September 4, 1955, 2S.
86. *Ibid.*
87. "Sport Thinks by Ed Orman," *Fresno Bee*, December 25, 1955.
88. "California Nisei Teams Will Open State Title Play," *Fresno Bee*, August 31, 1957, 4B.
89. "F.A. Homan Ex-Fresno Mayor, Dies," *Fresno Bee*, June 25, 1958, 1.
90. "Matsumoto Dies," *New York Times*, November 2, 1958; 89.
91. "Star Fresno Baseball Player of 20s Dies," *Fresno Bee*, January 27, 1959, 3B.
92. "Japanese All Stars Will Play in Fresno," *Fresno Bee*, August 12, 1959, 23B.
93. "He Arrived on Time," *Yuma Sun*, May 28, 1961.
94. "California Nisei Teams Will Open State Title Play," *Fresno Bee*, August 31, 1957, 4B.
95. "Fresno's Ken Zenimura, Dean of Nisei Baseball in US, Recalls Colorful Past," *Fresno Bee*, May 20, 1962, 3S.
96. *Ibid.*
97. *Ibid.*
98. "Fresno Will Honor Three Japanese Ball Players," *Fresno Bee*, May 3, 1964, 11S
99. "Reinoso Will Start for the Li'l Giants Against Bees," *Fresno Bee*, May 5, 1964, 1D.
100. "Fresno Athletic Hall of Fame," *Fresno Bee*, October 19, 1966, 6C.
101. Fresno Athletic Hall of Fame Inductees, 1950–69, http://www.fresnoahof.org/inductees.html.
102. "City News in Brief: Rings Stolen," *Fresno Bee*, May 22, 1968, 14A.
103. "Zenimura, Dean of Nisei Baseball, Dies," *Fresno Bee*, November 14, 1968, 4C.
104. "White Ashes," Japan: Life and Religion, http://nihonshukyo.wordpress.com/buddhist-texts/white-ashes.

Appendix A

1. "Japanese Win from Bees 6 to 4," *Fresno Bee*, March 10, 1924, 4.
2. "Fresno All-Stars Beat Los Angeles Crack Team, 9 to 4," *Fresno Bee*, July 5, 1926, 10.
3. "Royal Giants Swamp Fresno Japanese 9–1," *Japan Times*, April 21, 1927, from the Harvey Iwata 1927 Tour Scrapbook, National Baseball Hall of Fame.
4. "Colored Giants Defeat FAC Outfit," 12 to 7, *Fresno Bee*, March 19, 1928, 6.
5. "Japanese Beat Old-Timers, 12–6," *Fresno Bee*, October 15, 1934, 2C.
6. "Tokio Giants Defeat Fresno Japanese," 6–4, *Fresno Bee*, April 30, 1935, Sports Section, 1.
7. Game Score Sheet Courtesy of Carl "Scooter" Lopez, former Tucson High Badger player; Game Summary by the Nisei Baseball Research Project, May 2007.

Appendix E

1. "Top Batting Averages, 1943 Season," *Gila News Courier*, September 11, 1943.
2. "Major League Batting," *Gila News-Courier*, June 30, 1944, 6.
3. "Major League Pitching Avgs," *Gila News-Courier*, June 30, 1944, 6.
4. "Final Standings," *Gila News-Courier*, June 23, 1945, 6.

Appendix F

1. Nisei Baseball Research Project (NBRP), Fibber Hirayama biography, NBRP website: http://www.niseibaseball.com/html%20articles/Nisei%20Legends/hirayama.htm.
2. Documentary: *Diamonds in the Rough: The Legacy of Japanese-American Baseball*, Chip Taylor Productions, 1998.
3. "Japan, and Its Fans, Embrace New Title of World Champion," *New York Times*, March 21, 2006.

Bibliography

Records and Archives

California Passenger and Crew Lists, 1893–1957
Directory of the City and County of Honolulu, 1933–1934
Honolulu, Hawaii, Passenger Lists, 1900–1953
Kenichi Zenimura Family Archive
Mid-Pac High Administration Office, Honolulu, HI
National Baseball Hall of Fame, Cooperstown, NY
Negro Leagues Baseball Museum, Kansas City, MO
Nisei Baseball Research Project, Fresno, CA
Second Year at Gila, 1943 Yearbook, Rivers, AZ
Tets Furukawa Archive
United States Federal Census, 1910
United States Federal Census, 1920
United States Federal Census, 1930
World War I Draft Registrations Cards, 1917–1918

Books and Papers

Bloom, Leonard. Review of *Prejudice—Japanese-Americans: Symbol of Racial Intolerance*, by Carey McWilliams. *American Sociological Review* 10 (1945): 313–314.

Davis, Charlotte, and Edith Stickney, eds. *The Emerging Minorities in America: A Resource Guide for Teachers.* Santa Barbara, CA: ABC-Clio Press, 1972.

Findling, John E., et al. *Encyclopedia of the Modern Olympic Movement.* Santa Barbara, CA: Greenwood, 2004.

McNeil, William. *The California Winter League: America's First Integrated Professional Baseball League.* Jefferson, NC: McFarland, 2002.

Morgan, Joe. *Baseball My Way.* New York: Atheneum, 1976.

Nakagawa, Kerry Yo. *Through a Diamond: 100 Years of Japanese American Baseball.* San Francisco, CA: Rudi, 2000.

Nankivell, John Henry. *Buffalo Soldier Regiment: History of the Twenty-Fifth United States Infantry, 1869–1926, Blacks in the American West.* Lincoln: University of Nebraska Press, 2001.

Pearce, Ralph M. *From Asahi to Zebras: Japanese American Baseball in San Jose.* San Jose, CA: Japanese American Museum of San Jose, 2007.

Peterson, Robert. *Only the Ball Was White.* New York: Oxford University Press, 1992.

Sayama, Kazuo. *Black Baseball Heroes: The Rise and Fall of the "Nigro League."* Tokyo, Japan: Chuo Shinsho, 1994.

Schorzman, Tim W. "Caught in a Rundown: Baseball and the Japanese American Struggle for Acceptance" Master's Thesis, Northern Arizona University, 2009.

Tolnay, Stewart, and E.M. Beck. *A Festival of Violence: An Analysis of Southern Lynchings, 1882–1930.* Champaign: University of Illinois Press, 1995.

Vaughn, Stephen. *Ronald Reagan in Hollywood: Movies and Politics.* New York: Cambridge University Press, 1994.

Veeck, Bill, and Ed Linn. *Veeck—As in Wreck: The Autobiography of Bill Veeck.* Chicago: University of Chicago Press, 2001.

Interviews and Correspondence

Phone Interviews

Bailey, Lowell (pitcher, 1945 Tucson High Badgers)
Ferris, Bruce (reporter, Fresno Bee)
Fisher, Jr., Cornell (son of Cornell Fisher, pitcher, 1943 Phoenix Negro All-Stars)
Furukawa, Tets (pitcher, 1945 Butte High Eagles)
Ikeda, Fumio (infielder, 1930s–40s Clovis Commodores)
Ikeda, Kaz (catcher, 1943 Butte All-Stars)
Nakagawa, Kerry Yo (author, historian, filmmaker)
Saiki, Zac (grandson of Ty Saiki, pitcher, 1933–38 Fresno Japanese Ballclub)
Towns, Arnold P. (nephew of Ajay Johnson, pitcher, L.A. White Sox and Philadelphia Royal Giants)
Tsuhuko, Keiji (infielder, 1953 Fresno Japanese Ballclub)
Zenimura, Kenso (son of Kenichi Zenimura)

In-Person Interviews

Bailey, Lowell (pitcher, 1945 Tucson High Badgers)
Carey, Lee (third base, 1945 Tucson High Badgers)
Dodson, Jerry (catcher, 1945 Tucson High Badgers)

Furukawa, Tets (pitcher, 1945 Butte High Eagles)
Hall, Midori (former Gila River internee)
Inoshita, Mas (former Gila River internee, caretaker of World War II memorial at Gila)
Lopez, Carl (outfielder, 1945 Tucson High Badgers)
McCleve, Richard (second base, 1947 Mesa High Jackrabbits)
Nakagawa, Kerry Yo (author, historian, filmmaker)
Osada, Ralph (infielder, 1945 Butte High Eagles)
Rose, Pete (Major League Baseball's all-time hit king)
Shimasaki, Jack (infielder, 1945 Butte High Eagles)
Tomooka, James (outfielder/pitcher, 1943 Guadalupe YMBA Ballclub)
Weinstein, Bernie (infielder, 1945 Tucson High Badgers)
Wolf, Gary (son of Otto Wolf, shortstop/mgr., 1930s–40s Phoenix Thunderbirds)
Zenimura, Kenso (son of Kenichi Zenimura)

Correspondence Via E-mail

Doswell, Ray (Negro Leagues Baseball Museum)
Ellfers, James (author, historian)
Hendsch, David (son of Charles Hendsch, pitcher, 1927 Fresno Athletic Club)
Martin, Glynn (LAPD historian)
McNeil, William (author, historian)
Nagata, Yoichi (SABR member, Japan)
Nakagawa, Kerry Yo (author, historian, filmmaker)
Okihiro, Mike (author, historian)
Pearce, Ralph (author, historian)
Stivers, Wayne (Negro Leagues historian)
Yoshida, Kyoko (writer, professor Keio University)
Zenimura, Kenso (son of Kenichi Zenimura)

Newspapers and Periodicals

Afro-American (Baltimore, MD)
Arizona Republic (Phoenix, AZ)
Atlanta Constitution (Atlanta, GA)
Auburn Bulletin (Auburn, NY)
Baseball Magazine
Chicago Daily Tribune (Chicago, IL)
Chicago Defender (Chicago, IL)
Chicago Heights Star (Chicago, IL)
Desert Sentinel (Desert Hot Springs, CA)
Elyria Chronicle (Elyria, OH)
Evening Herald (Syracuse, NY)
Evening Independent (Massillon, OH)
Fresno Bee (Fresno, CA)
Fresno Bee-Republican (Fresno, CA)
Fresno Morning Republican (Fresno, CA)
Fresno Republican (Fresno, CA)
Galveston Daily News (Galveston, TX)
Gila News-Courier (Gila River, AZ)
Hartford Courant (Hartford, CT)
Hawaiian Gazette (Honolulu, HI)
Hayward Review (Hayward, CA)
Heart Mountain Sentinel (Heart Mountain, WY)
Honolulu Star-Bulletin (Honolulu, HI)
Kingsport Times (Kingsport, TN)
Lincoln Sunday Star (Lincoln, NE)
Long Beach Press (Long Beach, CA)
Los Angeles Times (Los Angeles, CA)
Lowell Sun (Lowell, MA)
Modesto News-Herald (Modesto, CA)
New Castle News (New Castle, PA)
New York Times (New York, NY)
Nikkei Heritag
Oakland Tribune (Oakland, CA)
Ogden Standard-Examiner (Ogden, UT)
Olean Evening News (Olean, NY)
Pacific Commercial Advertiser (Honolulu, HI)
Poston Chronicle (Poston, AZ)
Rafu Shimpo (Los Angeles, CA)
Reno Evening Gazette (Reno, NV)
San Antonio Express-News (San Antonio, TX)
San Mateo Times (San Mateo, CA)
San Jose Mercury (San Jose, CA)
Sporting Life Magazine
Sports Illustrated
Stars and Stripes
The News (DesMoines IA)
Time Magazine
Tucson Citizen (Tucson, AZ)
Tucson Daily Citizen (Tucson, AZ)
Vidette-Messenger (Valparaiso, IN)
Washington Post (Washington, DC)
Woodland Daily Democrat (Woodland, CA)
Yuma Sun (Yuma, AZ)

Online, Digital and Multimedia

Arizona Interscholastic Association http://www.aiaonline.org
Arizona Republic, http://www.azcentral.com
Around the Horn in KC Blog http://royals.mlblogs.com
Baseball Almanac http://www.baseball-almanac.com
Baseball-Reference.com http://www.baseball-reference.com
Baseball Think Factory http://www. baseballthinkfactory.org
BaseballGuru.com http://baseballguru.com
Becoming Arizona http://www.becomingarizona.org
Chronicling America, Library of Congress http://www.loc.gov/chroniclingamerica
The Daily Bruin http://www.dailybruin.com
Densho Archive http://archive.densho.org
The Diamond Angle http://www.thediamondangle.com
Diamonds in the Rough: The Legacy of Japanese-American Baseball. Derry, NH: Chip Taylor Communications, 1998. DVD, 35 min.
EricEnders.com http://www.ericenders.com
The First 100, *Las Vegas Review Journal* http://www.1st100.com
Fresno Athletic Hall of Fame http://www.fresnoahof.org

Google Books
http://books.google.com
Hawaii Medical Library
http://hml.org
Hawaiian Historical Society
http://www.hawaiianhistory.org
HawaiiHistory.com
http://hawaiihistory.com
Hokubei.com
http://www.hokubei.com
Japan-Guide.com
http://www.japan-guide.com
Japan: Life and Religion
http://nihonshukyo.wordpress.com
Japanese American National Museum
http://www.janmstore.com
Japanese American Veterans
http://www.javadc.org
Japanese Baseball Hall of Fame and Museum
http://english.baseball-museum.or.jp
KOLD News 13 Tucson
http://www.kold.com
LA84 Foundation
http://search.la84foundation.org
MinorLeagueBaseball.com
http://web.minorleaguebaseball.com
MLB.com
http://www.mlb.com
National Baseball Congress
http://www.nbcbaseball.com
National Baseball Hall of Fame
http://www.baseballhalloffame.org
Newspaper Archive
http://www.newspaperarchive.com
Nisei Baseball Research Project
http://www.niseibaseball.com
Paper of Record
http://www.paperofrecord.com
ProQuest Historical Newspapers
http://library.lib.asu.edu
Rafu Shimpo
http://www.rafu.com
SABR Asian Baseball Committee
http://asianbb.sabr.org
U.S. Census Bureau
http://www.census.gov
U.S. Open Golf Tournament
http://golf.about.com
University of Arizona News
http://uanews.opi.arizona.edu
University of California Irvine Libraries
http://content.cdlib.org
Westegg Inflation Calculator
http://www.westegg.com
WorldBaseballClassic.com
http://www.worldbaseballclassic.com

Index

Abo, Takeshi "George" 149, 150, 151, 153–157, 159–162, 166, 173–179, 183, 186, 232
Aburamen (Fresno Athletic Club, 1934, util.) 92, 98
Adams (L.A. White Sox, 1925, 1b) 210
Adams, Maurice "Lefty" 67, 212, 222, 223
Aizawa, Dave 129
Akimoto, George 189
Akizuki, Chi 137, 153, 160, 186
Alameda Japanese Club 39, 55, 58, 71, 72, 82, 87, 89, 101, 102, 114, 115
Alameda-Kono All-Stars 104, 108, 160, 188, 216, 217, 218, 220
Alexander (Aratani Guadalupe, 1930) 80
Alexander Field (Honolulu, HI) 24
All-Chinese 18
Allen, Newt 55
Alleruzo, Marion 103
Allison, Paul 102–104, 223
Alvarez, Lefty 94, 96
Amache (CO) All-Stars (baseball team) 149, 150, 163, 181
Amache Internment Camp 149, 150, 163, 181
Amachi, Shunichi 233
Anderson, "Doc" 32, 33
Anderson, Merle 84
Aoki (Fresno Athletic Club, 1927) 59
Aoshiba, Kenichi (Bowles Japanese, 1939, cf) 94, 95, 213
Arakawa (Tokyo All-Stars, 1934) 108
Aratani, George 87, 121
Aratani Guadalupe Packers 80, 87, 219, 224
Arizona Compress 122, 123, 139, 141, 230
Arizona Diamondbacks 235
Arizona Softball Hall of Fame 141
Arizona state semi-pro baseball tourney 123, 134, 148
Arizona State University ix, 134
Arlett, Buzz 58
Armstrong (Sun Maids, 1927, c) 67
Arroyo Grande Ballclub 128
Arthur, Parks 90–91
Aruki (Stockton Yamato, 1926, p) 56
Asano, Tosh 137, 156
Ashford, Emmett 194
Asplund, Don 192
Atkinson, Alfred 112, 119
Atlanta University 30
Augie Fries Service Nine 108
Averill, Earl 93

Bailey, Lowell ix, 140, 149, 168, 169, 171, 214
Baker (Fresno Twilight Leagues All-Star, 1927, cf) 67, 211
Bakersfield Ballclub (Caucasian) 200, 222
Bakersfield Ballclub (Japanese American) 39, 71
Bakersfield Colored Cubs 86, 88, 100, 108
Barry, Sam 187
Barton, C.M. (Pop) 84, 107
Baseball as America exhibit 236
Baseball Reliquary Shrine of the Eternals 236, 239
Baseball Saved Us 235
Baylis, I.M. 98
Beard, Dave 84, 116
Bechtold (Fresno All-Stars, 1935) 94
Beck, E.M. 81
Becker, Beals 84
Beene, Charley 193
Beiden, Pete 186, 189, 190, 192, 193, 195, 196, 200–204, 206, 233
Bell, James "Cool Papa" 7, 52
Berdoy, Pete 74, 80
Berg, Moe 93
Berra, Yogi 204
Berry, Charlie 93
Bessho, Takehiko 193
Bidwell, Oliver "Hasty" 67, 80, 84, 196, 212, 223
Bier, Al 68, 69
Bier, Dick 67, 84, 107, 212
Big Six University System (Japan) 81, 109
Block 16 Field, Canal Camp 125
Block 28 All-Stars (baseball team) 125–128, 132, 134, 136–138, 143, 148, 149, 166, 172–178, 181, 231
Block 28 Field 120, 121, 123–126, 128–130, 134–136, 142, 144, 147, 166, 174, 176, 177, 179, 180, 182, 214, 246
Bloom, Leonard 162
Blunt, Charles 210
Bobo, Willie 52
Boekhoff, Terri ix
Bonner 141
Bonzagni, Martin 74
Bordagaray, Frenchy 204
Bost, Chester Arthur "Chet" 32, 33, 40, 41, 66, 88, 184, 230
Bourdet, Len 193
Bowles Japanese Ballclub 71, 78, 108, 109, 110, 181–183, 185
Brandon, Em 75
Brandt, George 107
Braves (All-Portuguese) 18, 20
Bricker, Don 193
Britton, George 55
Britton, Mose 91
Broderson 67
Brooklyn Dodgers 122, 137, 185
Brown, Clint 93
Brown, D. 80
Brown, G. 80
Brown, James 108, 200
Brown, Zip 189
Buck Lai's Hawaiian All-Stars 98
Burgess, Larry 192
Busch, Connie 74, 84, 107
Bush, Connie *see* Busch, Connie
Butcher, Spencer 52, 212, 226
Butler, Bill 42
Butte All-Stars 132, 137–141, 143, 146, 147, 148, 149, 160, 161, 166, 179
Butte Baseball Association 126, 127, 128, 131, 133, 134, 136, 148, 165, 231
Butte High School Eagles 11, 122, 128, 129, 131, 146, 164–173, 175, 180, 185, 214, 230, 231, 236
Butte Major League All-Stars 132, 148, 161, 166, 179, 230
Butte Old Timers 174, 176

Cade, Joe 74, 212, 226
Cal Poly 130, 189, 191
California Japanese Baseball League 55, 56, 89, 96, 99, 100, 101, 106, 215
California State Japanese League *see* California Japanese Baseball League
California Winter League (CWL) 4, 5, 8, 26, 33, 51, 54, 55, 59, 62, 71, 74, 101, 107, 110, 232, 224, 226, 227, 228
Camp Stoneman 183
Canal All-Stars 132, 138
Canal Athletic Society (CAS) 121, 123, 138, 148
Canal Camp Athletic Club (2CAC) 126, 135, 138, 140
Canal Cardinals All-Stars 166, 173–176
Canal High School 126, 129, 166, 167, 173, 231
Cano, John "Moose" 68, 74, 91, 212, 223
Cantrell, Ken "Lefty" 139
Carey, Lee 168–170, 185, 214
Carlos, John 205
Carr, Wayne "Tank" 55, 184, 212
Cartwright, Alexander 26
Cartwright, Joe 31, 43, 53, 58, 68, 75, 84, 107, 212, 223
Cartwright's Pruners (baseball team) 31
Cascarell, Joe 93
Cassidy, Harry 107
Castro, Patsy 80
Central California Japanese League 78, 86, 97, 109
Central Coast Japanese League *see* Central California Japanese League
Central Valley Baseball League 94
Cepeda, Orlando 204
Chance, Frank 19, 132, 204, 233
Chang, B. 99
Chiba Lotte Marines 235
Chicago American Giants 33, 227, 228
Chicao Cubs 30, 39, 55, 122, 220, 222
Chicago White Sox 67, 122, 138, 193, 219, 221, 222
China 3, 15, 19, 48, 58, 61, 63, 65, 67, 104, 106, 107, 216
Chosen *see* Korea
Christian (DePrima's All-Stars, 1932, c) 86
Chum Chun Shu Sat (The Searching for the Truth Institute) 22
Clark, Will 119, 233
Cleary (Salt Lake Bees, 1924, 3b) 210
Cleveland Indians 1, 88, 169, 170, 185, 220, 221, 222
Cleveland Spiders 15, 190
Cleveland Stars 74
Clevenger, Truman 192, 193
Clifford, Larkins 90
Clovis Commodores 109, 110, 185
Clovis Nisei Nine 185, 186
Cobb, Ty 3, 7, 19, 47, 74, 94
Coffman, Johnny 58, 68, 74, 75, 81, 84, 212, 223
color lines in baseball 2, 3, 8, 15, 16, 30, 32, 43, 141, 162, 184, 191
Colorado State A & M 189
Columbia University 60, 215
Combs, Melvin 196
Comiskey, Charles 19, 26, 28
Comiskey Park 180
Congressional Commission on Wartime Relocation and Internment of Civilians (CWRIC) 9, 240
Cooper, Andrew "Andy" 2, 33, 54, 59, 62, 71, 74, 211, 226, 227, 238
Cooper, Gary 144
Cooper, Sam 74, 226
Cooperstown, New York 7, 8, 235
Cooperstown Symposium on Baseball and American Culture 6, 238
Costas, Bob 4
Couch (Gila River staff team, 1945, p) 174
Coumbe, Fred "Fritz" 44, 221
Cox, Bobby 233
Craghead, Howard 58, 67, 68, 80, 212, 220
Crawford (Sun Maids, 1927, p) 67, 212
Creacy, Dewey 52
Cropsy (Jaynes & Sons, 1930) 79
Currie, Rube 55
Curry (Sun Maids, 1927, 3b) 67, 212

Daimai Baseball Club 53, 63, 217, 229
Dai-Nippon Baseball Club 97
Damon Field (Honolulu, HI) 24
Daniels, A.D. 108
Daniels, Roger 10
Date, Maseo 234
Davis, George 102
Davis, Willie 191
Day, Connie 55, 226
Dean, Dizzy 88
Dean, Paul 88
Delahanty Joe 19
Delano Japanese Ballclub 99
Delozier (Fresno Tigers) 46
Demery, Art "Nooky" 108
Densho ix, 10, 243
Denver Nisei Ballclub 188, 189, 203
DePrima's All-Stars 86
Derr, Wilber 175
Detroit Colored Giants 90, 91
Detroit Tigers 47, 54, 66, 122, 206
DeVinno (Hollywood Japanese, 1934, ss) 92
Dihigo, Martin 7
DiMaggio, Dominic 220
DiMaggio, Joe 2, 88, 94, 95, 96, 110, 115, 122, 200, 218, 220, 222, 225
Dixon, Rap 55, 59, 61, 62, 211, 212, 226
Dodson, Jerry 214
Doi, Hunter 128
Doi, M. 78, 86, 92
Dolan, Mike 42
Draklich (Jaynes & Sons, 1930, p) 80
Drilling, Bob 193
Drilling, Dick 193
Duchalisky, Jimmy 221
Duncan, Frank 62, 211, 226

Ebell, Harry 98
Ellsworth, Dick 204
Emoto (Fresno Athletic Club, 1936, util.) 98
Evans, Alexander "Showtime" 57, 74, 211, 226, 227
Ewing Field (San Francisco, CA) 39
Excelsiors of Hawaii 18
Executive Order 9066 5, 111, 113, 114, 115, 233, 234, 241
Exeter, California 184

FAC Old Timers 93, 213
Fagan, Robert 20, 32, 54, 55, 57, 74, 210, 211, 212, 226, 227, 228
Ferriera, Mike 74
Ferris, Bruce 195, 206
Fink-Smith Playground 31, 32, 196
Firemen's Ballpark 40, 45–47, 52, 57, 68, 69, 75, 80, 83, 87, 88, 210–212
Fisher, Cornell ix, 141, 142
Fisher, Cornell, Jr. 141
Fisher, Mike 19
Florin Japanese Ballclub 39, 186
Flournoy, Jesse "Pud" 71, 226
Flowers, Okey 139, 140
Foote, Bill 52, 54, 210
Ford, Ernie 98
Ford, Gerald 233
Ford, Roscoe 84, 107
Ford, Whitey 204
Fort Lewis 183, 189
Fort Ord Warriors (baseball team) 192, 201
Foster, Rube 7, 13, 33, 226
Fowler, Bud 7
Fowler, California 58, 71, 217, 224
Fowler Firemen (baseball team) 53
Foxx, Jimmie 7, 55, 93, 110
Frank Chance Field (Fresno, CA) 84, 92, 96, 98, 100, 105, 107, 108
Frank H. Ball Playground 196, 206
Frazee, Harry 30
Frazier, Foy 68, 74, 98, 205, 212, 223
Fresno All-Stars 56, 57, 70, 80, 86, 87, 90, 211, 230
Fresno American Legion Post 67, 77, 84, 96
Fresno Assembly Center 115–119, 178
Fresno Athletic Club (FAC) 3, 11, 31, 32, 34–36, 39, 41–47, 51–54, 56, 58, 61, 63, 67, 72–74, 79, 82, 83, 85, 89, 92, 96–101, 104, 105, 109, 117, 164, 183, 193, 210–212, 227, 228, 236
Fresno Athletic Hall of Fame 117, 189, 204, 205
Fresno Auto Wreckers 84

Fresno Bee All-Stars 43
Fresno City Baseball League 39, 95, 106
Fresno Colored Athletic Club 86, 88, 89, 100, 230
Fresno Colored Cubs 75, 95, 230
Fresno Colored Giants 32, 66, 87, 230
Fresno Colored Monarchs 108
Fresno Cubs 52, 53
Fresno Grizzlies 236
Fresno Indians 196
Fresno Japanese 11, 34, 36, 204, 213, 217, 219, 220
Fresno Japanese All-Stars 88, 90, 94, 95
Fresno Japanese Ball Park 51, 52, 53, 55, 56, 66, 71, 72, 74–76, 82, 83, 87–91, 99, 101, 105, 207, 213
Fresno Junior College 196
Fresno Monarchs 66
Fresno Nichi Bei (baseball team) 191, 192
Fresno Nisei 186, 188, 190, 193, 196, 197, 200, 201, 202
Fresno Police Dept. Club 98
Fresno Sciots 56, 75, 76, 84, 88, 223–225
Fresno Shadow Giants 32
Fresno State 51, 60, 71, 98, 102, 182, 183, 186, 188–193, 195, 196, 199, 200, 203, 206, 215, 216
Fresno Taiiku Club 83
Fresno Tigers 39, 43, 46–48, 50–53, 71–73, 78, 100, 224, 225
Fresno WCNBL Team 184
Fries, Augie 68, 84, 107, 212, 233
Fuchs, Lefty 91, 94
Fuji Athletic Club 13
Fujioka, George "Lefty" 150, 152–154, 156–157, 159, 160, 177, 178, 188
Fujita, Jimmy 148, 149
Fujita, Nubuo 81, 82, 85, 109, 199, 232
Fujita, Tom 93, 94, 213, 215
Fukai, Masani 167, 168, 170, 173, 175, 214
Fukuyama (L.A. Nippons, 1935, 2b) 96
Fulice (Phoenix Colored Nine, 1943, 2b) 141
Funkner, Phil 74, 75, 79, 80, 213, 214
Furubayashi, Kenichi "Ken" 48, 51, 59, 60, 73, 211, 215
Furukawa, Stacey 172
Furukawa, Tets ix, 11, 146, 150, 151, 153, 154, 156, 157, 159–162, 164, 166–168, 170, 172, 174, 175, 176, 178, 214

Garcia, Al 193
Garcia, Rudy 192
Garcia, Sergio 186
Gates, Jim ix
Gehrig, Lou 2–4, 67–70, 84, 85, 93, 110, 144, 185, 212, 225, 226, 239
Gehringer, Charley 93
Gibson, Bob 206
Gibson, Josh 7, 236, 239
Gila Jr. All-Stars 152–159
Gila River Indian Community ix
Gila River Internment Camp ix, 11, 22, 47, 112, 114–185, 188, 209, 214, 219, 230–232, 235, 236
Gillespie (Salt Lake Bees, 1924, rf) 210
Given, Alison "Banty" 22, 23, 28, 37, 192
Go, Meisho 100
Gomez, Lefty 93
Gonzales (Mexican All-Stars, 1933, p) 88
Goodrich, Joe 52
Goodrich, Warren 191
Goodwin, Lorenzo Alfonzo "Lonnie," "Lon" 52, 54–59, 61, 62, 65, 71, 184, 226, 227, 230
Goto, Hiroshi 108
Goto, Sanga 165
Graff (Salt Lake Bees, 1924, ss) 210
Green, Julius "Junior," "John" 74, 211, 227
Green Light Letter 5, 124
Griswol, Arthur L. 148
Guadalupe Japanese *see* Aratani Ballclub
Guadalupe YMBA 86, 87, 90, 99, 123, 124, 125, 128, 133, 136

Haiyama (Shogyo-Hiroshima High, 1931, p) 82
Hall, Midori ix
Hamaguchi, Ken 125
Hamazaki, Shinji 60, 64, 72, 233
Hamilton (Phoenix Colored Nine, 1943, c) 141
Hammaker, Atlee 12
Hammett Park (Livingston) 39
Hanford Blue Sox 109
Hanford Japanese All-Stars 78, 79, 98
Hanford Mexican All-Stars 91, 96
Hanford YMBA 110
Hankyu Braves 64
Hannah, Jack 193
Hansen, Jimmy 58, 72, 84, 212, 224
Hanshin Tigers 217
Hanson, Joe 148
Harada, Tsuneo "Cappy" 187, 188, 193–195, 203
Harding, Warren G. 30, 33
Harol (Phoenix Colored Nine, 1943, util.) 141
Harris (Phoenix Colored Nine, 1943, rf) 141
Harris, Bucky 86, 87, 96, 105, 106
Hasaki (Fresno Athletic Club, 1921) 34
Hasegawa, Shigetoshi 236
Hasegawa, Tets 150, 153, 159, 161, 166, 167, 168, 170, 173, 175, 178, 214, 232
Hashimoto, Ichi 137
Hassey, Bill 214
Hatafuku (Tokyo Giants, 1936, p) 97
Hawaii Asahi (All-Japanese) 18, 20
Hawaiian All-Stars 37, 217
Hawaiian Asahi 15, 18, 20, 22, 25, 26, 27, 33
Hawaiian Braves (All-Portuguese) 18, 26, 66
Hawkins, Lem 20
Hayes, Frank 192
Heart Mountain Internment Camp 135–137, 148, 149, 150–163, 171, 180, 181, 186
Heizenrader, Jackie 84, 88, 94, 205, 224
Heizenrader's All-Stars 88
Helmuth, Jake 193
Hendsch, Charlie 51, 59, 66, 211, 215
Henmi (Fresno Athletic Club, 1919, cf) 34, 39
Hepting, Ernie 210
Herb Hunter's All-Star 35
Hester (Salt Lake Bees, 1924, 1b) 210
Higashi (Stockton Yamato, 1926, c) 56
Hikida, Shotaro "Joe" 138
Hill (Fresno All-Stars, 1926, rf) 57, 211
Hill, Johnson 91
Hilldale Park 72
Hilo, Hawaii 20, 22, 37
Hinaga, George 90, 91, 186, 215
Hinaga, Noboru "Russell" 7, 53, 90, 91, 92, 94, 135, 137, 148, 151, 153, 154, 155, 156, 157, 158, 159, 160, 173, 188, 215
Hinds, Gene 66, 78, 89, 230
Hinodes (baseball team) 126, 128
Hiramatsu, Charles 102
Hirano, Jenichi "John" 37, 39, 216
Hirano, Takeo "Tom" 37, 39, 46, 48, 216
Hirano, Yoshi 124, 128, 232
Hirasuna (Fresno Athletic Club, 1935) 94
Hirata (Fresno Athletic Club, 1924) 48, 92
Hirayama, Satoshi "Fibber" 6, 8, 184–186, 188–192, 200–202, 204, 206, 233, 234
Hirayama, "Truck" 185
Hirokawa, Hisa 13
Hirokawa, Katsue "James/Jimmy" 37, 48, 50, 51, 53, 59, 60, 61, 102, 210, 216
Hiroshima Carp 197–202, 233–235
Hirota, Y. 232
Hitsuna (Fresno Athletic Club, 1935, 2b) 97
Holland, Elvis "Bill" 71, 212, 227
Hollerson, George 67, 68, 212
Holley (Fresno All-Stars, 1935) 94
Holloway, Crush 55
Hollywood (PCL) 68, 193, 220–223
Hollywood Japanese 42, 92, 218, 219
Holmes Playground 108, 196, 223
Homan, Frank 47, 91, 125, 132, 203
Homan Sporting Goods *see* Homan, Frank

Honda, Henry 137
Hong Kong 104
Honolulu, Hawaii 7, 13–17, 19, 20, 22, 27, 30, 31, 33, 34, 36–38, 48, 50, 51, 58, 59, 60, 65, 66, 73, 74, 76, 77, 88, 93, 98, 102, 103, 105, 112, 157, 193, 195, 196, 213–215, 217, 218, 220
Honolulu Asahi ix, 50, 65, 103, 217, 219, 222
Honolulu City League 20
Honolulu Star Bulletin 24, 26
Horino, Min 155, 156
Horio, Jimmy 77, 93, 213
Horio, John 188, 197
Horitz (Gila River staff team, 1945, rf) 174
Horton (Salt Lake Bees, 1924, 2b) 210
Hosei University 60, 81, 82, 85, 234
Hoshizu, Jack 149
House of David 71
Hoyt, Waite 35
HR442, formal apology 234
Hubbard, Jess 55, 212, 227
Hudler, Rex 233
Hudspeth, Bob 55
Hulvey, Hank 210, 220
Hunt, Donnie 58
Hunt, Eldridge 51, 58, 59, 66, 67, 75
Hunter, Herbert 35
Hushino, Tadashi 99
Huso (Gila River staff team, 1945, cf) 174

Ichishita (San Jose Asahi, 1934, p) 91
Iguchi, Shinjiro 235
Ikeda, Fumio 109
Ikeda, G. 89
Ikeda, Juice 125
Ikeda, Kaz 126, 139, 142, 184, 231
Ikeda, Masumi 179
Ikeda, Seirin 139, 231
Ikeda, Tak 156, 159, 160, 161
Ikeda, Tom ix
Inai, George 123
Ino, Ryo 88
Inoshita, Mas ix, 117
Inouye, Horse 126, 128, 137, 138, 140
Inouye, Yoshite 108
International Boys League 234
Irabu, Hideki 235
Irie, George 59
Iriyama, Masao 125, 137
Iriyama, Noboru 137, 139, 140
Iriye, M. 96
Iseri, George 156, 157, 161
Ishida, Bill 78, 89, 93, 94, 96, 213
Ishida, Wilson 93, 94, 96, 97, 99, 101, 102, 108, 213, 216
Ishimoto, Kay 150, 152, 153, 154, 155
Ishitani, George 153
Isleton Japanese Ballclub 39
Itan (Seattle Asahi, 1934, ss) 92
Ito, Frank 159
Ito, Tokugoro 7
Itwo, Teiji 126, 128
Iwahashi, N. 230
Iwahashi, Tut 89, 102
Iwano (Fresno Athletic Club, 1924) 48
Iwasaki, George 39, 108
Iwasaki, Ted 39, 128
Iwata, Satoru "Harvey" 2, 7, 39, 44, 46, 48, 56, 57, 59, 60, 62, 66, 67–70, 75, 80, 81, 82, 86, 89, 92–94, 203, 210–213, 216

Jackson (Gila River staff team, 1945, 1b) 174
Jackson, Isiah 193
Jackson, Milt 179
Jackson, Tut 72
Jacobs, Phil 139
Jacobsen, "Big Jake" 80, 84, 91, 108, 224
Jacobsen, Doc 68, 80, 212, 224
Jacobsen, Earl 80, 224
Jacobsen, I. 68, 80, 212
Janes, Leroy Lansing 15
Japanese All-Stars (FAC/Meiji combo) 75
Japanese American Citizens League (JACL) ix, 80, 115, 242
Japanese Baseball Hall of Fame 35, 44, 45, 63, 72, 94, 98, 189, 204, 233–236
Japanese Times 3
Jaynes & Sons 79–81, 223, 224
Jefferson, Thomas 129
Jeffries (Fresno Sciots, 1925, p) 56
Jenkins, Geoff 233
Jerome Internment Camp 42, 116, 119, 146, 151, 165, 178, 218, 219
Jewett, Gene 67, 68, 84, 107, 212
Jio, Joe 137
Johnson, Ajay 32, 54, 55, 65, 210, 211, 227
Johnson, Ban 35
Johnson, Earl 122
Johnson, Ernie 122
Johnson, Oscar "Heavy" 20
Johnson, Walter 228
Jorgensen, Don 80

Kageyama, Chimaki 99
Kajikawa, Bill ix, 134
Kakebe (Fresno Athletic Club, 1921, mgr.) 34
Kaku, Art 128
Kanagaki, George 139, 229
Kansas City Monarchs 54, 122, 227
Kasai, Jack 126, 129
Kasakami (Fresno Athletic Club, 1934, ss) 89
Kashiwagi, Bill 126
Kataoka, George 167, 170, 176–179, 214, 232
Kato, Kisaku 35
Katyal, Neal 239
Kavai, Shig 137
Kawada (Guadalupe, 1934, p) 90
Kawakami, Shiro 93, 94, 96, 99, 102, 108, 116, 206, 213, 2116
Kawakami, Tetsuharu 193, 194
Kawakami, Yukio 86, 89, 92, 93, 96, 99, 213, 216
Kawamura, Jiro 99
Kawamura, Noboru 34, 39
Kawasaki, Richard 59, 60, 65, 211, 216
Kawasaki (Seattle Asahi, 1934, cf) 92
Kawasaki (Stockton Yamato, 1934, 1b) 89
Kebo, George 78, 82, 92, 115
Kebo, Johnson 78
Keio University ix, 13, 52, 59, 60, 64, 71, 72, 229
Kelley, George 35
Kelly, Frank 107
Kelly, Pat ix
Kennedy, Robert F. 205
Kerita (Tokyo All-Stars, 1935) 94, 213
Kerman Nine 91
Kigomura, T. 96
Kilburn, Shan 55, 72, 74, 84, 107, 184
Kilner (Sunmaids, 1927, 1b) 67
Kimura, Taka "Smokey" 149, 150, 186
King, Ed 196, 200
King, Martin Luther, Jr. 205
Kingsburg Vikings 121, 125
Kinoshita, Masato 124, 125, 128, 134, 136, 139, 143, 148, 179, 181, 186–188, 231, 232
Kinoshita, Min 125
Kintetsu Buffaloes 235
Kitamura, Dick 189
Kleim, Mike 98
Knight, Dypper 91
Kobayashi, Key 126, 143, 150, 153–156, 159, 161
Koch (Jaynes & Sons, 1930, p) 80
Kodama, Sadao "Suds" 96, 109
Kodomi, Takeo 108
Koerner, Phil 84, 107
Kohl, Jackie 46, 58, 67, 68, 74, 80, 212, 224
Kolovare, Hal 139
Komai (Hollywood Japanese, 1934, p) 92
Komatsu, Harry 131, 139, 143, 144
Komosky, Walter 98
Komura, Kay 128
Komura, Koizo 137
Komura, Tosh 138
Kondo, Kanemitsu 99
Kondo, Pete 86, 87
Kono (Fresno All-Stars, 1932, ss) 86
Kono, Harry 82, 87, 101, 102, 114, 115, 121, 125, 126, 132, 133, 135, 138, 149, 150, 160
Kono Alameda All-Stars 102, 103, 104, 108, 160, 161, 165, 198, 214, 217, 222
Korea 3, 15, 54, 58, 61, 63, 65, 67, 183, 189, 227, 239
Kozuki, Sinchi 26
Kozuki, Sindo 26
Kumano, Kats 82, 85, 89, 93, 94, 176, 213
Kunihisa, Lee 98, 103

Kunitomo, Anthony 56, 59, 60, 211, 216
Kurima, Herb "Moon" 116, 118, 143, 165, 173
Kurosaki, Ryan 233
Kurumatsu (Hollywood Japanese, 1934, p) 92

Landis, Judge Kenesaw Mountain 5, 26, 35, 67, 114, 122, 162, 162
LaRoux, George 74, 80
Larry, Lyn 58, 67
Larsen, Don 118
Lauderdale (Jaynes & Sons, 1930, p) 80
Lawless, Toby 196
Lawrence, Charles 108
Lawson, Ty 84, 98, 211, 224
Lazzeri, Tony 39, 44, 53, 160, 210, 220, 234
LeGrand (baseball team) 95, 101
Leonard, Dutch 84, 107, 204
Leslie, Roy 210, 220
Lewis (Phoenix Colored Nine, 1943, ss) 141
Lewis, Duffy 38, 39, 44, 45, 160, 210, 221
Lewis, Glen 192, 193
Lincoln, Abraham 13
Lincoln Giants 33
Lincoln Links (baseball team) 43
Livingston, California 11
Lodi Japanese Ballclub 39, 186, 201
Lompoc 126, 128, 134, 136, 137, 161, 231
Lopez, Carl "Scooter" ix, 168, 214
Lorenzo, Peter 90
Los Angeles Dodgers 235
Los Angeles Nippons 32, 34, 35, 75, 86, 87, 96, 97, 216, 219
Los Angeles Tigers 71
Los Angeles White Sox 52–57, 62, 74, 109, 184, 210, 211, 226, 227, 228, 230
Low, Ed 25, 26
Lowry, Dr. Frederick 20
Lowry, Nell 20
Lung, Dan 98
Lung, Ed 87
Lynn, Fred 236

MacAlpine (Gila River staff team, 1945, 3b) 174
Mack, Connie 80, 85, 93, 185
Mackey, James Raleigh "Biz" 2, 3, 33, 55, 59, 61–63, 65, 71, 107, 110, 184, 210, 227, 238
Madokora (Alameda Japanese, 1934, 2b) 89
Maglia (Aratani, 1930) 80
Mails, Walter 221
Mainichi Orions (baseball team) 189
Major League Tourists 18, 19, 35
Makel (Fresno Cubs, 1925, p) 53
Malone, Les 74, 98
Maloney, Earl "Hands" 78
Maloney, Jim 78, 204
Mamiya, Taketo "Tom" 59, 60, 211, 216
Manchuria 15, 73
SS *Manchuria* 13
Mantle, Mickey 204
Manzanar Internment Camp 217, 233
Marich, Martin "Pug" ix
Marichal, Juan 204
Marley, Lew 56, 75, 97
Martenson (Gila River staff team, 1945, ss) 174
Martin, Pepper 88
Martinez, Bernard 192
Maruyama (Fresno Athletc Club, 1935) 94
Matsuda (Hawaiian Asahi, 1919, cf) 26
Matsuda, George 143, 173, 174, 232
Matsui (Fresno Athletic Club, 1932, 3b) 70, 86, 92
Matsui, Hideki 3, 12, 236
Matsui, Ryozo "Rosie" 92, 137, 153
Matsumoto, Kiyo 31
Matsumoto, Sutosaburo 31
Matsumoto, Tadashi 108
Matsumoto, Takizo "Frank" 31, 58, 60, 74, 85, 100, 185, 202, 203, 215, 236
Matsuno, Kaname 126
Matsuno, Morio 80, 87
Matsura, Benny 121
Matsura, G. 96
Matsuzaka, Daisuke 3, 12
Mays, Willie 204
McCann, Cline 107
McCarthy, Ray 196
McCleve, Richard ix, 179
McCovey, Willie 204
McFarland (Old-Time Professionals, 1938, cf) 107
McGraw, John 13, 15, 16, 19, 22, 32
McKeg, Philip 20
McKenry, Pete 53, 68
McKinley High School (Honolulu, HI) 23, 24, 60, 217, 219
McMurtry, Ed 71, 84
McMurtry, Elbert 97
McMurtry, Orville 71
McNair, Eric 93
McNair, Hurley 52
McNeely, Earl 42
McNeil, William ix
McWilliams, Carey 119
Meadows, Hillary "Bullet" 30, 41
Meehan, Tom 4, 204
Meiji Shrine Stadium 35, 45, 46, 50, 58, 59, 60, 61, 62, 74, 75, 76, 85, 107, 137, 224, 227, 229
Meiji University 234
Merced Bears 72
Merced Cubs 11, 39
Merced Merchants 99
Merrit (Salt Lake Bees, 1924, 2b) 210
Mesa High School Jackrabbits ix, 173, 229
Mesa Junior American Legion Post 179
Metzler, Alex 55, 58, 67, 68, 70, 81, 84, 88, 204, 205, 212, 221
Meusel, Irish 35
Mexican All-Stars 88, 91, 92
Meyer, Jerry 193
Meyers (Phoenix Colored Nine, 1943, p) 141
Mid-Pacific Institute (Honolulu, HI) 22
Miller, Bing 67, 80, 93, 212
Miller, Herb 112
Miller, Leighroy 43
Miller, Pat 107
Mills High School (Honolulu, HI) 20, 22–28, 37, 59–60, 88, 217, 219, 220, 222
Mimura, Kazuo "Pug,""Tandy" 60, 206, 210
Minamimura, Yuko 194
Mirikitani, Sunto "Frank" 82, 102
Mitani, Mas "Mits" 126, 128, 139, 231, 232
Mitchell (Sunmaids, 1927, c) 67, 212
Mitsuyoshi, Ben 197–199
Miya, Frank 34
Miyahara, Taijiro "Ty" 26, 27, 35, 46, 48, 59, 60, 211, 215
Miyake, Juichi "George" 108
Miyamoto, Ky 108
Mizote, Roy 34, 39, 78
Mizuhara, Shigeru 94, 95, 194, 233
Mizukami, Kazuo "Scotty" 143, 150
Molis, John 140
Moncrief, Charley 81
Moniz, Bob 193
Montana State College 119
Monterey Japanese 101
Montez, Antonio 80
Montez, Pete 80
Moore, Alice 20
Moore, Allen 90
Moore, Caroline 20
Moore, Eloise 20
Moore, Nell L. 20
Moore, Walter "Dobie" 20
Morehead, Albert 90
Morgan, Joe 8
Mori (Hollywood Japanese, 1934, c) 35, 92
Morihisa, Shoji 108
Morinaga, Masa 176
Morioka, Jimmy 190
Morioka, Jiro 233
Morishita, Irving 125
Morishita, Ted 128, 138, 231
Morita, Pat 125, 136, 182, 235
Moriyama, G. 89, 91, 94, 96, 215
Moriyama, Irving 125
Morris, Bob 179
Morris, Harold "Yellow Horse" 41, 74, 184, 227
Morris, John H. 148
Morse, John 193
Morton, Harry 52
Moto (Filipino All-Stars, 1934, p) 92
Mt. Whitney Brewers 95, 96, 100, 101
Mujanishi (Stockton Yamato, 1934, 2b) 89
Mulcahy, Phil 44, 210, 221

Munishi (Stockton Yamato, 1926, p) 56
Murakami, Masanori 12, 204, 235
Murakata, Masao 99
Muranishi, Johnny 230
Murashima, Fred 78, 82, 86
Murashima, Yushio "Yosh" 72, 75, 82, 86
Murata, Gekitaro 76
Murata, Tom 150, 157, 159
Murayama (Fresno Athletic Club, 1934, p) 89
Muyamoto, K. 101
Myers, Dillon 162
Myers, Elmer 220

Nagai, Kiyo 178, 231
Nagasawa, Fujio 94
Nagata, Saburo 100
Nagata, Yoichi ix
Nagoya Dragons 197
Nakagawa (Alameda Japanese, 1934, 2b, rf) 89
Nakagawa, Junichi "Johnny" 2, 7, 34, 39, 40, 48, 56, 59–62, 65–72, 80, 81, 92, 93, 204, 206, 210, 211–213, 215
Nakagawa, Kerry Yo ix, 1, 2, 4, 6, 116, 125, 151, 172, 199, 235
Nakagawa, Miyoshi 234
Nakahara, George 92
Nakamura, M. 70, 215
Nakamura, Roy 136, 150, 176, 232
Nakamura, Tad 128, 176, 232
Nakamura, William 34, 37, 70, 93, 210, 211, 213, 215
Nakamura, Y.K. 7, 92
Nakamura, Yoshio 86, 96
Nakano, L. 89
Nakano, Makito "Mike" 59, 60, 126, 139, 211, 217
Nakano, Mas 89
Nakatogawa, Joe 149
Nakayama, Takeshi 98
Namura, Babe 153
Namura, Kaz (fictional) 238
Nanba (Alameda Japanese, 1934, ph) 89
Napolitano, Janet 236
Narushima, Hichiza 31
Narushima, Takizo "Frank" *see* Matsumoto, Takizo "Frank"
National Baseball Congress tournament 108, 122, 123, 141, 217, 220
National Baseball Hall of Fame ix, 3, 6, 8
Negro Leagues 3–8, 19, 33, 51, 55, 59, 64, 65, 90, 91, 110, 141, 209, 226, 227, 228, 230, 238
New Orleans Winter League 19
New York Giants 8, 15, 19, 32, 34, 42, 98, 122, 190, 193
New York Lincoln Giants 91, 122
New York Lincolns 54
New York Yankees 30, 34, 63, 85, 110, 117, 122, 144, 204, 220, 221, 222, 235, 234
Nidegawa, Nobuaki 233
Nippon Professional Baseball League 2, 4, 6, 35, 97, 209
Nisei Baseball Research Project (NBRP) 2, 70, 235
Nishi, Nik 108, 183, 184
Nishijima, Masao "Lefty" 149
Nishikawa (Hollywood Japanese, 1935, rf) 92, 96
Nishikawa, Jack 126
Nishimura, Lefty 138, 231
Nishino, James 128, 231
Nishino, Koi 137, 231
Nishino, Toshino "Tosh" 150, 153, 154, 167, 168, 174, 175, 177, 178, 232
Nitta, Shoichi 56, 211, 217
Noda, Gikaku "Steere" 18, 74
Noda, Hideo 149
Nogami, Kiyo 89, 102
Nomo, Hideo 12, 233
No-No squad 135, 138, 142
Northern California Japanese Baseball League 83, 91
Nozomi Park, Chandler, Arizona 236
Nushida, Kenso "Roy," "Boy Wonder" 7, 17, 22–25, 37–39, 42, 46–48, 54, 56, 58, 80, 82, 87, 89, 90, 100–102, 204, 210, 217, 222

Oahu-Service Leagues 14
Oakland Independents (PCL players) 42
Oakland Larks 184
Oakland Pierce Giants 33, 40, 43, 54, 57, 184, 227, 230
Oana, Henry "Hank," "The Hawaiian Prince" 66, 216
Obata, Chiura 13, 181
O'Doul, Frank "Lefty" 44, 45, 80, 85, 93–96, 114, 150, 185, 188, 190, 221, 236
Oh, Sadaharu 236
Okada (Fresno Athletic Club, 1935) 95
Okada (Stockton Yamato, 1934, rf) 89
Okada, Gensaburo 75
Okagaki, Tom "Chesty," "Ghosty" 137, 154, 197
Okai, Hank 125
Okajima, Hideki 3
Okazaki (Seattle Japanese, 1937, p) 92
Okazaki, Maino 128, 140
Oki, Nobu "Nob" 134, 136, 137, 139, 231
Okida, Harry 86
Okihiro, Mike ix
Okino (Stockton Yamato, 1934, cf) 89
Okino, Hisashi 37
Okino, Yoshi 37
Okuhara, Mas 124, 128, 134, 231, 232
Okuhara, Tosh 128
Okuharu, Ejji 124
Okuharu, Keizo 124, 139, 231
Okumura, Rev. Takie 18
Olympic Summer Games, Baseball 235
Omachi, Hatsuo "George," "Hats" 114, 118, 119, 184, 192, 202, 203, 231
Omachi All-Stars 233
Omata, Jiro 86
Omata, S. 108
Omoto, Mits 149
Omura (Stockton Yamato, 1934, ss) 89
O'Neil, Buck 51, 239
Onitsuka, Adrian 92
Ono, Michimaro 35, 63
Ono, Tad 149
Ono, Yonami 149
Orman, Ed 4, 68, 102, 105, 106, 135, 136, 185, 195, 202, 204, 205
Osada, Joe 174, 176
Osada, Ralph 150, 153, 157, 168, 170, 178, 214
Osada, Tom 150, 161
Osaka Tigers 97
Oshita, Kenichi 99
Ostenberg, Leo 68, 70, 74, 91, 97, 98, 212, 225
Osumi, Kango 121
Osumi, Keso 155
Ota, Harry 126
Outlaw Leagues 19
Overall, Orval 107, 204

Pacific Coast League (PCL) ix, 4, 5, 13, 19, 30, 34, 38, 39, 42–45, 52–54, 58, 67, 70, 74, 88, 94, 101, 102, 105, 117, 122, 186, 190, 193, 209, 210, 215, 216, 218, 220–225, 227, 236
Paige, Satchel 7, 90, 101
Para (Shan Kilburn's All-Stars, 1928) 74
Parks, Arthur 90, 91
Parret, Eli 68, 94, 212
Pasadena White Sox 137, 138, 232
Pearce, Ralph ix
Pearson, Monte 80, 94, 88, 97, 204, 222
Pepperdine 191
Perez, Timon 235
Perkins, Jim 193
Peterson, Robert 6, 7, 8
Pettus, Bill 54
Pfyl, Monte 107
Philadelphia Giants 13
Philadelphia Hilldale Colored Giants 71, 212
Philadelphia Royal Giants ix, 3, 54, 55, 58, 59, 61, 63, 64, 65, 70, 74, 86, 88, 100, 107, 108, 211, 226–228, 230, 238
Philippines 19, 104
Phoenix Thunderbirds 123, 138–141
Piggozzi (Merced Bears, 1928, p) 72
Pinelli, Babe 117–118, 185
Pittsburgh Pirates 13, 122
Placer (CA) Japanese Ballclub 186, 201
Policemen and Firemen's Ballpark *see* Firemen's Ballpark
Porterville American Legion Post 43
Portland Rosebuds 184
Poston Internment Camp 117, 119,

122, 129, 130, 132–135, 146, 148, 149, 163
Poston Yankees (baseball team) 148, 149
Pullen, O"Neal 52, 54, 55, 62, 64, 65, 74, 86, 88, 100, 108, 210, 211, 226, 227, 228
Punahoua High School (Honolulu, HI) 22–24
Purdue University 122
Puyallup Assembly Center 9, 240

Rakutani (Alameda Japanese, 1934, p) 89
Ramage, Art 46, 48, 53, 68, 71, 72, 84, 223
Reagan, Ronald 234
Reece, John 52
Regis College 60, 216
Reid, Charles 237
Reid, Mrs. George 144
Renna, Joe 86
Renna, Tom 86
Reynolds (Gila River staff team, 1945, 2b) 174
Reynolds, Deal E. 200
Riddle, John 33, 54, 55, 210, 211, 228
Riggs, Norman 102
Rikkyo University 61, 239
Ritchie (Fresno All-Stars, 1926, 2b) 211
Rivers, Jim 117
Robbins, Harold "Blondy" 138–140
Robinson, Frank 1
Robinson, Jackie 1, 4, 7
Robinson, Sharon 3, 6
Rodriguez (Fresno Colored Athletic Club, 1933, c) 88
Rogers, George 80
Rohwer Internment Camp 142
Roosevelt, Franklin 5
Rose, Pete 8, 170
Rosenthal, Joe 175
Ruth, George Herman "Babe" 2, 4, 7, 12, 30, 34, 53, 67–70, 84, 86, 90, 93, 98, 110, 146, 204, 211, 224, 237
Ryan (Aratani, 1930) 80
Ryono, Paul 173, 178, 230

Sacramento Mikado Club 58, 74, 82, 83, 99
Sacramento Salons (PCL) 94, 96, 105, 193
Sadamune, Saturo "Al" 89, 102, 216
Saeki, Tatsuo 234
SafeCo Field 2
Saiki, Taro "Ty" 82, 86, 87, 89, 91, 92, 94–99, 111, 115, 213, 218
St. Louis Browns 200, 201, 221, 222, 223
St. Louis College (Honolulu, HI) 24
St. Louis Colored Giants 51, 52
Saito (Fresno Athletic Club, 1931, util.) 83, 86
Sakagami (Seattle Japanese, 1934, p) 92
Sakai (Fresno Athletic Club, 1923) 39
Sakamoto, George 126
Sakamoto, Harry 149
Sakamoto, Sanji "The Japanese Wonder" 32
Sakamoto, T. 230
Sakata, James 34, 48, 63, 209
Sakata, Len 12
Sakata, Masako Zenimura 63
Sako, Hideo "Alfred,""Al" 39, 40, 42, 44, 45, 48, 56, 57, 70, 92, 160, 210, 212, 218
Sakoguchi, Ben 236, 237
Sakuma, Junius 136, 231
Salazar, Joe "Lefty" 139, 140
Salinas Japanese Ball Club 89, 90
Salisbury (L.A. White Sox, 1925, ss) 210
Salt Lake City Bees 38, 43–45, 160, 188, 210, 221, 235, 236
San Diego State University 191
San Diego Tigers 184
San Francisco Filipino All-Stars 92
San Francisco Giants 204, 235, 236
San Francisco Sea Lions 184
San Francisco Seals 40, 43, 94–97, 188, 189, 193, 218, 222
San Joaquin Old-Timers 84
San Joaquin Valley Baseball League 43
San Joaquin Valley Japanese All-Stars 37
San Joaquin Valley Japanese Baseball League 78
San Joaquin Valley Japanese Track Meet 39
San Jose Asahi 39, 45, 53, 89, 90, 91, 94, 97, 106, 135, 137, 159, 160, 215, 220
San Jose Zebras 148, 186, 188, 196, 197, 201, 202
San Pedro Skippers 109, 137, 190
Sandburg, Carl 146
Santa Ana Junior College 191
Santa Barbara Japanese Ball Club 108
Santo, John 157
Santos, Mike 31, 68, 72, 210, 212, 225
Santos Pirates 31, 225
Saperstein, Abe 91, 184
Sasaki (Seattle Japanese, 1934, 2b) 34–37
Sasaki, Kazuhiro 235
Satake, Taichi 99–100
Savage, Azel 54, 74, 210, 211, 216
Savory, Jack "Big Jack" 84, 205, 215
Sawamura, Eiji 94, 95, 97, 195
Schmidt, Walter 107
Schneider Aviation Club (baseball team) 86
Schofield Barracks (Honolulu, HI) 19
Scott, Marvin "The Marvel" 179
Searcy, James 122, 141, 230
Seattle Asahi 34, 40, 41, 42, 43, 50, 92, 101, 105, 204
Seattle Japanese *see* Seattle Asahi
Seattle Mariners 1, 93, 235, 236, 239
Seattle Rainiers 122, 220
Seattle Steelheads (Steelies) 184
Seaver, Tom 233
Seibu, Lions 238
Seki, Henry 108
Sera (Mills High, 1918, rf) 24
Sera, Morio "Duke" 53, 90
Sera (CA) Ballclub 96
Sewell, Luke 35
Shan Kilburn's All-Stars 74
Shepherd, Pete 67, 74, 84, 107, 212, 225
Sherman Indian School of Southern California 34
Shibata, Kazo 92, 101, 108
Shibata, Mistura 109, 218
Shibata, S. 108
Shimada, Fuzzy 154, 159, 161
Shimada, Joe 128
Shimada, Mori 152, 156, 160, 161, 167
Shimada, Y. 241
Shimamura (Fresno Athletic Club, 1924) 48
Shimasaki, Shosan "Shim," "Jack" 136, 167, 168, 170, 214, 231
Shimazu, Tom 149
Shinmoto, Hiroshi 177
Shintaku, Ben 31, 32, 34, 36, 53, 225
Shintomi, Usaburo 94
Shirachi, Ty 102
Shirakawa, Katsutaka 100
Shiraki, Frank 153
Shiraki, George 152, 160
Shiro, Bob 149
Shironaka, Tadao 89
Shogyo High School (Hiroshima, Japan) 82
Shoriki, Matsutaro 90, 93, 187, 188
Shundo, Billy 152, 153, 157, 160
Simons, Justin "Jud" 56, 58, 59, 62, 66, 68, 80, 84, 104, 107, 174, 211, 218
Sisler, George 93, 147
Skaisgir, Joe 204
Slagle, Hanley "Hank" 122, 170–172, 174, 179, 204, 238
Smith, A.J. 90
Smith, Bill "Big Bill," "King Kong" 91
Smith, E.R. 121
Smith, Ford 122
Smith, Tom 214
Smith, Tommie 205
Sommers, Fred 193
Sorackichi (Cleveland Spiders, 1897, recruit) 15, 16
Soriano, Alfonso 235
Spalding, Albert G. 18–19
Spalding & Goldsmith 123
Sperry Flours (Baseball team) 34
Sporer, George 107
Stacks, Kenny 192
Stanford University 53, 71, 199
Starffin, Victor 94, 95
Steinhauer, Johnny 56
Stengel, Casey 35
Stephens (Sun Maids, 1927, rf) 67
Stewart, Jack 74
Stivers, Wayne ix

Stockholm (Fresno Cubs, 1925, 1b) 53
Stockton Japanese *see* Yamato Stockton
Stockton Ports 192
Stockton Yamato 7, 39, 45, 46, 55, 56, 58, 75, 78, 80, 82, 89, 90, 100, 102, 133, 159, 217, 222
Stoker, Bill 79, 80
Storms (Fresno All-Stars, 1935) 94, 96
Stringer (Gila River staff team, 1945, c) 174
Sugi, Saturo "Half-Pint" 88
Sugimoto, Shumza 15–16, 32, 190
Sugiyama, Tak 153
Sukita (Fresno Athletic Club, 1926) 56
Sullivan, Ted 19, 28, 76
Sumida, Takayashi 75
Sumii, Kiyo "Paul" 126, 147
Supher Dell Field (Nashville, TN) 55
Suski, J. 96
Suzuki, Rev. D. 117
Suzuki, Ed 103
Suzuki, Ichiro 3, 8, 12, 93, 239
Suzuki, Kiyoshi 100
Suzuki, Kurt 3
Suzuki, Mac 235
Suzuki, Minoru 193, 194
Suzuki, Roy 153
Suzuki, Sotaro 233

Tabe, Takeo 84, 94, 95, 98, 213, 233
Tachino, Yoshio 70, 75, 82, 86, 87, 93, 213, 218
Tacoma Tigers 19
Taiyos Ballclub 173–176
Takagi, Noboru 89, 92, 94, 97, 102, 108, 213
Takahara (Fresno Athletic Club, 1924) 48
Takahashi, Sam 86, 96
Takasu, Kiyoshi 100
Takata, H. 85, 86
Takemoto, Jim 190
Takemoto, Yamishima 115
Takeuchi, Takejiro "Tokyo," "Ike" 108, 174, 176
Takokura (Alameda Japanese, 1934) 89
Tamaki (Fresno Japanese, 1930) 80
Tamayo, Al 80
Tamura, Nobu 108
Tamura, Sam 174, 176
Tamura, Tomochi 108
Tamura, Yoshizumi "Butch" 86, 90, 94, 125, 126
Tanaguchi (Bowles Japanese, 1939, rf) 108
Tanaka (Stockton Japanese, 1934, c) 89
Tanaka, Frank 149
Tanaka, Ken 129
Tanaka, Zuke 87, 96, 126, 176
Tanaki (Seattle Japanese, 1934, 3b) 92
Tani (McKinely High, 1919, p) 24
Taniguchi, Goro 233
Tanizawa, Nobuyashi "Ben" 89, 101
Tebeau, Oliver "Patsy" 15
Telephone Company (baseball team) 196
Templeton, Cam 73
Terao (Seattle Japanese, 1934, rf) 92
Thomas, Carl 191
Thomas, Jeri ix
Thomas, Mary ix
Thomas, Norman 162
Thurston, John Hollis "Sloppy" 220
Tischilar, John "Chilly" 139
Tobita, Chujun 50
Tocher, Lloyd "Joy," "Doc" 80, 84, 223
Tokuda (Hawaiian Asahi, 1919, lf) 26
Tokugoro, Ito 7
Tokumoto, Shigeo 86–91, 93–102, 108–110, 116, 207, 213, 228
Tokunanga, Duke 134
Tokyo All-Stars *see* Tokyo Giants
Tokyo Giants 94, 97, 98, 158, 188, 191, 193, 194, 195, 203, 213, 215, 218, 233, 234
Tolleson High School (baseball team) 166, 167
Tollhouse Cubs 71
Tolnay, Stewart 81
Tominaza (Hawaiian Asahi, 1919, ss) 26
Tomiyama, Isamu "Tom" 39, 48, 53, 71, 92, 218
Tomooka, James "Step" ix, 90, 124, 131, 132, 136, 137, 176, 231
Tomooka, Massy 137, 231
Tomooka, T. 231
Tono, Jackson "Jack" 137
Topaz Internment Camp 125, 236
Topping, Al 117
Toshiyuki, Taizo "Howard" 69, 70
Toyama, George 190, 192, 201
Toyama, L. 96
Toyoda, Bob 231
Toyoda, George 129
Tsuda, Kozuo "Fred" 22, 24, 26, 46, 47, 48, 80, 87, 133, 137, 139, 174, 176, 207, 210, 217
Tsukimura, Hideichi "Ed" 39, 44, 48, 53, 70, 75, 80, 82, 86, 87, 89, 93, 94, 100, 104, 105, 116, 206, 210, 212, 213, 219
Tsukinkawa (Stockton Japanese, 1934, lf) 89
Tsukiyama, Chomatsu "Wilfred" 23, 27, 38
Tsuruzaki, Toshiatsu 100
Tsusimi, Ben 137
Tucson High School 166, 167, 168, 172, 214, 236, 238
Tucson Junior American Legion Post 148, 149, 163
Tully, Joe 168, 169, 170, 214
Turner, C.E. "Tiny" 107
25th Infantry Wreckers (baseball team) 19, 20, 32, 54, 226
Twilight All-Stars 58
Twilight League Hall of Fame 78, 84, 205

Uchibori, Tamotsu 94
Umekubo, Bob 149
U.S. Congress 9, 13, 30, 135, 233, 240
University of Arizona 112, 119, 122, 132, 204
University of Arkansas A&M 142
University of California 34, 191, 193
University of California at Berkeley 181
University of California at Los Angeles (UCLA) 191
University of California Santa Barbara 191
University of California at Santa Clara 191
University of Chicago 55
University of Maryland 122
University of Michigan 20
University of San Francisco 192
University of Southern California (USC) 22, 33, 44, 71, 191, 228
University of Washington 34
Ushiro, Yoshio "Muscles" 167, 168, 170, 173, 175, 177, 178, 214
Usil (Hollywood Japanese, rf, 1934) 92
Utsumi (Alameda Japanese, 1934) 89
Uyesaka, Caesar 108
Uyesaka, Hideo 108

Valenzuela, Fernando 236, 239
Vanderlaan, Bill 193
Vasey, Chet 214
Vasquez (Filipino All-Stars, 1934, 3b, p) 92

Wa Sung Chinese Ball Club 98, 99
Wachenfeld, Walt 210
Wada, Otomatsu 165
Wada, S. 93, 213
Wagner, Honus 7
Wah Han (Mills High, 1918, 3b) 23
Wakaba Club of Sacramento 83
Wakabayashi, Tadashi "Bozo" 65, 84, 85, 189, 219
Wakahara, Shoza 99, 100
Wakamatsu, Don x, 1, 2, 3, 12, 234, 239
Walker (Aratani Ballclub, 1930) 80
Walker, Jesse "Hoss" 74, 211, 228
Walker, John 193
Walker, Moses Fleetwood 7
Walnut Grove Deltans of Sacramento 202
Walnut Grove Japanese Ballclub 186
The Wanderers (All-Caucasian) 18
War Relocation Authority (WRA) 17, 130, 146, 240–243
Warfield, Frank 212, 228, 230
Warstler, Harold "Rabbit" 93
Waseda University 13, 33, 50, 53, 70, 99, 100, 137, 229
Washio, Jiro 75

Watanabe, George 159
Watanabe, Joe 108, 128
Watanabe, Min 86, 96
Watanabe, Texie 156, 159
Watsonville Apples 97, 99
Webb, Del 117
Weinstein, Bernie 168, 170, 214
Wells, Willie 52
West Coast Negro Baseball League (WCNBL) 184
Westbrook(s), Luther Leon "Sugar" 122, 184
Western Compress (Fresno) (baseball team) 110
Wheat, Buck 107
White (Gila River staff team, 1945, lf) 174
White, Sol 7
White, Wilford "Whizzer" 179
White Sox Park 86, 210
Whitehill, Earl 80, 93
Whitney, David 91
Williams (Phoenix Colored Nine, 1943, lf) 141
Williams, Harry A. 37, 70
Williams, "Smokey" Joe 7
Williams, Ted 110, 220
Wills, Ted 193
Wilson, Horace 15
Wilson, Woodrow 30
Windell (Twilight League All-Stars, 1930) 80
Wolf, Gary ix
Wolf, Larry ix
Wolf, Otto 122, 139, 140, 141
Woods, Jesse 19
Workman, Bill 179
World Baseball Classic (WBC) 236, 239

Yajima, Kumeyasu (Tokyo All-Stars, 1935) 94
Yamada, Goro "George" 143, 154, 156, 157, 159
Yamada, Sab 134, 139, 143, 232
Yamada, Shak 121, 125
Yamada, Tad 76
Yamada, Ted 176
Yamada, Yoshio "Frank" 102
Yamaguchi (Hawaiian Asahi, 1919, 3b) 26
Yamaguchi, George 174, 178
Yamamoto, Bobby 174
Yamamoto, Kenichi Russell "Ken" 101, 219
Yamamoto, Tadashi 108
Yamanaka (Seattle Japanese, 1934, lf) 92
Yamanaka, H. 231
Yamasaki, Bob 35, 39, 78, 80, 82, 86, 87, 89, 92, 93, 94, 126, 143, 180, 183, 213, 219
Yamasaki, Kahn 176
Yamasaki, Kaz 176
Yamasaki, Kiyoko Lillian *see* Zenimura, Kyoko
Yamasaki, Sam 34, 53, 59, 60, 61, 62, 75, 78, 86, 92, 93, 94, 99, 104, 126, 134, 139, 143, 204, 211, 213, 219
Yamasaki, Torjiro 35, 76, 110, 181, 183
Yamashiro, Masayoshi "Andy" 7, 26, 217
Yamashita, Minoru 234
Yamato, Kiyosho 92, 93, 94, 213
Yano, Ben 190
Yano, Masao 89, 93, 94, 96, 97, 102, 108, 130, 133, 213, 219
Yano, Ted 160, 161
Yasuda, Yoshinobu 75
Yasuhara, Yuso 154
Yasui, Norman 153, 159
Yellow Peril 7, 243
Yes-Yes squad 135, 138, 142
Yokohama Bay Stars 235
Yokozawa, Sabur 50, 63, 232
Yomiuri Giants 236
Yonamine, Wallace Kaname "Wally" 6, 7, 8, 188, 193, 194, 195, 199
Yong Lim, Chang 239
Yorioka, Ken 125
Yoshida, B. 92
Yoshida, Kyoko ix, 35, 59, 229
Yoshida, N. 92
Yoshikawa, B. 78, 82
Yoshikawa, Henry 78, 79
Yoshikawa, Shinichi "Fred" 2, 24–26, 39, 45–48, 56, 57, 59–61, 66–70, 72, 74, 75, 79–82, 84, 86–90, 92–94, 97, 98, 116, 186, 203, 204, 206, 210–213, 219, 223, 224
Yoshimoto, Bob 230
Yoshinaga, George 154
Yoshinaga, K. 180
Young, Cy 7
Young Men's Buddhist Association (YMBA) 39, 71, 78, 82, 86, 93, 110, 123–126, 128, 131–133, 136, 138, 231
Young Yuen (Mills High, 1918, 1b) 23

Zellerbach Ballclub 79
Zenimura, Kenji "Harry" 27, 51, 52, 73, 77, 94, 104, 142, 189, 197, 199
Zenimura, Kenshi "Harvey" 6, 8, 27, 73, 74, 76, 77, 93, 94, 108, 110–112, 114, 118, 126, 127, 132, 135, 139, 140, 142, 143, 150, 153, 155, 161, 165–168, 170, 174, 175, 177, 178, 180, 181, 183, 185, 188–195, 197–203, 214, 232
Zenimura, Kenso "Howard" ix, 8, 24, 27, 47, 53, 56, 63, 66, 67, 69, 70, 73, 76, 77, 81, 82, 86, 89, 91, 93, 96, 108, 110–112, 114–116, 118–120, 123, 131, 132, 134, 135, 139, 140, 142, 143, 150, 153–157, 159, 160, 161, 166, 167, 170, 174, 175, 177–183, 186–194, 196–199, 201–203, 214, 232, 234
Zenimura, Kyoko Lillian Yamasaki 27, 35, 48, 49, 50, 51, 52, 73, 76, 94, 108, 111, 119, 120, 125, 181, 183, 187, 205, 235
Zenimura, Masakichi 13, 15, 48, 73, 76, 93
Zenimura, Masako *see* Sakata, Masako Zenimura
Zenimura, Tatsumi 35, 60, 74–76
Zenimura, Waka 13, 31, 73, 76, 93
Zenimura Field *see* Block 28 Field

www.ingramcontent.com/pod-product-compliance
Lightning Source LLC
LaVergne TN
LVHW081258100826
845148LV00005B/905
9780786461349